International Brand Management of Chinese Companies

Sandra Bell

International Brand Management of Chinese Companies

Case Studies on the Chinese Household
Appliances and Consumer Electronics
Industry Entering US and Western
European Markets

Physica-Verlag

A Springer Company

Author
Dr. Sandra Bell
Trappenbergstr. 35
45134 Essen
Germany
bell.sandra@bcg.com

ISBN 978-3-7908-2029-4   e-ISBN 978-3-7908-2030-0

DOI: 10.1007/978-3-7908-2030-0

Contributions to Economics ISSN 1431-1933

Library of Congress Control Number: 2008923751

© 2008 Physica-Verlag Heidelberg

zgl. Dissertation der Mercator School of Management, Universität Duisburg-Essen, Germany

Cover design: WMXDesign GmbH, Heidelberg

Printed on acid-free paper

9 8 7 6 5 4 3 2 1

springer.com

Foreword

China is certainly doing its best to keep the world mesmerized by its economic achievements. The Chinese economic growth story that begun 30 years ago has in terms of dynamics and duration long since surpassed all those "economic miracles" which have brought Germany, Japan, and the South East Asian Tigers into the top–league of the industrialized world. The rapid expansion of the Chinese economy has gone along with a full-fledged re-integration of China into the global economic system. In the course of the last 30 years China has become a major player in the global economy and today is on a trajectory towards even greater prominence.

In recent years, the Chinese economy seems to have reached an important threshold line of economic development and global integration. In the first quarter century of reform and global opening, Chinese enterprises have been largely confined to a 'passive' role in the global division of labor. Foreign enterprises as the proprietors of greatly superior business models, production technologies, management models as well as very competitively established brands have been integrating Chinese players in their value chains and global operations. Lacking the necessary production technologies, products as well as marketing knowledge to successfully address OECD-consumers, Chinese enterprises have been hardly able to enter the global markets without such guidance. Now, this constellation is changing. An increasing number of Chinese enterprises has already acquired a critical mass of production and management know-how and is venturing out on the global markets in order to directly cater to the customers of the OECD markets and gain a larger share in the profit pools until recently monopolized by the established brand owners of the triad economies.

The study presented here by Sandra Bell is dealing with these new Chinese 'global players'. Focussing on the Chinese household appliances and consumer electronics industry she is taking a very detailed look at the brand management of China's new 'multinationals'. The establishment of strong brands in the OECD markets will be of fundamental importance for a successful market entry by Chinese enterprises. But the successful placement of new brands is known to be a very complex and resource consuming exercise, requiring very advanced management skills. However, the mere concepts of 'marketing' or even more so 'branding' have only recently become common features in China's transition economy: Are Chinese players already in a position to deliver on the challenge of international brand positioning? How successful are they? What strategies do they employ, and to go one step further, is there something like a 'Chinese way' of going global and conducting international branding?

Sandra Bell provides answers to all of these questions. Founded on thorough field research in China she presents a highly enlightening analysis of how Chinese enterprises have ventured out in order to conquer the global markets. By doing so she provides us with highly valuable insights in the realities of brand management in China's new corporate elite. With enormous detail Sandra Bell dissects the international branding activities of some of the most prominent Chinese enterprises and provides the reader with an insider perspective not to be found elsewhere. Obviously most Chinese enterprises are still in an early stage of their pro-active globalization and are still paying a high price for learning from the markets. However, the learning curves seem to be steep and it does not appear to be too far fetched to assume that Chinese brands will be soon a regular feature of the European and American consumer markets.

Duisburg, November 30th, 2007

Univ.-Prof. Dr. Markus Taube
University of Duisburg-Essen
Mercator School of Management
East Asian Economics / China

Preface

Sun Tzu says: One who knows the enemy and knows himself will not be in danger in a hundred battles. One who does not know the enemy but knows himself will sometimes win, sometimes lose. One who does not know the enemy and does not know himself will be in danger in every battle ("The Art of War", chap 3).

The motivation for this doctoral thesis has its origin in my childhood, when my father invited Chinese colleagues to our home in Germany, and I, then ten years old, became fascinated by their Chinese difference in appearance and culture. I therefore owe my father, Dr. Wolfgang Steinwarz, not only thanks for his great support during the thesis itself, but finally my education path as well. I would not have studied Sinology and the Chinese language, and would not have chosen a China-related topic without him.

I would also like to express my gratitude to my sponsor Jürgen-Manchot-Stiftung, who constantly supported my research, living and travelling with generous funding in both Germany and China. Special thanks also due to the DAAD and the Chinese Scholarship Council who enabled my research period at Shanghai Fudan University.

I am also extremely indebted to the representatives of the participating Chinese companies, namely Haier, TCL, Hisense and Lenovo, for volunteering their time into my in-depth interviews. Special thanks to Haier for a fantastic exhibition tour. I would also like to especially thank Valinna, Simon Zhao, Guillaume de Lavallade, Ying Zhang and Wei Ke, who enabled these interviews. The study could not have been completed without the contributors and interviewees: Liu Zhenyu, Liu Zhanjie, Wang Ruiji, Stacey Sun, Meng Yutian, Zhang Ying, Roland Gerke, Dr. Steffen Stremme, Prof. Lu Xiongwen, Prof. Zhou Dongsheng, Prof. Allan K. K. Chan, Prof. Hang Zhonghe, Rüdiger Burkat, Isabelle Gras, Prof. Sven Müntel, Dr. Michael Meyer, Holger Gottstein, Jim Hemerling, David C. Michael, Collins Qian, Joseph Wan, Paul French, Laurie Underwood, Benedikt Sobotka, Dr. Marc Bieling, Dr. Christian Schmidkonz, Dr. Matthias Schramm, Ponpon Zhan, Dunja Saleh-Zaki, Andreas Günther and Laurence Bagot. Also invaluable was everyone who filled in the online survey.

Very special thanks are due to The Boston Consulting Group who enabled my thesis by a supportive leave of absence and strong global networks. I am especially grateful to Heidi Huang and Jacqueline Joliet who have always served my research requests, regardless how strange and challenging they were, during their spare time.

I also owe large debts to Prof. Dr. Markus Taube, my doctoral father, with whom I have discussed many of the ideas in this thesis and whose influence should be apparent. I would like to express special thanks for his encouragement and invaluable comments throughout the research process. I thank my friend Anja Wollschläger for her great support, since she was never tired off sending me literature from German libraries to my home in Shanghai.

Finally, I owe a great deal and ultimately my sanity to my family and husband John Daniel Bell who have supported me during all stages of my thesis. I thank John for his never-ending overwhelming support, encouragement, inspiration, and editorial contribution. Thank you for moving with me to Shanghai. The thesis is dedicated to you.

Shanghai, February 10th, 2008

Sandra Bell

For any feedback and comments feel free to email to the author at bell.sandra@bcg.com.

Contents

operating with French *Thomson* since November 2003. Shanghai Automotive Industry Corp (SAIC) bought the design rights of *MG Rover* and plans to launch its first self-branded family car by end of 2006 (Jing 2006).

Lenovo Group purchased the IBM Personal Computer (PC) division for US$1.25bn in 2005, and caused excitement not only in the global computer industry (Lenovo Deutschland 2005). The new Lenovo Group is now the third largest manufacturer of PCs in the world and enjoys global brand awareness through the brands of *ThinkPad, ThinkCentre,* and *IBM,* and through *Lenovo*'s own brand popularity in China (fig. 1-2).

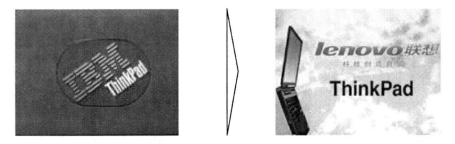

Fig. 1-2. Lenovo Group acquires IBM ThinkPad (own illustration)

Taking these recent developments of Chinese companies into account, are brand acquisitions thus the successful market entry strategy into developed markets? Do we have to expect more cross-border acquisitions in future? Will the notebook *IBM ThinkPad* be re-branded into *Lenovo Think-Pad*? Will IBM customers and employees accept the new Chinese ownership? Haier Group, China's largest manufacturer of household appliances, however, decided against brand acquisitions, and has already demonstrated reasonable success in the US-market by self-branded products. What can developed markets finally expect from Chinese brands and their global brand management? What are the challenges facing these Chinese branded companies going global? And, what strategies and operational capabilities do they have in place to succeed?

These and other questions are very new and pose a great challenge for both the established multinational companies and the scientific brand management research. They may change the overall look of the developed and worldwide markets, and therefore, it is worth to investigate what is behind the emerging Chinese branded companies and their ambitions of taking their home brands global. Before starting the investigation, however, the next sections will shortly introduce the general role of a brand when a firm goes international and gives reasons why there has been insufficient research about Chinese brands on global markets so far. The introductive section will close with the outline of the research approach, including its limits, aims, theoretical and empirical access, and the structure of the study.

1.1.2 Role of brand management when going-international

Relevance of brands

The last decades have seen growing market saturations in US and WE markets, a huge variety of similar products, globalisation processes and an accelerating speed of innovations (Langner 2003: 6-12; Esch 2004: 27-59). As a result companies have been forced to differentiate their products from competitors in order to remain competitive, attract customers, and finally to secure future profitability. A Delphi-survey among company managers identified that the brand is regarded as one of the central value drivers within corporations (Kricsfalussy/Semlitsch 2000: 28). The brand value can be up to 82% of a company's stock market price, as found for the *Kodak* brand in 2004 (Esch et al. 2004: 1).

Whereas commodity and non-branded products promise functional quality and are primary purchased on the basis of price and availability, brands typically embody emotional benefits beyond functionality. They can create prestige, status and social acknowledgement, and can guarantee long-term product quality and market orientation. A brand can therefore be defined as a psychological construct of images and relationships in the mind of a consumer which is responsible for product identification and product differentiation, and which influences customers' purchase decisions (Esch 2004: 23).[3]

Although one could argue that a brand is a psychological phenomenon and its emotional benefits are intangible, the relevance of brands has already been proven as real and checkable in the market (Meffert et al. 2003). For instance, in an empirical study Chernatony and McDonald (2003: 14-15) asked several test persons to compare *Diet Coke* and *Diet Pepsi* firstly in a blind test scenario and secondly in an open test scenario. The results show that *Diet Coke* obtained a higher consumer preference score, although the pure taste was considered less attractive than *Diet Pepsi's* taste (fig. 1-3). The power of a brand can have impact on customer's purchase frequency, willingness to pay and thus directly on corpo-

---

[3] Other authors stress the means of brand visualisation within their definitions of a brand. They say a brand is a name, a symbol or even a coherent marketing approach that is added to a functional product offer. Berndt (2005: 37-38) listed up brand definitions of several known marketing experts.

rate profits and return on sales. For instance, *Miele* is the market leader in terms of price and volume in washing machines in Germany, although their washers are up to 70% more expensive than equivalent competitive goods (Biel 2001: 64; Esch 2004: 11-12).

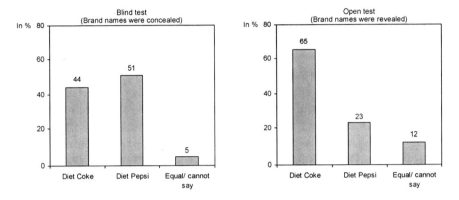

Fig. 1-3. Comparison of *Diet Coke* and *Diet Pepsi* in a blind and open test scenario (Chernatony/McDonald 2003: 14-15)

Even though brand building sounds promising for a company, young and new brands have to face strong difficulties particularly in developed markets. Customers are swamped with information and promotional communication. They take little notice of advertisements, and even at the point of sale they take little time to deal with products (Langner 2003: 10-11).[4] A company thus has to design and manage its brands very carefully: Which units and products shall become brands? Which company-objectives shall they fulfil? How are they named and communicated to the consumers? (Chernatony/McDonald 2003: 53-54; Berndt 2005: 131-132).

Brands on international markets

The management of brands gets an additional dimension when adding the international perspective. On the one hand customers in other country markets may have different preferences and tastes than in the home market (e.g., Remmerbach/Walters 1994: 658; Meffert/Bolz 1998: 186-188). Nationally successful brand massages thus may not be appropriate there.

---

[4] Kroeber-Riel and Esch (2004: 141-149) found out that an one-page advertisement is often looked at less than 2 seconds. Experiments from Russo and Leclerc (1994) showed that in a supermarket customers screen a 16 brand-sizes shelf of consumer nondurable goods on average 3.44 seconds.

Moreover, different product and advertising regulations may demand brand adaptations (Quelch/Hoff 1986; Kelz 1989; Baumgarth 2001: 331). On the other hand, there is evidence that customer habits seem to homogenise worldwide through modern information technology and individual mobility (Bukhari 1999: 17-20; Keller 2003: 684). The ongoing liberalisation and deregulation of many industries and changed political-legal conditions have also resulted in a more joint and globalised market place (Kotler/Bliemel 2001: 259-260).

In the last years, the penetration of multinational brands in domestic markets has caused increasing competition and crowding-outs. For domestic companies it has often been a case of Hobson's choice: Whether they liked it or not, they had to enter global markets by themselves in order to survive the market in the long-term (Sattler 2001: 109). On the other hand, to go international is typically complex and challenging, since it has direct impact on the firm's brand strategies and organisational processes in the home market (Meffert/Bolz 1998: 22-23; Backhaus et al. 2003a: 98-99). It may also require a new management skill set (Meffert/Bolz 1998: 175), since companies have to deal with so far unknown country markets and incomplete information about social-cultural conditions, consumer behaviour and their respective information sources (Backhaus et al. 2003a: 50-51).

Chinese brands on the international stage

Discussing the presence of Chinese brands in the global markets, one can say that they have just started to go international. The communist system and social market environments had forbidden trading with foreign countries such as the US and Western Europe until 1978 (Harding 1987; Bell 1993; Chai 1997; Qian 2000). However, as table 1-1 indicates, a couple of Chinese companies already became visible in some world markets and have made Western players listen attentively to them. Further, companies such as Lenovo, Haier and TCL recently demonstrated some commitment to a global brand building (e.g., Business Week 2004). But what is their long-term brand potential? Which other brands in PR China have international ambitions? What defines a Chinese brand? Professor Zhou Dongsheng from the China Europe International Business School (CEIBS) in Shanghai (2005) said that the expression of Chinese brands refers to two criteria. Firstly, Chinese brands are manufactured and owned by a Chinese company. And secondly, Chinese brands have grown and are known in China. Zhou explained that it is thereby not important where the brand is manufactured, in or outside China, as many international brands are manufactured in China for years, but are still regarded as US- or European brands.

Company	Product market	Country market	Market share in 2002
BYD Battery	Rechargeable batteries for mobile phones	Worldwide	72%
China International Marine Containers	Reefer containers	Worldwide	50%
Galanz	Microwaves	Europe	40%
Haier Group	Small fridges	USA	50%
Huawei Technologies	Routers	Worldwide	3%
Lenovo Group	Motherboards	Worldwide	20%
Pearl River Piano	Pianos	USA	10%
Shanghai Zhenhua Port Machinery	Quayside container cranes	Worldwide	35%
Sichuan Changhong Electric Group	Projector TV sets	USA	10%

Table 1-1. Selected Chinese companies with remarkable global market shares (according to Zeng/Williamson 2004: 40-43)

As there is evidence that a couple of Chinese brands will 'attack' developed markets in the US and Western Europe within the next years, the global marketing and branding society is already excited and argues that Chinese companies are going to develop their brands even faster than Japanese and Korean companies did. Ogilvy & Mather chairman and CEO Shelly Lazarus said in an interview: "I think they're going to do it faster. They understand what they're trying to do. They're committed to brand-building. They're smarter and more pragmatic when it comes to brand-building. Indian consumers already have a preference for Chinese brands over Korean brands" (Business Week Online 2004; similar Weiland 2004).

As the next section will show, though the topic is relevant, scientific research into the going international of Chinese branded companies has been rare so far.

1.1.3 Insufficient research

The going global of Chinese companies – a new field of research

Initiated by the process of China's open door policy in 1978, size and dynamics of the Chinese market have increasingly attracted multinationals and academic researchers from worldwide. Though international organisations such as the UNCTAD (2003) had already pointed out some years ago that there are increasing ambitions to go international from 'the other way round', studies about Chinese companies and their going-international into Western markets are very limited.

There are three main reasons for the lack of research in this area. Firstly, within the last ten years academic research in business management has highly focused on the phenomenon of Western multinationals going China. In line with their economic ambitions, a huge amount of studies evaluated Chinese market environments and derived strategies how to 'grab the largest piece of the cake'. There are all types of works about entering and improving established China operations. For marketing topics see, e.g., Feldmann and BBDO (2005), Chen and Penhirin (2004), Dong and Helms (2001), Temporal (2000); for intercultural management, e.g., Guan (2004), Peill-Schoeller (1994); for operational improvements, e.g., BCG (2003); and for general business guidelines, e.g., Ambler (2004) and Luo (2000a; 2000b).

Secondly, instead of business management researchers, economic researchers have so far investigated China's going-international from a macro-economic and political perspective. This includes works about state-owned companies, which entered global markets in order to secure raw materials and to demonstrate China's political and financial power (e.g., Zhang/Bulcke 1996). There are also works about the development of China's foreign direct investments interlinked to the political developments of China's open door policy (e.g., Choosin 1996; Chai 1997; Cai 1999; Brahm 2001; Rui 2005) and to China's entry into the WTO in 2001 (e.g., Drysdale/Song 2000; Lardy 2002).

Thirdly, although the number of Chinese companies which are managed according to free-market economy principles is increasing, the going-international of these firms is a pretty young phenomenon. Market entries into developed countries such as the US and Western Europe can only be traced back into the end 1990s (e.g., UNCTAD 2003; Zhang 2003). For instance, Seeger (2001) and Schlevogt (1999) did some research about Chinese private and privatised companies, but did not touch international activities. Xu (2000) investigated corporate decision making of innovation management, Zhu (2005) focused on human resource management, and Alon (2003) investigated the Chinese corporate culture and traditional concepts.

Although academic research on 'Chinese companies entering developed markets' is still rare, the topic is currently dominating articles of daily newspapers, scientific and non-scientific business press (Publicis Sasserath 2006: 8). They are motivated by the recent actions of Lenovo, Haier, CNOOC (China National Offshore Oil Corporation) in the US markets[5]

---

[5] CNOOC tried to acquire US-Unocal, a Californian oil rival, for US$18.5bn in 2005. Since the US society was shocked that a Chinese state-owned company grabbed for American strategic assets, political opposition forced CNOOC to

and by several acquisitions of ailing medium sized businesses in Germany and elsewhere. Whereas some articles play with fear and danger of Chinese companies for Western home economies (e.g., Wirtschaftswoche 2003; Rosenbush 2005), others describe the Chinese companies and their international ambitions more precisely (e.g., Goodman 2004; Blume 2005; Economist 2005b). At least, the wave of press articles underlines that there is high public interest into the going-international of Chinese branded companies and that academic research should be done.

Choice and multidisciplinarity of the research topic

The topic of the study demands the integration of three different research fields: brand management, going-international and Chinese companies. Academic research about brand management and going-international is already sophisticated and manifold. Same is true for the integrated field of 'strategic marketing' and 'international brand management'.[6] In contrast, the topic of Chinese companies and the analysis of their global brand management are, as noticed above, a very new field of research.

Since there is such a lack of research on the going-international of Chinese companies, why does the research topic concentrates on the small section of international brand management? There is one major reason: According to Meffert (2000; 2005) marketing and brand management is defined as an overall corporate management approach which has impact on all corporate decisions, forms of corporate culture and corporate leadership, and is implemented under the care of the top management team. The investigation of international brand management in Chinese companies thus offers the opportunity to derive an understanding of Chinese corporate decision making and leadership with respect to corporate culture, traditional values and international markets. As a result, this study also touches the research fields of 'intercultural marketing', 'country-of-origin', 'China's open-door policy', and 'China's philosophy' amongst others.

---

withdraw its bid (Economist 2005b) For Haier, see case study as presented in chapter 5.2.1.

[6] An overview about the status quo of brand management research gives Keller (2001); major literature about brand management includes works of Meffert (2005); Esch (2004); Haedrich/Tomczak (2003); Keller (2003); Aaker/Joachimsthaler (2000); Kapferer (1992); for international marketing and international branding see Bieling/Wiechers (2004), Berndt et al. (2003); Backhaus et al. (2003a); Gregory/Wiechmann (2002); Usunier (2000) and Meffert/Bolz (1998), amongst others.

Author	Year	Type of work	Research focus
Biers, Dan	2001	Article in Far Eastern Economic Review	Presentation of Haier Group's business success and *Haier* brand in the USA
Gao, Paul Woetzel, Jonathan R. Wu Yibing	2003	Article in McKinsey Quarterly	Status analysis of Chinese brands with respect to OEM business; general international brand strategies
Gilmore, Fiona Dumont, Serge	2003	Case studies	Brand success stories of 15 selected Chinese companies in their domestic markets; global brand management is a minor issue
Ling Liu	2005	Book based on PhD thesis	Role and impact of Chinese national and local industrial policies on the domestic appliance industry including cases of Haier, Hisense and Aucma; brand management is a minor subject
Liu Hong Li Kequan	2002	Article in European Management Journal	The going-international of Haier company; brand management is a minor issue
Quelch, John Knoop, Carin-Isabel	2006	Harvard Business Case	The global brand building of Lenovo company after the acquisition of IBM PCs
Roll, Martin	2006	Textbook incl. selected cases	General insights into Asian brands; little sophistication regarding China-related specifics; China represented by *Li-Ning* brand
Yi, Jeannie Jinsheng Ye Shawu Xian	2003	Book	Company history of Haier Group, including *Haier* brand and international strategy

Table 1-2. Overview of works on 'international brand management of Chinese companies' (own research)

Table 1-2 lists already published works in English literature touching the topic of 'international brand management of Chinese companies'.[7] As the table shows, works are rare, and brand management mostly a minor topic. In addition, some experts are arguing that the already published case studies on Chinese branded companies lack context information and an objective commentary along with the cases (e.g., the review of 'Brand Warriors China' by Cohen 2004). Both aspects are expressly addressed aims of this study, as presented in the next chapter.

1.2 Limits and aims of the study

The pretty unknown area of Chinese companies is the major challenge of the topic of 'international brand management of Chinese companies'. While a detailed investigation on Chinese branded companies as a whole is

---

[7] Not included are short and non-scientific articles published in newspapers and specialised press, as well as academic works dealing exclusively with going-international processes of Chinese companies or exclusively with marketing and branding issues in the domestic market.

beyond the scope of this study, Chinese branded companies will be exemplified by the Chinese household appliances and consumer electronics industry due to three reasons:

First, the industry itself involves the necessity of international brand management activities, as it is regarded as a global industry (Porter 1999: 350-351; BCG 2005). Meffert and Bolz (1998: 64, 183) identified a generally high level of standardisation and thus a general basis for a global brand building. Known global brand names include *Whirlpool, Electrolux, Siemens, Sony, Samsung, LG, IBM* and *Dell*. Second reason is that customers are worldwide highly involved in the purchase of household appliances and consumer electronics goods. Buying decisions are therefore not only made on the basis of price and availability, but also on brand preferences and added-values (fig. 1-4, Meffert et al. 2003: 17-18). Last but not least, the Chinese household appliances and consumer electronics industry was chosen with respect to number, availability and potential of Chinese corporate cases. By 2006 the industry is considered China's cutting edge in terms of going-international (Gao et al. 2003; Ling Liu 2005: xiii), embodying also the most advanced brand management organisations among Chinese firms (BCG 2006c: 13; Zhang 2006).

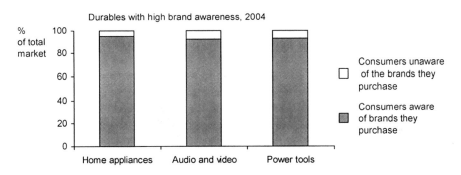

Fig. 1-4. Durables with high brand awareness in 2004 (figure taken from BCG 2005: 4)[8]

The goal of the study is to investigate selected real business cases of the Chinese household appliances and consumer electronics industry, and to

---

[8] Durables are consumer goods which intend to last more than a few years. They are particularly to be differentiated from fast moving consumer goods (FMCG) such as food, cosmetics, and clothes, amongst others. According to the study, the category 'power tools' includes air compressors, band saws, circular saws, grinders, orbital sanders, power drills power miter saws, radial-arm saws, routers, scroll saws, and table saws.

describe and identify their way of international brand management. It is the aim of the study to include all aspects and events that in some way have influenced the corporate decision-making regarding going-international and global brand building.[9] Since the developed markets in the US and Western Europe (WE) are considered the most difficult and most brand sophisticated markets in the world, market entries into US and WE markets are chosen as the focus of analysis.[10] As it would be beyond the scope of the study, the investigation does not cover details on international target grouping, business segment definitions, decisions on timing, or on optimal international pricing strategies. The study assumes that these decisions have already been made or are made at the same time independently. Although it simplifies reality, this limitation is necessary in order to fully concentrate on brand-related issues (Wöhe 1996: 36-37). Overall, the research question of the study can thus be formulated as follows:

How and why do Chinese branded companies of the household appliances and consumer electronics industry decide on certain brand management elements when entering developed markets in the US and Western Europe?

The research question involves four sub-questions which are investigated in the process of the study. First, what are general brand management options when a firm enters global markets? Second, who are the Chinese branded companies? When and how did Chinese brands fist emerged? Where are they coming from? Where are they heading for? What are their strengths and weakness? Third, when thinking about an appropriate global brand approach for those Chinese branded companies, how they should enter the developed markets in the US and Western Europe? Can they learn from Japanese and South Korean companies such as Sony and Samsung? And fourth, after having analysed selected Chinese branded companies, to what extend have they followed the recommended brand approach. What did they decide differently? Can we identify a Chinese way of international

---

[9] Bauer (2002: 28-29) and Björkman (1989: 59) define the requirements for the presentation of case narratives and their influencing factors by five criteria: a) relevance; all the data needed for the specific research aim is integrated; irrelevant data has been omitted; b) completeness; all the data that has been used for the analysis is presented; c) topicality, all the data that are recent and new is not missed; d) accuracy, all the data that are focus of study is described as close as possible; e) comparability, all the data is consistent across all case studies.

[10] The Japanese market is excluded, as a deep investigation of the Japanese market would require Japanese language skills which the author of the study cannot contribute in an appropriate manner. Western Europe i.e. includes Germany, France, Italy, Spain, Benelux and the UK.

brand management? Are there dominating decision factors, typical relationship structures, or cause-and-effect chains? Finally, in order to sum all those questions and answers, the aim of the study is to integrate all findings in a descriptive model[11]. It tries to explain the Chinese way of international brand management in the investigated companies and gives first rudiments to generalise it across and beyond the chosen household appliances and consumer electronics companies industry. See next sections for details on the theoretical and empirical access into the research question.

1.3 Theoretical und empirical access

1.3.1 The basic theoretical framework

The decision on the adequate theoretical access into the research question has to address the described lacks of research and aims of study. Whereas the research in the going-international of Chinese companies does not provide a satisfying theoretical basis, the Western theory of international brand management offers a reliable and comprehensive framework. From a corporation's point of view, the internal organisation of brand management is defined as planning, realisation and control, involving responsibility, competence and delegation of all types of brand management activities (Meffert/Bolz 1998: 175; Bieling/Wiechers 2004: 4; Esch et al. 2004). The study assumes that Chinese branded companies in principle use the same range of alternative international brand management elements as Western companies do. Thus, if one understands international brand management as a set of corporate decisions, it is adequate to choose *the decision making approach of the brand* as the underlying theoretical framework.[12]

The decision making approach of the brand originally comes from the research field called 'the decision making theory'[13], involving logical and empirical analysis of human behaviour. Precondition of the theory is that

---

[11] See for definitions and details chapter 1.3.2.

[12] Baumgarth (2001: 21-25) distinguishes six different approaches of brand management: the functional-orientated, the decision making, the behavioural scientific, the strategic, the identity-orientated and the approach of information economy. The theoretical directions are not contrary to each other. They rather emphasise different brand aspects and investigate them from different research perspectives.

[13] For a good overview and more details about the decision making theory see for example Bamberg/Coenenberg (2004), Laux (2003), Meyer (1999).

the human being heads for optimisation of individual aims and thus decides on the most promising alternatives (Wöhe 1996: 78-79; Bamberg/Coenenberg 2004: 1). According to Meffert (1994) and Baumann (2001: 22), the ideal structure of the decision making approach of a brand consist of four phases: a) brand aims; b) strategic brand decisions; c) operative brand decisions; and d) decisions on brand control and brand adaptations. The approach is well established in the scientific brand research and has already seen various applications (e.g., Baumgarth 2001; Esch 2004). Besides the structure of phases, the decision making approach of the brand also includes comprehensive evaluations of alternatives and thus the integration of internal and external influencing factors (Baumgarth 2001: 22). Consequently, the theoretical framework also satisfies the study's aim of discussing not only final results of decisions, but also the decision- making processes behind. The 'blank structure' will be filled with content in the course of the study, including specific options of the Western international brand management theory as well as Chinese cases on international brand management.

1.3.2 Development of hypotheses

Main objective of the study is to derive insights into the Chinese way of international brand management. Since the research field is not yet investigated in depth, several hypotheses are the study's main outcomes. Hypotheses can generally be developed by analogy, induction and deduction, or a combination of all three methods (Kopp 1972: 66-70).[14] The latter offers the opportunity to reduce disadvantages of single methods to a minimum (Brockdorff 2003: 22). In this study, hypotheses are derived in two steps: first, within a referential system and second, within a descriptive model.

A referential system is a theoretical aid which enables the researcher to structure complex real phenomena and to formulate questions by analysing a sufficient number of empirical data points over time (Kubicek 1976: 17-19; Kirsch 1997: 563). The hypotheses of the study's referential system are particularly developed by deduction and analogy. Basis for the deductive approach is a deep analysis of given brand literature and given material

---

[14] Analogy: Structural similarities are basis to conclude from one case to another; induction: single experiences are linked and extended onto superior and non-observable facts; and deduction derives specific hypotheses from pretty basic and global assumptions (for more details about scientific methods and requirements on the development of hypotheses see e.g., Kopp 1972: 67-69; Schneider 1978: 28-34).

about origin, experiences and competences of Chinese branded companies. Some analogue aspects are added with respect to international brand experiences of Japanese and Korean branded companies and how they had entered the developed markets in the US and Western Europe. Kubicek (1976: 20) recommended that "a referential system should have the tendency to be pluralistic and eclectic [...] Inconsistencies between single assumptions seem to be heuristically particularly fruitful."

In a second step, the formulated hypotheses of the referential system are tested by an empirical qualitative study. The goal is to improve, concretise and generalise the assumptions into a descriptive model. Compared to a referential system, a descriptive model includes more proven hypotheses, and assertions instead of questions. It explains how Chinese companies decide on global brand management elements in reality and what their reasons are behind. It includes the discovery and explanation of empirical relationships with respect to the Western brand management theory (Wöhe 1996: 156-157; Bamberg/Coenenberg 2004: 4-5). The descriptive model finally formulates first principles and cause-and-effect chains on the Chinese way of international brand management. The hypotheses are derived by comparative analysis[15] across cases and with the referential system (Glaser/Strauss 1967: 101-105). Analogies between different business cases as well as inductive developed hypotheses were used to describe the empirical findings. The referential system was always used to verify and confirm the inductive developed generalisations (similar approach Björkman 1989: 63).

1.3.3 Why case studies?

Case studies are most likely the preferred research method, when the research field deals with complex phenomena and 'how' and 'why'-questions (Yin 1994: 1). This is the case when the research field is not yet investigated in depth; and it is reasonable to choose research methods of a qualitative and explorative nature (e.g., Tomczak 1992). Borrowing the words of Glaser and Strauss (1967), case studies are a valuable approach, when a work is more interested in the "context of discovery" than in the validity of existing theories, the "context of justification".

The research method of case studies is characterised as communicative, naturalistic, authentic and open (Lamnek 1995b: 8). This implies that it can

---

[15] Comparative analysis is one way of content analysis. The content analysis is defined as a systematic analysis of documented communication with respect to a theoretical framework (for more details see Mayring 2003).

integrate investigations of contemporary and recent events, e.g., the merger between *Lenovo* and *IBM*, as well as contextual conditions, in this work e.g., China's open door policy or Chinese brand management experience (Yin 1994: 13). In addition, the method of cases studies do not require manipulation of relevant behaviours, like some experiments would do (Yin 1994: 6). The reader gets the opportunity to reinterpret the cases and draw conclusions by himself.

The most frequent concern about case studies is the lack of rigor: "the researcher's preconception of the phenomena influences his/her results" (Björkman 1989: 49); "[the] investigator has been sloppy and has allowed equivocal evidence [...] to influence the direction of the findings and conclusions" (Yin 1994: 9). In this work, this concern was taken into consideration in three ways. Firstly, the complaint of preconception is reduced to a minimum level by analysing the research question from two starting positions: the examination of theoretical brand management options and the examination of origin, experiences and competences of Chinese branded companies. In addition, the findings are challenged with experiences from Japanese and Korean branded companies, and real Chinese business cases. Secondly, the reader gets the opportunity to interpret and conclude himself, as the examinations and case studies include frequent citations and original comments from market experts and organisational members. However, which aspects are included in the case studies and which not, the researcher had to decide beforehand. Björkman (1989: 50) admitted "that the case narratives are to some extend already pre-analysed". Thirdly, feedback and suggestions from market experts and organisational members were used at any time to improve case narratives and final findings.

Besides lack of rigor, adversaries of cases studies argue that case studies do not satisfy the scientific interest of generalisation. However, as Yin (1994: 10) explained, a set of case studies does not have the claim to be a representative sample. It rather consists of a limited number of cases, which are chosen by the researcher by "theoretical sampling" (Glaser/Strauss 1967). Single cases are not unimportant, exchangeable objects as in quantitative works (Lamnek 1995b: 6-7), but they are regarded as relevant as long as they are typical, extreme, differentiating or promising with respect to the study's aims. Mayring (2003: 104) explained, the sample is completed when the "theoretical" saturation of a category or research object is achieved; this means nothing new is expected from an additional case. Case studies most likely result in a sophisticated description of interlinked factors, painting a holistic and most typical picture of the research object (Fuchs-Heinritz et al. 1995: 162). Analogously to the way scientists generalise from experimental results to a theory, case studies are used to generalise findings into a descriptive model (Yin 1994: 37).

1.3.4 Choice of data gathering methods

The study design involves data gathering on several topics. The establishment of the referential system requires, besides a theoretical international brand management basis, a deep investigation on origin, experiences and competences of Chinese branded companies as well as on major experiences of Japanese and Korean branded companies. The descriptive model additionally demands several different qualitative data sources in order to develop detailed case narratives (Lamnek 1995b: 5). Generally, there are the data gathering methods of field observations, group discussions, archival data and interviews, amongst others (Björkman 1989: 53; Lamnek 1995b: 7). Whereas field observations and group discussions are not appropriate in the context of this study, archival data and interviews are promising data sources.[16]

In this study, archival data are scientific papers, industry, market and company reports, consumer surveys, internal company material, business press articles and prior case descriptions of specific Chinese, Japanese and Korean companies. Archival data always involves the danger of incomplete information and manipulation (Björkman 1989: 53). For instance, the researcher has only limited access to internal transcripts of meetings and telephone calls; many decision making activities might also have taken place outside formal meetings and are thus not documented properly. Archival data from Chinese statistic offices and organisations have to be handled with care, because there has already been manifold evidence of manipulation (Bauer 2002: 152). This does not mean that these data points could not be use, but they have to be validated by other multiple sources of evidence (e.g., Lamnek 1995a: 245-257).

Besides archival data, the study relies on expert interviews. In an expert interview, the researcher is in direct contact with the test person and asks him/her questions verbally. In this study, the interviews are face-to-face and of an open-ended nature (Yin 1994: 81; Fuchs-Heinritz et al. 1995: 315-316). Face-to-face is an essential requirement in China, as surveys would highly depend on official approvals and are thus risky and very time-consuming. Open-ended nature means that interviewees can chose

---

[16] Field observations are out of question, as they demand real-time studies which would limit the number of research cases to one or maximal two cases, ruling out "the possibility of discerning patterns of between-case similarities and differences" (Björkman 1989: 52). The method of group discussions is generally a valuable approach of brand related research (Bauer 2002: 268-270), but, as this study focus on internal processes and corporate decision making, it is most likely respondents might not say the truth in front of colleagues, or would provide only shallow information.

relevant questions and aspects by themselves and can prioritise them by different detail levels. Moreover the researcher can be responsive to the interviewees, increasing their willingness of disclosure and spontaneity, and thus the plurality of answers (Bauer 2002: 265). The interview, though of an explorative character (Lamnek 1995b: 74), is conducted with respect to the study's research question. All conducted interviews thus include same question categories. They were individually adapted towards the interviewee's main field of expertise. See fig. 1-5 for question categories and appendix 2 for an exemplary interview guideline.

Brands in the Chinese market
- Origin of Chinese brands
- Customer brand behaviour
- Corporate aims

Corporate brand building
- Major brand building elements (e.g., advertising)
- Role of the Olympic Games in Beijing 2008
- Role of R&D and intellectual property

Brand management organisation
- Corporate structure and responsibilities
- Role of corporate origin and ownership
- Integration of international markets

Going international
- Market entry approach
- Governmental incentives
- Best practices (e.g., Samsung)

Fig. 1-5. Question categories of expert interviews

It is noted that all expert interviews were conducted in the respondent's native or fluent language – English, Chinese, or German, in order to reduce potential communication problems during the interviews. The interviews in Chinese language were supported by a professional translator; and in case of ambiguous statements and issues that were not fully understood, additional questions followed up in order to avoid misunderstandings (Björkman 1989: 56).

1.3.5 Chosen research objects

The focus of the study is the Chinese household appliances and consumer electronics industry. In total four research cases of this industry had been selected: Lenovo 联想, Haier 海尔, TCL, and Hisense 海信. Within the theoretical sampling, two sample criteria had been applied: a) functional brand management experience, and b) international market experience. Both sample criteria refer to O'Donnell and Jeong (2000: 22-23) who found that functional and international experience are the two key managerial characteristics with impact on organisation's international marketing strategy. 'Functional brand management experience' defines that the selected company owns at least one well-established brand in China. This means that the brands obtained revenues of more than US$1bn in 2004 (Beebe et al. 2006: 3); and consumer surveys, national statistics or other market reports confirm the company a remarkable brand success in the Chinese market place. The criterion 'international market experience' requires a certain amount of corporate FDI in the US and WE markets. Concretely, this includes at least the ownership of one production site, distribution & sales facility, or R&D centre in a US or WE market (BCG 2006c).[17] In addition, the company has to promote own Chinese brands in these foreign country markets, indicating that international brand building is a key corporate aim. Besides the two managerial characteristics, differentiating, typical and extreme cases had been selected. Moreover, feasible access to archival data, contact persons and interviews had been taken into consideration (Brockdorff 2003: 30).

The target interview partners of the study had been company representatives of the four selected cases as well as external company and market experts. They all held medium to top management positions in their respective organisations, including professorships at leading universities in Asia. Table 1-3 sums up 16 experts and their kind of contribution. In addition, the study was influenced by many informal talks with market observers who are not mentioned here.[18] One interviewee asked for confident information handling and is anonymously quoted as 'Brand Agency' in the course of the study. 10 of 13 interviews were face-to-face interviews; the interviews with Roland Gerke, Dr. Steffen Stremme, and Meng Yutian were telephone interviews. All interviews took between 1 to 2.5 hours. The interviews conducted with case representatives were recorded by a re-

---

[17] Production facilities can be located in Eastern Europe, as long as they serve Western markets.
[18] See section 'acknowledgements'.

cording machine[19]; the other interviews were truthfully recorded by the researcher.

Name	Institution	Position	Contribution
Rüdiger Burkat	Portelet AG	Member of the Board	Interview
'Brand Agency'	Anonymous brand consulting agency	CEO	Interview
Allan K.K. Chan	Hong Kong Baptist University	Professor of Marketing	Interview
Roland Gerke	Bosch and Siemens Home Appliances Group	President of Jiangsu BSH Sales Co., Ltd.	Interview
Paul French	Access Asia	Founder	Presentation
Hang Zhonghe	Shanghai Fudan University, Management School	Professor of Marketing	University course
Dr. Steffen Stremme	Media-Saturn-Holding GmbH	Managing Director	Interview
Liu Zhanjie	Haier Group	Director of Medical and Laboratory Instruments	Interview
Liu Zhenyu	Haier Group	R&D Director	Interview
Lu Xiongwen	Shanghai Fudan University, Management School	Professor of Marketing, Associate Dean of School of Management	Interview; university course
Meng Yutian	Lenovo Group	Senior Supervisor Brand Management	Interview
Stacey Sun	TCL Group	TTE Communication Director	Interview
Laurie Underwood	American Chamber of Commerce Shanghai	Director of Communications and Publications	Presentation
Wang Ruiji	Hisense Group	General Brand Manager	Interview
Zhang Ying	OgilvyOne Worldwide	Group Account Director Beijing	Interview
Zhou Dongsheng	CEIBS Shanghai	Professor of Marketing	Interview

Table 1-3. Overview about study's interviewees and contribution

---

[19] Sony Stereo Recording & MP3 Playback ICD-SX46.

1.4 Structure of study

The study is composed of seven chapters. After the introduction in chapter 1, chapter 2 deals with theoretical foundations and alternative options of international brand management. Along the decision making approach of the brand, the chapter discusses general brand aims of going-international, followed by strategic and operative brand management options. Chapter 3 deals with the origin, experiences and competences of Chinese branded companies. It discusses relevant context information of Chinese branded companies along the influencing factors functional brand management experience and international market experience. The chapter closes with a brief evaluation of both areas of experiences.

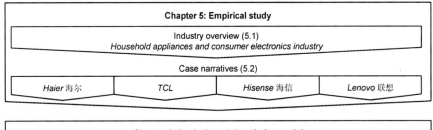

Fig. 1-6. Structure of the study

In chapter 4 the findings of both previous chapters are integrated in the referential system. It includes the hypotheses on a global brand approach for Chinese branded companies entering US and WE markets, and is structured in the same way as the theoretical chapter was. The hypotheses of the referential system are tested in chapter 5 and 6. Chapter 5 presents the empirical study of the Chinese household appliances and consumer electronics companies. It starts with a brief introduction into the global household appliances and consumer electronics industry, and is followed by the four case narratives of Haier, TCL, Hisense, Lenovo. Chapter 6 includes the analysis of the cases and the test of hypotheses. Further, it includes the development of the descriptive model, presenting first principles and cause-and-effect chains, and identifying first rudiments of the Chinese way of international brand management. Chapter 7 sums up the major results of the study and formulates starting points for future research. Fig. 1-6 illustrates the described structure of the study.

2 Theory of international brand management

The overall focus of the study is to investigate selected Chinese branded companies of the household appliances and consumer electronics industry. It is the aim to describe and identify their way of international brand management when they enter developed markets in the US and Western Europe. However, before focusing on these Chinese companies, this chapter reviews the major basic concepts of the Western international brand management theory. Which brand options do Chinese branded companies in general have when they want to enter developed markets? Do the options require certain corporate competences or given market conditions? To answer these questions, the chapter is structured along the decision making approach of the brand, starting with the review of possible aims of global brand building. It is followed by general strategic and operative brand options when a firm goes international, and closes with the section of control & adaptation of brand decisions.

2.1 Aims of global brand building

The long-term overall goal of each market-orientated firm is to secure and increase revenues, profits and thus profitability and corporate value (Hahn 1985: 13). Several studies and successful non-domestic brands, such as *Coca-Cola, IBM, Siemens,* and *Sony*, have already proved that brands are a crucial driver in this area (Kapferer 1992: 285). For instance, Swander & Pace (1997) found that the profitability on sales of branded fast moving consumer goods (FMCG) had developed by double the speed in comparison to unbranded FMCG products from 1990 to 1995, although sales had grown by similar growth rates. A study of McKinsey showed that stronger brands generated a 1.9% higher total return on shareholder compared to industry average and that weaker brands lag behind the average by 3.1% (Court et al. 1999). Consequently, one can conclude that firms with strong brands are more efficient, more competitive and more successful than other firms. They are quite protected against hostile takeovers and more likely attract high potentials, investors, sales partners and suppliers (Brockdorff 2003: 5-7; Chernatony/McDonald 2003: 18; Esch 2004: 61).

The success of strong brands basically refers to two variables: price premium and volume premium. See also figure 2-1. The price premium is the higher price per unit a strong brand realises compared to low-price players. The volume premium is the additional unit volume a strong brand realises compared to the average volume of major players (Joas/Offerhaus 2001: 9). Whereas some companies target either price premium or volume premium, there are others trying to realise both at the same time. Luxury brands such as *Porsche* and *Luis Vuitton* head for price premiums, whereas, for instance *Aldi*, Germany's branded food discounter, heads for volume premiums. Germany's brand for washing machines *Miele* is a prominent example of realising both premiums at the same time. Miele is market leader in Germany in terms of volume, although its prices are around 70% above market average (Absatzwirtschaft 2000).[20]

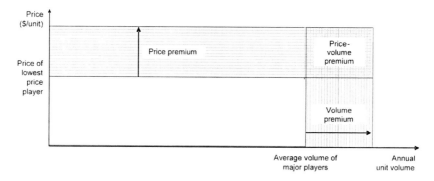

Fig. 2-1. Price and volume premium of a strong brand (own illustration)

Besides encouragement from successful brands and their premiums, a number of other forces have also contributed to a firm's motives in global brand building. Keller (2003: 683) particularly stressed five rationales: I) perception of slow growth and increase competition in domestic markets; II) belief in enhanced overseas growth and profit opportunities; III) desire to reduce costs from economies of scale, IV) need to diversify risk; and V) recognition of mobility of consumers (also Berndt et al. 2003: 93-94).[21] In addition, in more and more product categories the ability to establish a global profile is becoming virtually a prerequisite for success (Thomas et al. 1995). For instance, as in the US-liquor industry the US-consumption

---

[20] See same example in chapter 1.
[21] See also following chapters.

rate had constantly been decreasing, US-firms such as *Jim Bean*, *Jack Daniels* and *Southern Comfort* had been forced taking their brands into overseas markets. A market observer stated: "Spirits companies now view themselves as global marketers. If you want to be a player, you have to be in America, Europe and Far East. You must have world-class brands, a long-term perspective, and deep pockets" (quoted in Keller 2003: 683).

Beyond economic brand aims, it is to note that global brand building can also be initiated in order to increase personal power and prestige. Positive corporate brand images can, for instance, enhance the reputation of the firm's top management and CEO (Papendick 2002: 232; Berndt et al. 2003:94; Esch 2004: 4).

2.2 Strategic brand decisions when going-international

Ideally, the going-international of a brand would consist of the same brand values, the same product formulation, the same packing design, the same advertising program and so on as in the domestic market. It would be the firm's most efficient way for each and every country in which the brand is going to be sold. "Unfortunately, such a uniformly optimal strategy is rarely possible" stated Keller (2003: 683). This chapter gives reasons and shows which options generally exist to adjust the brand strategy towards global environments. This particularly includes alternatives in brand positioning and mode of market entry (Keegan 1999: 285-305).

2.2.1 Brand positioning

For existing brands, it is assumed that they know who they are, what they stand for and what makes them so unique in their home market. They have a brand identity – specified facets of the brand's uniqueness and values – as well as a brand positioning, meaning that the firm is used to actively emphasise the brand's distinctive characteristics that make it different from its local competitors and appealing to the national public in order to grow in market share (Esch 2004: 86; Kapferer 2004: 95-99; Kroeber-Riel/Esch 2004).[22] It is further assumed that the brands enjoy a certain brand image

---

[22] Brand identity is considered the starting point of all brand building. It is the self-image of a brand which has to be implemented and communicated to the public (consumers, employees, other third parties) by brand positioning and marketing mix elements. See Esch (2004: 89-120) for an overview about relevant concepts of brand identity building. See Haedrich and Tomczak (2003: 46-

among their local consumers which is ideally inline with the firm's brand positioning.[23] For instance, *Sony* stands for technology, *Rolex* for luxury, *Alessi* for design, *Miele* for quality, *Dallmeyer* for tradition (Baumgarth 2001: 124). When going-international and taking the home brands to foreign markets, the firm has in principle two alternatives: copying the national brand positioning as much as possible under the assumption that all markets are alike and the brands will thus become similar successful in the foreign markets, or adjusting the brand positioning to foreign market needs as far as it will not significantly damage the national brand success (e.g., Keegan/Green 2005: 347).

Brand differentiation or brand standardisation?

In the literature, the discussion of both alternatives is known as "the fundamental question of brand standardisation and brand differentiation" (Levitt 1983). It refers to two extreme scenarios. Brand differentiation means full product and brand adaptation to local needs up to and including separated local brands. In contrast, brand standardisation means a worldwide totally identical brand approach across all country markets (e.g., Meffert 1986).[24] Both scenarios comprise numbers of advantages and disadvantages which are exactly the opposite of each other. Figure 2-2 maps the major pros and cons from the standardised, global brand perspective.

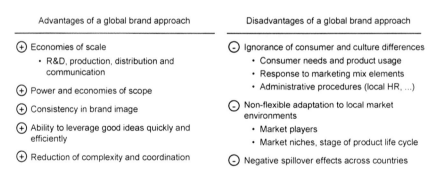

Advantages of a global brand approach	Disadvantages of a global brand approach

⊕ Economies of scale
   • R&D, production, distribution and communication
	⊖ Ignorance of consumer and culture differences
	   • Consumer needs and product usage
	   • Response to marketing mix elements
	   • Administrative procedures (local HR, ...)

⊕ Power and economies of scope	⊖ Non-flexible adaptation to local market environments
⊕ Consistency in brand image	
⊕ Ability to leverage good ideas quickly and efficiently	• Market players • Market niches, stage of product life cycle
⊕ Reduction of complexity and coordination	⊖ Negative spillover effects across countries

Fig. 2-2. Major pros & cons of a global brand approach (based on Keller 2003: 683-686; Schuiling/Kapferer 2004)

---

57) or Kroeber-Riel and Esch (2004: 51-67) for an introduction in the concept of brand positioning.

[23] Compare to chapter 2.4.1 for brand equity measurements.

[24] Synonyms of brand standardisation are global brand strategy (Keller 2003: 683-721; Meffert et al. 2005: 193-195) or world brand strategy (Kelz 1989).

It is widely agreed that the primary advantage of a global brand approach is cost efficiency by lower unit costs that derive from a larger scale of sales. According to Meffert (1986: 698), it is the goal to achieve a cost leadership by exploiting the experience curves in R&D, production, organisation, distribution and communication (Schiele 1997: 117-118; Sattler 2001: 111-112). This includes, for example, standardised global advertising campaigns and sponsorships brand presence at international communication channels, famous film and sports stars as testimonials of the brand, and fewer R&D staff, brand managers and sales partners per brand unit worldwide (Kreutzer 1989: 570-571; Kapferer 1992: 234; Schiele 1997: 118-199).[25]

A second advantage of the global brand approach is enhanced power and scope in both foreign and domestic markets. "A global brand profile may communicate credibility to the consumer. [...] The fact that the brand is widely available may signal that the product is high quality and convenient to use" (Keller 2003: 684). This is, as the economies of scope are theoretically grounded in information costs (Nayyar 1990). As it is costly for customers to acquire information about products, they likely seek to buy multiple products from the same vendor or manufacturer (Nayyar 1990: 516). The same is valid for financial investors and other third parties (e.g., Knudsen et al. 1997: 189; Zimmermann et al. 2002: 6).[26]

The consistency of the brand image is another advantage of the global brand approach. The consideration becomes particularly important when there is high consumer mobility and large cross-country media communication promoting the brand (Keller 2003: 684). Kapferer (1992: 239) noted that a global brand image is also able to address specific global consumer groups. He found, for instance, French workers and French managers less similar in consumer behaviour than French managers and German managers. Wagnleiter (2000) even found that the "colonisation" of US brands and proclaimed trends of the television channel *MTV* have built up an own global consumer generation of young people with same wants and needs (see also 'pub-culture', 'coffee culture' etc. in Keegan/Green 2005: 119-120).

In addition, the global brand approach comprises the ability to leverage good ideas quickly and efficiently through the organisation. In terms of corporate intelligence and international division of labour, this can be a competitive advantage of a firm. Finally, a standardised global brand approach can also reduce coordination and complexity within a company. A control of the brand performance measures could more easily be imple-

---

[25] Compare to chapter 2.3.2.
[26] Compare to chapter 2.1: 'aims of global brand building'.

mented and tracked in those countries, in which the brand is marketed (Keller 2003: 685).

On the other hand, a global brand approach also raises a number of potential disadvantages which a firm has to take in consideration. The most significant criticism is that a standardised brand ignores fundamental differences across consumers, countries and cultures. Critics argue, though a global brand is the most efficient approach, it is rather the least effective (Keller 2003: 685). Because of different cultural values, different income and price structures, economic development and other factors, consumer behaviour can likely be totally different across country markets (e.g., Remmerbach/Walters 1994: 658; Meffert/Bolz 1998: 186-188).[27] For example, marketing research at one time revealed that the French ate 4 times more yoghurt than the British, the British consumed 8 times more chocolate than the Italians, and Americans drunk 11 times more soft drinks than consumers abroad (Barwise/Robertson 1992; Sellers 1994). In addition, Keegan and Green (2005: 333) found that "growing national pride can result in a social backslash that favours local products and brands" (Arnold 1992: 315-316; Baumgarth 2001: 328-329; Schuiling/Kapferer 2004: 103).

Besides, consumers in foreign market can also response to marketing mix elements very differently. This is particularly a different understanding of symbols, names and colours as well as role of advertising, price promotions and usage of humour.[28] For instance, a comparative study of brand purchase intensions of Korean and US-consumers conducted by Lee and Green (1991) revealed that Americans' intensions were primarily affected by own brand and product beliefs, whereas Koreans' intensions were mainly affected by social normative beliefs and worries about what others would think of their decisions.

Similar cultural differences in behaviour are also true for administrative procedures and local employees. Keller (2003: 689) concluded that "in practice, it might be difficult to achieve the control necessary to implement a standardised global marketing program. Local offices may resist having their autonomy threatened." Moreover, a standardised brand approach disables a firm to act and react on market changes, local competition, sales and marketing institutions in an appropriate flexible way. Promising brand positions and niche markets cannot be targeted. Different stages of product life cycles cannot be addressed. Finally, potential brand failures in one

---

[27] E.g., Keegan and Green (2005: 117-146) gave a good overview and background information about different consumer behaviour in different countries, cultures and social environments.

[28] See also chapter 'Brand translations'.

country market could have immediate impact on the branded business in the home and other country markets (e.g., Schiele 1997: 142-145).

In practice, different degrees of standardisation

The pros and cons of both scenarios showed that brand differentiation primary means effectiveness, and brand standardisation primary means efficiency. In practice however, a firm does likely not choose either or, but targets an optimal degree of both criteria (Sattler 2001: 116-117; Backhaus et al. 2003a: 273). This means that a firm adapts its brand positioning to the needs of the foreign market in terms of 'how a brand looks like' (branding: brand name, brand symbol, etc.) and in terms of 'what the brand promises' (core brand values). Figure 2-3 distinguishes four typical degrees of international brand standardisation (Berndt et al. 1997: 133; similar Keegan/Green 2005: 347-348).

Fig. 2-3. Four typical degrees of international brand standardisation (based on Berndt et al. 1997: 133)

Strategy I is the approach of maximal brand standardisation and is illustrated by the corporate brand *BMW* and the product brands *Marlboro* and *Coca-Cola*. BMW promises dynamics, challenge and aesthetics under its corporate mission 'Sheer driving pleasure'. Consumers worldwide perceive brand values such as sportiness, fancy design and German quality (Baumgarth 2001: 42; Esch 2004: 93). Marlboro on the other hand stands for freedom and adventure, and Coca-Cola for fun, freshness and friendship. Although all three brands appear totally standardised having same branding and same brand values across all country markets, "closer examination reveals that the product is often far from standardised" (Kapferer 2005: 321). Marlboro, for instance, has to face different advertising regulations on cigarettes. Coca-Cola has to adapt colours and tastes according to national food regulations (Quelch/Hoff 1986; Kelz 1989; Baumgarth 2001:

331). BMW offers varying car models at different quality and price levels, e.g. in emerging markets. All three brands also have to translate advertising campaigns in local languages and according to local cultural values (Kreutzer 1989: 569; Arnold 1992: 315; Sattler 2001: 109).

Whereas in strategy I brand adaptation is very small, in strategy II major branding elements such as the brand name differs across country markets, though it promises same product and brand values. A famous example is the ice-cream of *Unilever* which is known as *Langnese* in Germany and which has been named *Ola, Frigo Algida,* and *Eskimo* in other countries (Berndt et al. 1997: 133; Baumgarth 2001: 331; Backhaus et al. 2003a: 215). Whereas Unilever's brand approach originates in M&A histories (compare to Sattler 2001: 110), the automobile *Vauxhall* in the UK is named *Opel* in Europe because of juridical trademark rights. The name was already owned by a competitor when entering the market (Kapferer 2005: 323).[29]

While strategy I and II comprise standardised brand values, strategy III offers varying brand values under the same brand name across countries. The approach is quite risky, since it can lead to unclear brand images, consumer confusion and thus to brand dilution and loss of brand credibility (Bieling/Wiechers 2004: 10). However, in practice, Kapferer (2005: 323) named cars as a product category that likely follow this brand approach: "The *Ford Fiesta* is a small car for the German market, but it is seen as a family car in Portugal". Market experts recommend a family brand approach in the case of such heterogenic product portfolios and brand values as long as they can be pooled into homogenous product lines (Berndt et al. 1997: 130-135; Esch 2004: 271-272, 406-407; Esch et al. 2004: 132-133). Under a family brand all products profit from same brand awareness and brand images without suffering brand dilution. Known examples are *Nivea* of *Beiersdorf, Kinder* of *Ferroro* or *Du darfst* of *Unilever. Nivea,* for instance, is worldwide associated with blue colour, silky skin care and family orientation, although they sell self-bronzer in Europe and promote skin whitener in Asia.[30]

Finally strategy IV is the approach of maximal brand differentiation: local brands for local markets. The brand is most likely a product brand, whose parent company behind it, is hidden (e.g., Aaker/Joachimsthaler 2000: 105; Baumgarth 2001: 138). Traditionally, US companies follow this brand approach, probably the most famous parent company is *Procter & Gamble (P&G).* Another example of such a parent company is Swiss

---

[29] See also the following chapter 'External factors'.
[30] See e.g., Esch (2004: 265-277) for details on family brands versus product and corporate brands.

Nestlé (Rüschen 1984: 47; Baumgarth 2001: 133). In Germany, P&G names their detergents *Ariel* which are similar to detergents named *Tide* in the USA and China. (Sattler 2001: 111; Kapferer 2005: 321) The brands are maximally orientated to local consumer needs and local competitors. They vary in product formulation, pricing schemes and brand values. Ideally, the products are perceived as local brands in the respective country markets, while they can still exploit cost efficiencies in terms of global R&D, production, supply chain, distribution and marketing power. (Keller 2003: 690-694)

Keegan and Green (2005: 351-354) noted that the four brand approaches of pure "brand extension and brand adaptation are effective for many but not for all country markets". They introduced the fifth strategy "product invention", arguing that to win global competition, companies have to think outside the box and create innovative new products that offer superior value worldwide. This includes inventions which address the market opportunity in low-income countries at lower price points, such as the hand-cranked radio of an English inventor, which generates energy by a short cranking session, instead of electricity and replacement batteries. These are inventions of emerging countries which raise their product design up to world-class standards in order to succeed in high-income countries. An example is the Indian *Thermax*, which has become world's largest maker for small boilers (Keegan/Green 2005: 352). Besides, product invention can also build up firm's global competitive advantage and unique selling proposition.[31] Gary (1990) identified *Motorola, Canon, Merck, Microsoft, Intel* and *Toyota* as such global companies which excel at new product development in fierce markets.[32]

2.2.2 Mode of market entry

Three alternatives

Besides the optimal degree of brand standardisation, a firm has also to decide on the optimal mode of market entry, when taking brands into global markets. Barwise and Robertson (1992) identified three alternative modes of market entry: a) exporting existing brands of the firm into the new market (geographic extension); b) acquiring existing brands already sold in the new market but not owned by the firm (brand acquisition); and c) creating

---

[31] Compare to Backhaus et al. (2003b: 35-37).

[32] For more details on global product development and global product launches see Czinkota and Ronkainen (1999: 540-551). See also Haedrich and Tomczak (2003: 95-113) and Keegan and Green (2005: 355-359) for brand innovations.

some form of brand alliance with another firm (brand alliance). All three alternatives comprise several advantages and disadvantages in terms of speed, control and investment. Barwise and Roberson evaluated them as seen in figure 2-5 and concluded that no one option dominates:

	Geographic extension	Brand acquisition	Brand alliance
Control	High	Medium	Low
Speed	Slow	Fast	Moderate
Investment	Moderate	High	Low

Fig. 2-4. Trade-off in modes of market entry (Barwise/Robertson 1992: 279)

For example, the major problem of the geographical extension is speed. Unless the firm is already a major global player both willing and able to roll out the brand from its home country to a large number of foreign countries simultaneously, globally expansion can be time-consuming slow and a market-by-market process. In a world of fast competition, the firm may no longer have the luxury time of rolling a brand sequentially into one country market after another (Barwise/Robertson 1992: 280). Brand acquisitions on the other hand, although they promise faster market entries, can be more expensive and difficult to control than it is typically assumed (Barwise/Robertson 1992: 280). The acquired brands are to be integrated in the firm's brand portfolio in terms of brand aims, branding and brand values (Brockdorff/Kernstock 2001: 55-56; Bieling/Wiechers 2004: 14).[33] In addition, internal brand management related units and departments have to be restructured and integrated into one organisation, most of the time under limitations of time, and financials and human resources (Brockdorff 2003: 3). M&A practices have shown that they often struggle and fail; studies estimated rates of failure of up to 85% (Jansen 2000: 223-226). 70% of all cross-country-mergers fail in the first three years (Müller/Gelbrich 2004: 737). M&As are considered failed if corporate and shareholder value is destroyed on the long run (Homburg et al. 2000: 6). Reasons of failure are often: not fitting company cultures, resistance of employees, different understandings of markets and consumer behaviour as well as personal ambitions of former top management teams (Brockdorff 2003: 60-62; Müller/Gelbrich 2004: 734-739; Keegan/Green 2005: 304). Cross-country-mergers are consequently the more successful, the more the acquiring company can rely on international acquisition ex-

---

[33] See chapter 'Brand transfers' for integrative opportunities.

periences, and the more it has thoroughly planned the acquisition in advance. It is also supportive, if the acquired brand contributes a strong economic market position as a basis for future growth, and if the firms' cultures, product portfolios, international scopes and company sizes are quite comparable (Link 1997; Müller/Gelbrich 2004: 739).

Finally, there is the third mode of market entry, brand alliances. They generally involve even less control than brand acquisitions, although they are likely much less costly (Barwise/Robertson 1992: 280-281). Esch (2004: 353-354) defined brand alliances (synonym: co-branding) as joint marketing of at least two existing brands in order to transfer brand images and to enhance brand success (similar Keller 2003: 360; Redler 2003: 16-21; Kapferer 2004: 91). In contrast to Barwise and Robertson (1992), the definition also includes alliances to brands of the same company. Generally, five types of brand alliances can be distinguished with respect to time of collaboration and degree of brand integration: I) co-promotions, joint communication of two brands for a short time period, e.g., joint promotion of *McDonald's* and *Disney*, or joint adverting of *Ariel* and *Whirlpool*; II) dual-branding, two brands are horizontally integrated in a new product, e.g., the ice-cream of *Häagen-Dazs* and *Baileys*, or the high-tech interactive toys of *Compaq* and *Mattel*; III) ingredient branding, two brands are vertically integrated in a new product; e.g., *Intel* chips inside *IBM* computers, *Lycra* inside *Falke*; IV) mega-brands, a bunch of brands are organised under one branded roof, e.g., *Star Alliance* promoting *Lufthansa*, *Austrian Airlines*, etc.; and V) joint ventures, shared ownership of at least two brands of a newly created business entity, e.g., *Moet Hennessey* and *Guiness* set up a sales and marketing joint venture that enabled *Guiness* to use *Moet Hennessey*'s established global distribution networks (Blackett/Russell 1999; Keller 2003: 363-364; Redler 2003: 12-14; Esch 2004: 352-354, 705; Kapferer 2004: 91-92).

Although brand alliances are widely viewed as a strategic enabler to enter new markets and consumer segments (they borrow needed market expertise, leverage equity the firm does not have, reduce costs of production launch, etc. (Sattler 2001: 106; Keller 2003: 361; Esch 2004: 358)), they have to be executed carefully. As Keller (2003: 362) described: "Fundamentally, there must be the right kind of fit in values, capabilities, and goals in addition to an appropriate balance of brand-equity. Executionally, there must be detailed plans to legalise contracts, make financial arrangements, and coordinate marketing programs. [...] The financial arrangements between brands may vary, although one common approach involves a licensing fee and royalty from the brand that is more involved in the production process."[34]

Ideally, the decision on the mode of market entry supports the chosen degree of brand standardisation. It is likely that geographical extension goes along with a high degree of brand standardisation, whereas brand acquisition and brand alliances likely involve some more differentiating brand elements, at least in initial stages.[35]

Separation from institutional entry modes

All three modes of market entry: geographical extension, brand acquisition and brand alliance, have to be distinguished from the institutional modes of market entry. Institutional modes are most likely discussed with respect to the firm's degree of involvement in overseas production capacities (e.g., Root 1994; Weiss 1996: 5-8; Oelsnitz 2000a; Keegan/Green 2005: 294). Basic institutional modes of market entry are export, contractual cooperation and foreign direct investment; addressing different levels of ownership and control (Keegan 1999: 288).[36]

Export is generally considered the first phase of corporate internationalisation. It is characterised by cross-border transportations, since the product is manufactured in another country than it is sold (Pausenberger 1994: 2; Perlitz/Seger 2000: 94). In the case that the product is sold through local sales agents and distributors, the export is indirect. This is in contrast to direct export where the product is directly sold to the end-consumer or marketed by company-owned subsidiaries (Keegan 1999: 288; Perlitz/Seger 2000: 94-96). In the case of indirect export, one has to decide whether to focus on a one-way distribution or to rely on several alternative channels in parallel (Meffert/Bolz 1998: 223).

Secondly, there is the 'contractual cooperation'. This especially includes the sub-variants 'licensing' and 'international franchising'.[37] In the case of licensing, a foreign independent company gets the permission to manufacture the firm's product in the local market for license fees. Contracts can vary, although they mostly include technology transfers in terms of pat-

---

[34] See for more details Esch (2004: 359-364), and Esch and Redler (2002).

[35] See chapter 'Brand transfers' and chapter 2.4.2 for details.

[36] See e.g., Perlitzer and Seger (2000), Root (1994), Pausenberger (1994) and the compendium of Oelsnitz (2000b) for more details and sub-variants of institutional modes of market entry. Systematic classifications are offered by Backhaus et al. (2003a: 175-197), Weiss (1996: 7) and Helm (1997: 36).

[37] In some works contract manufacturing, management contract and cross-border leasing are also discussed under contractual cooperation. See e.g., Perlitzer and Seger (2000: 102-105).

ents, employee trainings and other technical know-how from the licenser (Pausenberger 1994: 5). International franchising in contrast means a vertical licensing cooperation where foreign companies get the permission to use a certain kind of business concept for licensing fees.[38] Most famous franchisers are probably fast food chains such as *McDonald's* or retailers such as *Body Shop* (Meffert/Bolz 1998: 225; Keegan/Green 2005: 298).

Finally, there is foreign direct investment (FDI). It is often synonym for production in overseas markets (e.g., Pausenberger 1994: 8; Keegan 1999: 289). According to UNCTAD definition (2004: 345), FDI involves a long-term relationship and reflects a lasting interest and control by the foreign direct investor in an enterprise resident in an economy other than that of the foreign direct investor. FDI implies that the investor exerts a significant degree of influence on the management of the enterprise which is by operational definition an ownership of 20% and more (Keegan 1999: 294).

Dependent on the design of contractual cooperation and FDI, institutional modes of market entry may become difficult to be differentiated from brand-related modes of market entry. *Heineken*, for example, first enters a new market by exporting in order to build up brand awareness and image. If the market response is deemed satisfactory, the company will then license its brands to a local brewer in hopes of expanding volume. If that relationship is successful, Heineken may then take an equity stake or forge a joint venture (Keller 2003: 706). *Ford* motor company, on the other side, decided on the market entry mode of M&A in 1989 and acquired Jaguar PLC of Coventry, England in order to tap the luxury car market. Ford lacked a high-end luxury model for both the US and European markets, and the company was betting it could take a nameplate highly valued for exclusivity and sell it to more people by launching a new, less expensive line of Jaguars (Keegan 1999: 299). However, as the Ford history reveal, a firm has to make such market entry decisions very carefully. Since Ford name was synonymous with "bread and butter", it has since been a challenge to extend the Jaguar brand to less expensive segments without damaging the Jaguar's reputation (Keegan 1999: 299). By 2006, Ford shareholder are thus arguing to sell the luxury Jaguar brand (Financial Times Deutschland 2006).

2.2.3 Decision influencing factors

As the previous chapters reveal, strategic brand decisions have to be made carefully. They involve a multitude of different influencing factors that

---

[38] See e.g., Perlitzer (1997: 447) for different forms of international franchising.

may have to be considered: historical experiences, company internals, financial and strategic market opportunities, external market conditions etc. (Remmerbach/Walters 1994: 668; Doherty 2000: 237; O'Donnell/Jeong 2000: 20-21; Kapferer 2004: 412).

External decision influencing factors	Internal decision influencing factors
Product category	Production factors: real assets, financial assets, human resources
Possibility of internationalising brands	Existing brand portfolio
Role of domestic government	Core competence
Degree of consumer homogenisation	Functional and international experience of the management team
Brand images of competitive products	
Degree of globalisation of sales partners	Market experience of the firm (corporate history)
Image of the country-of-origin	Company culture and leadership

Fig. 2-5. External and internal influencing factors when taking brands on international markets (own illustration)

Even the same firms often use alternative options to enter new markets over the time (e.g., Alexander/Doherty 2004: 15). Figure 2-5 sums up the main internal and external brand management factors. Because of the number of individual situations the figure cannot qualify for guaranteeing completeness.[39]

External factors

First of all, there is the product category. Industrial goods and durable consumer goods likely have a higher potential of brand standardisation than FMCG. Durable consumer are particularly cultural-free and high-tech-products such as computer hardware, machine tools and consumer electronics (Sandler/Shani 1992: 28; Meffert/Bolz 1998: 183). As competition globalises, these product categories also often require a global perspective as a kind of prerequisite to survive the market (Thomas et al. 1995).[40] In contrast, product categories of high national identity, e.g., alcoholics, toilet articles, print media, and food are likely not qualified for successful brand standardisation (Meffert/Bolz 1998: 183; also O'Donnell/Jeong 2000: 21).

---

[39] It is explicitly stressed that the figure focuses on brand relevant factors. See Berndt et al. (2003) and Backhaus et al. (2003a) for an overview on more general factors such as macro-economic, political, socio-cultural and geographical factors. Compare also to chapter 1 'limits of study'.

[40] Compare to chapter 2.1: 'brand aims'.

One reason is that they likely lack the ability of product transportation, durableness and trade (Remmerbach 1988: 149-160).

A second factor is the "possibility of internationalising brands" (Bieling/Wiechers 2004: 11). This includes political and juridical regulations, technological product requirements as well as the possibility to protect brands in the respective countries. For instance, the German detergent *Persil* had to be renamed into *Le Chat* in France, as the brand name was already owned by a competitor (Seidler 1998: 12). Moreover, despite of progress in world trade organisations (WTO, EU, NAFTA and ASEAN), there are still trade barriers preventing the spread of global brands: unsure brand protection rights and brand counterfeiting in China (e.g., Sattler 2001: 113; Backhaus et al. 2003a: 129-144), anti-dumping taxes and import quota in US and European markets (e.g., Pausenberger 1994: 4; Pinzler 2006), limitations for foreign companies to have majority stakes into joint ventures, e.g., in China (e.g., Keegan 1999: 295).

Besides protectionism of foreign governments, the role of the domestic government can also play a crucial role in the firm's strategic brand decisions. Rautsola (1988: 93-96) found that a state has a multitude of possibilities to assist and enhance corporate competitiveness in direct and indirect ways. This includes export promotion, economy policy, and industrial policy in terms of subsidies and tax benefits. Rautsola (1988: 104-105) stressed the example of the European consortium *Airbus* that got large subsidies from the French and German governments in order to build up a European aircraft industry as a counterbalance to US-*Boeing*.

Last but not least, a firm has to evaluate the target country with respect to market players. There are local consumers and their degree of consumer homogenisation to national consumers, including local preferences, role of brands and size of consumer segments. The more similar consumers are across country markets, and the more the values of the established national brand suit them, the better can brands be standardised (Backhaus et al. 2003a: 201; Keegan/Green 2005: 338). In addition, the brand images of competitive products play an important role for the firm's own potential brand success in a foreign market. Whether a brand is perceived as independent and superior to competitive brands, it primarily based on consumers' associations with the competitive established brands in the market (Langner 2003: 22). Since brand values like price-value, innovation and trustworthiness are, though attractive for consumers, already pretty common and little differentiating in most markets, the implementation of the brand values gets increasingly crucial. For instance, the German insurance brand *Würtembergische* distinguished itself by the emotional key illustration and slogan 'firm as a rock' (original: 'Fels in der Brandung') (Thometzek 1995: 24-25).[41]

Besides consumers and competitors, there are also <u>sales partners and their degree of globalisation</u> that have impact on a firm's brand strategy. Large retail chains such as *IKEA*, *Wal-Mart*, *Carrefour*, and *Metro* run sales outlets worldwide and likely require standardised brands in each shop at a competitive price point (Schiele 1997: 146-147; Euromonitor 2006). *Unilever*, for instance, reduced its brands from 1,600 mainly national brands towards 400 more regional and global brands in order to meet the increasing pricing pressure. On the other hand, localised brands offer the opportunity to limit black market activities and re-imports (Sattler 2001: 112; Kapferer 2004: 406; Schuiling/Kapferer 2004: 98).

Finally, the <u>firm's country-of-origin</u> (COO) is another decision influencing factor when taking brands into foreign markets (Lampert/Jaffe 1996). Synonym is country image (Baumgarth 2001: 188).[42] Perceptions and associations about a country can be positive or negative (Keegan/Green 2005: 341). On the positive side, 'German' stands for quality engineering, 'Italian' for stylish and 'French' is synonym for chic (Milbank 1994). As industries globalise, COO becomes more complex. Whereas studies revealed that consumers likely do not pay attention to country-of-assembly and 'made in' labels (e.g., Gilmore/Dumont 2003: xvi-xvii), country-of-design and brand ownership is an important purchase decision factor (Papadopoulos 1993; Ahmed/d'Astous 1995).[43] Country stereotypes can consequently become a competitive disadvantage, if consumers show significant bias or the country image does not fit to the firm's brand values in terms of quality, price and benefits. On the other hand, in some product categories foreign products are just favoured because of their "foreignness" (Keegan/Green 2005: 343). Baumgarth (2001: 188-191) proposed to actively utilise the country image for global brand building, if it is positively differentiating from other regional images. If the brand belongs to a product category a country is known for (e.g., Germany: cars, Italy: shoes; Switzerland: watches), or if the image supports key brand values. It is

---

[41] Compare to operative chapters in 2.3.

[42] Nagashima (1970: 68; emphasis added by Amine et al. 2005: 120) defined country image "as the picture, the reputation, the stereotype that businessmen and consumers attach to products of a specific country. This image is created by such variables as representative products, national characteristics, economic and political background, history, and traditions".

[43] See, for instance, Ahmed and d'Astous (1995) for definitions and more details on country-of-design and country-of-assembly. See Usunier (2000: 318) for an overview about country, company and brand-related product images.

noted that COO effects are not absolute for a given country. They can vary across product categories, country markets and time (Amine et al. 2005; Keegan/Green 2005: 342-343).

Internal factors

In addition to external influencing factors, firms also differ in resources, capabilities and willingness to identify and implement optimal brand strategies (Keegan/Green 2005: 353). From the perspective of classical economy, corporate resources are the limited <u>production factors: real assets, financial assets and human resources</u>. After being allocated they cannot be used in alternative ways without causing extra costs (e.g., Agarwal/Ramaswami 1992: 3; Helm 1997: 43). With respect to going-international, these are particularly products, financial assets, technological know-how, and management capacities (Helm 1997: 44). It is likely, the larger the company size, production capacity, overall profitability and access to global financial markets, the larger the resources to support international brand ambitions (Remmerbach 1988: 167-172).

A specific kind of internal resource is the <u>existing brand portfolio</u> of a firm. A brand portfolio (synonym: brand architecture) is defined as the total of all existing brands in a company, including scope, roles and interrelationships of portfolio brands and co-brands with other firms (Kapferer 1992; Aaker/Joachimsthaler 2000: 134; Brockdorff 2003: 7; Aaker 2004: 13-17). There are two extreme architectures: the "house of brands" and the "branded house" (Aaker/Joachimsthaler 2000: 105). As the name indicates the house of brands refers to a company which operates through well-known product brands but remains itself discreet if not hidden. *P&G* is such a company or *Mars* that offers chocolates as well as dog food (Esch et al. 2004: 135). The branded house is the inverse case. A company itself is the one and single brand, acting as a banner and umbrella brand (Kapferer 2004: 319). *Vodafone, BMW, Siemens* and *Virgin* are such branded houses. Siemens, for instance, sells household appliances, telecommunication, medical engineering as well as power plants under its corporate brand name (Aaker/Joachimsthaler 2000: 105; Baumgarth 2001: 136; Esch 2004: 419; Esch et al. 2004: 135).[44] Between both extremes, Aaker and Joachimsthaler (2000: 105) found further types of brand architectures where either the corporate brand ("sub-brands") or the product brand ("endorsed brands") dominates, e.g., *'Courtyard* by *Marriott'* is an example for a "strong endorsement", *3M (Henkel)* is a "token endorse-

---

[44] See for more details i.e. Aaker and Joachimsthaler (2000), Kapferer (2004: 292-327), Baumgarth (2001: 127-141), and Laforet and Saunders (1994: 68).

ment", *Gillette Sensor* a "co-driver" or a dual-brand. In principle, the more the brand architecture is alike a branded house, the larger synergies among the portfolio brands (Esch 2004: 420-422). Kapferer (2004: 321-324; also Schuiling/Kapferer 2004: 98) argued that when going-international, a firm does not have to copy its national brand portfolio in each country. As the competitive status of brands can vary across countries and a brand might explicitly have been purchased for getting access into a market, a global brand portfolio should rather be managed in a flexible way (similar Aaker 2004; Esch et al. 2004).

Besides resources, a second important internal decision factor is corporate capabilities. One capability is the firm's <u>core competence</u> which comprises the relative competitive advantage of a firm that results in a positive consumer preference towards the firm's product and brand (Backhaus et al. 2003b: 43). Generally, a firm could achieve competitive advantages in all steps along the value chain. *Nike*, for instance, is reckoned to have its core competence in branding & consumer insights, whereas e.g., *Toyota* is known for organisational effectiveness and *Dell* for supply chain and distribution. As a result, a specific core competence can be the basis for the brand's unique selling proposition and brand positioning. The brand strategy of product invention is the more promising, the more core competences the firm has in technology and design (Keegan/Green 2005: 351-354).

Another capability of firms is experience. O'Donnell and Jeong (2000: 22) found that especially <u>functional and international experience of the management team</u> are crucial for international strategies. They understood functional experience as experience in marketing and brand management, and interpreted international experience as a proxy for the ability of a firm to reduce uncertainty, accumulate cultural knowledge, and internationalise the firm's management according to globalisation pressure (Sambharya 1996). They concluded that the greater the marketing experience of the employed subsidiary and country managers, the stronger the positive relationship between firm's standardisation and firm's performance (Quelch 1992; O'Donnell/Jeong 2000: 28-29).[45]

Other studies proved that the <u>market experience of the firm itself (corporate history)</u> also has an impact on brand strategies. Less internationally experienced firms, for instance, were found to choose overseas involvements of higher control than more experienced firms (e.g., Helm 1997: 85-88). The EPRG-concept of Perlmutter und Heenan (1974: 121-123; 1979: 17-22) showed that a firm tends to focus on domestic markets in the first

---

[45] See for international experience and perceived risk also Müller and Gelbrich (2004: 724-729).

phase of going-international (Ethnocentric). International sales are considered as adjunct to domestic business and as a source of quick profits. In a second phase (Polycentric), the firm expand its scope on local, most likely product brands in foreign markets. The local brands are grouped into regional brands across several country markets such as Europe in a third phase (Regional-centric). In the most experienced phase (Geocentric), the firm finally recognises the world as one relevant market and focuses on global brands.[46] As international company behaviour has revealed, the ethnocentric phase likely takes longer if the home market, in terms of consumer potential and market size, is larger. For example, US-companies tended to internationalise later in corporate history than companies from smaller countries such as from Switzerland and the Netherlands (Czinkota/Ronkainen 1999: 4). Further, Japanese companies typically skipped the polycentric and regional phases, and internationalised immediately towards a geocentric view (Meffert 1986: 690).

Interlinked to corporate experience is the decision factor of <u>company culture and corporate leadership</u>. For instance, companies with centralised power and an autocratic management style often tend to decide on majority or full control when going-international (Tse et al. 1997; Pan/Tse 2000; Mayrhofer 2004: 82). A promising basis for building brands across country markets is often seen in 'enlightened leaders'. Hewlett Packard CEO, Carly Fiorina said: "Leadership is not about hierarchy or title or status: [...] it is about empowering others to decide for themselves" (quoted in Keegan/Green 2005: 531). Leaders of organisations with international marketing focus, the CEO or top management team, are expected to be able to articulate values, policies and geographic scope of firm's activities, to know to actively leverage human resources and their ideas and complaints, to rely on globally experienced managers, to demand exposure to different languages and cultures, and to continuously rethink the companies goals from a global perspective (Aaker/Joachimsthaler 2000: 7-13; O'Donnell/Jeong 2000: 23; Keegan/Green 2005: 531-535; Van Gelder 2005). Keegan and Green (2005: 533) concluded that "the best person for top management or the board position is not necessarily someone born in the home market". Aaker and Joachimsthaler (2000: 8) added: "For organizations where there is marketing talent at the top, the brand manager can be and often is the CEO."

---

[46] See also Meffert (1986: 690), Meffert and Burmann (1996: 23), and Meissner (1994: 677).

2.3 Operative brand decisions when going-international

After a firm has decided on its adequate level of brand standardisation and mode of market entry, the firm has to implement these strategic decisions by operative brand measures in the respective foreign country markets. These are particularly decisions on branding, brand communication, brand distribution and brand organisation. Dependent on the choice of the strategic brand alternatives, corporate competences and given market conditions, design, role and relevance of the operative measures can vary across foreign markets and decision settings.

2.3.1 Branding

Brand translations

Branding is defined as the integrated brand design of brand name, brand illustrations (logo, symbols, key image, slogan, jingle etc.) and brand packaging, also including elements such as form, colour, taste, smell and material of the product (Kroeber-Riel 1993: 58-60; Baumgarth 2001: 160; Langner 2003: 4-6, 25-26; Esch 2004: 169-171). In general, nonverbal elements such as logos and symbols have to directly transfer into foreign country markets, as they do not require translations into another language (Keller 2003: 718; Kapferer 2004: 413). Famous examples for non-verbal brand elements are the red *Nike* swoosh, the green *Lacoste* crocodile, the design of the purple *Milka* cow or the *Marlboro* cowboy. However, as table 2-1 indicates, nonverbal elements such as brand colours can sometimes encounter translation problems, too. Whereas Chinese consumers likely associate red colour with festive and enjoyable brands, US consumers likely associate red with cheapness (Yang 2005: 119-120).[47] Brand symbols such as animals can also have different cultural meanings: Whereas the pig stands for happiness and wealth in Korea, Jews and Moslems consider the pig as unclean (Schiele 1997: 133-134; Müller/Gelbrich 2004: 343-344).

In contrast to nonverbal brand elements, the translation of the brand name, slogan and jingle is always highly challenging and critical for the success of a product in a foreign market (Usunier 2000: 331; Dong/Helms 2001: 99-100). The precondition is that the brand name has to be easily pronounceable. Backhaus et al. (similar Usunier 2000: 331; 2003a: 210) advised against local language specifics such as German umlaut, Slavic

---

[47] See also detailed works of Müller and Gelbrich (2004: 346-353), Jacobs et al. (1991), Grimes and Doole (1998) and Aslam (2006).

queues of consonants or French accents. Naturally, complicated brand names are difficult to memorise for most consumers in many countries, and are thus likely to be less preferred (Robertson 1987). Difficult brand names can also emerge as a serious obstacle when dealing with sales partners and other third parties in foreign countries, since they can create confusion particularly on the phone (Usunier 2000: 331-332).

	China	USA	Japan	Korea
Grey	cheap	valuable, top-quality	cheap	cheap
Blue	top-quality	sincere, reliable	sincere, reliable	top-quality, reliable
Green	immaculate, sincere	tasteful, adventurous	immaculate, tasteful	immaculate, sincere
Red	enjoyable, festive	cheap, love	enjoyable, adventurous	top-quality, love
Yellow	wealth & glory, lucky	welfare, immaculate	wealth & glory, welfare	welfare, reliable
Purple	valuable, mystic	cheap, aggressive	cheap	cheap, love
Brown	top-quality	cheap	cheap	cheap
Black	valuable, funeral	powerful, valuable	powerful, valuable	powerful, valuable
White	elegant, immaculate	top-quality	elegant, immaculate	new & fresh, top-quality

Table 2-1. Different understanding of brand colours across countries (own translation of Yang 2005: 119)

In addition to pronunciation difficulties, brand names activate various meanings and associations of the consumers' memories which can be positive or negative (Francis et al. 2002: 99). Backhaus et al. (2003a: 210-211) gave the example of car model *Chevy Nova* which was launched in Spain in the 1980s by US-*Chevrolet*. The brand, although considered a promising name because easily to pronounce in Spanish and of positive connotations: nova meaning new, did not sell well. The reason was that *Chevrolet* overlooked that Chevy Nova phonetically sounds like 'Chevy no va' – Chevy does not go/function (also Schiele 1997: 132-133; Usunier 2000: 336).

There is evidence that the more the language system and cultural background differ from the home country, the more brand names are translated into the new language and not kept in the original tone. A study of Francis et al. (2002: 108-109) revealed that the majority of US-brand names had adapted to the Chinese market, although they are likely known for English originals (Kapferer 2004: 419). In principle, there are three modes of translation: free translation, literal translation and creative translation (Dong/Helms 2001: 107-110; Francis et al. 2002: 102). Free translation is based on semantic equivalence and is the transfer of the original meaning in another language. Example is the US-hair care product *Silkience* of *Gillette* that is sold in France under the brand name *Soyance* and in Italy under *Sientel* (Usunier 2000: 332). Literal translation (synonym: transliteration) in contrast is based on phonetic equivalence and is the transfer of the original sound into another language. Examples are *Coca Cola* that is可口可乐 'kekou kele' and *Chrysler* which is 克莱斯勒 'kelai sile' in Chinese (Dong/Helms 2001: 107-108).[48] Finally, there is creative translation which is based on neither original meaning nor its sound, but intends to create a brand name that has the most desired meaning in the new culture and language. Dong and Helm (2001: 109) found the German car brand *BMW* as an example. Since Chinese consumers traditionally favour the image of 'horse', BMW is translated in 宝马 ('baoma') meaning 'precious horse' implying that it runs fast and runs for a long time.[49]

With respect to corporate names, Usunier (2000: 331) noted that it is symbolically difficult to change and translate such brand names, in the case they are closely associated with corporate history and related to the founder's name. *Siemens*, *Bosch* and *P&G* are such corporate brand names (Usunier 2000: 331; Esch et al. 2004: 132). In China, for example, Siemens thus uses the translated brand name 西门子 ('ximenzi') attached to the original brand name *Siemens*. Brand name translations are even more challenging if there is a link between the brand name and the brand symbol. Kapferer (2004: 419) gave the example of the French cheese *La Vache Qui Rit* which means the laughing cow. The brand symbol is a cow's head. In the case the brand name is not correctly translated and understood by the consumer, the cow can appear stupid and mad instead of smiling.

To circumvent translation difficulties, brand experts propose emphasising brand symbols and brand illustrations instead of the brand name itself when going-international (Kroeber-Riel 1993; Usunier 2000: 334; Kroeber-Riel/Esch 2004). For instance, the imagery of the IBM logo and its alternate slats of coloured bands are considered to be translinguistic. However, trademark legislation varies around the world. In some countries trademarks can only be composed of letters and their designs must be separately registered under the design and pattern law. In the US, for in-

---

[48] Whereas the translation of Chrysler does not comprise any meaning in Chinese, Coca-Cola got a meaning attached through the process of translation: "tastes good and make you happy".

[49] See Usunier (2000: 335) for linguistic details at creative translation such as phonetic, orthographic, morphological, and semantic devices.

stance, there is no such need for additional protection of the design (Usunier 2000: 334), but brand names have to meet a hierarchy of registration eligibility: "fanciful (*Kodak*), arbitrary (*Camel*), suggestive (*Eveready*), descriptive (*Ivory*), and generic (*aspirin*), the last being unprotectable" (Onkvisit/Shaw 1989: 30).[50]

Besides brand names, the verbal elements brand slogan and jingle can encounter similar difficulties. Slogans are short phrases which communicate descriptive and emotional information about the brand during its advertising (Baumgarth 2001: 170; Keller 2003: 204-206). They can and cannot include the brand name itself, examples from Germany are: 'Haribo macht Kinder froh und Erwachsene ebenso', or 'Geiz ist geil' *(Saturn)*. Jingles are musical brand elements which often supports the slogan by a certain melody, rhythm or tone. For example, the sail-away melody of *Becks* beer or the melody of *Bacardi*-feeling is famous in Germany (Baumgarth 2001: 170). Dependent on language system and cultural background, on has to evaluate whether free translation, transliteration or the creation of a totally new brand slogan and jingle is appropriate for the new country market. *Coca-Cola,* for instance, is considered to promote same slogans and jingles worldwide (Quelch/Hoff 1986; Kelz 1989; Baumgarth 2001: 331).

Brand transfers

Because of the desire to standardise globally, many firms attempt to uniform their branding across all foreign markets and reorganise their multibrand portfolios when going-international (Kapferer 2004: 356). According to Kapferer (2004: 419), this is especially changes in brand names, since worldwide standardised names are often seen as "the ultimate symbol of successful globalisation". Firms thus reduce the number of brands in the portfolio as well as the number of products under one brand name. Examples are *Raider-Twix, Anderson-Accenture, Pal-Pedigree*, as well as the creation of large groups such as *Novartis* and *Vodafone* (e.g., Kapferer 1992: 256; Esch et al. 2004: 130-132; Kapferer 2004: 355-356). Brand transfers (synonym: brand migrations) occur, if "products under brands due to disappear will have to be transferred to one of the remaining brands" (Kapferer 2004: 14). Brockdorff (Brockdorff/Kernstock 2001: 57-

---

[50] See Schiele (1997: 127-135) for details on international brand registration processes. He distinguished between application of a brand on the basis of national protection rights and international registration on the basis of cross-country protection agreements. Compare also to previous chapter 'Brand translations' for obstacles in brand protection.

58; 2003: 127) advanced the definition to "brand integration", also including brand transfers to newly created brand names such as *e.on* (former *Viag* and *Veba*) and brand combinations such as *DaimlerChrysler* or *AstraZeneca*.[51]

The approach of abandoning an existing brand and transferring it to a different brand is risky, since the market lose one of its benchmarks, choices or and consumers' favourites (Kapferer 2004: 353). On the company side, many examples have shown that besides pure name changes, brand transfers can also involve changes in marketing mix, product formulation, and organisational structure. The firm has to convince loyal customers, employees, and suppliers of the new brand name, and has to avoid brand damages which could lead to decreases in market shares (Kapferer 1992: 220-229; also Esch et al. 2004: 131; Kapferer 2004: 353). In principle, such risks varie whether it is a corporate brand name, a family brand name or a product brand name that is transferred, and whether it is a strong and valuable brand name or not (Bieling/Wiechers 2004: 17).[52]

In the literature, three alternative ways of brand transfers are distinguished with respect to speed and amount of information provided to customers (Kapferer 1992: 257-258; Liedtke 1994): a) progressive migration; b) information supported disruption; and c) clean break. The progressive migration involves a transition phase where the existing and the future brand are promoted together. The customer is introduced to the new brand name, while the old brand name serves as an anchor of recognition and guarantee. Positive brand images and brand values are ideally transferred and extended. Over the time, the old brand name is gradually eliminated and the new brand name starts dominating the brand (Kapferer 1992: 257). One has to note that progressive migration is likely more successful if the consumer is not aware of the transfer itself (Liedtke 1994: 806-807). Figure 2-6 shows the example of the brand transfer of *Créola* and *Chamby* (Kapferer 1992: 221-229): In 1985 *Nestlé* bought the product line *La Roche-aux-Fées* from *Unilever*. The product line offered the same range of products as Nestlé's family brand *Chambourcy* and had equivalent market shares of 11% in France. To reduce complexity, Nestlé decided to transfer all products to the family brand *Chambourcy*. Brand symbols, annexes and package design supported the re-branding.

---

[51] In the following, the terms 'brand transfer', 'brand migration' and 'brand integration' are semantically equally used in the sense of brand transfers.

[52] See Bieling and Wiechers (2004: 17) for details on risk evaluation methods and criteria.

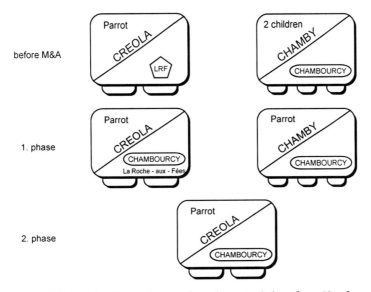

Fig. 2-6. Example of merging two brand names (taken from Kapferer 1992: 225)

Another possibility to implement progressive migration is inverting the hierarchical significance of the old and new brand. Graphically the size of the old brand name is reduced and finally eliminated, while the size and dominance of the new brand name increase. Figure 2-7 shows the example of *Vodafone* (Bieling/Wiechers 2004: 39-45). A third solution is to add same pre- or suffix to each brand. Later the brand names are eliminated and the pre- or suffix becomes the future brand name. *Alcatel* transferred its brands to the same corporate brand name in this way. Telic-Alcatel, Opus-Alcatel etc. (Kapferer 1992: 227). Many other steps and brand combinations are also possible within the transition phase. The more steps the transition phase include, however, the more expensive, the more complex and time consuming the transfer will be (e.g., Bieling/Wiechers 2004: 23).

The method of 'information supported disruption' involves not such a transition phase, but a phase of announcing the up-coming brand transfer to the public. Kapferer (1992: 257-258) mentioned the example of *Night & Day*, a decaffeinated coffee brand of *Jacobs*. The product was originally launched as *Nuit et Jour* in France and later internationalised in several country markets by free brand translation: *Tag & Nacht* in Germany, Austria and the Switzerland; *Night & Day* in the US and Canada. In 1987, Jacobs decided to build up a global brand name called *Jacobs*. In France they announced the brand transfer by etiquettes on product packages and the radio: 'Nuit et Jour is going to be called Night & Day soon'.

Fig. 2-7. Example of inverting hierarchical significance (based on Bieling/ Wiechers 2004: 41-46)

The third method of brand transfer is the 'clean break'. In contrast to both first methods, the consumer is not informed or introduced into the new brand name, but is confronted by a new name over night. The regional US-airline *Allegheny*, for instance, changed its name to *USAir* on the 28 October 1979. In December 1986 the sweets *Treets* were eliminated and *M&M's* was quasi launched as a new product brand, only using same slogans and jingles (Kapferer 1992: 228, 258). The option of clean break is considered risky and likely conducted if the old name has negative or zero brand images, or if the loss of the old brand value is consciously taken into account in order to achieve higher scores by the new brand name (Liedtke 1994: 805; Voeth/Wagemann 2004). However, there are also many bad experiences: The washing-up liquid named *Fairy* in Germany was suddenly renamed into the US existing brand name *Dawn* in 2000. As a result of confused consumers, the company lost revenues of around 50%. In 2002, the re-branding was therefore reversed to the old name *Fairy*. (Meffert 2002: 119; Bieling/Wiechers 2004: 20-21)

Whereas most of the mentioned brand transfers migrated to existing brands, it is noticeable that there are also companies that have internationalised their corporate brand names by brand abbreviations or creation of new brand names. Known examples of brand abbreviations are US-telecommunication firm *AT&T* ('American Telephone and Telegraph'), Germany's car maker *BWM* ('Bayrische Motorenwerke AG') or Korean's electronics company *LG (Lucky Goldstar)* (Keegan/Green 2005: 338). Today's *Danone* implemented a reverse strategy. They replaced its corporate abbreviation *BSN* by the newly created brand name *Danone*, because they have not seen chances to establish a basis for global recognition with an acronym (Kapferer 2004: 356). Overall, one can conclude that brand transfers require more thought of preparation and explanation to consumers, employees and other parties when the brand transfers are more radical (Kapferer 1992: 228-229). Also, transfers to brand abbreviations and meaningless fantasy names are likely more challenging and less successful than to existing brand names, as they cannot be connected to product categories and are thus more difficult to memorise (Endmark 2001; Backhaus et al. 2003a: 211; Esch 2004: 177-179).

2.3.2 Brand communication

Beyond brand names, a firm has also to decide on an adequate brand communication plan when it enters a new foreign market. Brand communication is defined as the appropriate placing of a brand into a market in order to positively influence the customers' buying behaviour towards the brand (Meffert/Bolz 1998: 189). The central communication aims are building brand awareness, and building and enhancing brand image (Esch 2004: 230). Brand awareness "refers to the strength of a brand's presence in the consumer's mind" (Aaker 2002: 10). Does the customer know and recognise the brand? Is the brand among the customer's top-of-mind alternatives? Brand image, in contrast, is the total of all memorised and learned brand associations in the consumer's mind (Aaker 2002: 25). What does the customer associate with a brand? Which pictures, which colours? Since brand communication can become very expensive and brand-intensive companies such as *L'Oréal* spend typically more than 30% of their global revenues on advertising and promotion each year (corporate websites), Keller (2003: 696) argued that when going-international a company first has to develop a hierarchy of brand associations. This defines the associations which are supposed to be held by consumers in all countries and which only in certain countries. In a second step, the company then has to establish some brand awareness before launching these brand associations in the new market.[53]

When deciding on appropriate communication channels, creativity has no limits; in principle any promotional carrier is possible including naked bodies or manholes.[54] To structure major brand communication channels, there are different possibilities provided in the literature (e.g., Bruhn 1995: 36; Rossiter/Percy 2001; Esch 2004: 236-237). Figure 2-8 differentiates between classical and non-classical communication. Non-classical is characterised by a high degree of newness in the market and direct communication to end-consumers (Baumgarth 2001: 194).

---

[53] See for brand awareness and brand image also chapter 2.4.1: brand controlling. The decision on key brand illustrations is interlinked to the decision on the optimal degree of brand standardisation as described in chapter 2.1.2.

[54] See e.g., Esch (2004: 239) for a list of criteria on how to choose the most appropriate channel.

Classical communication channels	Non-classical communication channels
Advertising (TV, radio, newspapers, magazines, billboards, cinema)	Events
	Customer clubs
Sales promotion (price reduction, sampling, couponing, etc.)	Product placement
	Internet presence
Public relation	Testimonials
Sponsoring (sport, culture, social)	Road-Shows
Trade fairs and exhibitions	Customer magazines
...	Telephone hotlines
	Direct mailing
	Mobile marketing
	Ambient Media (e.g., postcards)
	...

Fig. 2-8. Overview about major classical and non-classical communication channels (based on Baumgarth 2001: 194; Esch 2004: 237)

Across international markets the optimal choice and communication mix can heavily differ from the approach in the home market because of different media regulations and role of channels (Meffert/Bolz 1998: 200-211; Keegan/Green 2005: 477-499).[55] However, some communication rules are true for all markets: Advertising can faster reach larger numbers of potential consumers and is less expensive compared to direct communications in terms of costs per contact (Rossiter/Percy 2001; Esch 2004: 231). The more the consumer is involved in a product, the less repetitions of advertising are required (Kroeber-Riel/Esch 2004: 158). And, if more similar channels are broadcasted on, sold and used across countries (e.g., *Time, Newsweek, CNN, Eurosport,* etc.), the brand can profit from "cost-free" spillover effects (Meffert/Bolz 1998: 203).

In the case that a firm has decided on a standardised global brand approach, particularly those brand communication channels become interesting, which can push brand building activities across all country markets in a simultaneous way. These are especially: sponsoring, product placement, testimonials, and trade-fairs (Meffert/Bolz 1998: 216; Gould et al. 2000; Keegan/Green 2005: 495-498).[56]

---

[55] Compare to previous chapters.

[56] Compare to advantages of global brand approach as presented in chapter 'Brand differentiation or brand standardisation?'. Notice that the selection does not involve an evaluation which communication channels are the best in order to go international. For instance, classical advertising can be of course a valuable option in each market; but it is likely conducted on a country-by-country basis and involves little interrelationships with home and other foreign markets. For more details on the other communication channels see works of Keegan/Green (2005), Esch (2004), Bruhn (2003) and Meffert/Bolz (1998).

Sponsoring

Sponsoring means that a company pays a fee or provides goods, services and know-how to have its name associated with a particular event, team, association or facility in the area of sports, culture and social welfare (Baumgarth 2001: 186; Keegan/Green 2005: 495). Sponsorships, particularly large scale events, ensure that a brand name will draw considerable media attention and will be mentioned numerous times on-air. For instance, an Olympic Game or World Cup soccer sponsorship can help a company reach global audiences (Alonzo 1994; Keegan/Green 2005: 495). For more than 20 years, *Coca-Cola* has been the official soft drink sponsor of the World Cup soccer. For one year sponsorship, they pay around US$35m to the FIFA (International Federation of Football Association) plus an equivalent amount on promotion; broadcasted football matches reach around 44 billion viewers in more than 200 countries (Keegan/Green 2005: 495).[57] For sponsors of 2006 World Cup soccer figure 2-9.

Fig. 2-9. Sponsors of 2006 World Cup soccer (taken from FIFA websites)

---

[57] Compare to the story of *MasterCard* presented in Aaker and Joachimsthaler (2000: 198-203) or examples mentioned in Alonzo (1994).

Besides brand awareness, sponsored events also offer publicity for product launch or technology showcases that represent key associations of a corporate brand: For instance, *Panasonic* installed the largest video display in a US stadium at the Atlanta Olympics in 1996 (Aaker/Joachimsthaler 2000: 206); *Sony* became an official US-sponsor of the National Basketball Association with a signing of a US$10m per year deal in order to get priority air-time for Sony Music labelled musicians such as Pearl Jam and Mariah Carey during the games (Keegan/Green 2005: 495).

Similar to brand alliances, it is crucial for successful brand sponsorships how well the brand and the sponsored object fit together. Baumgarth (2001: 186-187) distinguished between the fit in performance (*Adidas* & sports), target group (*Krombacher* beer & football), image (sport sponsoring & dynamic, young, powerful) and regional focus (*Bayer* & football team Leverkusen). Moreover, small numbers of sponsors and some base amount of brand awareness are crucial to make the sponsorship be realised by target groups (Aaker/Joachimsthaler 2000: 222-227; d'Astous et al. 2000; Hermanns 2004).

Product placement

A special kind of cultural sponsoring is product placement. It involves the purposeful placement of the brand as a requisite in the story line of a movie, popular television program, and other types of performances (Meffert/Bolz 1998: 214). Particularly blockbuster movies are considered a popular entertaining medium which can equal worldwide audiences of tens of millions of people (Keegan/Green 2005: 496). For companies of a standardised brand approach, product placement then offers the opportunity to communicate a brand image which is "frozen" and will be seen without any adaptation everywhere in the world (Gould et al. 2000). In general, product placement fees are paid by financial assets. However, company practice has shown that product placement can also be accomplished by real assets, marketing and promotion support of the new production, or merchandising rights (Meffert/Bolz 1998: 214; Keegan/Green 2005: 496).[58] Fees are variable and usually depend on the relative exposure of the product in the movie. Most famous product placements have taken place

---

[58] Fees are the reason why product placement is not equivalent to surreptitious advertising. This occurs when promotional media is used free of charge and without approval, which is forbidden in many countries (Meffert/Bolz 1998: 214). See for further ethical and regulatory issues also Gupta and Gold (1997) and Gould et al. (2000).

with high profile projects such as *James Bond* films. There is research evidence that such placements are more effective than classical ads (Gupta/Gould 1997: 37).

As movies get more expensive, studios are increasingly looking for partnerships. The recent James Bond *Die Another Day* cost nearly US$100m to produce plus further US$20-30m on marketing spendings. In 1995 *BMW* launched its newly sportive car Z3 and placed it in *Golden Eye* (Keegan/Green 2005: 497). A market observer commented: "BMW has shaken, not just stirred, the auto industry with unprecedented media exposure and awareness for the Z3 and BMW in the US" (Rappoport 1996; also Burt 2002). In the following-up film *Tomorrow Never Dies* overall product placements have been estimated to US$100m: *Ericsson, Heineken, Omega, Brioni*, and *Visa International* have all showed up. *BMW* was replaced by an *Aston-Martin* (Keegan/Green 2005: 497), but came back with the Z8 model in *The world is not enough* in 1999. See figure 2-10.

Fig. 2-10. Product placement of BMW Z8 in James Bond *The world is not enough* (taken from www.jamesbond.de)

Testimonials

A testimonial (synonym: presenter, spokesperson, celebrity) is a known, not anonymous person among the target group who presents and recommends a brand during communication activities (Haase 2000: 56; Baumgarth 2001: 184). In most cases a testimonial is visualised on advertisements and on TV. Famous examples are Pelé for *MasterCard*, Boris Becker for *Nutella* and *AOL*, Claudia Schiffer for *L'Oréal* and *OTTO*, and Heidi Klum for *McDonalds*. Generally a testimonial can fulfil three functions (Haase 2000: 256; Koeppler 2000: 218; Baumgarth 2001: 184): a) guarding consumers' attention towards the communication channel; b) transferring image attributes from the testimonial to the brand; and c) intensifying the brand positioning by trustworthy guarantee. Similar to previous communication channels, the success of testimonials is highly dependent on the fit between the prominent person and the brand. This is most likely evaluated by the endorser's trustworthiness. A endorser is considered trustworthy if people perceive him to be honest and sincere, whereas an untrustworthy endorser is one, about which people feel scepticism and suspicion (Priester/Petty 2003: 408).

To estimate the degree of trustworthiness, consumers unconsciously evaluate the celebrity's know-how and experience with the brand and his/her overall reliability with respect to status, life attitudes and social behaviour (Baumgarth 2001: 184). Empirical research has shown that consumers' attitude to the brand's advertising can change and their perceived trustworthiness shrinks the more different brands a prominent person promotes at the same time (Tripp/Jensen 1994). It also shrinks, if the prominent person makes negative headlines. For instance, the report about Boris Becker's divorce and affair with a Russian beauty has not fit to the brand positioning of *AOL* towards happy families (Baumgarth 2001: 184). On the other hand, studies have also proven that in some occasions bad headlines and untrustworthy testimonials can also support brand awareness building, since bad headlines are sometimes more powerful than no headlines (Priester/Petty 2003: 408). Finally, research has shown that attractiveness of testimonials might be desirable with respect to 'sex sells' (Haase 2000: 58), but that pure beauty is not sufficient to enhance brand image in any case. For example, Solomon and Ashmore (1992) found that a sex-promising beauty fits to the magazine *Cosmopolitan*, whereas in contrast a classic-feminine beauty fits to the brand *Chanel* (similar Koeppler 2000: 224-227).

Trade-fairs

Trade-fairs are periodical events with a character of a market where several manufactures offer their products and brands in a competitive environment. From the customers' point of view, trade fairs reduce transaction costs, since they provide several kinds of information at a single place (Roth 1981; Fließ 1994; Selinski/Sperling 1995). This includes an overview about the market situation, company information, product orientation, price-performance comparisons, and contact to manufactures and vendors (Backhaus 2003: 448-449).

Dependent on the type of trade fair, the scope of information can vary. Typically, four types of trade fairs are distinguished: all-purpose exhibitions, multi-industry fairs, specialised fairs and virtual fairs (Selinski/Sperling 1995: 104; Backhaus 2003: 449). All-purpose exhibitions likely include one or more industries and their major products. Primary aim is often to represent the company towards a broad audience of visitors (Roth 1981: 64). Multi-industry fairs, in contrast, generally offer broad ranges of products of a limited number of industries. Visitors are likely professionals or interested parties who intend to compare products, prices and performances on a more detailed level (Beuermann 1976; Backhaus 2003: 453) Specialised fairs focus on one industry and address professionals and interested parties searching for detailed information for specific purchase decisions. Specialised fairs thus limit scattering losses of target audiences and can lead to immediate sales or orders (Backhaus 2003: 449). Known specialised fairs for consumer electronics are, for instance, the Internationale Funkausstellung (IFA) in Berlin or the Consumer Electronics Show (CES) in Las Vegas. Virtual fairs in the internet can complete traditional trade fairs and are not limited by space and time (Backhaus 2003: 449).

Although trade fairs are considered a crucial communication channel, particularly when a firm starts its going-international (Institut für Marketing 1996: 86), the choice to participate in a certain trade fair has to be decided with care and respect to company aims. A one-time attendance has probably not much power to influence brand awareness and brand image in a positive way (Meffert/Bolz 1998: 217). Moreover, participation is very challenging, since a number of different target audiences are likely to attend a trade fair (local and international sales partners, end-consumers and competitors) and additional capabilities on sale promotion, advertising and direct selling are required as well (Meffert/Bolz 1998: 216; Backhaus 2003: 449). Klein-Bölting (1989: 21) thus summed up the main decision criteria as follows: type of trade fair, quality and quantity of exhibitors, quality and quantity of visitors, costs of transportation and participance, infrastructure of fair grounds, political situation in the country, and economic potential of the local and regional markets.

2.3.3 Brand distribution

In addition to branding and brand communication, a firm has also to determine how the branded product is distributed to the customer into the new foreign market. Brand distribution thereby includes both the choice of the distribution channel as well as the physical distribution of the branded product (Meffert/Bolz 1998: 221). Distribution channels are generally selected due to potential of sales volume and market share, distribution costs and sales margin, market coverage, possibility of cooperation (e.g. brand alliances), speed and flexibility of market cultivation, influence and control of distributional activities, as well as image transfers from the distribution channel to the brand (Ahlert 1981: 46-47; Specht 1992: 144; Ahlert 1996:

174). The decision on the adequate distribution channels involves two se-
lections: vertical selection and horizontal selection. Vertical selection is
the choice between distribution channels (direct sale, retail, wholesale, ex-
porter/ importer) and determines the length in terms of number and types
of distribution layers.[59] Horizontal selection is the choice of sales partners
within a channel. It determines scope and depth of distribution, and thus
the intensity of distribution into the market (Meffert/Bolz 1998: 224).
Ahlert (1996: 157-160) distinguished three degrees of intensity: a) intensive distribution or high market coverage, distribution of the brand through
all possible channels, examples are daily goods such as cigarettes; b) selective distribution, selection of distribution channels along qualitative criteria
such as contractible sales volume, environment (size of shop, service quality, geographical location, etc.) and brand building support (image of the
channel, possibility of promotional cooperation, price level and promotions); and c) exclusive distribution, additional limitation of channels by
quantitative criteria, in order to closely control all brand building activities
and motivate sales partner for higher sales.

In reality however, a branded company can seldom decide on distribution channels on its own. As shelf space is limited and brands manifold, a
listening and promising placement in the shop means likely tough negotiations. It is to convince the retailer that the brand increases the attractiveness of the store and achieves higher profit margins than competitive products do (Esch 2004: 469). Generally, a firm can stimulate brand
attractiveness by three categories: pull, push, and cooperative stimuli. Pull
effects base on end-consumers and their preferences of a brand. It is the
more positive and established the brand is among end-consumers, the more
end-consumers demand the brand in the store. Pull effects are typically
built up by brand communication activities and ensure retailers higher fre-
quencies of consumers in the stores, enhanced store-brand-images and
therefore increased sales. Push stimuli, in contrast, address the retailers directly. They likely involve arguments in terms of price reductions, bonus
payments, improved cost structures, and add-on services such as merchandising, shelf care, and paid sales promotions. Cooperative stimuli go beyond such push-strategies and include partnerships between the manufacturer and the retailer in order to generate synergies along the supply chain
(Tomczak et al. 2001: 921-925; Esch 2004: 471).

An increasing cooperation is the "dual strategy" (Sattler 2001; Esch
2004: 479). Dual strategy means that the brand owner manufactures retail
or private labels in addition to its own brands. From the brand owner's

---

[59] For market entry decisions such as export versus own subsidiaries compare to
chapter 2.2.2.

perspective, dual strategies likely intensify the relationship to the retailer and improve to operate at full capacities. On the other hand, they comprise the risk of cannibalising own products in the store and damaging own brand images (Sattler 2001: 130). Known retail brands are *JA!*, *Salto* and *Ehrlenhof* in the German food sector and *TCM* (Tchibo) for consumer goods (Meffert 2000: 869-871) According to a grocery retail study conducted by Feige (1996: 201), consumer-pull effects have been the key success factor of convincing retailers. They contributed to the success 66%. Cooperative stimuli explained 19% and push-effects had only minor relevance. Tomczak et al. (2001: 930) confirmed these findings. Pure push-strategies and strategies without any over-proportional incentives are likely not successful, whereas a "cooperative pull-strategy" which combines cooperative and pull stimuli is found the most promising strategy.

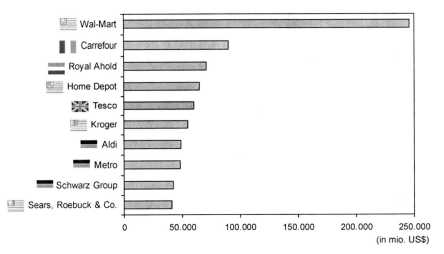

Fig. 2-11. World's top 10 leading retailers by turnover in 2003 (Euromonitor 2006)

Meffert and Bolz (1998: 227-228) added that in foreign markets the selection of adequate distribution channels is also determined by availability. When a country market becomes more advanced, the distribution layers and the number and different formats of channels in the market also increase. Additionally, the more advanced the country market becomes, the smaller the number of small stores and the larger the size per store. In Western European markets 70-90% of the revenues are made by the top five largest retailers (M+M Planet Retail 2006). These are particularly large-scale multiple food retailers such as *Wal-Mart* and *Carrefour* which are present in many countries and increasingly undermine the position of local specialist shops (Euromonitor 2006). Compare to figure 2-11. Since international retailers likely favour global standardised brands because of volume-orientated price advantages and standardised product ranges across markets, they are considered a valuable distribution channel for a fast and comprehensive going-international of brands (Schiele 1997: 146-147).[60]

2.3.4 Brand organisation

Since the implementation and success of the previous discussed brand decisions largely depends on the people in charge (Schaffer/Rhee 2005: 59), the brand organisation itself is another crucial operative brand decision. To maximise the brand's efficiency and effectiveness across all respective markets and countries, the brand approach has to be hierarchically and organisationally anchored by adequate organisational structures and systems (e.g., Macharzina/Oesterle 1995: 311; Aaker/Joachimsthaler 2000: 7-13; Meffert 2000; Meffert et al. 2005). This in particular includes the decisions on the optimal type of company organisation structure, the degree of centralisation and the origin of local management teams.

Types of organisation structures

The company organisation structure separates and clarifies corporate tasks and responsibilities (Macharzina/Oesterle 1995: 310; Meffert/Bolz 1998: 257). Dependent on the amount and stage of international business, companies most likely adapt responsibilities according to the following path (Welge 1980; Macharzina 1992; Meffert/Bolz 1998: 257)[61]: In the early beginning of a firm's going-international, international sales are typically made under an "unspecific organisation": overseas exports are little and seldom, varying managers of varying national departments are responsible in informal and sporadic way. Over the time, when overseas business increases and extends beyond the scope of a single person, companies then separate domestic from overseas activities. They implement differentiated (synonym: segregated) organisation structures which probably involve separated export departments, international divisions or holding structures. The executive in charge typically has a direct reporting relationship to the top management team or CEO (Macharzina/Oesterle 1995: 312-313; Keegan/Green 2005: 539). In the final stage of globalisation, firms then

---

[60] Compare to external factors as presented in chapter 2.2.3.
[61] Compare to the EPRG-concept as presented in chapter 2.2.3.

typically reorganise themselves towards integrated structures.[62] Integrated structures do not involve organisational separations between domestic and overseas markets in the parent company. Same managers are rather in charge of one specific function (R&D, production, sales) or object (products, consumer groups, regions) across all markets.[63]

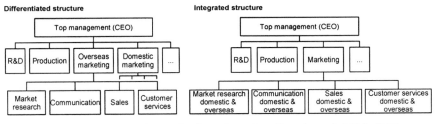

Fig, 2-12. Functional brand organisations (based on Berndt et al. 2003: 273)

Dependent on this overall business organisation, the functional areas of marketing and brand management are ideally integrated and organised in a corresponding way (Terpstra 1983: 597; Macharzina/Oesterle 1995: 312). Generally, functional and object-orientated brand structures are distinguished (Berndt 1995: 156-160; Berndt et al. 2003: 272). See figures 2-12 and 2-13.[64] Functional brand organisations refer to a separation of responsibilities according to different brand and marketing tasks such as market research, brand communication, sales & distribution, services etc. Object-orientated brand organisations refer to a separation of responsibilities with respect to products or brands, consumer groups (synonym: key accounts) or homogenous regions and country markets (e.g., Western Europe, South East Asia, Benelux, USA). The respective object manager is likely in charge of all activities (planning, implementation, control) which are related to the object (Berndt et al. 2003: 275-276). In the case that a firm can

---

[62] A study of Daniels et al. (1984) proved the opposite development among US companies. They had internationalised from integrated product structures into international divisional structures. See for discussions about these findings, i.e. Macharzina and Oesterle (1995: 313).

[63] As it is beyond the scope of the study, see for more details on overall business organisations e.g., Keegan and Green (2005: 539-544), Macharzina and Oesterle (1995: 312-326), Meffert and Bolz (1998: 257-267), Czinkota and Ronkainen (1999: 516-538), and Backhaus et al. (2003a: 62-65).

[64] In both figures, the first organisational layer is exemplified by functional integration or functional differentiation. In figure 2-12, the second layer of object-orientated marketing is exemplified by product-orientation. It is assumed that sales and service activities are separately management from pure marketing. (Compare to Berndt et al. 2003: 276)

group its brands, products and services into categories or topics, brand responsibilities can also be organised by category management structures (Köhler 1995: 1642; Baumgarth 2001: 207; Berndt et al. 2003: 277).

Functional brand organisations are likely used in firms of homogenous brand portfolios and industries of low market dynamics. They involve low coordination efforts because of structure-immanent high degrees of centralisation, but on the other hand, they typically lack market orientation, innovation ability and flexibility (Köhler 1993: 203; Berndt et al. 2003: 273-274). In contrast, product-orientated brand organisations have very often been implemented in consumer goods industries and in companies with heterogeneous product and brand portfolios (Berndt 1995: 158-162; Berndt et al. 2003: 277). In extreme scenarios, each brand in each country market has its own brand manager who is in charge of adapting strategies to local market needs and whose goal is to make the brand win, even if winning comes at the expense of other brands within the company (Aaker/Joachimsthaler 2000: 6).

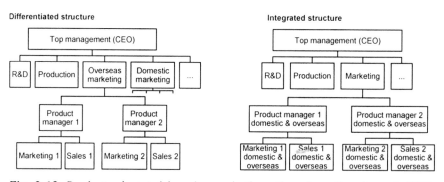

Fig. 2-13. Product-orientated brand organisations (based on Berndt et al. 2003: 273)

As worldwide markets are heterogeneous, regional brand organisations are sometimes also a promising option, since they group countries by homogenous consumer needs. Regional and country managers are typically in the local markets and are often in charge of the firm's local subsidiary. The biggest challenge of a regional orientation is the coordination of local business aims with global brand aims and corporate management decisions (Berndt et al. 2003: 277-278). As figure 2-14 on the right-hand side shows, mixed strategies between regional and product-orientated organisations are common as well. They typically include local sales offices while keeping the marketing activities (market research, brand communication, etc.) in the parent company (Berndt et al. 2003: 278).

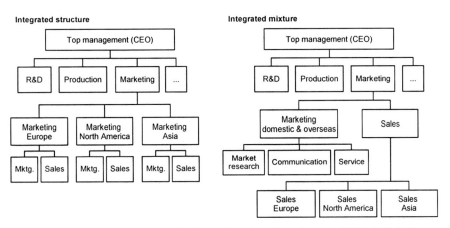

Fig. 2-14. Regional brand organisations (based on Berndt et al. 2003: 278-279)

Besides the traditional brand organisation structures, there are also many further company organisation structures in place: virtual brand organisations, marketing departments as matrix- or tensor organisations, hybrid organisations, and project and team structures.[65] Since re-organisation of a firm is expensive, time-consuming and typically leads to constitutive changes of employees' working places and company cultures, one has to note that continuous adaptations of organisation structures should be small and aligned to long-term corporate aims (Macharzina/Oesterle 1995: 310-311).

Degree of centralisation

Strongly interrelated to the decision on the appropriate company organisation structure is the decision on decentralisation versus centralisation (Meffert/Bolz 1998: 267). The degree of centralisation is defined by the number of tasks and responsibilities which are concentrated in one or few centres (Schanz 1994: 213-214). It determines the level and scope of autonomic decision-making in local market subsidiaries and the directive power of the parent centre (Hill et al. 1981: 275; Kieser/Kubicek 1992: 155). In practice, the power of centre can be designed in several ways: 'little power' implemented by continuous information exchanges and convincing communication up to 'strong power' implemented by rigid approval systems, strict guidelines and continuous control of activities (Quelch/Hoff 1986: 111-113).

---

[65] See for details Berndt et al. (2003: 281-288), Baumgarth (2001: 208), and Meffert and Bolz (1998: 264-267).

It is possible to say that the stricter the guidelines from the centre are, the more likely local brand and country managers are demoralised, since their competences are shortened to pure execution of sales and distribution. On the other hand, globally standardised brand approaches require tight coordination implemented by centralised structures across all country markets, because otherwise the company will suffer from inconsistent brand images and low spillover effects across markets (Quelch/Hoff 1986: 112-113; Macharzina/Oesterle 1995: 328; Meffert/Bolz 1998: 267-268). As a result, market research has shown that many companies have centralised brand elements such as product design, brand name, brand positioning, and brand control. Whereas responsibilities of sales promotion, sales agents, consumer focus and communication channels are likely decentralised and localised (Quelch/Hoff 1986: 115; Bolz 1992: 148; Meffert/Bolz 1998: 268; Marketing Leadership Council 2000: 5). With respect to going-international, one can state that a firm incidentally decentralises more if the decisions involved become more complex, and if the foreign market is unknown, fast decisions are required, communication is time-consuming between the subsidiaries and the centre, the employees in the local markets are qualified, and if the engagement in the foreign market is very intensive (Welge 1989: 1532-1534).

To overcome the disadvantages of centralisation and to integrate local subsidies to some extend into the global brand decision-making, the literature provides several coordinating instruments. These are particularly strategic working groups, international committees and the lead-country concept (Meffert/Bolz 1998: 273; Marketing Leadership Council 2000). Strategic working groups typically consist of representatives of the local subsidiaries as well as of the centre. The intension is to transfer market know-how and brand ideas across country markets, to create jointly accepted brand guidelines, and to implement standardised processes e.g., in brand control and market research. Potential working groups are for instance 'strategic planning', 'creative R&D', and 'creative communication'. International committees function similar to the strategic working groups. Beyond of formulating ideas and guidelines, however, they typically are also empowered to implement and control these issues in the respective local markets and report to the top management team or CEO (Quelch/Hoff 1986: 116; Macharzina/Oesterle 1995: 330-334).

A specific type of international committees is the lead-country concept (Kreutzer/Raffée 1986: 16; Kreutzer 1987). The base idea is to transfer the responsibility of designing and coordinating a regional or global brand approach to a specific corporate entity which can be a local subsidiary or the parent centre. The leading function likely refers to a certain product or product category and does not involve the whole firm's brand portfolio.

The developed brand approach is typically valid for all global markets and implemented in a standardised way. The allocation of the leading position likely depends on decision criteria such as the entity's competence in brand building and marketing, the strategic role of the country market, type of respective products and legal market environments (Macharzina/Oesterle 1995: 331-332; Meffert/Bolz 1998: 273-274). Besides the integration of the local subsidiaries into the corporate organisation, the lead-country concept typically also enhances the competition among the firm's entities in order to become a lead country and a country with authority, and thus the entities' overall performance. However, the firm has to ensure that the local brand managers are not punished for failed brand activities which have been implemented by the lead-country concept and have thus been beyond their responsibilities (Macharzina/Oesterle 1995: 332).

Origin of management teams

While both previous sections have explained the options of the overall corporate organisation structures, this section now focus on the employees themselves. Who should become the local manager in the new foreign country market? Should it be an in-country national or a parent-country national from the headquarters? The parent-country national is also know as an expatriate or expat, implying that he/she is sent from the home country to work in the foreign country market (Keegan/Green 2005: 480). Since the availability and choice of qualified managers and workers for the foreign market may be limited, the decision can become business crucial (Toh/DeNisi 2005: 133). Previous research has shown that poor staffing choices can lead to damages in brand image and relationships with customers, suppliers, and employees, whereas appropriate staffing can greatly enhance the firm's international competitiveness, profit basis and reputation (Valikiotis et al. 1994; Schaffer/Rhee 2005: 59-60; Lee/Liu 2006: 308). As corporate practice revealed, it is likely that firms following an ethnocentric approach fill important management positions with expatriates in their local subsidiaries, while polycentric organisations tend to hire in-country national managers (Deresky 1997; Cullen 1999; Schaffer/Rhee 2005: 61).[66] There are several advantages and disadvantages:

Expatriate assignments typically facilitate the communication between foreign subsidiaries and the parent company, since they are familiar with corporate policies, goals, brands and product lines, unique technologies

---

[66] See the EPRG-concept of chapter 2.2.3 for details on ethnocentric and polycentric perspectives.

and key decision makers (Deresky 1997; Schaffer/Rhee 2005: 60-61). In addition, expatriates are also considered an aid in order to form lasting linkages with host-country governments, domestic lobbyists, and other interest groups that may enhance the firm's overall position and competitiveness in the market. In return, expatriate managers gain international experience and market knowledge which they can transfer back into the parent company when their local assignment had run out (Lee/Liu 2006: 305-306).

On the negative side, it is likely that expatriates lack the ability to develop corporate loyalty among the in-country employees and cannot motivate them for corporate goals. This is because they often do not quickly assimilate into the foreign culture with respect to language, working environment and social bonds, and do not understand the very different local values, norms, and expectations (Adler 2002). Consequently they often wonder that policies and procedures he or she had set up to control the subsidiary may cause difficulties that can result in lower productivity, higher absenteeism, or other labour problems (Müller/Gelbrich 2004: 793-801; Schaffer/Rhee 2005: 60-61). Moreover, experiences from host countries like China have shown that there is also often much discontent among local staff and resentment towards expatriates because they often feel treated like second class citizens (inferior compensation, benefits, and developmental opportunities). This is especially so when expatriates do not have a clear advantage over the local employees in terms of work qualifications, expertise, or experience (Toh/DeNisi 2005: 133).

In-country national managers, in contrast, are familiar with the local culture, language, and business practices, and can often rely on local contacts and business relationships. A study of Volkmar (2003) also stressed that local managers can generally promise more control to the parent company than expatriates can, in situations where cultural asymmetries between the headquarters country and the host country are high and the operating environment is risky. However, employing in-country managers most times comprises disadvantages in terms of poor coordination between the parent company and the foreign subsidiary, which often involves conflicting loyalties of the local management team (Adler 2002; Schaffer/Rhee 2005: 61).

Finally, one should note that in the case that a company internationalises, in order to take advantage of certain corporate knowledge advantages and core competences, such as advanced technologies, there is often no other way than sending expatriates into the country. Since in-country manager miss this certain knowledge they cannot replace the expatriate (Rugman 1980; Schaffer/Rhee 2005: 61). Consequently, one can conclude that there is not 'the right choice' of the origin for local managers for all cases. Rather, the goal should be to combine both strengths in a multinational team, and to choose the best person for each situation, optimising effectiveness and maximising performance of the entire organisation (Lee/Liu 2006: 309).[67] Moreover, one has to develop and anchor both manager types in career paths and bonus payment systems which recognise excellent performance and long-term brand building in the host entities (e.g., Baumgarth 2001: 209-210).

2.4 Control and adaptation of brand decisions

As the previous chapters show, brand management options are manifold, strongly interlinked with each other and complex. For a firm, the decision on the optimal set of brand options can therefore become very challenging, expensive and crucial to business. As a result, firms tend to be very much concerned about their brand management decisions and want to control whether they meet the formulated targets or not. The next section reviews these options of brand control, and finally gives reasons why a chosen optimal brand approach might become suboptimal in the long-term run.

2.4.1 Brand control

Brand control includes all gathering, evaluation and distribution of all relevant brand data that support to control and coordinate international brand management decisions across the operating foreign markets. It ideally involves a comprehensive system of economic and psychological brand data, ex-ante and ex-post analysis, quantitative and qualitative as well as internal and external brand evaluations (Baumgarth 2001: 216; Meffert/Koers 2002: 406-409; Esch 2004: 481-483).

A common indicator of successful international brand management is the brand value approach. Brand values are estimated by numbers of market research and brand consulting companies each year (e.g., Bekmeier-Feuerhahn 1998: 62). The probably most accepted estimate and gold standard worldwide is the brand value annually awarded by US-market research company *Interbrand*. See table 2-2. The brand value is defined as a cash equivalent of all future surpluses of payments which the owner of a brand will earn compared to owners of non-name products (Kaas 1990:

---

[67] See also Tye and Chen (2005) for decision-making models on the 'right' choice of expatriates.

48).[68] In other words, the brand value reflects the monetary brand recovery costs, future profit expectations and the long-term price-volume-premium (Kapferer 1992: 298-321).

Brand	Country of ownership	Brand value 2005 in million US$	Brand value 2004 in million US$	Percent change
Coca-Cola	USA	67,525	67,394	0%
Microsoft	USA	59,941	61,372	-2%
IBM	USA	53,376	53,791	-1%
GE	USA	46,996	44,111	+7%
Intel	USA	35,588	33,499	+6%
Nokia	Finland	26,452	24,041	+10%
Disney	USA	26,441	27,113	+2%
McDonald's	USA	26,014	25,001	+4%
Toyota.	Japan	24,837	22,673	+10%
Marlboro	USA	21,389	22,128	+4%

Table 2-2. The world's ten most valuable brands in 2005 (Interbrand 2005)

Originally, brand values have been estimated in order to specify prices for brand acquisitions, brand licensing, accounting of brands, or assessment of brand claims because of brand piracy (Mussler/Mussler 1995: 135; Drees 1999: 14; Esch 2004: 63). Nowadays, a strong brand value also reflects brand's superiority towards competitors, consumers, employees, and other third parties (= brand flagship value). It also serves to measure the brand's potential to expand to other markets, countries and industries (= optional brand value) (The Boston Consulting Group, Aaker 2002: 9).

Brand value rankings typically favour corporate brands of large conglomerates and long histories, and indicate whether such brands develop better or worse compared to competitive brands and industry trends. They are likely not an appropriate controlling tool for young, niche market or product brands, and do not provide any information about why a brand is successful (Kapferer 1992: 291; Aaker/Joachimsthaler 2000: 16; Esch 2004: 408-415, 528-529). For the daily work of a brand manager, more significant and qualitative controlling tools are thus necessary. Tools which specify the brand equity (synonym: brand strength) in the mind of the customer and in the mind of other target groups (Keller 1993; Aaker

---

[68] See Interbrand (2005) and e.g. Esch (2004: 547-571) for details on Interbrand calculation method.

1995; Bekmeier-Feuerhahn 1998; Aaker 2002). Aaker and Joachimsthaler (2000: 17) defined brand equity as "the brand assets (or liabilities) linked to a brand's name or symbol that add to (or subtract from) a product or service." Although there are numbers of methods to measure brand equity in the market, they all base on similar brand assets such as brand awareness, perceived quality, brand associations and brand loyalty (e.g., Aaker 1991; Keller 1993; Bekmeier-Feuerhahn 1998; Meffert/Koers 2002).[69]

Brand awareness likely affects the perception and taste of a brand. One can say that people like the familiar and are prepared to ascribe all sorts of good attitudes to items that are familiar to them. Brand awareness is typically measured by brand recall tests (synonym: active or unaided brand awareness: What brands of this product category can you recall?) and brand recognition tests (passive or aided brand awareness: Have you been exposed to this brand before?) (e.g., Aaker 2002: 10, 16-17; Esch 2004: 230).

Perceived quality likely refers to the reasons why consumers buy a brand, to what extent they are satisfied with the brand, and whether they are going to advocate the brand to other people (Meffert et al. 2003: 36-37). Sources of market research can be consumer questionnaires or focus group experiments (e.g., Baumgarth 2001: 216-271; Aaker 2002: 8-9).

Brand associations are indicators for consumers' perceived brand image, brand personality and brand know-how. Long-term memorised brand associations can be visualised by mind-maps (Buzan/Buzan 2002). The more detailed and unique the brand associations show up, the better the consumer knows the brand and differentiates it from other products (Baumgarth 2001: 251-256; Esch 2004: 504-506). Other known methods of visualising brand associations are image profiles where consumers indicate on a scale from 1 to 5 to what extend certain attributes are fulfilled by a brand or not (e.g., Esch 2004: 494-497).

Brand loyalty is considered the heart of brand equity because a high rate of loyalty indicates a stable customer base and directly leads to assured future profits. A brand with a small but intensely loyal customer base can thus also have significant brand equity. Loyal customers typically are convinced of the brand, have a positive brand image and are immune against product and price offers launched by competitors. Moreover, keeping customers loyal is much cheaper for a company than acquiring new ones. This is one reason why frequent-buyer programs and customer clubs have in-

---

[69] As it is beyond the scope of the study to detail all possible brand equity methods, see for an overview about different concepts e.g., Esch (2004: 528-542) and Baumgarth (2001: 244-300). In the following process of the chapter, only some common methods are selected and presented.

creasingly emerged over the last decades (Aaker 2002: 21-26). Brand loyalty can, for instance, be measured by analysis of purchase-order, brand market share of total purchases, re-purchasing rates, or consumer's willingness to switch (see i.e., Baumgarth 2001: 272-281).

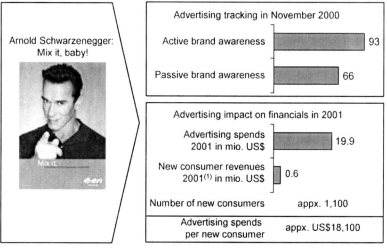

(1) €50 per monthly bill and consumer estimated

Fig. 2-15. Brand control of *e.on*'s campaign *Mix it, baby!* (Spiegel online 12.02.2002)

Though the brand assets are measured by separated instruments, it is necessary to analyse a brand's equity across all categories and with respect to long-term brand aims. As figure 2-17 shows, the market observer *Spiegel online* criticised the brand campaign *"Mix it, baby!"* of Germany's largest energy provider *e.on* very strongly, because they found that the advertising expenditure of the first year had not been paid back by new consumers in the same year (also Meffert et al. 2003: 16). However, as the scores of brand awareness are pretty high and consumers are considered reluctant concerning the switching of energy providers, the calculation does not show whether the marketing campaign might even have enhanced e.on's long-term brand equity aims.[70]

---

[70] For more promising and professional integrative brand evaluation tools see, for example, the iceberg model of Icon Consult, the brand potential index (BPI) of GfK, or the brand asset valuator of Young & Rubicam. Details are provided by Esch (2004: 531-542), Drees (1999), Esch and Andresen (1997), Andresen and Esch (2001).

2.4.2 Brand adaptation

In the case the brand controls signal that all targets of the global brand approach are going to be met in all markets they targeted to be, it might be assumed that no further decision-making and brand coordination is necessary. The firm continues with its defined brand strategy, and becomes an advanced player in the foreign market. The firm switches from a situation of going-international to a situation of which is called by Backhaus et al. (2003a: 303) "being-international". However, even though all brand targets are according to the global brand strategy, the strategy of being-international does only theoretically resemble the strategy of going-international. Since the respective country markets are dynamic and change in a permanent way, permanent brand adaptations are constantly necessary as well. Changes can generally occur in institutional environments, consumer behaviour, competitor landscape, and company internal factors (Sabel/Weiser 2000; Backhaus et al. 2003a: 303-304). This includes that countries become more homogenous (e.g., the expansion of the EU) or heterogeneous (e.g., the disintegration of the former Yugoslavia). Consumer behaviour changes, e.g. because of improved income levels, or new technologies such as the Worldwide Web. The competitive landscape develops due to advancement of technologies and unexpected players entering a market.[71] Alternatively the firm itself revises overall corporate strategies which effect the defined brand approach. For instance, many firms started favouring corporate brands instead of product brands over the last years, since they are considered to meet shareholder value requirements and top brand value rankings in worldwide comparisons in a better way (Esch 2004: 408-415; Esch et al. 2004).

Dependent on the origin of the change, size of coordination needs, and possible choice of decision-making, a firm might only adjust some brand positioning aspects, but might also be forced to revise the whole brand architecture, the brand communication approaches or other strategic and operative brand measures across markets. These decisions should, similar to those of the going-international, follow the ten key commandments of global branding, summed up in figure 2-19 (Keller 2003: 697):

---

[71] See for more details e.g., Backhaus et al. (2003a: 304-334).

1. Understand similarities and differences in the global branding landscape
2. Don't take shortcuts in brand building
3. Establish marketing infrastructure
4. Embrace integrated marketing communications
5. Cultivate brand partnerships
6. Balance standardisation and customisation
7. Balance global and local control
8. Establish operable guidelines
9. Implement a global brand equity measurement system
10. Leverage brand elements

Fig. 2-16. The ten key commandments of global brand building (taken from Keller 2003: 697)

3 The who is who of Chinese branded companies

As the last chapter shows, there are theoretically many different options when a company goes international with respect to brand management decisions. Some of these options require certain market conditions; others require certain corporate experiences of the internationalising firm. Which of these theoretical brand options are thus appropriate for Chinese branded companies to enter developed markets? What are their corporate experiences in the domestic market? Who are they? What are their strengths and weaknesses in terms of brand management competences? Why do they want to internationalise now? Which role does the Chinese government play in this decision? Are the Chinese branded companies ready to enter developed markets? Are their actions examples for best practice?

To seek answers to the above questions, this chapter is structured in three parts. Part one aims to examine all aspects relevant to China's domestic brand management experience, including the origin and competitive evolution of Chinese brands since 1978, China's top brands in 2005/2006, as well China's overall consumer and organisational behaviour towards brands. Part two investigates the experiences of Chinese branded companies with developed markets. This includes China's close relationships to foreign multinationals in terms of original equipment manufacturer (OEM) and retailing, and China's growing outward investments and global brand aims. It also includes China's country-of-origin, especially among German customers. The chapter closes with part three and a brief evaluation of both areas of experience.

3.1 Domestic brand management experiences

3.1.1 Landscape of Chinese brands

Origin and competitive evolution

The history of precious Chinese brands goes back to Chinese silk and Chinese porcelain about 2000 years ago. Both products have been unique, premium priced, and mesmerised Europeans for centuries. Qualities such as craftsmanship, creativity and innovation made Chinese silk, jade and porcelain the earliest brands worldwide (Buckley Ebrey/Liu 1996; Gilmore/Dumont 2003; Staiger et al. 2003). Due to political ideologies and internal wars, however, China secluded itself over the last five hundred years and has not been considered back in the world economy until the economic reforms, which had been initiated in 1978 by Deng Xiaoping. He shifted the emphasis away from socialist ideology and gave priority to economic modernisation over the building of socialism (Harding 1987; Bell 1993; Chai 1997; Qian 2000).

At this time China functioned as a rigid, centralised planned economy, modelled on the Soviet system.[72] Under this system, state-owned enterprises played the dominant role, leaving some room for collective enterprises[73] but virtually excluded private firms (e.g., Schurmann 1971; Tung 1982; Child 1994; Bettignies 1996; Chai 1997, 2000). Equipment and technologies lagged behind world standards 20 to 30 years, and the use of resources was rather inefficient and provoked serious shortages of transport facilities, energy, and industrial and construction material (e.g., Harding 1987: 33; Chai 1997: 3-4). Marketing and its efficacy were explicitly denied (Marx 1970), as commercial advertising was seen negatively as manipulating consumers to buy goods they do not need and thus as a misallocation of resources within a society. Since China had lower income levels and lower living standards than the other Chinese societies in Taiwan, Hong Kong and Singapore, and Chinese managers were rewarded by fulfilling their state plan rather than for taking risks in R&D or profit growth, there was also little incentive for the development of marketing activities (Deng/Dart 1995). All fundamental marketing decisions, as understood by Western brand management theories, concerning product lines, pricing and distribution channels were made by government officials. They set production targets for each company, assigned employees, allocated supplies and equipment, distributed their products, and retained all profits and covered all losses (e.g., Dembinski/Cook 1991; Chai 2000). Except for very limited discretion over product design, the Chinese man-

---

[72] Note that at the height of central planning in China, the system, however, was less centralised compared to that found in the Soviet Union or Eastern Europe (Shirk 1993).

[73] Formally, collective enterprises are owned by the urban or rural community in whose sphere they are active, while local authorities appoint and control the management. However, there is broad consensus that a large number of collective enterprises, especially those of the township-village enterprises (TVEs) in the rural area, can be expected to operate almost as independently as private enterprises (Opper 1999; Tian 2000; Chen 2004).

ager had little, if any, control over decisions involving the marketing mix (Holten 1985; Mahatoo 1990; Deng/Dart 1999).

In the first stage of reforms (1978-84), only partial reforms were carried out. They were primarily focused on institutional changes in the agricultural sector through the decentralisation of property rights and the upward adjustment of agricultural purchase prices (Ash 1993). Externally, the open door policy was initiated with the intention to increase foreign trade and to attract foreign investments, but both, the foreign trade and the foreign investment policy, were still heavily regulated (e.g., Chai 1997). As a result, the situation for marketing and brand management did not change significantly. Consumer goods were still rare, and Chinese customers had to queue for coupons and purchase allowances for items such as television sets at governmental offices. Each product, even of very low quality, was directly sold to the dictated customer (Dembinski/Cook 1991; Ding/Zheng 2005; Zhou 2005).

In the second stage of economic reform (1985-1991), the focus of reforms shifted to the urban sector, and comprehensive reform programme was launched. The official goal was to change China's economic system so that resource allocation would be done by markets and the government would exercise control only indirectly through the market (Chai 1997). This included the reduction in the scope of planning, the strengthening of enterprise autonomy and accountability, the liberalisation of product and factor prices, the creation of both product and factor markets, and the liberalisation of foreign economic relations. Many consumer markets were opened up and a wide range of foreign products and brands were the first time imported into the Chinese market place (Melewar et al. 2004: 452; Ding/Zheng 2005: 72). Moreover, first Sino-foreign joint ventures were established which often introduced Western capital, technology and management skills into the Chinese economy. It is said that Chinese consumers were stunned by the fact that almost all foreign brands were superior to the local Chinese offerings (Pan et al. 2003: 5). As a result, some Chinese firms began developing a consciousness for the power of brands. It was becoming common to copy foreign intellectual property, and to produce faked foreign brands. Many of today's Chinese brand names were also launched during these days (Ding/Zheng 2005).

The comprehensive reforms of stage two were, however, briefly interrupted by the Tiananmen Square tragedy in mid-1989,[74] before they accelerated dramatically after the southern tour of Deng Xiaoping and his proclamation to open up China further to the West in 1992. The 14th Party Congress finally agreed to replace China's centrally planned economy with

---

[74] See for additional reasons of the reform crisis e.g., Taube (2003b: 7-8).

a "socialist market economy" (Jiang 1992). As a result of these policy changes, the economy prospered by on average 8.4% between 1984 and 2005 (EIU 2006). Product supply as well as disposable income raised, and Chinese consumers began to demand better quality products and services, and thus initiated the shift from a seller to a buyer market since the mid 1990s (Pan et al. 2003; Ding/Zheng 2005: 73; Zhou 2005). Since many consumer industries suddenly suffered from overcapacities and functional similarities, price wars broke out and competition became so intense that even top producers struggled to make profit (e.g., Liu/Li 2002: 701). Since the majority of Chinese consumers were also preferring foreign brands over local offerings, as they were considered to provide better quality, fashionable designs and greater convenience, many local companies very quickly lost out or were forced to re-think their corporate strategy. Market and customer orientation became more important; technology, service and production quality was developed and caught up with foreign brands (Pan et al. 2003; Melewar et al. 2004: 451-452). In 2000, first Chinese product and company names finally got visible as recognised brands and begun to differentiate themselves as understood by Western brand management theory (figure 3-1, Wang 2005; Zhou 2005).

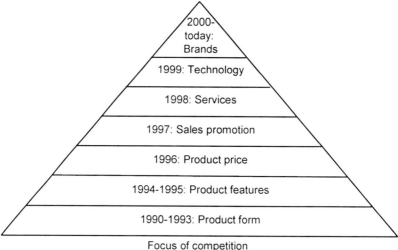

Focus of competition

Fig. 3-1. The competitive pyramid of the colour television industry in China 1990-2005 (own translation of Yang 2005: 16)

When China entered the WTO in November 2001, the competition in China became even fiercer. On the one hand, the accession required a further liberalisation of the Chinese market, larger transparency and uniform-ity in trade policies, stronger protection of intellectual property rights (IPR), and a stronger retreat from administrative and protective measures in favour of market measures in the management of trade. Most of the import tariffs were removed or reduced which made large-scale imports of foreign brands more likely and more usual (e.g., Drysdale 2000: 103-105; Goldman Sachs 2003: 23-24).[75]

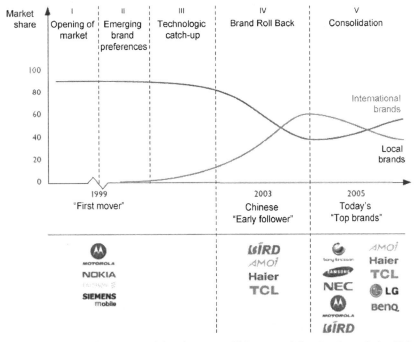

Fig. 3-2. Accelerating competition between Chinese and foreign brands in China, exemplified by the mobile phone industry in % market share 1999-2005 (own translation of Schramm/Spiller 2006: 25)

On the other hand, besides the larger availability of foreign brands, Chinese brands have become more popular among Chinese consumers. Compared to foreign brands, they typically provide a similar product quality at lower prices, often better addressed to local needs, and satisfy the desire of nationalism and cultural pride (Ewing et al. 2002; Melewar et al. 2004; Nan/Belk 2004; Schramm/Spiller 2006). As a result, many consumer markets in China are today very competitive, and both foreign and Chinese brands are considered equal rivals (figure 3-2). In the next section, it is

---

[75] See the references as presented in chapter 1 for further details on China's WTO accession.

thus the concern to present and characterise the most successful Chinese brands in more detail.

Top Chinese brands in 2005/2006

In Western societies a company or a product is likely to be named a 'brand', if it enjoys certain brand strengths or brand values in national or international rankings.[76] Similar to the international rating company Interbrand, 'Beijing Famous Brand Evaluation' evaluates Chinese brands in China each year since 1995 by monetary brand values (Wang 2005). As table 3-1 and figure 3-3 show, the national brand champion since 2002 is *Haier* 海尔 household appliances (US$7.34bn in 2004), followed by *Hongtashan* 红塔山 cigarettes (US$5.67bn), and *Lenovo* 联想 ('lianxiang') computers (US$3.71bn) (Beijing Famous Brand Evaluation 2004; Wang 2005).[77]

Brand name	Company of ownership	Major products	Brand value 2004 in bn US$
Haier 海尔	Haier Group	Household appliances	7.45
Hongtashan 红塔山	Hongta Tobacco Group	Cigarettes	5.67
Lenovo 联想	Lenovo Group	Computers	3.71
Wuliangye 五粮液	Yibin Wuliangye Group	Liquors	3.71
FAW 第一汽车	China FAW Group	Automobiles	3.71
TCL	TCL Corporation	TV sets, mobile phones	3.70
Changhong 长虹	Chonghong Electronics Group	TV sets	3.27
Midea 美的	Midea Holding Company	Electrical fans, air-cons, microwaves	2.43
KONKA 康佳	KONKA Group Company	TV sets, mobile phones	1.37
Tsingtao 青岛	Tsingtao Brewery	Beer	1.36

Table 3-1. The top ten Chinese brands by brand value in bn US$ in China in 2004 (own translation of Wang 2005: 116)

---

[76] See chapter 2.

[77] It is to note that the brand values measured by Beijing Famous Brand Evaluation are calculated by a different approach than Interbrand measures the world's top 100 brands every year. The Chinese method generally scores higher brand values. Otherwise, all Chinese brands starting with Haier brand (rank 1: US$7.45bn) to Midea brand (rank 8: US$2.43bn) would have made it among the top 100 world's most valuable brands in 2005 (Interbrand 2005). See on Interbrand also chapter 2.4.1.

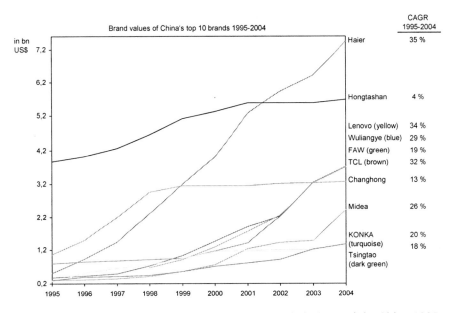

Fig. 3-3. Brand values of the top ten Chinese brands in bn US$ in China 1995-2004 (own illustration of Wang 2005: 130-131)

Other surveys confirmed *Haier* as China's leading brand. 'Worldbrand', another national brand rating company, annually awards the 'Chinese Brand Oscars' and ranked *Haier* first in 2005, followed by *Lenovo* (Yu 2006: 428). The 'Chinese University Students Career Guide' published by the Ministry of Education in 2005 Haier Group was recommended the most attractive employer for Chinese university graduates, followed by Microsoft, P&G, IBM and China Mobile (Haier Group 2006b).[78] Marketing professor Zhou Dongsheng (2005) of the CEIBS in Shanghai evaluated *Haier* as a strong brand because it is the leader of its product category, in all media, widely known and well-respected across entire China. A worldwide survey amongst readers of the Financial Times also ranked *Haier* as the most known Chinese brand in 2005, followed by *Lenovo* which internationally got famous by its acquisition of the IBM PC division including the *ThinkPad* brand in 2004 (Dyer 2005; Hirn 2005: 118-120).

---

[78] See also the survey of the newspaper Economics Daily in Ballhaus (2005: 32), the survey of the newspaper Beijing Youth in Yi/Ye (2003: 37), the survey of the magazine Fortune China mentioned in Haier Group (2006b), the evaluation of Zeng/Williamson (2004: 40-43) in the Harvard Business Manager, the ranking of the Blue Book of China's enterprises competitiveness (Jin 2004: 355), and the brand awareness scores of McEwen (2005a).

Besides *Haier* and *Lenovo*, it becomes evident that most of the top ten Chinese brands are also brands of the consumer electronics and household appliances industry (table 3-1). This is *TCL* (TV sets, mobile phones), *Changhong* 长虹 (TV sets), *Midea* 美的 ('meidi') (electrical fans, air-conditioners, microwaves) and *KONKA*康佳 ('kangjia') (TV sets, mobile phones). Even though they all hold top rankings in 2004, they have developed very differently since 1995 (figure 3-3). *Haier*, for instance, could rapidly increase its brand value by 35% a year, while *Changhong* is struggling with stagnation since 1998. Since the household appliances and consumer electronics industry is highly competitive in China, *Changhong* has probably suffered from fierce price wars and thus lost market shares.[79]

A brand which is also relatively loosing brand value, but is still a very powerful brand in China is *Hongtashan* 红塔山. *Hongtashan* is China's leading cigarette brand and China's second most valuable brand in 2004, although it was ranked at the top position till 2002 (figure 3-3). *Hongtashan* enjoys loyal customers throughout the country and at all levels of societies. It is famous for its typical taste and considered a status symbol among Chinese smokers. So far *Hongtashan* has also successfully competed against foreign global brands such as *Marlboro* at the higher end of the market (Access Asia Ltd. 2002: 3-10; French 2006). Similar successful are the Chinese alcoholic brands *Tsingdao* 青岛 beer and *Wuliangye* 五粮液 liquors. Both brands enjoy strong domestic brand recognition resulting in high levels of consumer loyalty. Tsingdao's success factor is said to be its nationwide expansion strategy of acquiring smaller regional breweries and its strong overseas sales mainly through Chinese restaurants. Wuliangye's best-selling product is the *Wuliangye Spirit* which consumers call 'pre-eminent' or 'empress-like' (Access Asia Ltd. 2002: 3, 28-29).

According to Beijing Famous Brand Evaluation, China's leading brand of the automotive industry is *First Automotive Works (FAW)* 第一汽车 ('diyi qiche'). FAW is China's first company to produce automobiles in 1953, and got famous though the joint venture with German Volkswagen (VW) since 1991. Main models are VW Jetta, VW Bora and Audi A6 (Goldman Sachs 2003: 36). Over the last years, however, FAW is challenged by national rivals such as Shanghai Automotive Industry Company (SAIC). SAIC has two large joint ventures with VW (VW Santana, Santana 2000, Passat and Polo) and American General Motors (GM) (Buick G, GL8, Buick Sail Compact). Moreover, SAIC has international

---

[79] See chapter 5 for details on the household appliances and consumer electronics industry. For Midea see also chapter 3.2.1.

ambitions and wants to become one of the world's six largest automakers by 2020 (Taylor/Dahong 2004).

Since none of these top Chinese brands have been chosen for the world's top 100 most valuable brands evaluated by Interbrand so far (Swystun 2006; Yu 2006: 382-383), they are widely considered as not globally important (e.g., Publicis Sasserath 2006: 15). However, the marketing research firm 'Millward Brown Optimor' (2006) very recently released a new ranking of the world's most powerful brands called BRANDZ, which ranked China's biggest wireless telecommunication operator, *China Mobile*中国移动通信 ('zhongguo yidong tongxin'), as the world's fourth powerful brand. China Mobile's brand value was estimated US\$39,168m and was only topped by the brands *Microsoft* (US\$62,039m), *General Electrics (GE)* (US\$55,834m) and *Coca-Cola* (US\$41,406m) (table 3-2). Apparently it is the first time a Chinese brand is listed in a global brand ranking. However, Millward Brown Opitmor admitted that *China Mobile* was not chosen because of its international relevance, but because of its immense domestic market power over 240 million customers and 4 million new customers each month in China (Hirn 2005: 115; CRIENGLISH.com 2006, company websites). In comparison, *Vodafone*, world's second largest mobile phone operator has 171 million customers across 26 country markets (company websites).

Brand	Country of ownership	Brand value 2006 in million US\$
Microsoft	USA	62,039
GE	USA	55,834
Coca-Cola	USA	41,406
China Mobile	PR China	39,168
Marlboro	USA	38,510
Wal-Mart	USA	37,567
Google	USA	37,445
IBM	USA	36,084
Citibank	USA	31,028
Toyota	Japan	30,201

Table 3-2. BRANDZ's top ten most powerful brands in the world in US\$ in 2006 (Millward Brown Optimor 2006)

Finally, beyond these Chinese brands listed in national and international rankings, which are all corporate brands of large conglomerates, there are also new aspiring Chinese consumer brands that are as well noticeable. Their origin is likely a private or privatised enterprise that started with a great idea and one or two employees during the 1990s. They are typically led by a charismatic manager who was often the founder of the same firm (Hirn 2005: 115). These Chinese brands are in particular *Li-Ning* 李宁 sportswear, *Yue-Sai* 羽西[80] cosmetics, *Mengniu* 蒙牛 dairy, *Wahaha* 娃哈哈 beverages, *GOME* 国美 ('guomei') consumer electronics, *Blocko* 宝高 ('baogao') toys, *Alibaba* 阿里巴巴 online market places and *Huawei Technologies* 华为技术 ('huawei jishu') (Gilmore/Dumont 2003; Roberts et al. 2004; Ballhaus 2005; Ding/Zheng 2005; Janke/Weiland 2005; Underwood/Wong 2005; Zhou 2005; Blume 2006; Roll 2006; Schramm/Spiller 2006; Yu 2006). As figure 3-4 exemplifies, these brands hold strong market positions and brand strength among Chinese consumers. *Li-Ning*, for instance, successfully competes against global brands such as *Nike* and *Adidas* in China (also box 3-1).[81]

To understand why and when Chinese consumers prefer local brands over foreign brands, and which underlying consumer concepts drive Chinese customers when purchasing brands, the next section will examine the Chinese consumer behaviour towards brands in more details.

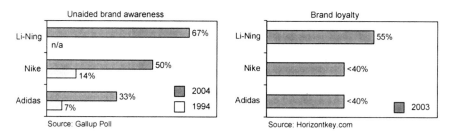

Fig. 3-4. Brand strength scores of the top three sports brands in China in % in 2003/2004 (McEwen 2005a; Schramm/Spiller 2006: 16)

---

[80] In Mandarin 羽西 is pronounced as 'yuxi', in Cantonese 'yuesai'.
[81] For more information about these brands see also the following chapters and appendix 3.

Li-Ning is China's most famous brand name for shoes, sportswear and sports accesso-
ries, and is also considered one of the most successful Chinese companies since the end-
1990s. Particularly over the last years Li-Ning has rapidly grown by 47% on sales each
year, resulting in total revenues of US$226.9 million, which is around 9% market share.
They have 2,800 independent brand stores in 2004.

The brand's identity bases on the personality and charisma of its founder Li Ning, who
was the star gymnast and the most honoured athlete of the Olympic Games at Los Angeles in 1984. Li Ning founded the company in the early 1990s and started with copying
Nike. Over the years, he emancipated the brand from Nike and developed own designs
and brand images. By 2006 the Li-Ning brand is able to compete successfully against the
global brands *Nike, Adidas* and *Reebok*, especially, by price-value propositions which
provide shoes of quality on a par with those of *Nike*, but at half the price of *Nike* and similar brands. Moreover, Li Ning's own popularity helped the brand to generate high levels of
awareness, acceptance and loyalty from his targeted markets. Li Ning was also able to
establish a strong distribution network not only in the major Chinese cities but also across
many of the rural Chinese cities. Over the years, Li-Ning company has also sponsored
several key sports events involving Chinese sports stars like the national Chinese Olympic team. It is also marketing partner of the Chinese National Basketball Association since
January 2005.

Although Li-Ning brand enjoys remarkable success in China, market observers are
arguing that it still has to go a long way to become a long-term brand as understood by
Western branding societies. They recommend to revise the brand image back from patriotism and national pride onto a clearer brand positioning of excitement, lifestyle and cool-
ness, especially attractive for the younger Chinese customers. Otherwise, the future of Li-
Ning would become difficult. In 2005, for instance, Li-Ning lost the market leadership to
Nike in China and lost the sponsorship for the Beijing Olympic Games 2008 to Adidas.

Box 3-1. Li-Ning sports brand (own summary of Roll 2006: 169-176;
Schramm/Spiller 2006: 15-16, company websites)

3.1.2 Chinese consumer behaviour towards brands

The Chinese consumer behaviour towards brands is highly influenced by
both traditional concepts and the recent economic growth through China's
30 years of modernisation. Accordingly, the section first reviews general
social consumer concepts in China with respect to brands, and will then
segment and characterise China's current major consumer groups by their
respective needs and purchase behaviour.

Social consumer concepts

In Western societies, the ownership of brands is nowadays seen as an expression of individualism, personal style and differentiation. When living

standards improved in the West in the 1950s and product quality became reliable, consumers began to seek for emotional stimulations when purchasing products (Karmasin 1993; Kroeber-Riel 1993; Esch 2004). In China and other Asian societies, however, brands function in a different way. Schütte (1998) explained that this goes back to the different underlying traditions and social concepts between Western and Asian societies which can be described by Maslow's hierarchy of needs. Maslow (1964) hypothesised that people's desires can be arranged into a hierarchy of five needs (figure 3-5). As an individual fulfils needs at each level, he or she progresses to higher levels. At the most basic levels of human existence, physiological and safety, Westerners and Asians search for same needs like food, shelter and clothing. At the three highest levels, however, Asians target   different   personal   desires.   While   Westerners   desire   self-actualisation, Asians typically favour status, admiration and affiliation (Schütte 1998). Affiliation needs in Asia are satisfied when an individual has been accepted by a group. Admiration can be satisfied through acts that command respect within a group. At the top of Asian needs is status, which is the esteem of the society as a whole. It likely involves luxury symbols (Schmitt et al. 1994), so that nearly the half of the US$35bn global luxury goods market occurs in Japan (20%) and the rest of the Asian Pacific region (22%) (Keegan/Green 2005: 341).

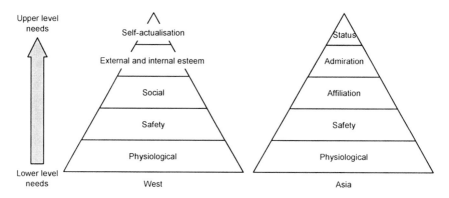

Fig. 3-5. Maslow's hierarchy of needs and the Asian equivalent (Maslow 1964; Schütte 1998: 23)

The Asian equivalent of Maslow's hierarchy reveals that Asians place much more emphasis on interpersonal relationships and social interactions than Westerns do, and consider autonomy and individuality not as crucial as in the West. Social psychologists name this behaviour also collectiveness, group orientation, or in-group versus out-group concepts (Hofstede 1980; Melewar et al. 2004: 451-452; Roll 2006: 48). In-group thereby refers to family members, co-workers, friends and the community around. The concept's idea is to live in harmony and to respect and support members of the same in-group (Markus/Kitayama 1998: 224-253). In China, a corresponding concept is named 关系 ('guanxi') (personal relationships). Guanxi is an integral part of the Chinese culture and resilient over a very long history (e.g., Fried 1953; Gold 1985; Hwang 1987; King 1991; Yang 1994). The essence of guanxi is that an in-group member "can capitalise on reciprocal obligation and trust implicit in strong social ties to facilitate the exchange of favours and informal influences outside the domain of the original social ties" (Chang/Tam 2004: 24).[82] Trustworthiness, social stability and security are almost taken for granted unless proven otherwise (Davies et al. 2003: 43-45). Closely interlinked to the concept of guanxi is that of face 面子 'mianzi'. "Face corresponds to either a personal's image or the respect in which they are held" (Davies et al. 2003: 44). Face is thought to be more important in China than in Western societies. It is a function of social control, and may be gained, lost, given or taken. Group pressure is used to ensure conformity through eliciting shame ("loss of face"), while an individual, who does a favour for another one, gains face. Overall, a good stock of face may be required to develop useful personal connections (Lockett 1988; Redding/Ng 1992).

While one can argue that individual success and more independent lifestyles are slowly getting more important in China due to 30 years of modernisation, there is evidence that the individual is still highly concerned about meeting collective expectations of family, friends, and the public in general (Leung 1996; Tse 1996; Melewar et al. 2004; Schaffmeister/Ziegler 2005). Furthermore, the speed of which China went from communism and social ideologies to an embracing capitalism has transformed the country in terms of material values. It has created a society of haves and have-nots (McGregor 2005: 18). As a result, many Chinese people nowadays place their complete trust in money, and regard the ownership of brands as one part of it. Luxury brands reflect scarcity, status, admiration and distance to the other lower income parts (Roll 2006: 51; Schramm et al. 2006: 122). Whereas in Germany or Scandinavian countries symbols of status are viewed as suspicious or negative, Chinese people like to show off what they have achieved (Worm 1997: 116-117; Brand Agency 2006).

Thus, the general price category of a brand is often one of the main purchase decision factors. Within a price category there is evidence that Chinese consumers do not decide on brand likes or dislikes, but tend to choose

---

[82] See for guanxi in terms of "social capital" also the literature review of Schlevogt (1999: 2-9). For a corporate perspective see chapter 'Chinese corporate culture and decision-making'.

the favourite brand of their corresponding social class in order to minimise the risk to loose face (Zhou 2005). Word-of-mouth is thus critical to brand success in China (Melewar et al. 2004: 452). A market observer found that a Chinese luxury consumer typically decide on a *Louis Vuitton* branded bag rather than, for instance, on a *Bree* branded bag of the same price group because all other Chinese luxury consumers had decided on a Louis Vuitton bag already (Brand Agency 2006). The trend towards these brand preferences in China, he explained, is thereby strongly influenced by the shopping patterns in Japan and South Korea.

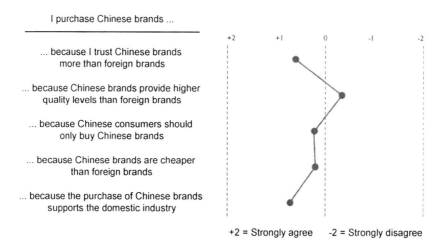

Fig. 3-6. Chinese consumer reasons for purchasing Chinese brands in 2005 (own translation of Schramm/Spiller 2006: 28)

Beyond luxury brands, which are preliminary provided by foreign brands and associated with status and cutting edge, Chinese consumers are also highly aware of Chinese brands and their social attributes (Ballhaus 2005: 32; McEwen 2005a). As figure 3-6 shows, Chinese brands are associated with good quality and an excellent price-performance ratio, and are often perceived as more trustworthy than foreign brands (Schramm/Taube 2006: 16). Another factor which is growing in influence on purchase decisions is the nationalism with the combination of a lingering anti-American sentiment. Most of the Chinese consumers feel obliged to buy local Chinese brands in order to support the national economy and local employment (Nan/Belk 2004: 63-64; Schramm et al. 2006: 122-123). Supported by governmental propaganda, Mingniu dairy, for instance, leveraged this tendency and sponsored the national 'Super-Girl' contest on TV and the

Chinese astronauts when they went into the space the first time in China's history (ABN-AMRO 2005: 16-17).

Probably motivated by the last years' achievements, it is notable that Chinese consumers are also ranked the most optimistic inhabitants in the world besides India. They feel "confident of an even brighter future ahead" (ACNielsen 2005), and are leading in the Asia Pacific region and considered very early adopters of shopping out-of-home-entertainment, new clothes and new technologies such as mobile phones (McEwen 2005b; Brand Agency 2006). In comparison, Western Europe was indicated to have the most pessimistic consumers (ACNielsen 2005).

Although these categorisations and concepts give first hints about Chinese consumer behaviour towards brands, the real picture is more complicated. The next section thus aims to segment the Chinese population of 1.3bn consumers in more homogenous consumer groups.

Chinese consumer segments

China is a large country, and against the general assumptions very heterogeneous. It includes 1.3bn inhabitants (one-fifth of the world's entire population), 31 provinces, 56 ethic groups, 80 languages, and various levels of education, income and beliefs. As figure 3-7 reveals, the consumer consumption levels also differ largely across China, particularly between the Eastern coast and the Western regions. Thus, although China has enjoyed 30 years of economic growth, only a fraction of the 1.3bn potential consumers have experienced the purchase of branded goods so far (Pan et al. 2003; Taube 2003a; French 2006). The average private consumption per head was US$548 in 2004 and is still alike a developing country's consumption. In comparison, in 2004 the average US-American consumed US$27,979, the Japanese US$20,686, the Western European US$16,440 and the Eastern European US$3,860 (EIU 2006). However, the private consumption along China's Eastern coast in the tier 1[83] cities Beijing, Shanghai and Guangzhou is considered as already quiet advanced. For instance, 65% of the consumers there are willed to pay more for their favourite brand, and feel already overstrained by masses of various product offerings (Ballhaus 2005; Zhou 2005; Schramm et al. 2006: 117).

---

[83] Due to their economy, consumption power and economic influence, the cities of Shanghai, Beijing and Guangzhou are usually labelled tier 1 cities; sometimes also the cities of Chengdu and Chongqing can belong to this category. Tier 2 cities are likely provincial capitals and developed coastal cities such as Xiamen, Shenzhen, Wuxi, and Suzhou. Tier 3 refers to prefecture-level cities and big country-level cities (The Boston Consulting Group).

Fig. 3-7. Per capita consumption by province in US$ in 2004 (own illustration of Guojia Tongji Ju [National Bureau of Statistics] 2005: 68)

The gap between haves and have-nots becomes also evident when comparing rural and urban areas in China (figure 3-8). Whereas the per capita urban consumption reached US$1,101 and increased by 5.8% each year between 1989 and 2004, rural households only consumed a third of it (US$317) and grew by 3.6% each year. There are two main reasons for this growing gap. First, the rural areas have mainly been excluded from China's economic growth, although there have been reform policies since the 1980s. And second, the country's immense economic growth has heavily relied on governmental investments, foreign direct investments and exports rather than on domestic demand (China Daily 2005a).

Overall, around 60% of the entire Chinese population are rural residents by 2006.[84] They are usually farmers or workers in town-village enterprises, have low incomes, and have only very basic education. They tend to be very price-sensitive, and little informed and sophisticated about brands. On the one hand, they might slightly favour local brands as considered less

---

[84] China currently undergoes immense urbanisation processes, particularly in the West. According to the National Bureau of Statistics, more than 40% of the Chinese population is already urbanised, which is up from 28% about a decade before (see for details also Zhang 2005).

expensive than foreign brands (Dong/Helms 2001: 106; Zhou 2005), but on the other hand, they could often not distinguish local brands from foreign brands, since both foreign and Chinese brands use Western stylish names and sound alike (Lu 2005). A study of Deutsche Bank additionally pointed out that China's rural population has often been refused access to brands, since they are not reachable in a cost efficient way due to poor physical infrastructure, week distribution systems and wide geographic dispersion (Shaw et al. 2003: 36; French 2006). As a result, though there are few global and national brand champions like Haier and Lenovo available across the entire country, each region is most likely dominated by its local manufacturers (Ayala/Lai 1996; Shaw et al. 2003: 46; Chen/Penhirin 2004; Credit Suisse 2006). For instance, there are more than 260 television makers in China, including foreign and overseas Chinese funded enterprises in 2004 (Huatongren Shichang Xinxiu [All China Marketing Research] 2004: 820).

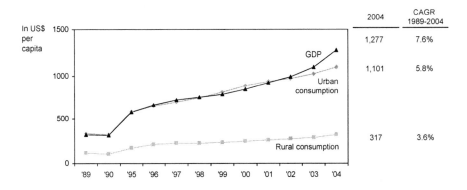

Fig. 3-8. Urban and rural per capita consumption versus GDP per head in US$ 1989-2004 (own illustration of Guojia Tongji Ju [National Bureau of Statistics] 2005: 53, 68)

While rural residents typically show simple shopping patterns due to very limited pockets, the around 525 million Chinese consumers living in urban cities can be separated into five different consumer segments (table 3-3, Dong/Helms 2001: 106): 'new riche' entrepreneurs, college graduates, urban middle class, little emperors, and urban underprivileged class.

	Characteristics	Share of population
'New riche' entrepreneurs	• Extremely rich, either from cities or countryside • Not necessarily with high education, thus little knowledge of English • Favour foreign, expensive brands to demonstrate social status	Minimal to small
Urban middle class	• Traditionally employees in government organisations and companies • Moderate education/income, little international and English knowledge • Value-orientated buyers, who tend to local brands and generic goods	Medium to large
College graduates	• Well-educated and well-paying jobs in multinational companies • Moderate English knowledge, few with international experience • Open-minded and sophisticated buyers of foreign and Chinese brands	Small to medium
Little emperors	• No own income, but sponsored by parents and grandparents • High level of education and good English, when getting older • Favour foreign brands, as considered more fashionable	Small to medium
Urban underprivileged class	• Low income; mostly low education; narrow knowledge of English • Very price sensitive, but with larger brand exposure and brand knowledge • Price-orientated buyers of regional and local products	Very large
Rural residents & farmers	• Low income; mostly low education; narrow knowledge of English • Very price sensitive and of limited product experience • Price-orientated buyers likely of regional and local products	Very large

Table 3-3. Six major customer segments in China (based on Dong/Helms 2001: 106)

'New riche' entrepreneurs are originally either from the city or the countryside (Dong/Helms 2001: 107), and caught a business opportunity during the Chinese transition process to become extremely rich (Zhou 2005). They do not necessarily have a higher education and knowledge of the English language, international markets and brands. They usually look for the most expensive brand in order to demonstrate their status, rather than reflect a certain lifestyle through their purchase behaviour (Think!Desk 2005; Zhou 2005: 4). Some of them thus may favour foreign luxury and premium brands, while some others may have problems re-membering foreign-sounding brand names (Dong/Helms 2001: 107). Ac-cording to a study of McKinsey, their corresponding consumer segment, which they call "economic elite", is estimated less than 10 million con-sumers in 2004 and shall reach 50 million till 2010. The individual shall have a purchase power of more than US$25,000 a year (McKinsey in Shaw et al. 2003: 36; Ballhaus 2005: 31). See also official consumer seg-ments and consumption levels as shown in figure 3-9.

The segment of the urban middle class is much larger then that of the new riche, and is developing fast. BBDO Consulting estimated 50 million households in 2005 and annual earnings between US$2,500 and US$5,000 (Schaffmeister/Ziegler 2005: 59). It is expected to rise by 15% each year and to obtain 45% consumer share by the year 2020 (Ernst & Young in

Wharton School 2005c). Members of this segment are traditionally employees in state-owned organisations and companies in big cities. They have moderate incomes with regularly paid jobs, moderate education (usually high school) and have little knowledge of English. They slightly favour foreign brands, but are not likely to pay a higher price for them. They usually evaluate and compare products carefully and decide on the overall provided product value rather than on the brand name and country-of-origin alone (Dong/Helms 2001: 106; Pan et al. 2003; Melewar et al. 2004: 452; Wharton School 2005c).

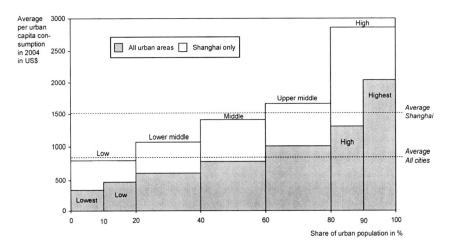

Fig. 3-9. Urban consumer segments by average per capita consumption in US$ in 2004 (own illustration of Guojia Tongji Ju [National Bureau of Statistics] 2005; Shanghai Tongji Ju [Shanghai Bureau of Statistics] 2005)[85]

Over the last years, an increasing part of the urban middle class is the college graduates. They are typically well-educated (often university degrees, very few with studies abroad in the US or Europe), have moderate levels of English knowledge and tend to have well-paying jobs in multinational companies. They often have chances to travel and have access to the

---

[85] Note that figures given by the mentioned different sources cannot be compared without care. They can refer to different reporting years, use different segmentation criteria and underlying definitions such as purchase power, (net/disposable) income, and consumption expenditures, amongst others. Moreover, the data given by the China Statistical Yearbook and Shanghai Statistical Yearbook might be adjusted due to political reasons (Bauer 2002: 152). Even though the absolute values might be difficult to compare, one can generally admit to different income levels as expressed through the figure.

internet and to other cross-country media. As a result, they are considered open-minded, fashion-conscious, and more sophisticated. They are usually well-informed about foreign and domestic brands, and also do not mind to pay a higher price for their favourite brand label (Tam/Tai 1998; Dong/Helms 2001: 106; Zhou 2005).

Since the Chinese government has launched strict rules of birth control in terms of the one-child policy in 1980, Chinese consumer markets are also increasingly influenced by the decision power of the so-called "little emperors" (Wharton School 2005c). The expression refers to the fact that a child may be supported by its parents and two sets of grandparents. While it has to meet the entire family's ambitions regarding school education, sports, and music, it is likely compensated by various consumer products and own disposable income. When the little emperors become college students, they typically have access to the internet and a good knowledge of the English language (Dong/Helms 2001: 107). They usually have a favourable feeling for the Western lifestyle and think it is fashionable to buy foreign global brands instead of local ones (Witkowski et al. 2003). Sponsored by parents and grandparents they are also willed to pay a higher price for their favourite brand (Brand Agency 2006; Schramm et al. 2006: 123).

The final consumer segment is the urban underprivileged class. Their consumer behaviour does not differ very much from those of the rural residents and farmers. They also have very low incomes and very basic education levels, and are very price-sensitive. However, in contrast to the rural areas, the urban underprivileged class has larger exposure to branded goods and can watch other people purchasing them. Thus, though they may have not purchased any branded good by themselves, they can be highly informed about brands and consumer trends.

It is to note that beyond these simple consumer categories, more specific brand preferences and loyalty patterns are rarely known in China so far. One reason is that China is still a transitional economy where tens of millions are continuously moving up the social ladder, changing their attitudes, preferences and living expenditures (Schramm/Taube 2006: 12). Another reason is that comprehensive market research has seldom been done in China so far (Think!Desk 2005: 2-3; Schramm et al. 2006: 115). However, figure 3-10 shows a first attempt of a more sophisticated consumer segmentation developed by the market research company Sinomonitor International in 2003 (Ma 2003: 1-17).[86] But, why is market research so

---

[86] Life orientation bases on factors such as family-, achievement-, and fashion-orientation, and basic personalities (independent, impulsive, price-conscious).

seldom in China? Which other means do Chinese branded companies use instead, to conduct their brand management decisions? These questions will be clarified in the next section on Chinese organisational behaviour towards brands.

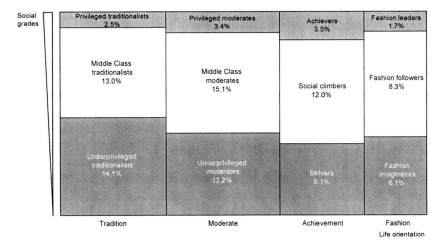

Fig. 3-10. 12er segmentation of urban Chinese consumers in 2003 (Ma 2003: 9)

3.1.3 Chinese organisational behaviour towards brands

The real picture of Chinese organisational behaviour is complex, and influences can be traced back to ancient times. In order to gain a profound basis of understanding of today's decision-making and organisational behaviour towards brands, this chapter first reviews ancient traditions of Confucian protocols, the era of Mao and the circumstances during the time of planned economy. In a second section, today's brand approaches of Chinese branded companies are then examined, and compared to Western organisational behaviour towards brands.

Chinese corporate culture and decision-making

As researchers stated that, more than any other countries, "in China culture pervades" (Hall/Xu 1990: 574), the doctrine of Confucius, apart from other factors and religions such as Buddhism and Taoism, is regarded as the un-

---

Social grades refer to education level, house size, income and ownership of durables.

derlying cultural concept of Chinese social relations and corporate culture over the last two thousand five hundred years (e.g., Yang 1961; Yau 1988; Fukuyama 1995; Lu 2003; Yu et al. 2003; Zhu 2003).

Management writers such as Lockett (1988), Xing (1995), Child and Lu (1996: 4) and Lu (2003), emphasised that Confucianism with its personal ethic principles was, besides from its social functions, also used in politics in order to build hierarchical organisation in China. So far there is little empirical evidence testing its importance for organisations (Lockett 1988: 486; Schlevogt 1999: 2-6), while in theoretical terms, Confucian authority patterns and legitimisation strategies may explain Chinese organisational structure (Hamilton/Biggart 1988; Lu 2003). More specifically, they tend to lead to organisations with a relatively high degree of centralisation and top-down command structures, since Confucian protocols place high value on social control and personal power (e.g., Child 1994: 31; Lu 2003: 33). According to Confucius, the king is the master of the minister; the husband is the master of the wife; and the father is the master of the son. Therefore, when the king gave an order, the minister could at best give some advice, and if the king insisted, the minister could do nothing but obey. Confucius also said that common people can be made to follow, but they cannot be made to understand (Confucius 1998: 9 book eight).

In addition, Confucianism doctrines emphasise ties of kinship and group loyalty (Wilson 1970: 20). The individual exist for the benefit of the group. Thus, Lu (2003: 28) explained that the leader of an enterprise does not only hold an administrative function, but also plays a morale role. If the leader is both, administrative efficient and morally 'good', it is thought that the employees refer to him as their 'parent leader' whom they are willing to trust in every sense, and regard the enterprise as their family (Lu 2003: 37). Social needs of employees in the workplace might thus be perceived more important than autonomy and self-actualisation needs (Xing 1995: 17). The aspect of group orientation may also be confirmed by China's old tradition of learning from good examples. Confucius said: "When three people are together, there must be one whom one can learn from" (Confucius 1998: 21 book seven). As a result, Chinese employees are typically considered to learn quickly by imitating, following role models and absorbing prescribed solutions for given problems (McGregor 2005: 260). Although there is little empirical evidence so far, Lu (2003: 32) stressed that this Confucianism principle may also be the reason why Chinese businessmen do not find it wrong to imitate what others do, and to produce imitated products and to violate intellectual property rights.

Although it is widely discussed whether Confucian cultural values were condemned during the Cultural Revolution (1967-76) led by Communist Mao Zedong, or are still vivid in today's Chinese society (e.g., Yau 1988;

Schlevogt 1999; Lu 2003; Yu et al. 2003; Zhu 2003), the extent of the consequences of the Cultural Revolution on the management elite and corporate decision-making is not imaginable (Wehrfritz 1996; Economist 2006).
So far only few management authors has discussed its impact (amongst
them, Laaksonen 1984; Walder 1986; Laaksonen 1988). Mao's era was essentially characterised by distrust, fear and terror. All power was centralised and concentrated in Mao's personality and ambitions. In order to im-
munise China against 'bourgeois and capitalist restoration', he called on
millions of patriotic youth to form the Red Guards with the mission to
clean the Chinese society from old culture and higher education. The
cleansing included much plunder, robbery and destruction of cultural
property such as books, paintings, music instruments, opera costumes, and
historical monuments. It also meant denunciation, torture and murder of
millions of intellectuals, artists and oppositional party officials. China's
schools and universities were closed and millions of educated youth and
professors were sent to the countryside to learn from the peasants and to do
physical work (e.g., Wehrfritz 1996; Shapiro 2001).

At firm-level, Mao collectivised the enterprise management, replaced
former 'capitalist' managers, and got people in leading positions ideologi-
cally trained up to 12 hours a week within the firm (Laaksonen 1977: 78).
Moreover, efforts were made to prevent personal managing power from
becoming too strong e.g., by multifaceted systems of self-criticism, by
revolutionary committees, and by forcing top managers to work part of
their time alongside their subordinates, doing the same tasks, often including physical exercise. Since the top managers often performed these un-
skilled tasks poorly, they lost face, and thus power, self-esteem and respect
among colleagues and subordinates (Laaksonen 1984: 6).

After the death of Mao in 1976, the new Communist party leaders abandoned the structures created by the Cultural Revolution, shifted away from
ideological to economic aims, one-man management systems, and extensive governmental control though rigid central planned systems
(Laaksonen 1984: 20; Chai 1997).[87] Firm-level decision-making was primarily focused on aligning with central administrative bodies, regulatory
bureaus and, in some cases, local governments (Tung 1982; Child 1994).
Main source of power and the highest organ in the country became the
Central Committee of the Communist Party which controls the resources
partly by themselves or through state organs and partly through top managers, who have been elected or approved by the Party through the so-
called "nomenklatura system" (Burns 1987). Nomenclature is a list which
includes the important positions in the political, economic and social sys-

---

[87] See also chapter 'Origin and competitive evolution'.

tem and the persons occupying them or persons who have been selected as potential 'crown princes' for them in the future. The top managers of the largest and strategically most important enterprises were usually also high Party officials who represented the power of the Party, implemented Party decisions, and kept personnel and organisational decisions in their hands in the first place to ensure that the Party keeps a tight hold on power (Schurmann 1971). As a consequence, middle managers often did not dare to make decisions independently, but rather waited for the decisions to be made by the top management levels. Hence decisions often had to wait and caused large inefficiencies (Laaksonen 1984: 17; Chou 2005: 43).

Since the reforms started in 1978, it has been the plan to separate the power of the Communist Party from the enterprise management, to down-size bureaucracy and to let employees elect the top management in order to give more independence to the firm (e.g., Laaksonen 1988; Burns 2001). On the one hand, there are official statistics indicating that the contribution of state-owned enterprises to the economy has decreased while private contribution is growing (figure 3-11). Further, more than 40% of the capital invested in China was raised at capital markets in 2004 (McKinsey 2005). Capital markets typically demand transparency and independent management in order to satisfy shareholder interests. On the other hand, there is wide consensus among China experts that the public sector and especially the government "remains as strong as ever" (Burns 2001: 420).

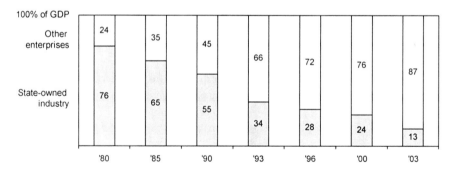

Fig. 3-11. Share of GDP hold by state-owned industry 1980-2003 (Guojia Tongji Ju [National Bureau of Statistics] 1998; 2004; 2005)[88]

---

[88] China Statistical Yearbook changed its reporting system of GDP data for the category 'state-owned industry' twice in 1996 and 2004. In order to show comparable data, figure 1 focuses on 'state-owned companies', a category which was phased out in 2004, and neglected 'state-holding enterprises'. The category 'state-owned and state-holding enterprises" would let jump up the state influ-

There are at least three reasons. First, the economic and enterprise reforms have been planned in details by an elite group of Communist Party technocrats and bureaucrats similar to the five-year plans that coordinate the Chinese overall economy (McGregor 2005: 227-228). Major industries, amongst them transport, telecommunication, energy, and banking are thus still dominated by state-controlled companies and are strongly supported by the government, partly to increase their power at the global level (e.g., Burns 2001: 424; UNCTAD 2003).[89] Second, the controlling shareholder, even of the publicly-listed Chinese companies are in most cases owned by a government entity (Lanzeni/Hansakul 2004: 13). This leads to the fact that many Chinese companies still focus on manufacture volume and sales growth rather than on individual profit strategies and modern management principles because this government entity finally covers all potential business losses ("soft budget constraints", Shaw et al. 2003: 13; Yang 2005: 8; Burkat 2006). And third, it is widely agreed that there is the informal policy of the Central Committee of the Party that assigns top management and CEO positions in state-controlled companies either to loyal party officials who worked their way up in the bureaucracy, or to children of senior party leaders who are expected to live and work in China (e.g., McGregor 2005: chap 2).

Overall, one may thus conclude that despite of 30 years of modernisation and reform, traditional Confucian principles as well as planned economic management systems are still widely in use in most of the Chinese companies, and determine Chinese decision-making. Market experts such as Deng and Dart (1999), Tan and Litschert (1994) and Yang (2005: 8) thus concluded that so far Chinese companies would lack substantial realignments in corporate governance and policies plus the development of organisational skills, especially those related to marketing and brand management functions. "The contribution of marketing in boosting China's once ailing economy has not yet become clear" (Deng/Dart 1999: 632). McGregor (2005: 261) added that organisational behaviour that is not dictatorship, treats others as equals, accepts responsibility for mistakes, shares information and rewards creativity and customer orientation, includes qualities which are still rare to find in Chinese corporations so far (similar Lu 2005).

---

enced GDP share onto 36% in 1996 and 50% in 1998 (Guojia Tongjiju [National Bureau of Statistics]).

[89] Compare to chapter 3.2.2.

Domestic Chinese brand approaches

Due to the described lack of own corporate marketing and brand manage-ment culture, how do Chinese branded companies then perform their brand management? It is said that Chinese managers regard brand management as an unknown intangible area (Lu 2005; Brand Agency 2006). Although they appreciate its power and success, they have typically denied to start dealing with it because they feel incalculable personal and economical risks (McGregor 2005: 260). There were no Chinese role models, no Chi-nese prescribed solutions and no Chinese brands to imitate at least until 2000.[90] Thus, if there were Chinese managers who had the heart to adven-ture into brand management, they took foreign brands operating in China as an example, and aimed to absorb their marketing strategies (Zhu 2003; Zhou 2005). Particularly Asian brands such as *Samsung* (South Korea) and *Sony* (Japan) has been taken as role models (e.g., Gao et al. 2003; Roll 2006).[91]

As a consequence, many Chinese companies have been accused to copy their way of business by providing imitations of foreign brands at lower-price levels (e.g., Carter 1996; Kong 2005; Sokianos 2006). Figure 3-12 shows three accused examples: *Li-Ning* 李宁 sportswear appears very similar to *Nike* (Economist 2003b; Schramm/Spiller 2006: 15-16); *Wan-danu* 万达奴 resembles *Adidas*; and the *Shanghai Xingbake* Coffee Bar 上海星巴克咖啡馆 ('Shanghai xingbake kafei guan') uses similar colours and the same Chinese brand name as the *Starbucks* which is 星巴克 ('xingbake') in Chinese characters (Müller 2006; Mure et al. 2006). Over-all, the Chinese government estimated the damage of piracy to US$25bn in 2003 (Blume 2006: 17). The US Chamber of Commerce estimated the costs to 15-20% of total US sales in China (Shaw et al. 2003: 31), while software companies like Microsoft and Adobe would even suffer from US$250bn a year (Fischer et al. 2004: 47; Zhu 2006). Main counterfeit product categories are fashion and design, computer software, DVD-movies and music, industrial parts and machines, Western drugs and food. Many fakes are said to be so good nowadays that even company execu-tives say that it takes a forensic scientist to distinguish them from the original. Chinese counterfeiters are considered "extremely ingenious, in-ventive, and scientifically oriented" (Balfour et al. 2005).

---

[90] Although one could argue that Chinese companies may have taken brands from Hong Kong, Taiwan and Singapore as their role models, there is not yet empiri-cal evidence, since they typically also lack globally successful brands (Roll 2006).

[91] See also case studies in chapter 5.2.

Fig. 3-12. Brand originals and Chinese copies (all photos taken on Shanghai Nanjing Road in September 2006)

Beyond pure imitations, however, there are also a couple of Chinese companies which have already "risked" to emancipate themselves and advanced the sole copies by own ideas and intellectual property. *Blocko* 宝高 (‚baogao'), for example, makes toys in the same category as *Lego* and is considered a significant competitor. While in the 1990s Blocko founder

David Cheng started with pure copies of Lego toys, the company is today proud to rely on own unique designs with international patent rights and global distribution through Wal-Mart and Toys'R'Us retail stores (Blume 2006, company websites). Another example is China's e-commerce leader *Alibaba.com* 阿里巴巴. The online marketplace operator was launched in 1999 by Jack Ma and basically relies on the same business concept as *Ebay*, but was adapted to local needs by a special online paying system which avoids payments by credit cards (Underwood/Wong 2005; Blume 2006). Today, the company includes three divisions – Alibaba International, Alibaba China (both b2b marketplaces) and Taobao.com淘宝 (c2c), employs 2,400 people and has registered members in over 200 countries and regions. In 2005 Alibaba also acquired *Yahoo* China, an underperforming division of the US web-media giant Yahoo (Underwood/Wong 2005).

Beyond such entrepreneurships, some other Chinese companies started professionalising the know-how transfer from foreign brand professionals into their companies, and developed more independent brand approaches since. They work together with international advertising and consulting companies (Madden 2001), and hire experienced brand managers or international designers from foreign multinationals (Huang/Du 2005; Zhou 2005). Li-Ning, for instance, is known to employ a former brand manager of P&G since 2004 (Madden 2004). Lenovo is known to get advice from McKinsey and JWT, China Mobile from Ogilvy, and GOME from BCG (Branigan 2005). In addition, Chinese companies increasingly tap the pool of native-born executives working abroad (BCG 2006c: 23), or that of Chinese students who were taught in marketing and brand management by international professors through American MBA programs at Chinese universities or abroad at elite universities such as Harvard and Stanford (McGregor 2005: chap 8).

Although there is therefore evidence that some Chinese companies have made progress in brand management over the last years, market observers still admit that the majority of firms have little adopted to the new market needs so far, and that well-educated and experienced personal remains a bottleneck (e.g., Yang 2005: 8). In most cases, brand management decisions are thus still made by the top manager or CEO, who is typically an engineer rather than a marketing expert, and who is used to base decisions on own strong beliefs rather than on market research or professional advice (McGregor 2005: 269-270). As a result, specialised marketing and brand management departments are usually seldom; and even though few companies have a marketing unit, it is said that the unit is typically focusing on short-term sales and promotional activities rather than on long-term marketing strategies and brand value building (Lu 2005; Zhou 2005; Brand Agency 2006). The cutting edge in brand management organisations in China is said to be Haier, Lenovo and TCL (Zhang Ying 2006). Figure 3-13 shows Haier's department of corporate values & communication 企业价值观统一处 ('qiye jiazhi guantong yichu') which is in charge of the group's domestic brand management including corporate values, advertising and public relation.[92]

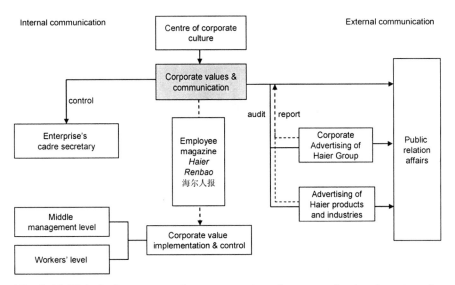

Fig. 3-13. Haier's department of corporate values & communication (own translation of OgilvyOne Worldwide 2006: 6)

As the Haier example confirms, one of the most important brand building channels used by the leading Chinese branded companies is classical advertising (Huang/Du 2005: 118; Yang 2005: 9). The annual survey of the Blue Book of China's Advertisers found that companies in China, both local and foreign branded companies, thus spent on advertising an average 41.4% of their marketing budgets (Huang/Du 2005: 119) which was on average 16.6% of total sales in 2005 (Huang/Du 2005: 117).[93] Marketing professor Lu Xiongwen from Fudan Management School in Shanghai (2005) gave reasons why leading Chinese brands tend to invest in advertis-

---

[92] For more details see Haier case study in chapter 5.

[93] According to the survey, the average marketing budget increased compared to previous years which was 12.9% in 2003 and 16.4% in 2004 (Huang/Du 2005: 117), while the share spent on advertising decreased from 45.1% in 2003 and 44.6% in 2004.

ing so heavily. He said that even leading Chinese managers would often understand brand building as equal to being "loud in the market" and would just push them in the market because they have the general belief that brands immediately mean larger sales (also Gao et al. 2003; Müller 2006). This may also be the same reason why most of the Chinese companies favour corporate brand names instead of product names. Most Chinese brands are currently stretching their name across as many product categories, regional territories and distribution channels as possible (Yuan/Dawar 2001: 3-4; Huang/Du 2005: 93; Zhou 2005). Major advertising channels in China are thus also channels with broad scope and large consumer reach. The top three advertising channels in 2005 were television (38.7% in 2005), newspapers (22.1%) and outdoor placements (13.0%) (Huang/Du 2005: 58; similar Shenzhen Daily 2005a). In total the advertising spending in China was more than US$15.3bn in 2004 (Fan 2005: 111). Table 3-4 maps the leading Chinese brands and their advertising expenditures. Although Chinese branded companies may put strong emphasis on advertising to communicate their brands, largest advertiser in China was however the US-multinational *P&G* in 2004. They spent US$572m on the cosmetic brand *Olay* 玉兰油 ('yulan you'), which is double as much than the expenditures of Chinese *China Mobile* (Huang/Du 2005: 436).

Brand	Industries of major ad spends	2004 in mio. US$
中国移动通信 China Mobile	Telecommunication	261.3
娃哈哈 Wahaha	Beverages	114.5
五粮液 Wuliangye	Liquors	81.4
国美 GOME	Retail	57.0
海尔 Haier	Household appliances	50.3
TCL	Household appliances, telecommunication	43.9
联想 Lenovo	Computer	29.7
美的 Midea	Household appliances	17.7
红塔山 Hongtashan	Cigarettes	12.1
李宁 Li-Ning	Sports wear	9.6

Table 3-4. Advertising expenditures of selected Chinese brands in 2004 (own illustration of Huang/Du 2005: 428-436)

In terms of advertising content, a study of Cheng and Schweitzer (1996) found that Chinese branded companies utilise a "melting pot" of Chinese and Western cultural values to promote their products in the mid-1990s. These values were particularly related to family, technology, tradition, modernity and youth. Moreover, the study stressed that Chinese advertisements were especially used to promote the functional "newness" of a product and to address governmental policies with respect to socialist modernisation and economic growth, while US advertisements focused on individual product benefits and emotional brand values. Although one could argue that the study is already ten years old and thus out-dated, market observers agreed that particularly Chinese symbolic values such as family and tradition still play a leading role in Chinese marketing. It is assumed that these are probably the only brand characteristic which are not copied from foreign brands, but are intrinsic for Chinese marketing.

Marketing professor Allan K.K. Chan (2006) of the Baptist University in Hong Kong confirmed that Chinese traditional and symbolic values remain particularly crucial when a company has to choose its Chinese brand name. Similar to the traditional choice of human names, Chinese people are very superstitious about brand names and regard them as the essence of the product and a symbol for their success (Schmitt 1995; Zhou 2005). Unlike other languages that use letters as components of words, the basic unit of the Chinese written language is the character. A character is an arrangement of strokes that form a syllabic unit. One character can have different meanings and multiple pronunciations. One phonetic sound can also have multiple written characters. Of the approximately 70,000 characters, 3,500 are in daily use (Dong/Helms 2001: 105). According to prior studies, the typical Chinese brand name is short, simple and restricted to the inventory of the 3,500 frequently used characters (Chan/Huang 2001, 2003). It is likely compounded of two characters (Chan/Huang 1997), a form which is alike to most of the usual Chinese vocabulary, and therefore easy for Chinese consumers to pronounce and to remember. For instance, computer 电脑 ('diannao') is compounded by electricity 电 ('dian') and brain 脑 ('nao'). Typically, the second character (脑) is a noun and the first character (电) a modifier of the noun. In terms of brand names, the noun likely indicates the product category, while the modifier adds to the name semantically positive attributes with respect to Chinese traditional values or symbols of beauty and significance. For example, the name of the TV brand *Changhong* 长虹 means 'long rainbow' (Huang/Chan 2002). Dependent on the product category, special Chinese characters and compounds are most likely. Bicycle brands, for instance, chose characters symbolising reliability and speed, such as 永 ('yong', forever), 久 ('jiu', a long time), 金 ('jin', gold), 飞 ('fei', flying). Known Chinese bicycle names are therefore 永久 ('always and forever'), 飞鸽 ('feige', flying pigeon) and 金狮 ('jinshi', golden lion) (Huang/Chan 1997; Chan/Huang 2001; Huang/Chan 2002).

It is to note that according to Chinese official regulations, Chinese and foreign companies are not required to choose a brand name in Chinese written language when operating in China. Although they have to register their enterprise by a Chinese corporate name, the brand name itself in advertising and on packages can be a pure English name (Brand Agency 2006). However, very few Chinese companies have abandoned their Chinese written names so far. As Marketing Professor Hang Zhonghe (2006) from Fudan University in Shanghai explained, most Chinese branded companies would chose a combination of both, English and Chinese written names in order to gain maximum brand building results. The English part is thereby used to enhance the brand image, as associated with fashionable, innovative, quality and probably a foreign country-of-origin, while the Chinese part is essential for the brand's recognition because most of the Chinese consumers have difficulties to pronounce and remember a sole English name (Brand Agency 2006).

In this chapter it has been shown that Chinese branded companies have a short history of brand management. However, they took foreign brands operating in China as their examples and have learnt quickly since. By 2005/2006, China has produced some powerful brand names in China. They combine Chinese traditional values with modern Western brand management concepts, and are very successful in their domestic markets. Since most Chinese consumer markets are very competitive, and increasing numbers of foreign brands are attracted by the large consumer potential, Chinese branded companies cannot take their market shares as granted. The next chapter will thus investigate whether and why some of these Chinese branded companies have already gone abroad to expand their markets, and what they have experienced particularly in developed markets so far.

3.2 Experiences with developed markets

Having examined the brand management experiences of Chinese branded companies in their domestic markets, the rationale of this chapter is now to investigate the experiences of Chinese branded companies with overseas markets, and there, especially with developed markets. There are two sections. The first section addresses international experiences and learnings that Chinese branded companies have gained though collaborations with multinationals through original equipment manufacturer (OEM, see next section) and retailing in China. The second section then examines China's presence in developed markets. This starts with a short review on China's government policies since 1978 concerning Chinese outward investments and global brand building, followed by a short study on general consumer attitudes and images towards China's country-of-origin among German customers.

3.2.1 Learnings from multinationals in China

Sino-foreign joint ventures and OEM

First contacts of contemporary Chinese companies with foreign multinationals and international market places occurred in the process of the open door policy in the late 1980s and accelerated after Deng Xiaoping's Southern tour in 1992.[94] Based on the examples of Taiwan, Singapore and Hong Kong, the Chinese government has employed foreign direct investments (FDI) as a key element in China's development strategy (Shi 2001). The aim has been to obtain foreign technology and capital that could then be turned toward export production in order to earn foreign exchange for China and to provide jobs for the Chinese people. In return for providing technology and capital, foreign companies were then allowed access to the Chinese market (e.g., Roehrig 1994; Naughton 1995; Lardy 2002; Buckley et al. 2004). In the early years of China's modernisation, however, this access was heavily restricted. Foreign companies were only allowed to set up offices in the special economic zones along the Eastern coast. The Chinese government intended that these zones could serve as study centres for Chinese companies to learn from the foreigners and to absorb techniques that would enable them to supply China's industry needs and to create the country's own brands and consumer products (e.g., Roehrig 1994; Yan 2000; McGregor 2005: 35). Moreover, foreign companies were, as a rule, unable to invest except via international joint-ventures with a Chinese partner. The Chinese partner was either imposed by the Chinese government, or freely chosen and then approved by the government. Additionally, local content requirements of 80% and constraints on importing components pressured the foreign companies to transfer their knowledge to China and to locally owned firms controlled by the Chinese government (Roehrig 1994; Luo 2000; Buckley et al. 2004: 34-35). Since the foreign companies were keen to establish factories in China in order to tap the immense market and to utilise the low labour costs for their international sales, hundreds of the world's largest companies accepted the Chinese restrictions, and es-

---

[94] Compare to chapter 'Origin and competitive evolution'.

tablished Sino-foreign joint ventures and representative offices in China. In 1993, for example, China signed nearly 85,000 contracts with foreign investors representing US$111bn investment (McGregor 2005: 37).

Although the intention of most of the foreign companies has been to copy the blueprints of their foreign parent firms into the Sino-foreign joint ventures, including all relevant technologies (product design, manufacturing process, product testing, and quality control), management skills (marketing, accounting and finance, planning, purchasing and supply, stock control) and product ranges, they typically started in a "from-easy-to-difficult" sequence (Buckley et al. 2004: 54). Since 'easy' likely meant assembling, testing and later production, Chinese managers and engineers learnt lessons particularly in sourcing and manufacturing (Buckley et al. 2004: 53-58). In addition, they were taught in foreign corporate cultures, organisational structures, technologies and consumer requirements related to global brands. They could also often improve their English language ability and gain international experience by stays abroad in the foreign partner's headquarters or even by sponsored American university degrees (Gao et al. 2003; Buckley et al. 2004: 46-52).

Over the years, Western companies started to outsource their manufacturing operations more aggressively into China (Yuan/Dawar 2001: 8; Roll 2006: 3). Many joint ventures contracts came to an end and Chinese companies began to buy out their foreign partners (BCG 2006b: 9). In addition, Chinese managers left the joint ventures and created own factories using the manufacturing and management know-how they have learnt from the foreigners (McGregor 2005: 255). As a result, China became the world's largest manufacturing country and second largest exporter in the world. 37% of China's GDP was export in 2005 (EIU 2006; MOFCOM 2006c). 40% of toys in the world are made in China, 50% of all shoes and 40% of all personal computers (Wang/Yin 2005).

At the same time, Chinese companies mostly became an original equipment manufacturer (OEM) for other foreign companies and global brands, ranging from toys and televisions to industrial machinery and fashion labels. The idea of OEM is basically to utilise each country's comparative advantage. The Chinese part provides low labour costs and economies of scale due to large volume manufacturing, and the Western part provides technologies, R&D, marketing and brand management (Gao et al. 2003). A known Chinese OEM is *Galanz* 格兰士 ('gelanshi'), that produces 30-50% of all microwave ovens in the world for more than 200 brands and retail private labels (Zeng/Williamson 2004: 42; Wang/Yin 2005). In 2004 they sold 18 million microwave ovens, of which 13 million were sold overseas. Galanz was founded in 1978 and started making microwaves in 1992, which it soon began manufacturing for OEM customers (Gao et al.

2003). Another known Chinese OEM is Midea 美的 ('meidi'). Midea was founded in 1968 and is today the world's largest manufacturer of electrical fans (50% world market share), making also air-conditioners and micro-waves for brands such as *SMC* in Hong Kong, and *Danby* and *Kenmore*[95] in Canada and the US (Yuan/Dawar 2001: 1). In 2004 Midea Group had revenues of US$3.8bn, 30% thereof abroad (company websites). Both firms have primarily targeted foreign companies which were keen on the low labour cost advantages, but were not yet ready to set up own operations in China themselves (Gao et al. 2003).

From the Chinese perspective, the key success factors in the OEM model are cost and quality leadership, the ability to support a number of global customers at the same time, and to acquire the needed technology and capabilities. The low costs, which are necessary to secure the initial contracts, must then be accompanied by excellent skills in supply chain management and sourcing. A number of customers are required to mini-mise dependence on any one of them and to gain scale. But while OEM seems to demand the lowest level of additional skills from the Chinese companies, it also offers the lowest upside from the market. Returns can only come through expanding scale to achieve a global dominating posi-tion in components and assembly (Gao et al. 2003; Roll 2006: 3-4). See as an example figure 3-14 that exemplifies a consumer goods industry. The brand margin in percent of the end-consumer retail price is in the example more than twice as high as the OEM margin.

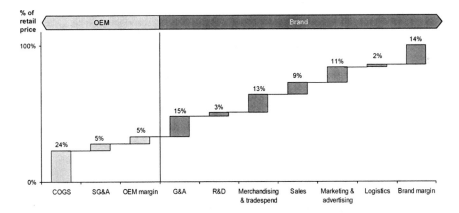

Fig. 3-14. OEM versus brand margins of an exemplified consumer good industry (based on Roll 2006: 3-4, and several expert and company inputs)

---

[95] Kenmore is a brand owned by Sears.

So far, many Chinese companies have been satisfied with the OEM approach. But, since the market conditions have gotten more competitive and price wars started to decrease margins,[96] many of these companies were forced to look for additional measures to survive and grow their business. Attracted by the large margins of their branded customers in international markets, these Chinese companies thus recently started to want to keep the margins for themselves (Yuan/Dawar 2001: 12-13; Lu 2005). But how shall they perform a brand approach without any know-how in R&D, technologies and innovation which is likely considered the basis for creating brands?

Despite the fact that China is the world's largest country by population, the world's sixth largest economy and the world's second largest exporter, the UNCTAD innovation capability index ranked China only at world's 74th position in 2001, two ranks behind its position of 1995, and behind developing countries such as Brazil, Malaysia, and Mongolia (UNCTAD 2005b: 114). China's R&D expenditures, though they increased from 0.6% to 1.23% of GDP between 1996 and 2004, are still small in comparison to Japan's and South Korea's 3% of GDP or America's 2.7% (Roll 2006: 6; Shanghai Daily 2006). At firm level, statistics show a similar picture. From 1991 to 2003, large and middle-sized Chinese companies invested between 0.4% and 0.8% of their revenues on R&D, while companies in developed countries usually spent 3% (Yi/Ye 2003: 58; UNCTAD 2005b: 120; China-Embassy 2006). As a result, Chinese companies lack international patents. According to a study of BCG (2006a), China does not rank in the top 15 patent holders in any major market in the world. Although China recently increased its patent filings in the US, Europe and Japan, statistics showed that China patent applications represent far less than 1% of patents filed in those countries in 2004 (also Wang/Yin 2005).

Due to this immense lack of Chinese companies in R&D, innovation and international patents, some market observers are arguing that Chinese companies may take the same path as in manufacturing, and will postpone their brand ambitions. Since recently hundreds of foreign companies are setting up R&D facilities in China at an accelerating rate (e.g., UNCTAD 2005b: 127-143; China-Embassy 2006) and the share of high-tech products of China's total exports has increased from 14% to 28% between 2000 and 2005 (MOFCOM 2006c), they assumed that the multinational research centres may again train thousands of Chinese researchers and designers, who may then leave the company and form their own R&D operations and technology companies based on their learnt foreign research skills (e.g., McGregor 2005: 255).

---

[96] See also chapter 3.1.1.

Huawei Technologies 华为技术 is China's most known B2B-brand and China's largest manufacturer of telecommunication equipment. Huawei is competing globally with other telecom equipment manufactures Cisco, Lucent, Alcatel and Ericsson and is to date world's number one manufacturer in switching and next generation network, number two in DSLAM and number three in integrated access and optical network. Huawei contracted sales in 2004 reached US$ 5.58 billion, an increase of 45% year on year, among which US$ 2.28 billion came from international sales. Its global network covers 90 countries and regions, serving 22 of the world's top 50 operators.

Key success factor and image builder is Huawei's excellence in R&D. Huawei invests over 10% of its revenue in R&D each year, holding 1,400 patents and cooperating with global players like TI, Motorola, IBM, Oracle and Intel both at home and overseas. They run international R&D centres in India, Russia, Sweden and the US. Their strength is said to be in tailor-made solutions that satisfy customers' specific requirements. Moreover, Huawei has created several digital technologies that are going to link PCs, TVs, stereos, and other devices to the Internet and among each other within the approach of a digital home. Besides innovation, Huawei profits from a distribution partnership with IBM and a good price-value-offer in the market. "When we first saw Huawei we couldn't believe a Chinese company could match on occidental one – we were wrong. Their technology was better and they were 30% cheaper", said Francois Paulus, head of the network division at Neuf Telecom in an interview with the Economist, using Huawei's optical transmission equipment to sell voice data and video services.

In future however, Huawei has to prove that critics like those of Hong Lu, CEO of UTStarcom, one of Huawei's biggest competitors in China, who said that "they are followers, not innovators. In the past, they have always done things that others have already done. [...] Real innovation will come from foreign companies opening their own research facilities on the mainland."

Up to now Huawei is a total B2B-brand which functions in a different way than the consumer brands Haier and Lenovo. However, some experts are already predicting that Huawei could emerge as a consumer brand as well. They have already started in developing third generation (3G) mobile phones and set top boxes for TV. In 2005 Huawei also won the licence to produce and sell mobile phones to consumers in China.

Huawei Technologies

"Craving connectivity?
We hear you."

Box 3-2. B2B brand Huawei Technologies (Einhorn et al. 2004; Roberts et al. 2004; Economist 2005a; Janke/Weiland 2005, and company websites)

However, it is to note that not all Chinese branded companies will take this path. There are already few Chinese companies that have proactively invested in own R&D facilities in order to be independent from foreign IP (Business Week 2004). Best R&D practice among Chinese companies is considered *Huawei Technologies* 华为技术 which invests around 10% of its total revenues on R&D and has already set up international R&D facilities in India, Russia, Sweden and the US (box 3-2, Roberts et al. 2004; BCG 2006c: 13-14; China-Embassy 2006). Moreover, it is to note that most of the typical OEM suppliers such as Midea and Galanz, though lacking own international IP, can already rely on own strong brands established in the domestic markets. As a reminder, Midea was ranked among the top 10 most valuable Chinese brands in 2004 by Beijing Famous Brand Evaluation.[97] As the next section shows, these brands have thus not only learnt about developed markets through Sino-foreign joint ventures and OEM arrangements, but could also already demonstrate their own brand power towards global retailers operating in China.

Global retailers

At the same time, when Chinese companies have learnt about international manufacture standards and Western basic consumer needs though Sino-foreign joint ventures and OEM arrangements, many of the same companies also got in touch with foreign sales culture and modern retail formats like hypermarkets, supermarkets and convenience stores in China. While prior to China's WTO ascension, the Chinese government had primarily owned and managed all distribution channels, and private wholesale and retailing had been marginal (Shaw et al. 2003: 45-46), global retailers such as Carrefour (France), Wal-Mart (USA) and Metro-Group (Germany) have opened up retail outlets at an accelerate pace since. It is said that they have grown by up to 50% a year (Hemerling et al. 2004: 1; Murphy 2005). Carrefour, for instance, was the first international retailer to establish presence in Asia. They began their experience in Taiwan in 1989 and started operation in China in 1995 by their first retail store in Beijing. In July 2006, Carrefour is China's leading foreign retailer running 79 hypermarkets in more than 20 cities and 242 hard discount stores, including franchisers and partners. In 2004, Carrefour had revenues of US$1,753m (table 3-5, company websites). The company expects that its sales in China will continue to grow by 25% to 30% each year at least till 2010 (Child 2006). Wal-Mart, the world's largest retailer, gained revenues of US$822m in China in 2004 and runs 51 supercentres, 3 Sam's Clubs and 2 neighbourhood markets by 2006 (annual report 2006). Metro Group has 30 cash & carry outlets and US$677m revenues in 2004 (company websites).[98] Other interna-

---

[97] See chapter 'Top Chinese brands in 2005/2006'.

[98] Cash & carry are superstores particularly selling its grocery and non-grocery items to resellers and commercials. Hypermarkets typically sell broad ranges of grocery and non-grocery items by sales area above 5,000m² per store; they are typically located outside city centres. Supermarkets likely have 400 to 2,500m²

tional retailers operating in China are IKEA (Sweden), Auchan (France), Ito-Yokado (Japan), OBI (Germany), Tesco and B&Q (both UK) (Dickens 2004; European Retail Digest 2006).[99]

Typically, the global retailers, among them Carrefour and Wal-Mart, are used to work with Chinese branded companies on OEM basis for their private labels that are sold in their international markets (e.g., Gao et al. 2003). Carrefour, for instance, created up 2,000 food and non-food products with different OEM-brand labels: *Carrefour*, *Carrefour Quality Line*, *Firstline*, *Frenchtouch*, and *Bang* (Carrefour websites). In China, however, the picture is different. Since Chinese consumers often prefer Chinese brands over foreign labels due to patriotism, trustworthiness and their competitive price-value-ratio,[100] Carrefour offers a modern retail format in China that is a mixed with local tastes as seen in figure 3-15:

Fig. 3-15. Food and electronics sections in Carrefour Shanghai Wuning store in October 2006 (own photos)

In the fresh-food sections there are tanks of live fish, eels, bullfrogs, and turtles, while vacuum-packed strips of bacon and slices of pepperoni lie in refrigerated cases a short distance away (Child 2006). In the electronics section Chinese brands including Lenovo, Haier, TCL, Hisense, Skyworth, Konka, Changhong, Midea and Galanz are dominating the shelves, while global brands like Philips, Nokia and Sharp complete the product portfolio (own store checks). Since the markets differ a lot across China's provinces,

---

sales area per store and offer broad ranges of non- and grocery items. Discounters typically offer limited grocery items and varying non-grocery items as promotion. They usually have simple store designs and sales areas of 400 to 1,000m^2 per store (M+M Planet Retail 2006).

[99] Compare to chapter 2 'brand distribution'.

[100] Compare to previous chapters.

in a hypermarket store in Shanghai, for example, 50% of the televisions would be flat-screen TVs, whereas in the middle and western China it would be only 10% because today's flat screens are too advanced and too expensive for those areas (Child 2006).

Although the relevance of global retailers for Chinese brands seems to increase in line with the growth of the retailers in China, it is to note that the total market share of foreign retail companies only added up to less than 2.6% of the entire market in 2004 (Schramm/Taube 2006: 23-24). The top three retailers Carrefour, Wal-Mart, and Metro-Group only accounted for total revenues of US$3,253m, which is not even half of the total revenue of China's retail giant Shanghai Bailian 百炼 (table 3-5).

Ranking by revenues	Chain store	Revenues 2004 in mio. US$	Revenue growth 2003/04 in %
1	Shanghai Bailian	7267	22.5
2	GOME Electrical Applaince	2563	34.3
3	Dalian Dashang Group	2479	27.0
4	Suning Applaince	2382	79.6
5	Carrefour (China)	1753	20.9
7	China Resources Suguo Supermarket	1487	44.9
15	China Resources Vanguard Supermarket	1270	6.7
20	Wal-Mart China	822	30.5
23	Metro Group	677	13.2

Table 3-5. Revenue of selected chain store companies in mio. US$ in China in 2004 (taken from Schramm/Taube 2006: 23)

Bailian is specialised in supermarkets and department stores and includes four companies: Shanghai No. 1 Department Store, Shanghai Huanlian Co. Ltd., Shanghai Friendship Co. Ltd., and Shanghai Materials and Logistics Co. Ltd. (Jiang 2004). With respect to electrical appliances, the Chinese retailers Gome 国美and Suning 苏宁 play also a growing role. Between 2002 and 2004, the privately-run chains more than doubled their combined stores and count now to over 500 (CCFA 2005). Moreover, traditional Chinese trade channel formats like traditional street markets and small, local department stores are still very important (Lo et al. 2001; Hemerling et al. 2004: 1). They accounted for more than 70% of the total retail sales in China in 2004 (table 3-6, Schramm/Taube 2006: 22).

Category	Example	Modern trade channels Market share in %	Traditional trade channels Market share in %
Personal care products	Shampoo	50	50
Durables	TV sets, microwave ovens	30-35	65-70
Home care products	Laundry detergent	30	70
Ready-to-drink beverages	Carbonate soft drinks	25	75
Snacks	Rice crackers	15	85

Table 3-6. Role of traditional and modern trade channels by product category in market share % in China 2004 (Hemerling et al. 2004: 1)

In order to maximise their own revenues, Chinese brand companies have thus often established a broad and sophisticated sales and distribution network, covering not only larger cities but also smaller cities and the fragmented rural areas. Midea, for instance, is said to run 24 regional offices and over 1,000 service locations, cooperating with small regional distributors to get access to the smaller cities, and with national and global retailers to strengthen its presence in the larger cities (Yuan/Dawar 2001: 4, company websites). But, what are the reasons that after more than 10 years of presence and growth in China, the relevance of global retailers is still so small?

One reason is that Chinese consumers still prefer Chinese retailers and acknowledge them a better image. Even though many foreign stores have adjusted their product range to Chinese buying habits, Chinese stores still enjoy perceived advantages concerning product range, freshness of products and pricing (Schramm/Taube 2006: 23). IKEA, for instance, struggles with its brand positioning in China, since they have just rolled out their usual global store blueprints and are now perceived as comparatively expensive (Dickens 2004). Another reason is that modern retail formats are not yet widespread across entire China, but rather concentrated in a small number of metropolitan areas. As prior research found out, global retailers would typically follow the expansion of China's purchase power, and would thus still be essentially non-existent in rural areas due to prohibitively high costs of set-up (Shaw et al. 2003: 46; Hemerling et al. 2004: 1; Schramm/Taube 2006: 22). Other market observers remarked that many foreign retailers suffer from central government regulations and market restrictions. While some global retailers, Carrefour among them, are reported to be bypassing them to open illegal stores by doing deals with local governments, other stores groups, such as Tesco, B&Q, and OBI, have entered the market through acquisition and joint ventures with local retail partners (Dickens 2004; Underwood 2006).

All in all, however, though global retailers may have difficulties to expand their market shares in China, it is safe to conclude that at least the Chinese branded companies have benefited form their presence in the Chinese markets. They could establish relationships to the global retailers' management, get to know their internal organisation structure, their perspectives on consumer satisfaction and branded sales culture, including product quality, design, pricing, merchandising, after-sales-service as well as storage, inventory and chill techniques (Shaw et al. 2003: 46). Moreover, Chinese branded companies could demonstrate their own brand power towards the global retailers and prove them that they are able to satisfy the needs of several different trade channels at the same time.

Since one could assume that Chinese branded companies are going to use their learnt competences and established relationships to enter the developed markets by their own brands, the next section aims to examine whether and to what extent Chinese branded companies are already present in developed markets.

3.2.2 China's presence in developed markets

The presence of Chinese branded companies in developed markets can generally be investigated from two perspectives: the Chinese organisational perceptive or the Western consumer perspective. Accordingly, the first section gives a short review on China's government policies since 1978 concerning China's outward investment and global brand building. The second section then examines China's country-of-origin in developed markets, exemplified by German consumer attitudes and associations with China, Chinese products and brands.

Government policies of outward investment and global brand building

Transnational operations of Chinese state-owned enterprises started long before 1978 in the areas of ocean shipping, financial service and trading, amongst them, the Chinese-Polish Joint Stock Shipping Company known as CHIPOLBROK that was established in June 1951 with each government holding 50% shares, and the China Merchants Steam Navigation Company, China Travel Ltd., and the Bank of China Hong Kong Branch that all had been established and state-owned in Hong Kong well before the establishment of the PRC in 1949 (Shi 1989: 450; Zhang 2003: 82-87).

However, it was after the Chinese government initiated its open door policy in 1978 that Chinese outward investment begun to develop (Choosin 1996: 91; Cai 1999: 859). Even in the first decade of China's open door policy, China's outward FDI was insignificant as a foreign economic activity (figure 1-1). The Chinese government felt rather ambivalent towards China's outward investment (Zhang 2003: 92), and gave priority to the nation's domestic economic restructuring by attracting inward FDI into the Chinese economy. Both market and capital conditions were considered not yet necessitate a strategy of investing abroad (Cai 1999: 859; Zhang 2003: 90-91). The few investment projects were in industries such as engineering, construction and finance/insurance (Choosin 1996: 91; Cai 1999: 859), mainly conducted by centrally controlled state-owned companies and purposely built multinational corporations (Zhang 2003: 88).[101] It is argued that most of these early investments were to a great extent motivated by governmental rather than by commercial interests, for example, to boost the confidence of foreign investors in the open door policy (Zhang/Bulcke 1996: 417).

Starting in the mid-1980s, however, there was a big jump in China's outward FDI. From 1985 to 1990, a total of 577 Chinese foreign non-trading affiliates were established, a figure which was over three times that for the period 1979-1985 (Choosin 1996: 91). The affiliates covered more than 90 countries and a wider range of industries such as metallurgy/minerals, petrochemicals/chemicals, electronics/light industry, transportation, finance/insurance, medicine and tourism (Cai 1999: 860-861). Affected by China's bid for the General Agreement on Tariffs and Trade (GATT) and WTO membership, first submitted in 1986, and the sanctions imposed on China by major economic powers in the wake of the government crackdown in Beijing in 1989, the transnationalisation of Chinese firms through outward investment was finally incorporated in the overall economic development strategy at the 14th National Congress of the Communist Party in 1992 (Jiang 1992; Zhang 2003: 80).

Since then, China outward FDI experienced a large booming development with a number of large outward investments, making China to one of the top FDI exporters among developing countries since (UNCTAD

---

[101] This includes the China State Construction Engineering Co. Ltd., the China Civil Engineering and Construction Cooperation, the China Road and Bridge Engineering Co. Ltd., the China Complete Set Equipment Import and Export Co. Ltd., and the China International Trust and Investment Corporation (CITIC). The Bank of China, for example, opened up a branch in Luxembourg in 1979. COSCO, China's national ocean shipping company started operation in 1979, first in Hong Kong and then in the UK.

2005b). The annual average of China's FDI outflow substantially increased from US$54m in 1984-89 to US$2,764m in 2001-2004. By 2004, China has accumulated an FDI outward stock of US$38.8bn according to UNCTAD country fact sheet (Cai 1999: 861; UNCTAD 2005a).[102] According to statistics of the Ministry of Commerce of the People's Republic of China (MOFCOM) (2006c), China's non-financial direct overseas investment was US$6.92bn in 2005. At the same time, China began also to seek to list parts of its state-owned companies on the international equity markets in order to rise funding for cross-border mergers and acquisitions. For example, in 1997 the sale of China Telecom (Hong Kong) raised US$4bn. In 2000, the three large oil giants China National Petroleum Corporation (CNPC), Sinopec and China National Offshore Oil Corporation (CNOOC) plus China's telecom giant, China Unicom, listed subsidiaries in Hong Kong and New York and raised a total of US$15bn (Zhang 2003: 101).

Ranking by foreign assets	Corporation	Industry	Assets in mio. US$ in 2003	
			Foreign	Total
1	Hutchison Whampoa Ltd.	Diversified	59,141	80,340
7	China Ocean Shipping (Group) Company	Transport, storage	8,457	18,007
10	Jardine Matheson Holdings Ltd.	Diversified	6,159	8,949
13	China National Petroleum Corporation	Petroleum exp./ref./distr.	4,060	97,653
16	Shangri-La Asia Ltd.	Hotels, motels	3,672	4,743
17	CITIC Pacific Ltd.	Diversified	3,574	7,167
18	CLP Holdings	Electricity, gas, water	3,564	9,780
19	China State Construction Engineering Corp.	Construction	3,417	9,677
26	China Resources Enterprises	Petroleum exp./ref./distr.	2,364	4,034
34	First Pacific Company Ltd.	Electrical & electronic equipment	1,910	2,074
38	China National Offshore Oil Corp.	Petroleum, natural gas	1,467	14,479
46	China Minmetals Corporation	metals mining & processing	1,150	5,352

Table 3-7. The TNCs headquartered in China and Hong Kong among the top 50 non-financial TNCs from developing countries, ranked by foreign assets in US$ in 2003 (UNCTAD 2005b: 271-272)

As a result, an increasing number of Chinese firms are now among the top 50 largest transnational corporations (TNCs) from developing coun-

---

[102] Note that all UNCTAD FDI figures exclude cross-border M&As.

tries. While in 1994 there were only seven companies from China and Hong Kong, in 2003 there were already twelve companies, not including corporations from Taiwan (table 3-7). Hong Kong conglomerate Hutchison Whampoa is also ranked 16th among the world's top 100 non-financial TNCs by foreign assets in 2003 (UNCTAD 2005b: 268-271). Among the world's top 50 financial TNCs 2003, there are three Chinese financial institutions, namely the Industrial and Commercial Bank of China (ranked 23), Bank of China (ranked 34) and China Construction Bank (ranked 39) (UNCTAD 2005b: 273). However, by global standards, China's outward FDI and cross-border M&A is still tiny. In 2004, China accounted for only 0.25% of the global FDI, ranking 28th among all countries (UNCTAD 2005b). Moreover, market-orientated outward investments into developed countries such as Western Europe and the USA, are also tiny so far (Zhang 2003: 108). Major recipient of China's outward FDI is Hong Kong which concentrates heavily on the service sector, and is partly influenced by geo-cultural affinity and strategic reasons such as raising funds in the capital market there, or using Hong Kong as a springboard for exploring other international markets (UNCTAD 2003: 4; Ke 2005). Other major investment recipients are natural resource-seeking projects which are basically situated in Australia, New Zealand, North America, Kazakhstan and Africa (Zhang/Bulcke 1996: 403, 410; BCG 2006b: 11; Grill 2006).

However, since 2000, there is some indication that Chinese manufacturing firms have also made aggressive investments overseas, in order to expand their market presence, to circumvent protectionism and to escape the sluggish domestic demand and overcapacities (UNCTAD 2003). One of their key market expansion regions is South Asia (Zhang 2003: 109), but Chinese FDI into developed countries is also rising. According to a EIU survey among 176 Chinese companies, 17% target Asia, 12% Europe and Russia, and 11% North America for future outward investments (EIU 2005: 14). The motives for investments in developed markets include access to new growth markets, advanced technology, global brand names, distribution networks and foreign management skills (UNCTAD 2003: 6; EIU 2005: 42-43; Beebe et al. 2006: 4-5).

With growing financial reserves, Chinese TNCs have in particular begun to focus on mergers and acquisitions abroad (UNCTAD 2003: 6; EIU 2005: 19). BCG (2006b: 8) estimated that from 1986 to 2005, they have invested some US$27.6bn in non-Chinese companies abroad, nearly a third of it in 2004 and 2005. According to MOFCOM, M&A also accounted for over 80% of Chinese companies' total outward investment in the first seven months in 2006 (Jiang 2005). In 2005, this includes Lenovo's purchase of the IBM PC division for US$1.25bn (Lenovo Deutschland 2005), SAIC's 50.6% acquisition of South Korea's Ssangyong and purchase of the design rights of MG Rover 25 and 75 for US$116m (Taube 2005: 4; Jing 2006), and CNPC's acquisition of PetroKazakhstan for US$4.2bn (Beebe et al. 2006: 1). Accessing foreign technology also takes the form of establishing R&D centres in developed countries. For instance, Huawei Technologies and ZTE Corporation have each established an R&D centre in Sweden, Konka an R&D facility in Silicon Valley, and Kelon a design centre in Japan (UNCTAD 2003: 6).

Aside from market factors, the Chinese government is becoming more supportive for Chinese companies to expand and invest globally, since they have acknowledged that being the cheapest assembly line in the world has limited future potential (Wu 2005; Müller/Turner 2006; Yu 2006: 377-393). Thus, over the past few years, various government agencies such as the National Development and Reform Commission (NDRC), the Ministry of Finance, the Ministry of Commerce (MOFCOM) and the State Administration of Foreign Exchange (SAFE) have all developed policies encouraging Chinese companies to expand overseas. Chinese firms are sanctioned by easier access to foreign exchange, to financing and insurance services from commercial banks and the Export-Import Bank of China, and to preferential policies such as corporate income tax exemptions (UNCTAD 2003: 9; China Daily 2004b; Beebe et al. 2006: 6). "The Chinese government has been preparing the top 100 to 150 companies to go overseas and expand," said Jack Huang, a chairman of the Chinba practice at the law firm Jones Day. "The government wants to use this as a testing ground, to see how well the companies stand up to international competition" (quoted in Barboza 2005). As a result, dozen of Chinese companies stand in waiting and already sixteen corporations from China and Hong Kong were ranked among the *Fortune* Global 500 companies in 2005, most of them from national monopoly industries such as electric power, petroleum and banking (table 3-8).

However, as the *Fortune* 500 reveals Chinese global brands are rather few (Wu 2005).[103] Therefore, the Chinese government has recently begun encouraging Chinese firms to build Chinese global brand names (Wu 2005). Premier Wen Jiabao said that brands made in China would represent the image of a nation, its economic strength, its result of scientific development and the solemn commitment to consumers (MOFCOM 2006b). In 2001, the Chinese government thus launched its so-called "brand strategy" (China Daily 2005c), and established the China Brand Name Promotion Committee, organised by the General Administration of Quality Supervision, Inspection   and Quarantine of the People's Republic of China (AQSIQ) (People's Daily Online 2001). As reported, the committee should

---

[103] Compare to chapter 'Top Chinese brands in 2005/2006'.

support Chinese companies to appraise, manage, advertise, and create China's brand-name products in order to make them influential and competitive on global markets, and to increase their technological innovation and quality to enhance the brand image of 'made in China' (People's Daily Online 2001; China Daily 2005c; AQSIQ 2006).

Rank	Company	Country	Revenues 2004 in mio. US$	Profits 2004 in mio. US$
1	Wal-Mart	USA	287,989.0	10,267.0
2	BP	UK	285,059.0	15,371.0
3	ExxonMobil	USA	270,772.0	25,330.0
4	Royal Dutch/ Shell Group	NL	268,690.0	18,183.0
5	GM	USA	193,517.0	2,805.0
20	IBM	USA	96,293.0	8,430.0
21	Siemens	Germany	91,493.2	4,144.6
23	Hitachi	Japan	83,993.9	479.2
25	Matsushita Electric Industrial	Japan	81,077.7	544.1
31	Sinopec	China	75,076.7	1,268.9
39	Samsung Electronics	South Korea	71,555.9	9,419.5
40	State Grid	China	71,290.2	694.0
46	China National Petroleum	China	67,723.8	8,757.1
47	Sony	Japan	66,618.0	1,524.5
115	LG Electronics	South Korea	37,757.5	1,403.8
212	China Life Insurance	China	24,980.6	74.3
224	China Mobile Communications	China	23,957.6	4077.9
229	Industrial & Commercial Bank of China	China	23,444.6	279.2
262	China Telecommunications	China	21,561.8	2,422.0
287	Sinochem	China	21,561.8	229.7
309	Shanghai Baosteel Group	China	19,543.3	1,537
315	China Construction Bank	China	19,047.9	5,846.2
316	China South Power Grid	China	18,928.8	231.4
339	Bank of China	China	17,960.4	2,529.0
347	Hutchison Whampoa	Hong Kong	17,280.8	2,070.7
397	Agricultural Bank of China	China	15,284.6	242.0
434	COFCO	China	14,189.4	121.4
448	China First Automotive Works	China	13,825.4	293.4
500	Masco	USA	12,431.1	893.0

Table 3-8. Selected Fortune Global 500 companies by US$ in 2005 (Fortune 2005)

In the 11th Five-Year Plan (2006-2010), the Communist Party also announced the establishment of Chinese global brands as a plan target: "By the end of 2010, China will have a group of enterprises that have strong international competitiveness, proprietary intellectual property rights and famous brands" (Xinhua 2005). As a part of the plan, the Chinese government adopted "a market-orientated technology strategy" (Wang/Yin 2005). This includes a national R&D budget of 2.5% of GDP till 2020 and respective R&D spending of China's large enterprises (Shanghai Daily 2006). Moreover, the Ministry of Commerce plans to build 100 export bases for "its creative and high-tech industries" and to support 100 big group companies and 1,000 others with strong R&D capability to build their own brands (Chen 2006). The aim is that China's reliance on foreign technology shall decline and the number of patents granted to Chinese nationals shall rank among the world's top five countries by 2020, including cutting-edge technologies in biology, information industry, materials technologies, and advanced manufacturing.

To support China's brand building, the Chinese government will also improve its intellectual property rights system, create a legal environment in which intellectual property is protected, increase awareness of IPR protection and crack down on IPR infringement (Roth 2005; Shanghai Daily 2006; Zhu 2006). Probably surprising for foreign companies is the fact that Chinese branded companies likely suffer more than three times more from China's widespread piracy than foreign multinationals (Balfour et al. 2005; Schramm 2005; Zhou 2005). A study of the Chinese Ministry of Information Industry even stated that 37% of the Chinese software industry was struggling with piracy in 2005 (Roth 2005). To advocate brand awareness and to inspire innovation and IPR in China, the Ministry of Commerce very recently also initiated its so-called "Brand Promotion Activity" in June 2006 (MOFCOM 2006a), which includes a brand promotion tour on 5 routes across entire China, "which are promotion of open brand in eastern area, promotion of brand rising in central area, promotion of brand development in western area, promotion of brand revitalization in northeast area and promotion of Chinese brand 'going abroad'"(MOFCOM 2006b, 2006a).

At firm level, a study of BCG (2006c: 13) forecasted eighteen Chinese companies with potential to take their domestic brands global. As table 3-9 indicates, these are particularly companies of the industries of home appliances, consumer electronics, computers and IT components, and automotive equipment. The going-international of the Chinese branded companies *Haier, TCL, Hisense* and *Lenovo* will also be investigated in chapter 5 in more detail.

Ranking by revenues	Company	Industry	Revenues 2004 in mio. US$
1	China FAW Group Corporation	Automotive equipment	15,088
2	Haier Group	Home appliances	12,244
3	Shanghai Automotive Industry Corporation Group (SAIC)	Automotive equipment	12,056
4	Lenovo Group	Computers and IT components	12,000
5	Dongfeng Motor Company	Automotive equipment	11,800
6	SVA Group Company	Consumer electronics	5,100
7	TCL Corporation	Consumer electronics	5,071
8	Midea Holding Company	Home appliances	3,620
9	Hisense Corporation	Consumer electronics	3,288
10	China National Heavy Duty Truck Group Corporation (CNHDT)	Automotive equipment	2,818
11	Gree Electric Appliances	Home appliances	2,642
12	Chunlan Group Corporation	Home appliances	2,373
13	Konka Group Company	Consumer electronics	1,610
14	Skyworth Multimedia International Company	Consumer electronics	1,490
15	Nanjing Automobile Group	Automotive equipment	1,339
16	Galanz Group Company	Home appliances	1,245
17	Tsingtao Brewery	Food and beverages	907
18	Erdos Group	Textiles	378

Table 3-9. Chinese firms with potential to take their brands global, ranked by revenues in US$ in 2004 (own illustration of BCG 2006c)

China's country-of-origin

As the last chapter shows, the Chinese government has great global brand ambitions, and few Chinese brands have already started to conquer developed markets. But, what is the feedback from the developed markets so far? What do Western consumers associate with Chinese brands? Do they know, like and purchase Chinese brands? Since China lags far behind developed countries in Western Europe and the US in terms of economic development, it is said that Western consumers usually have many prejudices against Chinese products, as they are unconvinced that a Chinese brand could manufacture and support products of a sufficient quality and reliability to match their needs (Gilmore/Dumont 2003; Amine et al. 2005: 140). In addition, because China is, despite of its 30 years of modernisation, still considered a Communist system with a different understanding of human and individual rights, there are many Westerners who feel animosity against China and Chinese products (Klein et al. 1998: 90; Amine et al. 2005: 124-126).

When you think of the country China, what are your first five associations and thoughts?

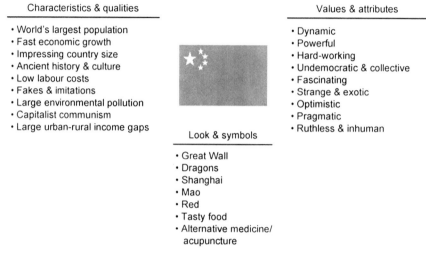

Characteristics & qualities	Values & attributes
• World's largest population • Fast economic growth • Impressing country size • Ancient history & culture • Low labour costs • Fakes & imitations • Large environmental pollution • Capitalist communism • Large urban-rural income gaps	• Dynamic • Powerful • Hard-working • Undemocratic & collective • Fascinating • Strange & exotic • Optimistic • Pragmatic • Ruthless & inhuman

Look & symbols

• Great Wall
• Dragons
• Shanghai
• Mao
• Red
• Tasty food
• Alternative medicine/
  acupuncture

Online survey in October 2006, n = 84 Germans

Fig. 3-16. Qualitative summary of the key associations with the country China in October 2006 (own research, similar Publicis Sasserath 2006: 37)

An unrepresentative online survey conducted in October 2006 among 84 Germans between 25 and 60 years old, mainly high-educated (university degree) and partly with previous China experiences, thus aims to detail attitudes and associations of Western consumers with China, Chinese products and brands.[104] As figure 3-16 shows, the surveyed German consumers associated with the country China sophisticated attributes which can be considered as partly positive and partly negative. On the positive side, there are the ancient Chinese culture & tradition, symbolised by the Great

---

[104] Publicis Sasserath, a brand consultancy in Germany, conducted a similar online survey with n = 64 in September 2005, although with a different focus. They did not differentiate associations with the country China from associations with Chinese products, and in particular asked Likert-scaled questions in order to compare 'Made-in-Germany' versus 'Made-in-China' images. However, the presentation of the survey results as seen as in figure 3-16 appears similar to their report's presentation (Publicis Sasserath 2006: 37).

Wall, dragons, tasty food and alternative medicine/ acupuncture, as well typical qualities of a developing country such as low labour costs (similar Publicis Sasserath 2006: 37). In addition, it becomes evident that the German consumers acknowledged China's modernisation progress from a developing country to a world powerhouse. Almost half of all respondents characterised China by its large population, more than every third respondent named China's economic growth as his/her key association. More than every seventh called China already a world power. Most often used adjectives were dynamic, powerful, hard-working, optimistic and pragmatic. The city Shanghai was indicated as China's symbol of the present, and was described as glamorous and with a large number of huge skyscrapers.

On the negative side, however, the survey confirmed that Westerners likely show an ambivalent feeling towards the Chinese government. The respondents criticised the government as inhuman and ruthless, since they would follow their economic modernisation process by all means, and would even behave more capitalistic and egoistic than the Westerners would do. Since individual freedom is self-evident and guaranteed in the West, the Germans named the Chinese system as collective, undemocratic and illiberal, in particular evaluating the situation of China's human rights, press liberty and security of intellectual property as very poor. They also negatively associated with China large environmental pollution and growing income differences between rural and urban areas, and seem to be partly scared of China due to its enormous population, immense country size and dynamic growth.

Whereas the associations with the country of China among the surveyed Germans may be evaluated as quiet sophisticated, the image of Chinese products is driven by typical prejudices and scepticism rather than by own product and brand experiences (figure 3-17, Frank 2005: 3; Swystun et al. 2005: 3; Publicis Sasserath 2006: 33). More than 70% of all respondents named Chinese products as cheap; almost every second criticised them as pure copies and fakes of Western originals, and perceived the product quality and design as poor, low-tech and made of plastic. The respondents also indicated that Chinese products have in their eyes poor serviceability and are more junk goods & trash rather than reliable consumer goods. Textiles, shoes, consumer electronics and IT hardware were typically associated Chinese product categories (similar Publicis Sasserath 2006: 20).

When you think of Chinese products, what are your first five associations and thoughts?

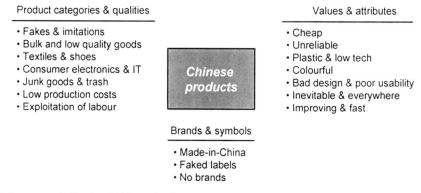

Product categories & qualities

- Fakes & imitations
- Bulk and low quality goods
- Textiles & shoes
- Consumer electronics & IT
- Junk goods & trash
- Low production costs
- Exploitation of labour

Chinese products

Values & attributes

- Cheap
- Unreliable
- Plastic & low tech
- Colourful
- Bad design & poor usability
- Inevitable & everywhere
- Improving & fast

Brands & symbols

- Made-in-China
- Faked labels
- No brands

Online survey in October 2006, n = 84 Germans

Fig. 3-17. Qualitative summary of the key associations of Germans with Chinese products in October 2006 (own research)

Across all industries and product categories, which Chinese brand names do you know? (maximal 5 brand names)

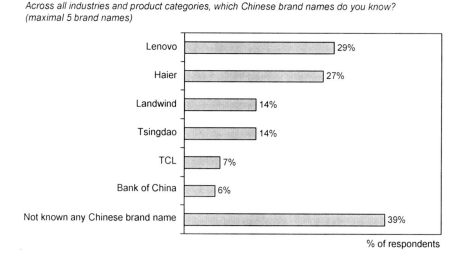

Lenovo 29%
Haier 27%
Landwind 14%
Tsingdao 14%
TCL 7%
Bank of China 6%
Not known any Chinese brand name 39%

% of respondents

Fig. 3-18. Unaided brand awareness of Chinese brand names in October 2006 (own research)

However, as the study also reveals, almost 40% of the same respondents were not able to remember one Chinese brand name at all (figure 3-18). Those respondents, who have known a Chinese brand name, partly admitted that they would not know the brands from own product experiences but only from media reports. Lenovo and Haier were the most known brands.

Surprisingly, the brand *Landwind* scored also relatively high in brand awareness. Landwind is a cross-county vehicle created by the Chinese car maker Jiangling Motors which was introduced as the first Chinese car in the German market for the price of €15,000 during the IAA (International Automobil-Ausstellung) in Frankfurt in September 2005. In a crash-test conducted by the German automobile club ADAC, however, it failed to measure up to the European safety standards (ADAC 2005; Spiegel online 2005). Jiangling Motors, though having rejected the critics, finally cancelled the car launch into the German market (Sedan 2006). Although this market failure is already one year ago, the surveyed Germans kept the Landwind brand in their minds, probably because Germans are generally highly informed and involved in automobiles, and the poor performance combined with a cheap price has confirmed their general prejudice against Chinese products.

Imagine you have bought a Chinese electrical product (TV set, refrigerator, computer, mobile phone, etc.), what was the main reason of purchase?

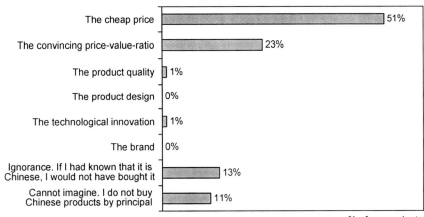

Fig. 3-19. Chinese electrical products - main reasons of purchase in October 2006 (own research)

This prejudice can also be confirmed in the electronics sector. Figure 3-19 reveals that the main reasons of purchasing a Chinese electrical product among German consumers are a cheap price (51%) and a convincing price-value-ratio (23%). 24% of all respondents even indicated that they want to prevent buying a Chinese electrical product by all means.

However, on the positive side, the survey revealed that many respondents already acknowledged the fast progress of Chinese products and their improvements in quality, design, and technology over the last few years (figure 3-17). Some Germans already associate with Chinese products "high quality", "innovation", and "good design" (similar Publicis Sasserath 2006: 19). Since Chinese companies would constantly shift their production focus towards high-tech goods such as IT, computers and mobile phones and would increase own R&D and innovations, already 6% of all respondents already believe that Chinese products will get ahead of Western products in near future.

To enhance and accelerate this "new" image of China and Chinese products and brands, the Olympic Games hold in Beijing in 2008 may help. Publicis Sasserath (2006: 26) expects that the local Chinese sponsors of the Olympic Games will strengthen their brand image, relevance and trustworthiness of Chinese products in the world. The Beijing Organizing Committee (BOCOG) expects that "the Olympic Games provide an honourable opportunity to enhance their image and demonstrate their strengths in key technologies, products and services while gaining recognition for their commitment to China's national quest for professional excellence and in all realms of business" (BOCOG 2006). As figure 3-20 shows, these Chinese brands are amongst others *Lenovo* (Worldwide Olympic Partner), *China Mobile*, *Bank of China*, *Air China* (all Beijing 2008 Partners), *Haier* and *Tsingdao* (Beijing 2008 Sponsors).

Fig. 3-20. Partners and sponsors of Beijing 2008 Olympic Games, as announced by October 2006 (BOCOG 2006)

China's capital Beijing was awarded the right to host the 2008 Olympic Games in 2001 and since then the Chinese government and the BOCOG begun "to invite the world in and introduce China to the world" (BOCOG 2006). They chose the slogan "One world One dream, 同一个世界

同一个梦想", the five mascots called "Friendlies" (figure 3-21), and started promoting the Games in and outside China by thousands of posters, merchandising articles, media announcements, and several impressive construction sites in Beijing (host city) and its co-host cities in Shanghai, Tianjin, Shenyang, Qinhuangdao (all football), Qingdao (sailing) and Hong Kong (equestrian) (Schmidkonz 2005; BOCOG 2006; Yu 2006: 330-346).

Fig. 3-21. The five Olympic Mascots "Friendlies" (BOCOG 2006)

3.3 Brief evaluation of both areas of experience

In the previous chapters many different aspects about China and Chinese branded companies with respect to their domestic brand management experiences and experiences with developed markets were discussed. This section now aims to sum up the key issues of both areas of experience and to briefly evaluate the major strengths and weaknesses of Chinese branded companies by 2006.

As China's history and modernisation since 1978 reveal, Chinese brands and Chinese branded companies, as understood by Western marketing societies, did not emerge until 2000. Since then, however, they made rapid progress in domestic brand management through primarily copying Western marketing approaches and learning from multinational brands operating in China. As a result, by 2005/2006, China has produced some powerful Chinese brand names, amongst them the conglomerates Haier and Lenovo as well as few aspiring consumer brands like Li-Ning, Mengniu, and GOME, which all held leading positions in their respective local markets. Compared to foreign brands operating in China, Chinese brands thereby typically provide similar product qualities at lower price levels, address local needs in a better way, and satisfy the desire of nationalism, traditional values and cultural pride. For instance, Chinese branded companies take the role of brand names very seriously and decide on names which are a combination of both a Chinese written name with traditional positive connotations and an English name with associations of fashion and innovation. Moreover, in contrast to most foreign brands, leading Chinese branded companies are also well established in China's rural areas and across all distribution channels in China. However, since increasing numbers of foreign brands are attracted by the large potential of 1.3bn customers particularly since China's WTO accession in 2001, Chinese brands' success is not granted, but challenged by fierce competition through overcapacities, price wars and low profitability every day.

As a result, as the previous sections show, a few Chinese branded companies have already started seeking additional market opportunities in overseas markets since 2000. Based on the fact that China is the world's second largest exporter and the world's largest manufacturing site, Chinese branded companies can typically rely on an efficient supply chain, fast production-cycles and competitive prices. In addition, the large presence of multinationals in China has taught Chinese branded companies lessons in manufacturing competences, foreign sales cultures and basic Western consumer needs, and has enabled them to establish relationships to global distribution partners. While before the early 1990s, China's outward investments were restricted to natural resource seeking projects and to boost the confidence of foreign investors in the open door policy, the Chinese government now supports the going-international of Chinese brands by all means. They offer funding and tax-reductions, established the China Brand Name Promotion Committee, improve China's IPR, and won the right to host the 2008 Olympic Games, amongst others.

However, despite of China's rapid development and global brand ambitions, the previous sections also reveal that Chinese branded companies still lack some of those corporate competences which are considered crucial for long-term brand success by Western marketing societies. Even though most of the Chinese companies have already acknowledged the power and relevance of brands, most of them are still lost when it comes to the creation and implementation of effective brand approaches. Chinese branded companies typically lack own R&D, innovations and patents. Chinese managers, particularly those of state-run enterprises, are often bureaucrats and high party-officials who are used to fulfil governmental orders and are not willed to venture into new management concepts and long-term profit strategies such as marketing and branding. As a consequence, brand management is widely understood in China as equal to being 'loud in the market' and as another opportunity to push products in the market and to make larger sales in a shorter time frame. Chinese branded companies thus also lack organisational structures such as marketing departments and market research, and regard broad advertising as its major communication channel. Most advertising messages only promote functional product benefits and a mixture of Chinese and Western values or just governmental propaganda messages.

Since most of the Chinese consumers are not yet very sophisticated on brands due to limited pockets and group-orientations, Chinese branded companies have been very successful in China despite of these weaknesses so far. However, as the study on China's country-of-origin among German customers indicates, these weaknesses may become a bottleneck for Chinese branded companies when entering developed markets. Western consumers have large prejudices against Chinese products and are unconvinced that a Chinese brand could manufacture and support products of a sufficient quality and reliability to fit their needs. How can Chinese branded companies thus be successful in the USA and Western Europe? Are there possible brand strategies? To address these questions, the next chapter's rationale is to discuss and formulate hypotheses on an appropriate global brand approach for Chinese branded companies entering developed markets in the USA and Western Europe.

4 Hypotheses – How to enter developed markets

The last chapter introduced Chinese branded companies and their overall strengths and weaknesses with respect to domestic brand management and international market experience. Along the theoretical brand options as presented in chapter 2, the rationale of this chapter now is to hypothesise a global brand approach for these Chinese branded companies when they want to enter developed markets in the USA and Western Europe (WE). The aim of this chapter is to discuss and choose from all theoretical brand options, the option, which is considered the most appropriate choice for Chinese branded companies and their areas of experience, and which promises them the largest brand success in terms of long-term revenues and profits in the US and WE markets. Best practices of Japanese (*Sony*, *Toshiba*) and South Korean (*Samsung*) companies are used to support the hypotheses.

Since global markets change fast and Chinese branded companies learn quickly, the following hypotheses refer to the situation of Chinese branded companies as described in chapter 3 and assume market entries by October 2006. According to the theoretical framework, the chapter starts with hypotheses on global brand aims, followed by hypotheses on strategic and operative brand decisions, including, if relevant, aspects on brand control & adaptation. All hypotheses are going to be tested in chapter 5 by real Chinese case examples.

4.1 Aims of global brand building

H1: Under the current conditions, Chinese branded companies have two main motives of global brand building and entering US and WE markets. First, they aim to use brand building as an additional channel to increase their sales by entering new growth markets. And second, they aim to enlarge their corporate size to fulfil the target, set by the Chinese government, to establish Chinese brands as significant global players as a prove of China's economic and political power in the world economy.

As chapter 3 shows, Chinese branded companies have competitive advantages in manufacturing, sourcing and pricing. They benefit from China's low labour cost advantages and can typically realise economies of scales due to large volume productions (Gao et al. 2003; Buckley et al. 2004). Though one can argue that China's OEM experiences has demonstrated and taught Chinese branded companies that global brands are likely to achieve higher profit margins because of larger brand price premiums and higher general price levels in developed markets (Lu 2005), there is evidence to hypothesise that Chinese branded companies regard global brand building only as an additional channel to increase their sales basis rather than their profits:

In China many consumer markets are characterised by fierce competition, price wars and overcapacities. To survive the market and to gain critical size, many leading Chinese branded companies are thus extending their brands to as many related and non-related industries as possible (Huang/Du 2005: 93; Zhou 2005). To extend the brands onto new markets in US and WE would therefore continue their growth strategy. In addition, most of the brands lack own R&D, innovations and experienced brand managers (UNCTAD 2005b: 114; BCG 2006a). Many of the top managers are party officials who are used to fulfil governmental output targets, and regard brand management as an unknown intangible area (Lu 2005; Brand Agency 2006). Even if these companies attempted to target brand price premiums instead of brand volume premiums in the US and WE, they would be possibly not yet ready to compete with the existing brands. They would lack outstanding designs, innovations and appealing brand images.

Since larger brand volumes would also immediately result in larger corporate sizes, which can be proven by national and international statistics such as the ranking of the *Fortune* Global 500 (figure 3-16), it is also hypothesised that the Chinese government favours brand volume premiums over brand price premiums. It is supposed that the Chinese government demands successful market entries of Chinese brands in US and WE markets to demonstrate China's economic and political power towards the world economy (compare to MOFCOM's brand building efforts and the establishment of the Brand Promotion Committee).

4.2 Strategic brand decisions when going-international

H2: Under the given conditions and not interfered by legal brand regulations, Chinese branded companies decide on a global standardised brand approach and a brand architecture of a branded house with very limited adaptations in branding and brand values across all operating country markets.

A global standardised brand approach involves per definition a high degree of consistency in visual, verbal, sonic and tactile brand identity across all country markets and assumes that all markets are alike (e.g., Meffert 1986). It is the goal of the approach to achieve cost leadership by lower unit costs that derive from larger volumes (Sattler 2001: 111-112). Taking in account that Chinese branded companies already hold the cost leadership in manufacturing, brand standardisation is hypothesised to be optimal. This hypothesis is also supported by the fact that Chinese branded companies typically conduct a brand architecture of a branded house in China, most times with the company itself as the one and single brand (Huang/Du 2005: 93; Zhou 2005). The geographical extension of the identical home brand onto developed markets would therefore continue the existing brand portfolio and would reduce complexity and coordination need.

In addition, Chinese branded companies have little experience in global markets (Zhang 2003; Wu 2005), a fact that categorises them as ethnocentric. They can also be characterised by autocratic management styles, centralised power, and large involvement of the Chinese government (e.g., Tse et al. 1997). According to the brand management theory, a global standardised brand approach, in the sense that it is conducted as a copy of the home brand with high control from the headquarters, would usually suit these company characteristics best (Helm 1997: 85-88).

Although one can argue that the underlying assumption that all markets are alike is incorrect when comparing Chinese markets with those in the US and WE, Japanese companies have demonstrated international similarities and the potential of brand standardisation by their success of worldwide standardised, reliable products to competitive prices since the 1980/90s (Arnold 1992: 314). As competition globalises, these products also often requires a global perspective as a kind of prerequisite to survive the market (Thomas et al. 1995). Moreover, a high degree of brand standardisation enables Chinese brands to maximise their marketing spillover effects across countries and to utilise global marketing efforts (Swystun et al. 2005).

Furthermore, as most Chinese consumers in China are not yet sophisticated when purchasing brands, Chinese branded companies have still large room and flexibility to adapt the home brand approach in a way that suits all local and foreign markets appropriately. However, as differences in income and economic power are large across entire China, Chinese branded companies may be required to offer cheaper and more low-tech products under the same brand for China's lower income classes. Since many leading global brands also offer different products at different price levels under the same corporate brand (Berndt et al. 2003; Esch 2004), it is assumed that this necessity should not impact the overall brand approach.

H3: Given that Chinese branded companies lack own innovations, advanced technologies and international patents, they promote their brands globally as 'clever brands', positioning them as a brand of quality, me-too technology and low price, while being perceived advanced to pure discount goods.

Chinese branded companies typically lack own innovations, advanced technologies and international patents (BCG 2006a). When creating a promising standardised brand approach for all operating markets in China, the US and WE, they can consequently seldom compete on unique technologies and extraordinary designs. Brand promises such as *Sony's* 'Go create' would be unrealistic and not reliable. However, despite of this lack, it is hypothesised that Chinese branded companies can develop a unique brand positioning, which is called "clever brands" (Publicis Sasserath 2006: 22): Clever brands would combine characteristics of classical brands such as quality, after-sales service, trustworthiness and modernity with the consumer need for low prices. Since Chinese branded companies have comparative advantages in low price manufacture and in fast cycles of product imitations, Publicis Sasserath (2006: 19), a leading brand consultancy in Germany, recently acknowledged that Chinese brands democratise many product categories and innovations for lower income levels and make the newest technologies and status symbols affordable for a larger group of consumers.

As many Western consumers are currently captured in ambivalent consumer behaviour, Chinese clever brands could become an attractive option (Publicis Sasserath 2006: 16). While in the past Western consumers have purchased luxury articles and status symbols such as an old Cadillac to show that they have class, the same consumers now drive a Mercedes-Benz and shop commodity goods at a discounter to show that they are smart. Today cheap is good ("Geiz ist geil"), and consumers who are trading up are also trading down to good quality at low prices (BCG 2006d).

However, as one can argue that the brand positioning itself is not new, and can easily be copied by companies from other emerging countries, speed in product imitations and in production cycles combined with a powerful unique brand execution is crucial to the success of the Chinese brand approach. Moreover, a good product and service quality must be ensured at all times in order to prevent that Western customers would find any proof of China's general poor country-of-origin (COO), as experienced in the market failure of *Landwind* in Germany in 2005 (chap 3.2.2.2, ADAC 2005). Chinese branded companies are therefore supposed to establish sophisticated quality controls that approve their products according to all relevant Western official and consumer-related quality standards.

H4: Given that own innovations and own international IP are regarded as crucial for a long-term brand success globally, Chinese branded companies invest heavily in R&D in order to catch up with the global market players (dependent on the industry, a R&D budget of at least 7-8% of total revenues may become necessary to catch up).

A unique brand positioning as clever brands is supposed to be a short- and mid-term approach for Chinese branded companies entering US and WE markets. For the long-term run it is hypothesised that they need to advance their products by own innovations and designs to gain own international IP in order to become more proactive and more independent from foreign technologies and licensing agreements. Further, own IP may also enable Chinese branded companies to shift their brand aims from pure brand volume premiums to brand price premiums. In general, innovation can be conducted with respect to product, process, or business model (McGregor 2006).

As a recent study of BCG (2006a) explained, lack in international IP can imply several crucial business risks for Chinese branded companies. They may be excluded from key export markets due to IP barriers. They may be relegated to the 'low-end' of product and technology markets because of a lack of international IP assets. And they may be forced to pay an increasing portion of their profits to foreign companies through royalties for high technology access, which under certain circumstances may reverse China's low cost advantages to cost disadvantages, and make them uncompetitive on the world market as clever brands. For example, analysts estimate that the total cost of IP licensing for 3rd Generation (3G) cellular phone manufacturers who do not own 3G patents may be as high as 25-35% of the final selling price.

As the fact of lacking international IP that China is facing today is not new, but was already overcome by Japan and South Korea in recent decades Chinese branded companies are supposed to learn from these experiences and decide on similar solutions. According to BCG (2006a), Japan especially took the path of IP orientated M&A. They completed at least 450 acquisitions of US companies with valuable intellectual property in the computer, biotechnology, advanced materials, chemicals, electronics, semiconductor and other high-tech industries in their IP seeking phase. South Korean company *Samsung* has also invested in IP orientated partnerships and joint ventures to develop an own IP portfolio over the years (BCG 2006a). While in 1990, Samsung was granted 60 US patents and was nowhere near ranking in the top 100 companies awarded US patents, Samsung had increased its position all the way to number 5 on the US Patent & Trademark Office's (USPTO) annual list of patent grantees with 1,641 patents by 2005. According to the company's annual report in 2005, Samsung has set a goal for itself to reach number three on the USPTO's list by 2007. Samsung was also ranked the twelfth most innovative company in the world in 2006 by BCG and Business Week for excellence in product and process innovation (McGregor 2006).

To catch up with the leading global players, BCG (2006a) estimated that Chinese branded companies have to overcome a relevant patent portfolio of their competitors that has an advance of probably five to ten years, and would require a 30 times increase of their current international IP investments. In terms of general R&D investments, the required increase may depend on the industry. Since *Samsung* has a R&D budget of 6-7% and *Sony* of 7-8% of total revenues (annual reports), it is hypothesised that Chinese branded companies operating in similar industries require at least a budget of 7-8% to catch up. This would mean a 10 times increase of the average Chinese R&D budget as given for 2003 (Yi/Ye 2003: 58). Since many Chinese branded companies suffer from low profitability and may be reluctant to invest in R&D due to China's poor IPR, it is assumed that the Chinese government will ensure the funding as a part of their "market-orientated technology strategy" for the most promising branded companies (Wang/Yin 2005).

H5: Given that Chinese branded companies target a global standardised brand approach in all stages of their going-international in US and WE markets, they decide on geographical brand extension as their mode of market entry. Given that there are external market forces, unplanned market opportunities, or political reasons which are considered more crucial to business, Chinese branded companies decide on brand acquisitions combined with brand transfers at a later stage.

In general, the mode of geographical brand extension suits companies that favour higher control, lower costs and lower financial risk of investment when going-international (Barwise/Robertson 1992). As already described, Chinese branded companies are typically very centralised, autocratic, inexperienced in international markets and thus reluctant against financial risks (McGregor 2005; Zhou 2005). Therefore, if Chinese branded companies could choose freely, not interfered by any external market forces, it is hypothesised that they would decide on geographical brand extension as their mode of market entry in US and WE markets. In addition, they are supposed to seek for a powerful brand alliance to already well-established Western brands to accelerate the market entry and to profit from their brand equity. However, since brand alliances always need two parties to sign a contract, Chinese branded companies may have difficulties to find a promising Western brand that is willing to join a partnership. Chinese brands suffer from a poor COO and may thus be considered a risk for the partner's own brand equity. On the other hand, Chinese branded companies may attract Western brands for an alliance, in which they expect to get a better access to the Chinese market in return. Since Chinese markets are already very competitive, one has to question whether this kind of alliance would suit the interests of the Chinese branded company and those of the Chinese government.

In industries of strong competition, Chinese branded companies may no longer have the time for geographical brand extension (Barboza 2005). Brand acquisitions may therefore become an option of market entry. However, promising M&A objects are rare and difficult to identify. Despite of deep investigations and advanced planning, M&As remain risky (Müller/Gelbrich 2004: 737), can hardly be controlled, and require brand transfers at later stages, if targeting a global standardised brand approach. Since Chinese and Western corporate cultures are supposed to be extremely different, and Chinese branded companies lack experience in cross-border M&As and brand transfers, it is hypothesised that they decide on brand acquisitions only due to external market forces, unplanned market opportunities or political reasons partly triggered by the Chinese government to demonstrate economical and political power to the West.

4.3 Operative brand decisions when going-international

H6: Given H1-H5, Chinese brand companies introduce their global standardised brand approach in the US and WE markets by a unique and powerful, but cost-clever brand execution, including excellence in branding, brand communication and brand distribution (dependent on the industry and foreign market, a marketing budget of around 20% of total revenues may become necessary in the first three years).

The idea of the brand positioning of "clever brands" implies that Chinese brands shall be perceived as brands of quality, me-too technologies and low price, and not only as pure discount offers. To ensure the superiority towards no-name discount goods, a unique and powerful brand execution with excellence in branding, brand communication and brand distribution is hypothesised to be crucial. The brand execution has to ensure to build both brand awareness and to create a brand image and a brand preference. Since a brand is not a brand in Western countries unless it competes along emotional dimensions (Swystun et al. 2005), Chinese branded companies decide on a hierarchy of unique and emotional brand associations that are supposed to symbolise the brand promise of clever brands, and appeal to their consumers worldwide.

Since Chinese brands are typically unknown in US and WE markets and can quickly be hurt by China's general poor COO, it is hypothesised that a market entry in US and WE markets is expensive (Dolan/Hardy 2002). Roland Gerke (2006), president of *Bosch-Siemens* Home Appliances in China, assumed that dependent on the industry and foreign market a marketing budget of around 20% of total revenues would be necessary in the first three years of market entry. He assumed that the marketing budget may be reduced to 4-5% in year four, if some brand awareness is established and the Western consumers are persuaded by the brand's quality and trustworthiness. Among market experts *Samsung* is considered best practice for a successful repositioning of a brand from a poor COO manufacturer to a brand of class and quality (e.g., Keegan/Green 2005: 328-329; Roll 2006: 153). Samsung won several marketing prices, amongst the 2004 Gold Award winner for best international consumer promotion by investing around US$3bn a year in an integrated marketing approach, including mass media advertising, sports sponsoring, and product placement amongst others (Keegan/Green 2005: 497, annual report 2005). Samsung's brand slogans were 'Challenge the Limits' and 'Everyone's Invited' (Roll 2006: 155-156).

Whereas Samsung is one of the most profitable companies in the world by 2006 (Roll 2006: 152), Chinese branded companies likely suffer from low profitability. They are supposed to have limited marketing budgets that can probably not afford the Samsung path. Though market observers argue that funding is not an issue for Chinese companies due to soft budget constraints (e.g., Burkat 2006), it is hypothesised that they are required to develop a "clever" brand approach that maximises the brand approach's effectiveness by a given smaller amount of funding. The "clever" brand approach should satisfy at least the following three conditions in terms of branding (H6a), brand communication (H6b) and brand distribution (H6c):

H6a: Chinese branded companies choose a global standardised brand name that does not sound Chinese and does not include Chinese characters in the US and WE markets.

Since China's COO is poor in Western markets and Chinese names are supposed to be difficult to pronounce and remember for Western consumers, it is hypothesised that Chinese branded companies choose a brand name that does not sound Chinese or is associated with a Chinese country of origin. Though Marketing Professor Allan K. K. Chan (2006) recommends that Chinese branded companies should not try to hide their COO or even fool Western consumers that they come from another country, it should probably not be actively communicated by the brand name either (Baumgarth 2001).

Japan's Sony, for instance, decided on a global brand name which does not include any "Japanese-ness" as a part of their going-international strategy (Hang 2006). In 1955, they registered *SONY* as an official trademark and re-branded their corporate brand name from *Tokyo Tsushin Kogyo* into *Sony Corporation* three years later. At this time the re-branding was considered an innovative step. It was highly unusual for a Japanese company to spell its name in Roman letters (or, when Sony is written in Japanese, in phonetic script rather than in Chinese characters). Though *Tokyo Tsushin Kogyo* held a brand awareness of 91% in Japan (Hang 2006), the management knew that the name was not readily understood overseas. According to Sony, they had tried translating the name as *Tokyo Teletech* or *Tokyo Telecommunications* in the past, but this had not worked. The name *Sony* is easy to pronounce and read in any language. Moreover, it has a short lively ring, which is said to match the corporate values of spirit of freedom and open-mindedness. According to Sony, the name *Sony* was neither derived from anything connected with the electronics industry, nor from the names of the company's two founders. At the time it was introduced, the name was considered by many Japanese to be quite strange (Sony 2006).

H6b: Chinese branded companies decide on one or two sponsorships in large scale events, amongst them the 2008 Beijing Olympic Games, in order to establish global brand awareness and to build brand image in US and WE markets.

With the aim to become a global standardised brand, Chinese branded companies have to communicate to a global audience. It is hypothesised that they decide on sponsoring large scale and international sporting events, amongst them 2008 Beijing Olympic Games, to achieve global brand awareness and to build brand image, similar to the way Samsung started their global brand building in the end-1980s (e.g., Park 1995; Hang 2006):
Samsung started its debut on the international stage in 1988, when the Olympic Games were hold in Seoul, South Korea, and Samsung became a

major local sponsor of the Games. In 1998 Samsung extended its sponsorship in the Games and is a Worldwide Official Partner since. Samsung has
also been the chief sponsor of the Asian Games since 1986, main sponsor
of the Samsung Nations Cup (equestrian) since 1988, official sponsor of
the Asian Football Confederation and the official club sponsor of Chelsea
FC since 2005. Besides financials, Samsung has contributed to each event
through its products and technologies, and was able to successfully showcase its brand performance to a worldwide audience (Samsung 2006). As a
result of their sponsoring efforts, Samsung was ranked the 20th most valuable brand in the world by *Interbrand* in 2005 and the third biggest brand
winner with a 19% growth rate of their brand value (Interbrand 2005).

As Chinese branded companies are supposed to have smaller marketing
budgets compared to that of Samsung, it is hypothesised that they decide
on only one or two key global sponsorships and may reduce the spending
for brand communication activities such as trade fairs and advertising to a
necessary minimum in US and WE markets. A sponsorship in the 2008
Beijing Olympic Games is considered crucial, as it is a unique platform to
promote Chinese brands as a part of modern China and to demonstrate
corporate governance.

*H6c: Chinese branded companies decide on distribution channels of large
consumer reach and brand fit. In the area of electrical appliances, they
therefore decide to take the electronics chains MediaMarkt and Saturn for
WE markets. Given that speed of market entry is more crucial to business,
they chose Carrefour and Wal-Mart as their favourite initial distribution
partners in US and WE markets.*

The brand approach of "clever brands" implies that Chinese brands are
perceived as superior to pure discount goods. Thus, hard discounters (in
Germany: e.g., *Aldi, Lidl*) and cheap image stores (e.g., do-it-yourself
stores) should be excluded as distribution channels at any times (Stremme
2005). Instead, Chinese branded companies are hypothesised to choose
distribution partners which provide a brand image that fits to the brand positioning of "clever brands", including a reliable after-sales service and a
permanent product portfolio, combined with the opportunity to advance
the product portfolio by own innovations in the long-term run.

For Chinese electrical brands large surface area electrical chains, such
as *MediaMarkt* and *Saturn* in Germany, are hypothesised to be reasonable
partners for US and WE markets.[105] MediaMarkt made revenues of

---

[105] Best Buy may be the respective large surface electrical chain in the US. Best
Buy is North America's largest specialty retailer of consumer electronics, PCs,

US$5.9bn in 2004 and runs more than 420 stores in thirteen European countries thereof 215 in Germany by June 2006.[106] MediaMarkt offers a product portfolio of 45,000 items in telecommunication, computer, photo, hi-fi, and electrical appliances. Saturn offers a similar product portfolio, runs 161 stores in Europe thereof 116 in Germany by June 2006 and gained revenues of US$2.4bn in 2003.[107] Both chain stores target the same ambivalent customer, who wants to buy qualitative brands for smart prices, as the brand approach of Chinese clever brands does. MediaMarkt's slogan is "I am not stupid" (original: "Ich bin doch nicht blöd"), Saturn's slogan is "cheap is good" (original: "Geiz ist geil") (BCG 2006d; Wikipedia 2006).

Chinese branded companies are supposed to win these distribution partners by an initial product that convinces with a very competitive price-value-ratio and can be pushed in the market to gain large market shares. Over the time, when the Chinese brand has built up some brand awareness and could advance their products and technologies by own international IP, they may ad more advanced and expensive products, and may finally be able to offer a complete product portfolio of several different prices and quality offers. *Toshiba*, a Japanese computer brand, took this path and is now selling 6-8 different computer models between €799 and €3,000 at MediaMarkt and Saturn stores in Germany in 2005 (Stremme 2005).

Furthermore, MediaMarkt and Saturn are hypothesised to be promising distribution partners because they both belong to the German *Metro Group*. Many Chinese branded companies have already worked with Metro Group in China and have established valuable relationships that might help to gain a foothold in the Western chain stores and to speed up negotiations. However, since each MediaMarkt and Saturn store is run as a single enterprise where the manager can decide on its own product portfolio and prices (Wikipedia 2006), the prior relationships may not be convincing enough. Given that competition in many industries runs fast, Chinese branded companies may thus be forced to find faster distribution solutions. *Carrefour* and *Wal-Mart* are then hypothesised to be reasonable choices. Both retailers are known by Chinese branded companies from op-

---

entertainment software and appliances. Best Buy ran 742 stores in the US in 2006, and estimated revenues at US$2.27bn. Further, Best Buy was represented in China by its electrical chain 'Five Star', which ran 131 outlets in China in 2006 (Best Buy 2006).

[106] Germany, Austria, Switzerland, Hungary, Poland, Spain, Portugal, the Netherlands, Belgium, Italy, France (Hypermédia), Greece and Sweden.

[107] In addition, 10 stores in Austria, 2 stores in Spain, 3 in Poland, 23 in France (Planète Saturn), 5 in Italy and 2 in Hungary.

erations in China and are considered to sell more globally standardised product portfolios (Euromonitor 2006). According to Dr. Steffen Stremme (2005), managing director of Media-Saturn-Holding in Germany, global retailers such as Carrefour would also not prevent building brand awareness and brand image nor would they immediately exclude later partnerships with Saturn and MediaMarkt. Brands such as *Philips, Toshiba, Sharp, Acer* etc. are all sold in Carrefour, MediaMarket and Saturn stores. However, he admitted that both chain stores would require the same low price as Carrefour gets when deciding on a listing of Chinese brands.

H7: Given H1-H6, Chinese branded companies establish a corporate brand department which is in charge of aligning, steering and controlling all brand management decisions across all world markets. Given that Western and Chinese markets demand different marketing qualities, sales & marketing of the region "US and WE markets" is organisationally separated from the region "China".

To ensure a global standardised brand approach with excellence in branding, brand communication and brand distribution across all operating and target markets, it is hypothesised that Chinese branded companies establish a corporate brand department which is in charge of aligning, steering and controlling all brand management decisions. This in particular includes the responsibility for corporate brand growth, cross-brand perspective and insight, resource allocation, branding standards and guidelines, and global marketing strategy. The corporate brand department is also in charge of advertising, sponsoring events, market research, new product development, major promotions, and relationships to global distribution partners such as *Carrefour, Wal-Mart* and *Metro Group* (Marketing Leadership Council 2000).

While Chinese branded companies are supposed to enjoy large brand equities and leading market positions in China and can rely on a profound customer understanding and strong distribution networks, they may lack these advantages in US and WE markets. While in China marketing and brand activities may thus aim to retain and enhance the well-established brand, marketing in US and WE markets may aim to build up brand equity from scratch. Given this scenario, one can assume that both regional markets may also require totally different marketing and personnel qualities, and promotion plans. Given that US and WE consumer markets are considered quite homogenous and alike, Chinese branded companies organisationally separate the sales & marketing unit "China" from the sales & marketing unit "US and WE markets". The latter might be detailed further, if the company has increased its overseas sales and generated larger volumes in each developed market (Berndt et al. 2003: 278-279). The sales & marketing activities of both units are supposed to be aligned, coordinated and approved through the guidelines of the corporate brand department.

H8: Given that Chinese branded companies lack Western market knowledge and experienced brand managers, they seek for external support to run the corporate brand department and the sales & marketing unit "US and WE markets".

As Chinese branded companies typically lack experienced marketing personnel and brand managers to be assigned to leading positions in the brand management organisation, they are hypothesised to seek for external brand support (e.g., Ballhaus 2005: 31; Yang 2005: 8). It is assumed that the head of the corporate brand department may be a former experienced brand manager of a Western multinational (Aaker/Joachimsthaler 2001). It is also imaginable that external brand consultancies may support a Chinese, less experienced brand manager to establish the department and to set up a global brand and marketing strategy. Further, as the Chinese staff often lacks experiences and insights into Western consumer markets, it is assumed that Chinese branded companies decide on in-country nationals and local market experts to run the sales & marketing unit "US and WE markets". Once established, they would also run the local subsidiaries in these markets (Quelch 1992; O'Donnell/Jeong 2000: 28-29). Since most Chinese branded companies are very ethnocentrically orientated and autocratically managed, one can assume that the company leaders would typically not agree to trust foreigners in a pure in-country national marketing team, of whom probably none can speak any Chinese. Instead, it is therefore hypothesised that Chinese branded companies will employ Chinese expats and in-country nationals in a Sino-foreign managing team, similar to the way *Samsung* started their global business in the 1980s:

Samsung established their first overseas subsidy in Portugal in the 1980s by a majority joint venture with two other partners. One partner was a Portuguese manufacturer which was an OEM contractor of Samsung in Portugal, and the other partner was an English marketing company and importer to the UK market. Samsung and its 7 Korean managers were in charge of the corporate management, financials, technology, sourcing, and marketing into Western markets except UK. The chairman of the joint venture was a Portuguese, who was in charge of production, domestic marketing, and human resources that were in total 200 local Portuguese at this time. The English marketing company was in charge of sales & marketing into the UK, overall market research, consumer insights and local designs. To ensure productivity and strong relationships with the headquarters, Samsung established training courses at and job rotations with the production sites in South Korea for the Portuguese workers (Choi 1991: 110-111; Park 1994: 403).

5 Empirical study

After an appropriate global brand approach for Chinese branded companies entering US and WE markets have been hypothesised in the last chapter, the approach is now going to be tested by real case examples. Four
case studies of the Chinese household appliances and consumer electronics
industry have been chosen as the study's objects of research. These are
namely *Haier, TCL, Hisense* and *Lenovo*. Before presenting the company
cases, however, the chapter takes a closer look at the global household appliances and consumer electronics industry by benchmarking China
against the US and Western European markets.

5.1 The global household appliances & consumer electronics industry

The household appliances and consumer electronics industry is one of the
world's largest consumer goods industries in the world (Euromonitor
2006). Since there is not a uniformed industry definition, for the purpose
of this research, it includes large kitchen appliances (synonym: white
goods), TV & video (synonym: black goods), and personal computers
(PCs). The section aims to give a short overview about all three industries,
including market sectors, major players, brands and consumer behaviour,
and to benchmark China against the markets in the US and Western
Europe (WE). Besides a look at the global level, regional focus is thus
USA, WE and China.

Large kitchen appliances

According to Euromonitor (2006), the world market for large kitchen appliances made up a value at US$132bn in 2005. The major market sectors
are refrigeration, home laundry (i.e. washing machines), large cooking appliances and microwaves. As table 5-1 and table 5-2 indicate, Western
Europe is the most lucrative regional market and accounted for around
32% of the global market in 2005, while China is relatively small and ac-

counted for around 7%. The largest single sector in terms of value was worldwide refrigeration with around 33% market share, although it was topped in Western Europe by large cooking appliances.

	Retail value in US$ mio. in 2005			
	World	USA	WE	China
Total	132.477	25.941	42.612	9.508
Refrigeration	43.455	7.583	11.610	3.173
Home laundry appliances	37.426	6.357	11.474	2.901
(Washing machines)	*(24.415)*	*(3.828)*	*(8.447)*	*(2.520)*
Large cooking appliances	32.823	5.529	12.546	2.683
Microwaves	8.654	3.173	1.966	577

Table 5-1. Global white goods market and its major market sectors at retail value in US$ mio. in 2005 (Euromonitor 2006)

		2001	2002	2003	2004	2005	CAGR 01-05	CAPU 2005
World	'000	301,921	311,521	329,202	349,413	364,226	3.8%	
	US$ mio.	95,832	98,142	110,968	123,592	132,477	6.7%	$363.72
USA	'000	57,011	60,449	63,924	68,337	68,540	3.8%	
	US$ mio.	21,391	22,599	23,508	25,429	25,941	3.9%	$378.47
WE	'000	79,437	79,330	82,208	84,196	85,210	1.4%	
	US$ mio.	28,710	29,836	36,241	40,553	42,612	8.2%	$500.08
China	'000	45,764	49,064	52,102	56,595	61,044	5.9%	
	US$ mio.	7,111	7,532	8,127	8,806	9,508	6.0%	$155.76

Table 5-2. Global large kitchen appliances at retail volume ('000 units) and retail value (US$ mio.) 2001-2005 (based on Euromonitor 2006)[108]

Global market leaders in large kitchen appliances are Whirlpool Corp, Electrolux AB and Bosch-Siemens Hausgeräte (BSH). All three companies accounted for 21% volume share in 2003 (table 5-3), and have long traditions and a number of well-established global, regional and specialised brands. Since large kitchen appliances are capital intensive in manufacturing, assembling and distribution, the realisation of economies of scale and economies of scope are considered business crucial. Large industry con-

---

[108] China retail value 2001-2005 at 2005 exchange rates. See appendix 1 for the exchange rate.

solidation has therefore taken place since the 1980s in the US and WE markets (Ling 2005: 62), and the today's leading manufactures begun to ensure their strong market positions by additional performance factors such as branding, product innovation, relationship building to retailers and after-sales service (Ling 2005: 59).

	Global retail volume in %		
Company *(brands)*	2001	2002	2003
Whirlpool Corp	8.6	8.2	7.9
(Whirlpool)	*(5.5)*	*(5.7)*	*(5.7)*
Electrolux AB	7.2	7.0	6.8
(Electrolux)	*(1.9)*	*(1.8)*	*(2.0)*
(Frigidaire)	*(1.3)*	*(1.4)*	*(1.3)*
Bosch-Siemens Haushaltsgeräte GmbH	6.0	5.7	5.5
(Bosch)	*(2.8)*	*(2.8)*	*(2.8)*
(Siemens)	*(1.7)*	*(1.6)*	*(1.6)*
General Electric Co (GE)	4.4	4.7	4.7
(GE)	*(3.7)*	*(3.9)*	*(4.0)*
Haier Group	3.1	3.9	3.9
(Haier)	*(3.1)*	*(3.7)*	*(3.6)*
LG Group	3.2	3.7	3.9
(LG)	*(3.0)*	*(3.5)*	*(3.6)*
Merloni Elettrodomestici SpA	3.4	3.4	3.6
(Ariston)	*(1,1)*	*(1.1)*	*(1.2)*
(Indesit)	*(0.9)*	*(0.9)*	*(1.0)*
Maytag Corp.	3.0	3.1	3.1
(Maytag)	*(2.3)*	*(2.3)*	*(2.3)*
Matsushita Electric Industrial Co. Ltd.	2.7	2.8	2.7
(National)	*(1.7)*	*(1.8)*	*(1.7)*
Samsung Electronics	2.1	2.2	2.4
(Samsung)	*(2.1)*	*(2.2)*	*(2.3)*

Table 5-3. World's top 10 largest manufacturers of large kitchen appliances and their brands in % of retail volume 2001-2003 (Euromonitor 2006)[109]

However, over the last few years, companies from Asia like Haier Group, LG Group, and Samsung Electronics have made strong advances at the global level, as their Asian home markets are growing fast (table 5-2), and they have become more active in marketing their products and were more successful or more willing to compete on the price. Price discounting and thus a substantial pressure on operating margins has been a conse-

---

[109] Note that Haier is the world's forth largest appliance maker, including OEM since 2004; and since August 2005, *Maytag* brand belongs to Whirlpool Corp. See case study Haier Group for details.

quence of increasing competition in the whole industry, with the result that many Western companies currently tend to shift their production facilities into lower labour cost counties such as Eastern Europe (Euromonitor 2006; Gehrmann 2006).

In terms of consumer demand for large kitchen appliances, the markets in the US and Western Europe are sluggish and mainly driven by the replacement cycle (table-5-2). The product penetration is high and close to 100% for certain product types like refrigerators and washing machines. Moreover, the overall product life expectancy is relatively long, on average 10-15 years. Thus, innovation is considered important both to comply with environmental legislation and to stimulate consumer demand by providing more sophisticated appliances. This may include the production of novel versions of old products with advanced technologies such as electronic control for washing processes, the introduction of new product categories, or the development of 'connected' appliances (Datamonitor 2005b).

Even though one could expect that US and WE consumers would have similar product demands and brand preferences, the markets have remained relatively isolated from the others. While, for instance, US consumers traditionally prefer top-loading washing machines and large free-standing refrigerators, consumers in Germany favour front-loading washers and built-in appliances. As a result, each market is much dominated by its local, traditional brands, though not all are in local ownership (Stremme 2005). In the US, the leading brands are *Kenmore* (Sears, Roebuck & Co.), *GE. Whirlpool, Maytag* and *Frigidaire*. In Germany, there is *Bosch, Siemens, AEG* (Electrolux AB), *Bauknecht* (Whirlpool Corp.), *Liebherr* (Liebherr-International AG), *Miele* (Miele & Cie. KG). France is dominated by *Whirlpool, Brandt* (ElcoBrandt Group), *Ariston, Bosch, Scholtes* (Merloni Electroménager SA); and UK is dominated by *Hotpoint* (Indesit Co UK), *Bosch, Whirlpool,* and *Zanussi* (Electrolux AB). Customer brand loyalty is likely to be high, although, white goods are not considered as status symbols, as they are neither portable (in contrast to mobile phones and notebooks) nor considered as decorative for living rooms (in contrast to televisions). Share of voice in terms of advertising is therefore also low, while product experience, durability, and reliable after-sales service are regarded as key purchasing criteria (Stremme 2005).

Despite of different brand preferences, in both US and WE markets there is recently a trend towards high quality, better designed and technologically more advanced appliances. In the US, for instance, each large appliance brand has therefore made major investments in premium products, with brands such as *Kenmore's Elite*, *GE's Profile* and *Monogram*, and *Maytag's Jenn-Air* all well-known to many consumers (Euromonitor

2006). In Western Europe, a similar trend may be confirmed by its impressive value performance: 8.2% growth in 2001-2005, and a calculated average price per unit (CAPU) at US$500 in 2005 (table 5-2). At the same time, however, also price-aggressive distribution formats such as large surface area electrical chains (e.g., *MediaMarkt, Saturn*), hypermarkets and online discounters including *eBay*, have grown rapidly over the last few years. As, for instance, in Germany the rate of unemployment is high and people feel economically unstable, they often postpone replacements, while the importance of price as a purchasing criterion increases (Euromonitor 2006).[110]

	Bicycle	Washing machine	Refrigerator	Dishwasher	Colour TV	Black & white TV	Computer
Urban	140.2	95.9	90.2	0.6	133.4	n/a	33.1
Rural	118.2	37.3	17.8	n/a	75.1	37.9	n/a
Twelve Western provinces	74.8	25.9	7.7	n/a	62.6	37.2	n/a

Table 5-4. Ownership of selected durables goods in China 2004, per 100 urban and rural households (Guojia Tongji Ju [National Bureau of Statistics] 2005)

While US and WE markets are quite mature, in China, the market of large kitchen appliances is growing rapidly in both volume and value, on average 6% each year in 2001-2005 (table 2-3), together with China's growing middle class and growing incomes. Chinese consumer demand is thus not stimulated by replacement cycles, although washing machines and refrigerators already have nearly 100% penetration in urban households. Besides, there is a large urban-rural polarisation of consumption patterns in China (table 5-4), with low-cost models favoured in rural areas. Overall prices are thus very low, on average at US$156 per appliance in 2005 (table 5-3). Due to their strong distribution networks, which also extend into the rural areas, the top three leading brands of large kitchen appliances in China are local brands, namely *Haier, Midea* (GD Midea Holding Co. Ltd.) and *Shuaikang* (Zhejiang Shuaikang Co. Ltd.). They accounted together for more than 36% volume share in 2005 (Euromonitor 2006).

While overall competition may be on price, China is planning laws on electrical equipment recycling and other environmental issues similar in scope to those of the EU. These are likely to be introduced in the next couple of years, and will add to the costs of foreign and domestic companies.

---

[110] See for this ambivalent consumer behaviour also chapter 4, hypothesis 3.

According to Datamonitor (2005e), the Chinese market will become one of the world's largest appliance markets in terms of retail value by 2009.

TV & video

According to Euromonitor (2006), the global market for TV & video has a similar market size as the market of large kitchen appliances and accounted for US$118bn in 2003.[111] Its major market sectors are televisions, television combinations, video cassette recorders, DVD/DVDR players, camcorders, and digital cameras. As table 5-5 indicates, Western Europe and USA accounted for almost 50% of the global market in 2003, while China is relatively small and accounted for around 8%. The largest single sector in terms of value was worldwide televisions with around 59% market share, followed by DVD/DVDR players with 14% market share.

	Retail value in US$ mio. in 2003			
	World	USA	WE	China
Total	118.066	24.126	31.920	9.922
Televisions	69.258	12.601	14.881	7.596
Television combinations	3.265	888	628	---
Video cassette recorders	4.180	570	2.065	211
DVD/DVDR players	16.563	4.585	6.665	1.374
Camcorders	9.823	2.263	3.090	389
Digital cameras	14.976	3.219	4.590	352

Table 5-5. Global TV & video market and its major market sectors at retail value in US$ mio. in 2003 (Euromonitor 2006)

As table 5-6 shows, the global market is predominated by Asian-based multinationals and their brands. According to Datamonitor (2005d), the reasons for their pre-eminence in the market are several. They can make use of production facilities in countries selected for optimal labour and transport costs. They can negotiate favourable prices from suppliers because of their purchasing power. And they can afford those sizeable investments in research which are vital if new technologies, and the products based on them, are to be developed. The leading global brand is *Sony* with around 10% market share, followed by Matsushita's brands *Panasonic* and *JVC,* and *Philips* and *Samsung.* Despite of minor loss of market share in

---

[111] More recent data not yet published by Euromonitor. Instead Datamonitor provides 2004 market data on the global TV & video industry, but lacks a country split into USA, WE and China, and company and brand market shares.

2003, Sony is acknowledged as an upmarket, high-margin and innovative brand.

Rank	Company *(brands)*	Global retail volume in %	
		2002	2003
1	⊡ Sony Corp	10.1	9.8
	(Sony)	*(10.0)*	*(9.7)*
2	⊡ Matsushita Electric Industrial Co. Ltd.	10.1	9.5
	(Panasonic)	*(6.5)*	*(6.1)*
	(JVC)	*(3.3)*	*(3.2)*
3	⊡ Samsung Electronics	4.4	4.9
	(Samsung)	*(4.4)*	*(4.9)*
4	▬ Koninklijke Philips Electronics NV	4.8	4.7
	(Philips)	*(3.4)*	*(3.6)*
	(Magnavox)	*(1.4)*	*(1.2)*
5	⊡ Toshiba Corp.	3.2	3.1
	(Toshiba)	*(3.1)*	*(3.1)*
6	⊡ LG Group	2.5	2.6
	(LG)	*(2.5)*	*(2.6)*
7	▮▮ Thomson SA	2.3	2.0
	(RCA)	*(1,1)*	*(1.0)*
10	▨ Konka Group Co. Ltd.	1.5	1.9
	(Konka)	*(1.5)*	*(1.9)*
11	▨ Sichuan Changhong Electronics Group	1.9	1.6
	(Changhong)	*(1.9)*	*(1.6)*
13	▨ TCL Group	1.5	1.5
	(TCL)	*(1.5)*	*(1.5)*
16	▨ Shenzhen Skyworth-RGB Electric Co. Ltd.	1.1	1.2
	(Skyworth)	*(1.1)*	*(1.2)*
20	▨ Qingdao Hisense Co. Ltd.	1.2	1.0
	(Hisense)	*(1.2)*	*(1.0)*

Table 5-6. World's leading TV & video manufacturers and their brands in % of retail volume 2002-2003 (Euromonitor 2006)[112]

Based on strong leadership positions in their home markets in Asia-Pacific, Sony was ranked amongst the top three brands in all US and WE markets. In the USA, *Sony* was ranked first in 2003, followed by *Panasonic* and *Apex* (Apex Digital Inc). In the UK, *Sony* was ranked first, fol-

---

[112] Since 2004, *TCL* and *RCA* brand are marketed by TCL-Thomson-Electronics (TTE), a wholly-owned corporation of TCL Multimedia Group (e.g., TMC 2006a). See also case study TCL Group.

lowed by *Philips, Panasonic, Samsung* and *JVC*. In Germany, *JVC* was ranked first, followed by *Sony, Philips, Samsung* and *Panasonic*. And in France, *Samsung* led the market, followed by *Philips, Sony* and *Thomson* (Thomson SA). Although the expansion of lower priced brands, such as *Konka* and *Samsung*, particularly in televisions, may have undermined Sony Corp's wider share in video products, it becomes evident that in contrast to large kitchen appliances, the industry of TV & video is much more globally standardised and dominated by global corporate brands.

		1999	2000	2001	2002	2003	CAGR 99-03	CAPU 2003
World	'000	142,284	144,739	140,270	149,682	156,692	1.9%	
	US$ mio.	63,181	62,433	59,172	63,724	69,258	1.9%	$442.00
USA	'000	18,345	18,706	16,920	18,861	19,941	1.7%	
	US$ mio.	9,009	9,777	9,989	11,647	12,601	6.9%	$531.91
WE	'000	27,342	28,096	27,727	28,018	28,563	0.9%	
	US$ mio.	12,369	11,546	11,005	12,215	14,881	3.8%	$521.01
China	'000	32,097	31,690	31,765	35,016	37,198	3.0%	
	US$ mio.	9,111	7,687	6,991	7,615	7,596	-3.6%	$204.20

Table 5-7. Global televisions market at retail volume ('000 units) and retail value (US$ mio.) 2001-2005 (based on Euromonitor 2006)[113]

Meanwhile, however, Sony Corp. has already withdrawn its televisions form the Chinese market by 2005 due to shrinking profit margins (Underwood 2006). The Chinese market is very price competitive. In terms of value, the market decreased by 3.6% each year in 1999-2003, resulting in an average price of US$204 per television (table 5-7). As a consequence of low price levels, combined with strong distribution networks, the top five leading brands in China are locals, namely *Konka, Changhong, TCL, Skyworth* and *Hisense*. They accounted together for more than 42% volume share in 2003.[114] In terms of volume, the Chinese market is growing healthily by 3.0% each year in 1999-2003, since numbers of prosperous Chinese middle class citizens can enjoy television (table 5-4, Datamonitor 2005d). According to Euromonitor (2006), colour television sets accounted for over three-quarter of the total TV & video sales in 2003.

---

[113] China retail value 1999-2003 at 2003 exchange rates. See appendix 1 for the exchange rate.

[114] In 2005, TCL is China's leading TV brand and accounted for 18% market share (Huang/Du 2005).

Due to a high penetration rate of over 130% (table 5-4), colour televisions in urban areas become almost a mature product and consumers begin to replace old versions or to buy additional TV sets. For upgrading, Chinese consumers tend to buy larger screens, better picture quality and more stylish models. Large-sized, flat screen Cathode Ray Tube (CRT)-based televisions are the best selling items in 2003. Interestingly, the share of foreign brands in this category increased significantly. The four leading foreign brands had more than 30% market share of CRT television sales in 2003 (Euromonitor 2006).

In contrast to the Chinese market, table 5-7 reveals that the markets in the USA and Western Europe are very sluggish in terms of volumes, but growing in terms of values. Although in both regions the price levels are also nearly en par at around US$525 per television, consumer behaviour is not identical in each country market. In Germany, for example, the market for traditional CRT televisions is generally saturated, as every German household owns at least one television set. Due to the general low consumer confidence, existing sets are generally only purchased out of necessity. This hampers the sales of innovations and pushes demand down to the replacement rate. In the USA, in contrast, technological innovation can stimulate consumer demand: higher priced digital formats and flat screen TVs using LCD or plasma displays are such developments, and the combination of slim profiles and large screens make them popular among consumers. Further, American households usually hold several sets, sometimes more than one for each member, while Europeans traditionally have fewer TV sets. Since both digital and high definition (HDTV) television sets are still few in volumes, their sales can only be expected to have an impact on the mass market once digital broadcasting becomes the norm and product replacement starts to occur. Digital broadcasting is planned to become standard in the USA by 2007, in the UK and Germany by 2010 (Euromonitor 2006).

Besides, the high price points of most digital TVs have so far kept most consumers away, but this is beginning to change as prices drop, because competition is becoming fiercer in the category. New companies such as Dell and Gateway have introduced lower priced plasma TVs to a number of major markets, while most existing TV manufacturers, such as Sony, Samsung, Panasonic and Philips, greatly expanded their product lines during 2003. In the US, for example, average digital projection TV prices have fallen from highs in 1999 of US$2,650 to just over US$1,300 in 2003. Similarly, plasma TVs have nearly halved in average price since their introduction in 2001, according to the Consumer Electronics Association, falling to under US$4,000 in 2003 (Euromonitor 2006). The flood of new products, compounded with large price drops, has thus made the digital TV category much more viable. As Datamonitor (2005d) concluded, those manufacturers who have increased production capacity appropriately will be able to profit from the changeover to digital televisions in future.

Personal Computer (PC)

The third industry that belongs to the study's definition of the household appliance and consumer electronics industry is the global PC market. According to IDC (2006), the global PC market accounted for US$218bn in 2005. In general, PCs can be classified in terms of users and distribution channels, and in terms of hardware types. In terms of PC users, the products fall into three categories: home users, small & medium enterprises (SME), and large enterprises. Interlinked to these categories, PCs can also be split up by distribution channels into sales through retail channels, including internet and mail order, and sales at business-to-business (B2B) (Stremme 2005). In terms of hardware types, PCs fall into three categories: desktops, portables (i.e. notebooks), and servers (x86 servers). As table 5-8 shows, the largest regional market is the USA that accounted for almost 30% value share in 2005, while the Chinese market is relatively small and accounted for around 6% market share. The largest single sector in terms of value was desktop computers, though the sales of portables were already almost en par in the USA and Western Europe.

	Value of PC shipments in US$ mio. in 2005			
	World	USA	WE	China[1]
Total	217,742	63,570	58,807	14,099
Desktops	109,159	29,491	27,109	8,087
Portables	68,378	23,240	25,356	4,673
(Notebooks)	*(59,851)*	*(20,107)*	*(23,829)*	*(3,923)*
x86 servers	26,545	10,389	6,342	1,339

(1)   Calculated by IDC growth rate 2005 as provided for Asia/Pacific excluding Japan, and China 2004 market sizes as given by Datamonitor (2005), PCs in China

Table 5-8. Global PC market and its major market sectors, at value of PC shipments in US$ mio. in 2005 (IDC 2006)

The global market leader in PCs is the American *Dell Inc.* that held almost 19% market share in the first quarter of 2005, followed by two other American vendors *Hewlett-Packard (HP)* (15%) and *IBM* (5%) (table 5-9). Since May 2005, however, when Chinese *Lenovo* acquired the IBM PC division, Lenovo is the third largest PC vendor in the world (Lenovo Group 2005b).[115]

Vendor	Branded PC shipments in % volume share		
	1Q 2004	4Q 2004	1Q 2005
Dell	18.4	16.8	18.5
Hewlett-Packard (HP)	15.4	15.8	15.1
IBM	5.5	5.7	5.0
Fujitsu/Fujitsu Siemens	4.5	3.9	4.5
Acer	3.3	4.3	4.0
Toshiba	3.3	3.3	3.6
NEC	2.9	2.7	3.2
Apple	1.8	2.0	2.3
Lenovo	1.9	2.4	2.1
Gateway	1.1	2.3	2.0

Table 5-9. Global branded PC shipments by top ten vendors in 1Q 2004-1Q 2005 in % volume share (IDC 2005)

Whereas Dell and HP were ranked first and second in both sectors desktops and portables, there are other vendors that are specialised in one sector. For example, *Toshiba* consciously focuses on portables, and was ranked third in this category with 11.8% market share in the first quarter of 2005 (IDC 2005). In contrast, *Lenovo* and *Gateway*, offer both portables and desktops, but are only among the world's top ten leading vendors in desktops. According to Datamonitor (2005a), PC vendors may be successful and gain strong market shares if they can use brand leverage, have large advertising budgets and the ability to build and maintain consumer trust. As a consequence, the world's leading vendors primary focus on marketing their PCs by a global standardised and corporate brand, partly combined with product line names such as *Dell Optiplex* and *HP Pavilion*, although some product lines have already emerged as quite independent brands such as *IBM ThinkPad* (portables), *IBM ThinkCentre* (desktops) and the *iMac* from *Apple* (Quelch/Knoop 2006).

---

[115] For details see case study Lenovo in chapter 5.2.

As table 5-10 shows, the global PC market is dynamic with a peak in 2005 and is forecast to remain so until 2007. The US market remains the world's largest in terms of both volume and value, while China overtook Japan in 2004 to become the largest volume market in Asia-Pacific and the world's second largest, after the US (Datamonitor 2005c). In terms of average price per PC, Western Europe is the most lucrative market with US$1,211 per PC. Interestingly, in contrast to the industries of large kitchen appliances and TV & video, the overall price level of PCs in China (US$810) is relatively high and not as much lower than the US price level (US$995).

		2003	2004	2005	e2006	e2007	CAGR 03-07	CAPU 2005
World	'000	155,667	179,218	207,804	229,735	257,366	10.6%	
	US$ mio.	181,338	199,901	217,742	226,224	241,520	5.9%	$1047.82
USA	'000	52,699	58,285	63,874	67,840	73,915	7.0%	
	US$ mio.	57,045	59,417	63,874	65,632	69,849	4.1%	$995.24
WE	'000	35.964	41,790	48,551	51,428	56,399	9.4%	
	US$ mio.	51,197	57,085	58,807	56,794	57,964	2.5%	$1,211.24
China[1]	'000	13,000	14,900	17,403	20,553	23,842	12.9%	
	US$ mio.	11,100	12,600	14,099	15,975	17,556	9.6%	$810,16

(1)   2003-2004 taken from Datamonitor (2005), PCs in China; 2005-2007 calculated by IDC growth rates provided for Asia/Pacific excluding Japan

Table 5-10. Global PC market at PC shipments ('000 units) and at value of shipments (US$ mio.) 2003-2007 (based on IDC 2006).

According to IDC (2006), a key driver for the global market growth until 2007 is the portable PC adaptation. Although desktop PCs remain a mass-market product in many markets, particularly the growth in developed markets is determined by portables. Besides a home user trend to portables, also many small & medium businesses replace and advance their systems by portables. Besides, consumer demand in US and WE markets is stimulated by falling PC prices, attractive digital bundles and the decline of broadband prices. However, PC penetration rates differ heavily across the WE markets. Datamonitor (2005a) stated that the fact is partly a reflection of differing internet penetration rates. Southern Europe has low internet usage and PC ownership rates, Italy and Spain are amongst the lowest.

High internet penetration rates, combined with the development of legalised music and film download sites, are thus considered crucial to market high specification, multimedia PCs, and premium-price systems to gamers and other demanding users, that can create higher margins to PC vendors. At the meantime, mass-markets and price conscious consumers can benefit from the rapid pace of development in the market, that leads to the quick obsolescence of products, and thus to dropping prices towards the budget end of the price spectrum. Particularly, Dell's popularity demonstrates the willingness of consumers to embrace the internet as a distribution channel in order to save money and to gather information about the product before the purchase. Dell operates solely through the internet and mail order channels, a business model that has considerable consequences for common retailers, whose higher overheads and maintenance costs inhibit their ability to price competitively. Point of sale displays and packaging have also become less important in the face of internet retail competition (Datamonitor 2005h).

Although price levels are not significantly lower and price droppings not larger in China than in all US and WE countries, the market is dominated by local firms, with the major exceptions of Dell and HP. Lenovo holds almost a third of the total market since 1999 (IDC), and have gained additional ground at home and abroad with their recent purchase of IBM's PC division. Other leading players include domestic firms such as *Founder Electronics* and *Great Wall Group*. While the US and WE market are quite mature, Chinese consumer demand has mainly been stimulated by expansion of both business-to-business and business-to-consumer sectors. Due to China's open door policy, there has been a large influx of multinational companies within the country, and together with the modernisation processes of Chinese firms that lead to a demand of commercial PCs. Moreover, the home user market has seen rapid growth, as the consumers' disposable income has grown, particularly in the urban areas. Because in terms of numbers PCs are still few in China (table 5-4), market growth is forecasted to be healthy in the next couple of years (Datamonitor 2005g). In 2003, John Antone, Intel general manager Asia Pacific has forecasted that China would equal if not exceed the US as consumer consumption PC market by 2010 (Daily Times 2003).

Conclusion

The overview about the household appliances and consumer electronics industry shows that the market in China compared to the markets in the US and Western Europe may demand different brand approaches from a company. Whereas in China, it may be sufficient to attract Chinese consumers by competitive price offers and simple brand promises, consumers in the US and WE are supposed to expect more sophistication, as penetration rates are high and purchases are likely made due to replacement cycles. In addition, the overview reveals that the three sectors of large kitchen appliances, TV & video, and PC may require different brand approaches in order to gain strong market shares. In large kitchen appliances, a key success factor may be a local, well-established brand, combined with a reliable after-sales service and strong relationships to retailers. In TV & video and PCs, a global standardised brand may be crucial, combined with large advertising budgets, and speed in innovation. While large kitchen appliances and PCs are mainly dominated by Western companies, Chinese branded companies might benefit from the overall Asian dominance in TV & video, in terms of positive spillover effects on the brand image. On the other hand, they may have the opportunity to gain a foothold in the PC market, as products are not yet considered commodity. Whether these suppositions and the hypotheses of chapter 4 can be confirmed by brand realities in Chinese branded companies, the next sections and the following four case studies will show.

5.2 The case studies

For the purpose of this research, four case studies of the household appliances and consumer electronics industry have been chosen. These are namely Haier Group (i.e. large kitchen appliances), TCL Corporation, Hisense Group (both i.e. TV & video), and Lenovo Group (i.e. personal computers). The aim of the case narratives has been to include all aspects and events that in some way may have influenced the companies' brand decisions concerning their market entries into US and WE markets, and are thus considered necessary to test the formulated hypotheses, and to identify a Chinese way of international brand management. Own comments on certain brand decisions are explicitly indicated.

Each case study is separated in the three sections: 'aims of global brand building', 'strategic brand decisions when going-international' and 'operative brand decisions when going-international'. The section 'aims of global branding' includes a short company overview and the firm's motives of global brand building. The section 'strategic brand decisions when going-international' presents the company's mode of market entry, brand positioning, and brand innovations.[116] The section 'operative brand decisions when going-international' presents the company's branding, brand communication, brand distribution, and brand organisation. Each case study closes with a short summary of all nine sub-sections.

---

[116] Due to story telling reasons of the cases, the section 'market entry' is discussed ahead the section 'brand positioning'. Compare to brand theory as presented in chapter 2.

5.2.1 Case study 1: 海尔集团 Haier Group

Aims of global brand building

Company overview

海尔集团 Haier Group was incorporated in Qingdao in 1984 as a collective-owned enterprise producing refrigerators. Based on a joint venture with German *Liebherr*, they advanced their refrigeration quality and have grown rapidly since (box 5-1), on average 35% each year in 1998-2004 (figure 5-1). Since the 1990s, Haier Group has differentiated into many related white and black goods, and non-manufacturing industries. Today, Haier Group is China's market leader in large kitchen appliances (i.e. in refrigeration and laundry), and China's most valuable brand. Haier Group accounted for 17.4% volume shares in 2005 (Euromonitor 2006), and gained, according to own data, revenues of US$12.29bn of which 8.3% were made abroad.

Due to the fact that Haier Group is also the world's forth largest appliance and world's largest refrigeration maker including OEM (Haier Group 2005a), Haier has also been considered China's most global and prominent company (e.g., Hirn 2005: 122; Ling 2005: 125). Since Lenovo purchased IBM PCs in 2005 and became the world's third largest PC vendor, Haier's title may however be challenged. Haier Group is particularly quite successful in US-niche markets, competing there against Whirlpool, Electrolux, Bosch-Siemens and LG, and gaining market leadership and 50% market shares in wine cellars and small refrigerators by sales of US$229.7m in 2004 (Dolan 2004; Hoover's online 2006). Although Haier Group is also relatively known in Western Europe (figure 3-19), they still struggle with difficulties in launching their product portfolio there (e.g., Wurm 2005).[117] Haier Group obtained revenues of US$136m in Europe including OEM, thereof US$5.5m in Germany (Weiland 2004).

Since Haier Group considers its corporate strengths in customer-tailored product designs and innovation speed, they are strongly convinced to enhance their performance in near future (Liu 2005; BCG 2006c). Haier manager Liu Zhanjie evaluated Haier Group's corporate strengths compared to world-class level as seen in figure 5-2.

---

[117] Haier Group itself claims market shares of 10% in the European air-conditioning market (Ling 2005: 100; China Economic Review 2006: 39). Since this significant number could not be confirmed in any major WE market by external market sources, the reliability of this market share has to be questioned. Compare to section 'brand positioning' and table 5-2.

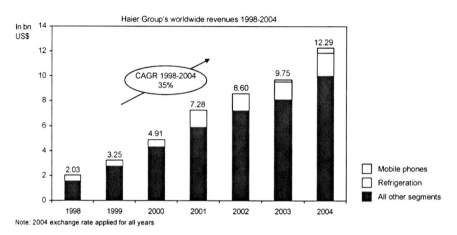

Fig. 5-1. Haier's worldwide revenues in bn US$ 1998-2004 (company data)[118]

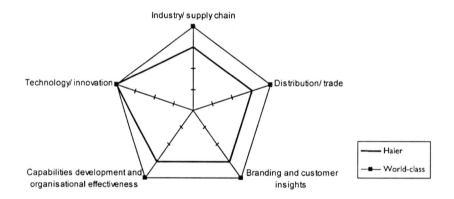

Fig. 5-2. Haier Group's perceived core competences on a scale from 1 (basic industry level) to 5 (world-class level) (estimation of Liu 2005)

---

[118] Data base on annual reports 2000-2004 of Qingdao Haier Co., Ltd. and Haier Electronics Group, as well as on Yi/Ye (2003: 237-240) and Haier Group (2006b). See appendix 1 for exchange rates. Since only 18% of Haier Group's revenues are publicly-listed, treat overall revenue data with care.

[119] Compare to Yi/Ye (2003), Gilmore/Dumont (2003), Gu (2002), Ling Liu (2005), Ding/Zheng (2005: i.e. 45), Liu/Li (2002: 704), Haier Group (2006b) and Hoover's Online(2006). See Haier case as given by Harvard Business School for the acquisition of Red Star (Paine 2001a, 2001b, 2001c).

Although officially incorporated in 1984, Haier had its origin in 1955 when a group of people formed a handicraft-producers' cooperative. In 1979, it was named into 'Qingdao Home Appliance Factory' manufacturing washing machines. Though the company switched to the more profitable refrigerator business in 1984 and was renamed into 'Qingdao General Refrigerator Factory' with the approval of Qingdao Economic Committee, the factory, employing about 800 people, was almost bankrupt by end of 1984.

Zhang Ruimin, a former bureaucrat in the municipal government, was appointed director by the Qingdao Municipal Governmental Household Appliance Division and turned around the money losing business. He focused exclusively on refrigerators and decided to develop a national brand, addressing product and service quality as the top aims of corporate mission. In a pretty known event in 1985, at a time when refrigerators were in high demand and sold at prices of two years workers' salaries, he ordered the destruction of seventy-six defective refrigerators with a sledgehammer in order to bring awareness of quality and discipline to the workers. In addition, Zhang concluded a seven-year licence contract with German appliance maker Liebherr in order to profit from their advanced refrigerator production line. When the joint venture contract ran out in 1991, the 'Qindao-Liebherr Refrigerator' was a known product name in China.

In accordance with guidelines from the central government, Qingdao General Refrigerator Factory was merged with several local freezer and air-conditioner companies to form 'Qingdao Haier Group' in 1991. In 1993, the today's 'Haier Group' was formed and Zhang Ruimin became the president of the group. To fund the construction of the new Haier Industrial Park in Qingdao, which was completed by 1995, Haier went public on the Shanghai Stock Exchange Market in 1993. In the same year, Haier diversified into the washing machine sector by forming a joint venture with Italian company Merloni Elettrodomestici and acquiring 'Qingdao Red Star Electric Appliance Company'. Red Star, also a collective enterprise, is said Haier's most critical acquisition, since they had debts in seize of Haier's total profit at this time. It was given to Haier free of charge by an arrangement of municipal government officials to cure business and to keep the 3,240 workers in employment.

Inline with governmental encouragements, Zhang made a 'ten-year-plan' aiming at expansion through further diversification and cross-provincial acquisitions of troubled manufactures, entering the Fortune 500 before 2010. By 1997, Haier was merged with eighteen factories and entered the air-conditioner, TV and computer market. In 1999, Haier got the approval to produce mobile phones. To acquire the technology they entered into a joint venture with China Construction Telecommunication Company (CCT) in Hong Kong and build up a production plant in Qingdao in 2000. In 2003 Haier mobile phones went IPO in Hong Kong and were renamed into Haier Electronics Group in 2005. To diversify risk and fully utilise the value of the established Haier brand in China, Haier has also expand to industries other than appliances, such as medicine, real state, financial and travel service. In 2002, Haier also invested in the retailing sector by forming joint ventures with OBI, Germany's largest Do-it-yourself retailer, and with Chinese Suning Appliance Chains. By 2006, Haier is looking into further overseas stock market listings such as in New York.

Box 5-1. Haier's corporate history and domestic growth (own summary)[119]

By end of 2005, Haier Group is still a quite traditional Chinese collective-owned enterprise, although they run two publicly-listed entities to fund corporate growth: Haier Electronics Group is listed at Hong Kong stock market and includes Haier mobile phones and since January 2005 one of Haier Group's core businesses, washing machines.[120] Qingdao Haier, Ltd. is listed at Shanghai stock market and includes Haier refrigeration covering refrigerators, freezer and air-conditioners. Since only 18% of Haier Group revenues are listed till end of 2004, overall figures on profitability can only be estimated. An industry observer named them flat (Bremner/Roberts 2005); president of Jiangsu Bosch and Siemens Home Appliances Roland Gerke (2006) estimated the profit margin to less than 3-4% by 2005. Although national and local governments may ensure Haier Group's overall profitability, this margin defines the bottom line compared to competitors such as *Whirlpool* who has around 6-8% profit margin.[121]

Haier Group has set up 15 manufacturing complexes, 30 overseas factories including industrial parks in the USA and a factory plant in Italy, eight design centres outside China and 58,800 sales agents worldwide. Haier Group has a workforce of 50,000 thereof 320 in the USA (Haier Group 2006b, 2006a). Haier Group's corporate goals for the future are to become a global top 3 white goods giant, a member of Fortune 500 before 2010, and a world-famous brand name such as *GE*, *Sony* or *Nike* (Haier Electronics Group 2005a: 2; Haier Group 2005b; Ling 2005: 94; Liu 2005).[122] In 2002 Haier USA president Jemal announced "We're looking to build a brand [...] We'll do it faster than Panasonic did" (quoted in Dolan/Hardy 2002).

Motives of global brand building
It is told that Haier Group's international brand strategy was born in the mid-1990s, when former group president and today's CEO Zhang Ruimin was disappointed with the market conditions in China. Price wars had led to shrinking profit margins in the home appliance industry. Haier's net profit margins dropped from 8.8% in 2000 to 5.4% in 2001, to 3.5% in the first six months of 2002 (Yi/Ye 2003: 149, 229; Haier Wenhua Zhongxin [Haier Cultural Centre] 2005: 57; Ling 2005: 99). In addition, Zhang had considered that China's entry into the WTO in 2001 would be more a chal-

---

[120] Haier washing machines had not been publicly-listed until end of 2004; thus it still belongs to 'other business segments' in figure 5-1.

[121] Due to restructuring processes, Electrolux, world's number two appliance maker, has currently a pretty weak profit margin of 4% which will likely be improved in near future (Gerke 2006).

[122] Target for 2005 has been to gain US sales of US$1 billion, probably including OEM (China View 2003; Ling 2005: 100).

lenge than an opportunity for Haier. He expected that profit margins would get worse, because of stronger competition from foreign multinationals in the domestic markets and critical anti-dumping regulations and non-trade barriers on the global markets (Yi/Ye 2003: 233). Zhang thought that the multinationals would have the same advantages of low cost as Chinese companies have in addition to their existing superior technology, as soon as they have established themselves in China (Gilmore/Dumont 2003: 75). To overcome these difficulties, Haier has thus targeted to establish international sources of innovation and R&D, overseas manufacturing facilities and the creation of a global brand: "If not developing a brand now, it could only become more difficult in future", Zhang concluded, "[…] in order to meet the challenge of the multinationals, Haier must become a multinational itself" (Yi/Ye 2003: 174; Haier Wenhua Zhongxin [Haier Cultural Centre] 2005: 57; also Ling 2005: 115). After being asked if Haier does not worry about the Chinese image of 'being cheap and low tech' in developed markets, CEO Zhang answered that Haier Group have chosen to enter international markets with its own brand exactly for the purpose to change the negative image of 'Made in China' products (Yi/Ye 2003: 198). "We have a dream. China should have world-famous brands on its own … letting the people of China hold their heads high in the world" (Haier slogan quoted in Ling 2005: 110).

Zhang's international initiative has also strongly been encouraged by the Chinese central and local governments. They has announced Haier as a "national champion" (Nolan 2001) and supported it by "priority access to capital, including interest-free loans and stock market flotation; export subsidies and political status; preferential policies including allocation of land and tax exemption" (Ling 2005: 56, 89). In 2001, Haier also got the approval to enter the domestic market for financial services, on condition that its going-international would be actively pursued (Liu/Li 2002: 701, 705). Since Haier is a collective enterprise, it has typically received more benefits from the local than from the national government. For instance, Qingdao city took pains in 2001 to receive the approval to organise an annual China International Electronics and Electrical Appliances Exhibitions (Ling 2005: 56).

To transfer the ambitions of an international brand into a market strategy, CEO Zhang announced a balanced country portfolio: one third manufactured and distributed in China, one third manufactured in China and distributed overseas, and one third manufactured and distributed in foreign countries (Gilmore/Dumont 2003: 63-64; Liu 2005). In the domestic market Haier considered a 25-30% market share for all types of home appliances as maximal target (Liu/Li 2002: 702). Whereas domestic sales and sales in emerging markets will primary involve Haier branded products, there is strong evidence that sales into developed markets are most likely dominated by OEM so far (compare to Ling 2005: 100). Reason is that Haier is still manufacturing a large amount of parts and appliances for global brands such as Whirlpool, Sanyo, LG, and Samsung by end of 2005. See also Haier's OEM product range at http://haiermarket.manufacturer.globalsources.com.

Strategic brand decisions when going-international

Market entry mode

Prior to mid-1990, Haier Group's international business was very small. In 1989 export sales were under US$700.000 (Ling 2005: 97). When competition in the domestic markets became fiercer, Haier accelerated exports and particularly sold OEM into developed markets (Yi/Ye 2003: 205). According to "market first, profit second", CEO Zhang found gaining large market share and cash flow much more important than the corporation's net profit margin at any stage (Yi/Ye 2003: 11, 104). In 1994, when Haier got suddenly the offer to sell refrigerators under own Haier brand name into the US market, Zhang took his chance to sell branded products besides OEM labels in overseas markets. Michael Jemal, at this time vice president of the import company 'Welbit Appliances' based in New York, was searching for a supplier of major appliances. As it is told, he found Haier by coincidence by a large billboard in a Chinese airport. Zhang and Jemal agreed to start with 150,000 compact refrigerators in the US market. In the end of 1994, Jemal sold 165,000 units and gained a market share of over 10%. Zhang rewarded him and granted exclusivity and the promise of a long-term relationship (Yi/Ye 2003: 205-209).

Based on the initial success in US, Haier Group formulated three phases to achieve its balanced country portfolio: phase one 'seeding', focus on revenues, but also first brand building activities through local sales agencies in foreign countries; phase two: 'rooting', increase of market shares and establishment of own manufacture plants in foreign countries; and phase three: 'harvesting', establishment of own local sales and R&D facilities in foreign countries in order to leverage the full range of local resources and brand building elements (Liu 2005; Haier Group 2006a). By Zhang's words "difficult things first, easier steps later" (Yi/Ye 2003: 90), he had planned to enter developed countries in the first place and emerging countries in the second place. He had the idea that once having established a competitive position in the difficult markets and having developed world-class technology and management skills, it would be pretty easy to conquer developing countries (Yi/Ye 2003: 188; Ling 2005: 98).

As table 5-11 reveals, Haier did not follow this strategy immediately. After the initial step into the US, Haier firstly set up 'Haier Middle East' to penetrate some emerging markets before investing further into the US and European markets in the end 1990s (similar Liu/Li 2002: 702).

Year	Country	Brand mode	Institutional mode	Name	Initial products
1992	Indonesia	OEM	JV	manufacturing plant with Sapporo Company	RF
1994	USA	Own brand	Sales alliance	Welbit Appliances, New York	RF
1997	Philippines	Own brand/OEM	JV	manufacturing plant with LKG Electric Company	RF, A/C
1997	Malaysia	Own brand/OEM	JV	Haier manufacturing plant	RF, A/C
1997	D, NL, I	Own brand	Export	External sales agencies	RF
1999	United Arab Emirates	Own brand	Greenfield	Haier Middle East Trading	RF, A/C, WM
1999	USA	Own brand	JV	Haier America Trading	RF, FR, A/C, W/C
1999	USA	Own brand	Greenfield	Haier Industrial Park Camden	RF
2000	Europe	Own brand	Greenfield	Haier Europe Trading, Italy	RF, A/C
2000	Bangladesh	Own brand/OEM	JV	manufacturing plant with Hayes Bangladesh Company	A/C, RF
2000	Iran	Own brand/OEM	JV	Haier manufacturing plant	RF, A/C, WM
2000	Vietnam	Own brand/OEM	n/a	Haier manufacturing plant	RF
2001	Pakistan	Own brand/OEM	Greenfield	Haier Industrial Park Pakistan	WM
2001	Italy	Own brand/OEM	M&A	RF plant of Meneghetti Equipment	RF
2001	USA	Own brand	Purchase	New HQs for Haier America	RF, FR, A/C, W/C
2002	Japan	Brand alliance	JV	Sanyo Electric Company (trading, manufacturing)	WM, RF
2002	Taiwan	Brand alliance	Alliance	Sampo Electric Company (trading, manufacturing)	TV, RF, A/C, WM
2002	Italy	Own brand	Greenfield	Haier A/C Trading Italy	A/C
2002	Spain	Own brand	Greenfield	Haier A/C Trading Spain	A/C
2003	Germany	Brand alliance	Alliance	Distribution through OBI	RF, FR
2003	UK	Own brand	Greenfield	Haier A/C Trading UK	A/C
2004	F, D, I, E	Own brand	Greenfield	Regional sales offices of Haier Europe Trading	TV, MP
2004	Italy, Germany	Own brand	Greenfield	Sales office Haier Electronics Europe, Italy	TV, MP
2004	Australia	Own brand	Greenfield	Sales office Haier Australia – HAEC	WM, RF, A/C, TV
2005	Russia	Own brand	Greenfield	Haier Russia Trading	TV, MP, A/C
2005	NZ	Own brand	Greenfield	Sales office Haier Appliances New Zealand	WM, RF, A/C, TV

RF - refrigerator	FR - freezer	MP - mobile phone	
A/C - air-conditioner	WM - washing machine	W/C - wine cellar	

Table 5-11. Haier's mode of market entry (own illustration of major steps)[123]

In 1999, Haier and US-distributor Jemal intensified activities in the US. They formed the joint venture 'Haier America Trading' in New York for

---

[123] Table refers to proven FDIs. It does not include countries which have been entered by pure export business. It is assumed that OEM is conducted in each of Haier's overseas factories, probably besides the Camden industrial park, USA. Compare illustration to Du (2003: 261).

US$1m and invested US$40m to build up a wholly-owned manufacturing facility in Camden, South Carolina, making Haier branded compact refrigerators. Reasons for the local factory are said to be reduction of costs, circumvention of anti-dumping laws and shipping from China, as well as the opportunity of selling Haier products under 'made in U.S.A.' stickers. In 2001, 'Haier America Trading' expanded and purchased for US$14.5m headquarters at 1356 Broadway, New York. There has been evidence that demonstration of corporate power and national pride had been major motives of this investment (Yi/Ye 2003: 216-217, 221; Economist 2004; also Gerke 2006).

In June 2005, Haier Group placed a bid for US appliance giant *Maytag*, firstly of US$1.28bn, later of US$2.25bn. Intention had been to make Haier Group to the third largest appliance maker in the world and the owner of an American brand. Haier finally withdrew the bid "because of the intervention of the US government" said Haier R&D director Liu Zhenyu (2005). The bid had made waves across all American society and politicians, fearing the sell-off of American assets and know-how, after Chinese *Lenovo* had already taken IBM's PC business. Finally, American *Whirlpool*, world's largest home appliance maker, acquired Maytag for US$2.7bn in August 2005 (Bremner/Roberts 2005; Dyer 2005; Giesen/Vougioukas 2005: 20). Roland Gerke (2006), president of Jiangsu Bosch and Siemens Home Appliances, commented that Haier's bid had probably mainly been driven by political rather than by business reasons. He assumed that Haier Group enjoyed the public attention as a kind of international promotional event, and has not intended to carry out a real take over at any stage. By end of 2005, Haier is planning to expand the manufacturing capacity in the Camden factory by organic growth. The aim is to invest into side-by-side refrigerators, large-capacity freezers and central-air-conditioning units in the USA within the next few years (Haier Group 2006a).

In Western Europe, Haier started launching its own brand name in 1997. Since they could not rely on a Haier loyal distributor such as Michael Jemal in the US, they had to find local sales agents on own initiatives. They finally started selling refrigerators in Germany, the Netherlands and Italy (Yi/Ye 2003: 198). In 2000, Haier expanded its European activities by founding 'Haier Europe Trading' with headquarters in Varese, Italy. Instead of the prior external sales agents, 'Haier Europe Trading' became in charge of distributing Haier branded white goods; they extended their focus onto seventeen European countries (Yi/Ye 2003: 199; Haier Europe

2006).[124] One year later, in 2001, Haier Group spent US$8m to purchase the Italian refrigerator plant belonging to Meneghetti Equipment Company, which was later renamed into 'Haier (Italy) Appliances'. The factory produces built-in refrigerators and freezers under 'Made in Italy' sticker primary for European markets (Liu/Li 2002: 702). There is evidence that besides Haier branded products the factory also makes OEM items.

Whereas in the US, Haier has expanded its product portfolio under the organisation of 'Haier America Trading', Haier established additional regional 'Haier Air-Conditioning (A/C) Trading' subsidiaries in Italy and Spain in 2002, and in the UK in 2003. In addition, Haier entered the German kitchen furniture and appliance market by a brand alliance with *OBI*, Germany's largest retail chain in the Do-it-yourself sector in 2003. Haier already knows OBI from a sales partnership in China: OBI and Haier Group had jointly entered the Chinese retail market in 2002 (Haier Group 2006b). In 2004, Haier Europe Trading extended its structure of white goods' distribution and opened up national offices in the major countries France, Germany, Italy and Spain (Haier Europe 2006). In addition to white goods and air-conditioners, Haier has been going to launch A/V businesses and mobile phones through Western Europe since 2004. They established a new European sales subsidiary with 'Haier Electronics Europe' headquartered in Vimercate, Italy and two sales offices in Germany and Italy (Haier Group 2006b).[125] By 2006 it is reported that Haier Group is negotiating with Eastern European countries and potential joint venture partners to set up a new factory for refrigerators and kitchen appliances in Eastern Europe which should also provide Western European markets with products (Mysan.de 2005).

After more than ten years of branded business activities in developed markets such as the USA, Haier Group's market entry mode can be characterised as follows: Haier has primarily entered US and WE markets by its own Haier brand and organic growth. In order to overcome lacks in market know-how, Haier has searched for partnerships and alliances with locally established distributors and retail brands (compare to conclusions of Liu/Li 2002: 703). For the US market, Haier has relied on the market expert Michael Jemal and his established distribution networks. In Western Europe, Haier started leveraging its relationship to Germany's *OBI*. In future, however, it is also possible that Haier will place a second bid for a leading

---

[124] The seventeen European countries are UK, Ireland, Germany, the Netherlands, Belgium, France, Luxembourg, Greece, Spain, Portugal, Switzerland, Austria, Italy, Denmark, Norway, Finland and Sweden.

[125] See for an overview about Haier subsidiaries and offices in Western Europe also section 'brand organisation'.

brand such as *Maytag* to grow faster and to meet the industry requirement of a well-established local brand.

Brand positioning

In the domestic market, 海尔 *Haier* is China's most valuable and leading consumer brand. It is known for innovative, personalised and high-quality product designs and a reliable after-sales service (e.g., Gilmore/Dumont 2003: 67; Ling 2005: 109; Yang 2005: 134). Haier Group primary positions themselves as an internationally leading brand of Chinese origin as seen in the advertisements of figure 5-3 (also Gerke 2006). Haier Group's president Yang Mianmian summed up: "Haier brand evolution is like that: refrigerator brand – household appliance brand – Chinese brand – global brand. The message of the change is: high product quality – good service – individuality – high speed" (own translation of Haier Wenhua Zhongxin [Haier Cultural Centre] 2005: 108).

Fig. 5-3. National advertising promoting Haier's going-international in 2005 (OgilvyOne Worldwide 2006: 15-16)

Whereas Chinese consumers believe in Haier Group's international competence, its presence in the US and WE markets is not such strong so far. Despite of more than 10 years of market experience, Haier brand is mainly known for niche markets and low priced refrigerators in the US so far. When having entered both US and WE markets in the mid-1990s, Haier intended to focus on one product at a time, the same way Haier had started in its early Chinese days. But in contrast to the Chinese market,

CEO Zhang tried to begin with niche markets and categories in which local competitors would be pretty weak (Yi/Ye 2003: 214). The goal has
been to address local market needs and being perceived as a local brand.
Similar to the domestic market, Zhang's long-term approach has been to
develop Haier into a brand of high-quality and a leader for market and
consumer trends (Gilmore/Dumont 2003: 63-64). Haier R&D director Liu
Zhenyu (2005) further specified Haier's overall brand positioning and
stressed that customers like the new and hate the old. He proudly explained
that Haier would address this overall customer psychology, since they are
more innovative and more personalised than their competitors: "We have
the smallest washing machine, the smallest freezer and the most stylish
wine cellars" (own translation). Price should thus not be the selling argument of Haier branded products in national and overseas markets (Yi/Ye
2003: 188, 203).

In the US market, Haier carried out its strategy of niche markets and of
continuous expansion of the product portfolio. In 1994 Haier started with
the distribution of three models of compact refrigerators. They have been
positioned for student apartments and offices, as being smaller and less
expensive than standard-sized refrigerators (Biers 2001: 52). The total
market for that type of appliances was less than 1.5 million units at this
time and the target was to achieve 10% market share. As expected from
Zhang, Haier's US competitors did not pay much attention to the segment
of compact refrigerators and left the business to Haier Group. Based on the
success in compact refrigerators, Haier Group expanded its product portfolio onto wine cellars, freezers and domestic air-conditioners in 1999
(Yi/Ye 2003: 206, 214-215).

Although almost the full Haier product range is available in the US by
2006,[126] compact refrigerators and wine-cellars still make up the major part
of Haier US-revenues. They are market leaders and hold about 50% volume shares in both markets (Dolan 2004; Haier America 2006). In contrast
to both niche markets, global competition is huge in the US-standard white
goods and consumer electronics segments. Although Haier Group insists
that they are going to win market shares by innovative designs, and reliable services and quality, the factor 'price' is a key selling argument
against the global and well-established competitors from the US and
Europe (Yi/Ye 2003: 210-211; Zeng/Williamson 2004: 41; Euromonitor
2006). An US store manager confirmed that Haier Group is "a company
that largely competes on price" (Biers 2001: 53). See also figure 5-4:

---

[126] Including large-size refrigerators, washing machines, audio-video and mobile
phones; only Haier laptops and desktop computers are not yet launched by beginning of 2006.

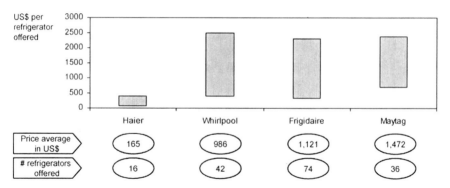

Fig. 5-4. Haier brand's price position in comparison to three US-brands in the US refrigerator market in US$ in February 2006 (company websites)[127]

Within the low price segment, however, general manager of Haier Group's factory in Camden Tymkiw expected competitive advantages because of Haier's 'Made in U.S.A.' stickers: "[…] the label of origin is still an important factor for some U.S. consumers choosing between products of similar product and price. For consumers now, I think 'Made in the U.S.A.' is a tie-breaker" (Biers 2001: 54). In 2005 Haier brand achieved 1.2% volume share in large kitchen appliances, and 6.5% market share in refrigeration in 2003 (table 5-12).

In contrast to the US market and overall strategy, Haier entered the Western European markets not by niche markets, but by highly competitive and more standard business segments. For instance, in France, Italy, Spain and the UK, Haier first launched its air conditioners. In Germany, Haier started with standard-sized refrigerators (Liu/Li 2002: 703). As market shares in the German refrigerator market are settled and dominated by domestic players such as *Bosch-Siemens*, managing director of MediaSaturn Holding Dr. Steffen Stremme (2005) had to confirm that Haier Group is still heavily struggling in the market. They are forced to offer its branded appliances at low prices, and have not yet built strong brand awareness (chap 3.2.2.2, Gerke 2006). See also table 5-12 as an indicator.

Haier Group's consumer electronics are in a similar situation in Western Europe. Even though officially started in 2004, Haier Group delayed launching their TV sets, for instance, in Germany several times and skipped the launching of mobile phones in 2005 completely (Wurm 2005).

---

[127] Refrigerator prices were taken from USA company websites in the internet on 23rd February 2006; Haier refrigerators prices are taken from Wal-Mart (US-prices), as Wal-Mart is Haier Group's most important distribution channel (Yi/Ye 2003: 212-213; Euromonitor 2006).

As president of Jiangsu Bosch and Siemens Home Appliance, Roland Gerke, commented (2006), Haier Group has difficulties to meet the European product regulations such as the environmental protection laws (also Ling 2005: 83). Despite of the delays, Haier Electronics Europe however remains confident. In 2005 they announced to become a top 3 brand name of LCD and plasma flat screens in Europe till 2008 (Heise.de 2005).

	Large kitchen	Cooking	Cooling	Dish washers	Freezers	Microwave ovens	Washing machines	Domestic air-cons
Germany[2]	0.002	0.001	0.602	0.042	1.099	0.083	0.002	n/a
France	<0.2	n/a	n/a	n/a	n/a	n/a	n/a	n/a
Italy	0.6	narrow[5]	narrow[5]	narrow[5]	narrow[5]	narrow[5]	narrow[5]	narrow[4]
Spain	<0.1	narrow[5]	narrow[5]	narrow[5]	narrow[5]	narrow[5]	narrow[5]	1.83[3]
UK	1.1	narrow[5]	1.8[1]	narrow[5]	1.8[1]	narrow[5]	narrow[5]	n/a
USA	1.2	narrow[5]	6.5[1]	narrow[5]	6.5[1]	narrow[5]	narrow[5]	n/a

(1)   2003; one figure for cooling and freezers (=refrigeration)
(2)   Share of retail value 2005 , source: GFK panel for major domestic appliances Feb 2005 – Nov 2005
(3)   Share of retail value 2005, source: Alimarket
(4)   Haier not among top 12 brands in April 2006, source: Altroconsumo
(5)   Haier not among Euromonitor's listed brand names

Table 5-12. Haier brand presence in white goods and air-conditioning in US and WE markets in % of retail volume in 2005 (Euromonitor 2006)

Brand innovations

Liu Zhenyu (2005), head of Haier Group R&D department, pointed out in an interview that Haier Group believes that a strong brand is mainly created by customer satisfaction. Thus, he said, Haier has concentrated most corporate efforts on product quality, customer understanding, and innovation speed. For instance, Haier Group has improved its production processes by introducing modern management systems like Japan's 'zero tolerance error' and 'Six Sigma' over the years as well as CEO Zhang's own management concept of OEC (overall every day control) which shall ensure quality and employees' commitment (Yi/Ye 2003: 29, 39). However, Roland Gerke (2006), questioned how advanced Haier Group really is. Though Haier set up a Consulting and Certification Centre devoted to getting various quality certifications to access international markets such as the ISO 9001, ISO 14001, the American Underwriters Laboratories, the French CSA, and the European GS, VDE and EMC (Yi/Ye 2003: 33-34, 202, 237; Ling 2005: 99), he said that Haier has still difficulties to pass European requirements of recycling and has, for instance, not yet dealt with cost efficiency measures such as combinable assembly or platform manufacturing.[128]

Whereas one can argue about Haier Group's performance in the organisation of production processes, Haier's strength of customer-tailored product innovations is widely recognised (e.g., Gerke 2006). They gather consumer needs in 45 domestic information centres and regular feedback processes with sales managers, after-sales services and dealers along slogans like 'Never say no to a market' or 'Watch the market and create superior quality'. Haier R&D division also sends out their own designers into the market to learn from consumer expectations directly (Gilmore/Dumont 2003: 66; also Ling 2005: 110; Liu 2005). Though Haier has a deep knowledge of Chinese customer needs, they had only a limited understanding for local needs when they entered the US and Western European markets in the mid-1990s. For instance in the US, they heavily relied on the experience and research input of Haier America president Michael Jemal. In Western Europe, Haier had mainly been dependent on information from their local dealers and sales agents (Liu 2005). By end of 2005 however, Haier R&D director Liu Zhenyu (2005) is quite confident that Haier Group has developed deep insights into Western European and US customers too. Haier established 16 information centres around the world and a global analysis centre for receiving and evaluating customer, competitor and market information. Haier also established eight design centres in the USA, Canada, Japan (2), South Korea, France, the Netherlands and Germany, and decided on regular market visits of their designers, similar to the approach in China.

As a consequence of going-international, increasing competition and fast changing market needs, Liu Zhenyu (2005) explained that Haier Group has also continuously raised its R&D spends onto 6% of its global revenues till 2005, resulting in 5469 domestic patents or on average 1.2 new products and 2.3 patents every day (Liu/Li 2002: 704; Liu 2005). See also figure 5-5. Haier has also invested in close connections with more than 120 domestic universities and research institutions to overcome the shortage of own talent available (Ling 2005: 118). Liu Zhenyu (2005) gave reasons and explained that innovations have two sides of the same coin: If Haier is innovative, they risk to be imitated by Chinese piracies, but they are more competitive against global players. If Haier were not innovative, their international competitors would fear that Haier could copy them, and as a pirate, Haier would not be allowed to enter developed markets due to patent rights. He stressed that in the case Haier has own patents, their global competitors have to be careful not to violate Chinese patent rights

---

[128] Compare to section 'brand positioning'.

when entering the Chinese market. However, despite of increasing R&D efforts, Haier is still lacking technology patents in the developed markets. Liu and Li (2002: 704) thus concluded that Haier "has remained highly dependent on foreign key components and technologies. These include high-performance electro-motors, compressors, controllers, magnetrons, and sensors".

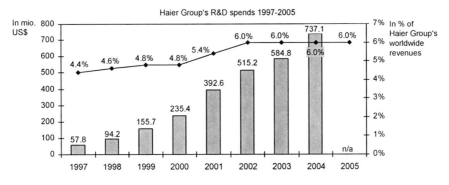

Fig. 5-5. Haier Group's R&D expenditure 1997-2005 (based on Liu/Li 2002: 704; Liu 2005)[129]

As Haier Group has fully been aware of this weakness from early days onwards, they have continuously formed partnerships to absorb advanced technologies from global players. In the high-tech sectors, these are particularly partnerships with Microsoft (computer software), CCT (mobile phones), LG and Philips (digital television), Toshiba, Lucent Technologies and Ericsson (Bluetooth and GSM technologies), Fujitsu and Hitachi (plasma television) (Yi/Ye 2003: 201; Ling 2005: 95, 118; Haier Group 2006a; Hoover's online 2006). "First we observe and digest the new methods, then we imitate them. In the end, we understand them well enough to design them independently" (Haier quoted in Ling 2005: 115). In addition to partnerships, CEO Zhang concluded that Haier can only compete against multinationals' superior technology by higher speed in product development and a quicker innovation-to-market time. It is told that the re-invention of the chest freezer for the American market is a prominent example for Haier's fast product development. According to own figures, Haier only needed seventeen hours from the blueprinted variant, created by

---

[129] R&D spends 1997-2000 base on Liu/Li (2002: 704), 2002 on Yi/Ye (2003: 58), 2005 on Haier interview. (Liu 2005) Figures for 2001 and 2004 are extrapolations.

America's president Michael Jemal, to the prototype product (Yi/Ye 2003: 215-216; similar Ling 2005: 109).[130]

Though Haier's inventions are manifold and widely recognised, it is to question, if Haier can manage its manufacturing complexity of product variants in the long-term run efficiently (compare to "lack of focus" in Economist 2004; Economist 2005a). Moreover, it might be difficult to remain competitive in the developed markets without own advanced technology patents. License fees might increase and certain cutting-age technologies might not to be licensed at all.

Operative brand decisions when going-international

Branding

Haier Group decided on the brand name 海尔 *Haier* in 1992. The joint venture contract with German Liebherr had run out in 1991 and CEO Zhang was not satisfied with the corporate name 琴岛青岛海尔 'Qindao Qingdao Haier Group' which they had established between 1991 and 1992.[131] At this time, Haier's international activities were few and under OEM model. Although some experts believe that international market aspects had already been included in the brand name decision (Yi/Ye 2003: 32-33), this could be questioned. There is evidence that 海尔 *Haier* corporate name was more likely chosen by the following four reasons: First, *Haier* 海尔 brand name kept some brand awareness and brand reputation of the prior refrigerator product name 琴岛利勃海尔 'Qindao-Liebherr ' which was quite popular among consumers in China at that time. Second, the corporate brand name was simpler and more user-friendly than 琴岛青岛海尔 'Qindao Qingdao Haier Group', and offered a platform for blanket family names under the corporate *Haier* umbrella. CEO Zhang said Haier had modelled its brand architecture on other multinational appliance companies such as GE or Siemens. Third, the Chinese characters 海尔 had positive connotations in terms of Chinese traditional values. 海尔 means 'like a sea', endless and living. Same pronunciation 'haier', but written 孩儿, means 'brothers' and 'lots of sons'. And fourth, 海尔 *Haier* corporate name was chosen to demonstrate its independence as a Chinese appliance maker from its German bonds (Yi/Ye 2003: 32-33; also Ding/Zheng 2005: 63; Liu 2005).

---

[130] Instead of the traditional style of chest freezer providing an uneasy access to frozen items at the bottom, Haier freezer's top half can be accessed through a conventional top-opening lid and the lower half by a pull-out drawer.

[131] Qindao is the ancient name of today's city Qingdao.

When Haier Group then started using its brand name in the US in 1994 and formulated its international brand strategy in the end 1990s, Haier was probably very pleased that *Haier* brand name also suits international markets. As Haier is pronounced like 'higher' in English language, they only had to eliminate the Chinese characters from logos and packages. A Haier employee proudly explained that Haier does not sound Chinese (Yi/Ye 2003: 9) which is confirmed by the following episode: "Somewhere in [… an] American wholesale store, […] we asked about [Haier] origin, and were told by a young salesperson, a student […] that Haier was a brand the store has recently started to carry. 'Maybe a German brand?' the salesperson offered" (Yi/Ye 2003: 2). By May 2006, Haier brand name is registered in China, Germany, France and Russia, but interestingly not in the USA so far (WIPO 2006). Figure 5-6 sums up Haier's path to a global brand name:

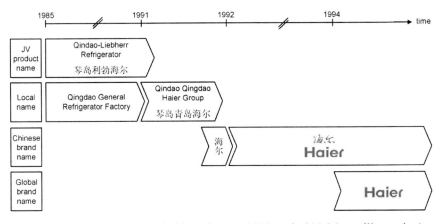

Fig. 5-6. Haier's path to a global brand name 1985-early 2006 (own illustration)

Besides the brand name, which is written in bold letters of red, pink, or purple colour, Haier branding also includes a brand visual as seen in figure 5-7. Haier has introduced the two little "Haier Brothers" in the mid-1980s. The Haier brothers are two boys - one Chinese and one German, symbolising the fact that Haier started business with technology investment from the German company Liebherr and symbolising the meaning of 'hai er' in terms of 'brothers'. They typically held an ice-cream between them, again symbolising the fact that Haier started business with manufacturing refrigerators. To enhance brand image, the two little brothers has been used to explain each other the values of Haier products during advertising spots on Chinese TV (Gilmore/Dumont 2003: 72; Yi/Ye 2003: 32; Liu 2005). Later, Haier created a cartoon series telling mystical adventures around the

Haier brothers and their friends, which have made them famous in China. As Access Asia (2002: 18-19) reported, "the cartoon series has not only been a commercial success in its own right, but has done wonders for the credibility of the Group's brand and corporate image. This has been one of the most shining examples of creative marketing to have come out of China in recent years, and is indicative of the creativity of the Group's management."

Fig. 5-7. Haier brand visual "The Haier Brothers" in 2006 (own photos)

Brand communication

In the domestic market, Haier has promoted its corporate identity and brand values since 1984. Besides 'The Haier Brothers' and advertisements on Haier's going-international, Haier has built its brand image by the slogan 真诚到永远 'zhencheng dao yongyuan' ('Sincere and forever'), addressing customers' endless demand and Haier's trustworthiness (Yang 2005: 134). According to own figures, Haier Group spends on average 5% of its worldwide revenues on marketing; this would have been US$614.3m in 2004. Haier R&D director Liu Zhenyu (2005) explained that the budget is much higher in international markets as Haier brand is not much known in Western Europe and the US. According to Yi/Ye (2003: 213), the overall US-advertising budget had been 6% of American sales or less than US$10m in 2001.

In the beginning, when Haier Group had just entered the US market, they had concentrated brand communication on trade buyers and distributors. Haier attended several trade shows, such as the Consumer Electronics Show (CES) in Las Vegas, the House Wares Show, and the Kitchen/Bath Industry Show. End-consumer marketing was little and low-budgeted. For instance, Haier started advertising on the luggage carts at New York's JFK airport. Rent and design cost about US$200,000 a year (Yi/Ye 2003: 213).

Since 2001, however, Haier America has increased its end-customer marketing. In Arkansas, where Wal-Mart is located, and in South Carolina, where Haier has a factory, Haier put up billboards. In 2001, a TV spot promoting a Michael Jordan film was also tied up with Haier's new DVD players (Biers 2001: 53). The current slogan of Haier advertisements in the US is 'What the world comes home to'. It is assumed that Haier may intend to address its large product portfolio and increasing integration into US-households by this slogan (Haier Group 2006a). According to Gilmore/Dumont (2003: 72), Haier Group had also plans in 2003 to debut the carton series 'The Haier brothers' on a US TV channel, after it was successfully televised to a test audience of American children in cooperation with AOL-Time Warner Co.'s cartoon network, the largest cartoon channel in the US (Access Asia 2002: 18).

Similar to the US market, Haier started communication into Western Europe with selected trade shows and fairs. Haier firstly participated in the Cologne Appliance Exhibition 1997 and 1999. Haier has then intensified presence since 2000, and attended the Cologne Appliance Exhibition (2001, 2004), the HomeTech exhibition in Berlin, Milan's ExpoComfort Fair, the Electrical Retailing Show in UK, Germany's MOW Fair, and the Exhibition for Hotel Consumables and Daily Necessities Britain in London in 2003. In contrast to the US market, however, Haier has already spent a certain amount of money in several end-consumer marketing activities from the beginning onwards. According to Yi/Ye (2003: 200) Haier launched a corporate-image campaign promoting Haier's high-quality and design in the UK in 2000. Additionally, Haier has set up eye-catching pink-cube displays in retail outlets throughout Europe. At the Cologne Appliance Exhibition in 2001, Haier also invested in advertising to be positioned side-by-side to the German brand *Miele* at the entrance door. In Paris, Haier established neon advertising on the top of a building and in Milan Haier erected an advertisement billboard by the expressway near Malpensa Airport (Yi/Ye 2003: 200; Haier Group 2006b).

Even though Yi/Ye (2003: 200) announced that Haier doubled the European budget for advertising and promotion in 2002,[132] it is to comment that a clear communication strategy has not yet become apparent. Haier has rather invested sporadically and in many different end-consumer activities across several Western European countries. For instance, Haier started promotions into the French market by the 'Haier Train'. The Haier train was established in collaboration with the Chinese embassy and Chinese Tourist Agency in order to introduce Haier products and the Chinese

---

[132] There are no details about Haier's current European marketing budget available.

culture to French citizens. The train was composed of seven wagons and toured around France for 20 days. It started in Paris and stopped at 11 large and medium-sized cities such as Lille, Strasbourg, Lyon and Marseille, for one to three days. Final station was Rennes. At each stop, visitors could win prizes like a tour to China or a Haier appliance (Yi/Ye 2003: 202). In 2005, Haier also increased activities in Spain. Haier erected an advertisement billboard at the Santiago Bernabeu stadium in Madrid, the home football field of Real Madrid and one of the 'holy palaces' of football games in Europe (Haier Group 2006a). By 2006, brand messages of Haier advertisements in Western Europe are 'Haier and Higher', 'Head held high' and most recently 'Haier. Believe it' (DTK Computer 2006; Haier Group 2006b, 2006a), playing with the word game Haier and higher.

Due to Haier's sporadic brand communication, market experts typically consider its impact on end-consumers in WE markets as marginal (e.g., Frank 2005: 4; Gerke 2006). On the other hand, the unrepresentative online survey among 82 Germans acknowledged Haier a score of 27% unaided brand awareness in 2006 (chap 3, figure 3-19), a score which is quite significant. Given that this brand awareness is not a result of own brand building activities, it may then come from the fact that currently China and Chinese companies are subject in many media in Western Europe, and are discussed with respect to production shifts and low labour cost advantages.

Another reason may be that Haier has also made efforts at the global marketing level. Since January 2004, Haier sponsors the Australian basketball team 'Melbourne (Haier) Tigers'. The sponsorship is reported to be the first foreign sports event that a Chinese company has ever undertaken (Haier Group 2006b; Hoover's online 2006). In addition, Haier Group was elected by the Olympic committee as an official Beijing 2008 Sponsor in the category of white goods for the 2008 Beijing Olympic Games in August 2005 (Haier Group 2005c). Though one can argue, if a national sponsorship which is restricted to domestic activities only and is therefore inferior to the category of Worldwide Olympic Partners (figure 3-21), can contribute to building a global famous brand (China Economic Review 2006: 39), Haier R&D director Liu Zhenyu is optimistic. He expects that the sponsorship will increase the national and worldwide brand awareness and will enhance the Haier brand image: "First, we have the chance to prove the world that we are both a Chinese brand and a global brand. And second, we can demonstrate public welfare and corporate governance" (own translation of Liu 2005). Concretely, the sponsorship allows Haier to immediately promote and sell products in China until the end of the Games in 2008 under the Haier-Beijing Olympic label as seen in figure 5-8. Moreover, Haier may receive special promotional opportunities during the Games on TV and within sport arenas.

Fig. 5-8. Haier Olympic logo on a billboard in Shanghai in 2005 (own photo)

Brand distribution

Haier Group generally described the access into foreign distribution networks as the most challenging aspect of its going-international (e.g., Liu
2005). Whereas in China Haier products are sold in all major cities and
appliances chains, and Haier can even force its customers to prepay for
their customised orders (Yi/Ye 2003: 118-119; Liu 2005), Haier is a new-
comer in the US and WE markets. Yi/Ye (2003: 224) explained that Haier
had the negative example of Taiwan's *Acer* in mind when they defined
their own distribution strategy for the US market in 1999. Acer is Taiwan's
leading PC vendor and a well established brand in many parts of Asia.
Acer entered the US market in the 1980s. At its peak, the company's US
share was 5.4% in late 1995, but in 2001, Acer had to retreat from the US
market because of dwindling sales and weak distribution networks at both
the retail chain and mass outlet levels. To learn from them, Haier thus decided on an intensive distribution approach through large volume retailers
that would get the products "into as many markets as possible, and expand
distribution channels, especially in the chains, where sales were considered
significant" (Yi/Ye 2003: 209; Ling 2005: 99).

Although the strategy was clear, Haier Group admitted that it has been
quite hard to achieve. It is reported that besides competitive prices and
product differentiation, in particular patience and perseverance were
needed to convince US retail stores to put Haier brands on their shelves.

The most famous retailer that Haier could convince is American *Wal-Mart*. According to Haier America's president Jemal, it was nothing but regular phone calls, even though "it took us a whole year just to get an appointment".[133] Finally in July 1999, Haier Group got an appointment to show their room air-conditioners. After quality checks and a visit of Wal-Mart managers at Haier manufacturing facilities in Qingdao, Wal-Mart placed an initial order of 50,000 air-conditioners. In the following year Wal-Mart doubled the order and in 2002 the total already increased to 400,000 units, including compact refrigerators, washing machines and air-conditioners (Yi/Ye 2003: 212-213). By 2002, Haier products were also sold by Lowe's, Best Buy, Home Depot, Office Depot, Target, Fortunoff, Menards, Bed bath & Beyond, BJ's, Fry's, ABC, BrandsMart and by over 7,000 independent stores. By 2006, Haier products are distributed by nine of the top 10 chain stores in the US (Yi/Ye 2003: 223; Haier Group 2006a). Due to the fact that Haier only enjoys a volume share of 1.2% in the US market in 2005 (Euromonitor 2006), there is evidence that the retailers, except Wal-Mart, are mainly selling Haier manufactured OEM labels instead of Haier branded products.

In Western Europe, Haier's distribution approach was probably the same as the approach in the US, targeting mass markets and large volume retailers. One of Haier manager Liu Zhanjie (2005) explained that Haier had a lot of trouble in the beginning to find local sales companies. Finally, they started with twelve import agents in the countries Germany, the Netherlands and Italy in 1997. Haier CEO Zhang had set the following directive: "Our goal is to build a global brand name. Any distributor who shares our goals and promotes our brand-name products along that line is eligible" (quoted in Yi/Ye 2003: 198). Haier planned to attract potential retailers by an additional profit margin. Among the developed markets, Haier described Germany as the toughest market, as the distributors were arguing whether a Chinese brand would actually be accepted into the German market, since the Japanese refrigerators had not yet been successful (Yi/Ye 2003: 189). Haier requested a blind test in order to prove quality towards the German distributors. It is reported that the result was a 9^+ which would have placed Haier products on the same high quality level as other major brands in Germany. Although Haier R&D director Liu Zhenyu (2005) commented that after the test Haier refrigerators have gradually been ac-

---

[133] There are lot of rumours about Haier's access into Wal-Mart in the yellow press. In the conducted interviews, it could not be confirmed that Haier got in contact with Wal-Mart by putting a large neon billboard directly in front of the office window of Wal-Mart's chief buyer. According to the rumour, the buyer was impressed by the billboard and asked for the unknown company behind it.

cepted in the market, it is to note that market shares remain narrow in Germany in 2005 (table 5-12).

In contrast to the set distribution approach and probably a reason for the narrow market shares, Haier-branded products are mainly sold by several independent specialist retailers in WE markets so far. Managing director of Haier Europe Casilli tried to find reasons and explained in 2002: "In big stores we would simply be one of the many products available, whereas in small outlets, the specialist staff are able to underline our unique characteristics" (Yi/Ye 2003: 203). The assumption that Haier had probably tried to also obtain listings in Europe's large volume retail stores at all stages is also supported by Göttgens (2005). He found that some Haier refrigerators were sold in few German electronic discounters in 2006 and that Haier kitchen equipment started cooperating with Germany's do-it-yourself chain, OBI. Managing director of Germany's leading electronic retailer MediaSaturn Holding, Dr. Steffen Stremme (2005) also confirmed Haier's ambitions: "We have sold some promotional offers of Haier-branded washing machines, but we have not planned any permanent listings so far" (own translation).

Brand organisation

Haier Group's organisation has originated with Haier Group CEO Zhang Ruimin, an economic engineer and former bureaucrat of the Qingdao municipal government (China View 2003; Ling 2005: 108). In the early days, Zhang was mainly influenced and inspired by Confucius' and Sun Tzu's principles.[134] In the 1990s, he studied Western management styles of leading CEOs as those of the General Electric's CEO Jack Welsh (Gilmore/Dumont 2003: 73). It is reported that Zhang has led his employees by strong guidance and self-discipline and a mixture of fear and reward: "The manager must lead by example, while the employee must follow and excel" (Yi/Ye 2003: 94); "any Haier manager who is not head over heels in love with Zhang's thinking risks being marginalized or relegated" (Yi/Ye 2003: 128). It is said that despite of constant government involvement in the Haier collective, Zhang has enjoyed a high level of

---

[134] The name of Sun Tzu is known due to the work of 'The Art of War', covering sophisticated treatise on philosophy, logistics, espionage, strategy and tactics. The core text was probably written during a time of expanding feudal conflicts early in the Warring States period (c.453–221 B.C.). This work has deeply influenced Chinese, Vietnamese, and Japanese military thinking and has enjoyed growing popularity among businessmen. It stresses the unpredictability of battle, the importance of deception and surprise, the close relationship between politics and military policy, and the high costs of war. The best battle, Sun Tzu says, is the battle that is won without being fought (Columbia Encyclopaedia).

managerial independence and has utilised government resources according to his needs: "In fact, the more successful Haier has become, the more political status could obtain higher levels of governments, and the more independence it receives from the municipal government" (Ling 2005: 114).

Facing the challenges brought by electronic commerce and China's entry into the WTO, Zhang decided to modernise Haier Group and introduced a management restructuring program in 1998 (Haier Group 2006b). The big goal has been to achieve consistent profitability across all operations, while transforming the organisation from a domestic manufacturing company into an international service provider (Ling 2005: 103). Zhang launched the Haier 'Market-Chain System Practice' in order to minimise costs and inventory by resource integration and just-in-time-concepts (appendix 4). The concept intended to reinforce individual accountability and market focus. Moreover, the re-organisation has involved centralisation of management responsibility, and a switch from a profit centre organisation to a more functional organisation structure. Zhang set up four Promoting General Business departments (overseas, transport, products, capital) in order to separate the sectors finance, purchases and sales from the pure production and R&D processes (Ling 2005: 106-107; Haier Group 2006b).[135]

By end of 2005, Haier Group is a complex, diversified conglomerate. Complicated ownership structures, non-transparent relationships to different governmental entities and hundreds of different subsidies make it difficult to understand (Ling 2005: 122-123).[136] Figure 5-9 is therefore a simplification of reality and focuses on brand related structures with respect to US and Western European markets.[137]

---

[135] See for details about Haier's reorganisation Yi/Ye (2003: 139-162), Ling Liu (2005: 102-108), Gu (2002: 61-102) and Denison (2001).

[136] In 2004, main shareholders of the listed entity 'Qingdao Haier Ltd.' were the Qingdao Haier Investment and Development Co. Ltd. (29.945%), Haier Group Corporation (12.00%), Qingdao Collective Industry Association, a non-governmental organisation (1.651%), and several Chinese banks such as the China Construction Bank, Developing Bank and Industrial Bank (Qingdao Haier Dian Bingxiang [Qingdao Haier Refrigeration] 2006: 8-9). Main shareholders of 'Haier Electronics Group' were Qingdao Haier Collective Asset Management Association, Haier Group Corporation, Qingdao Haier Investment and Development Co. Ltd., Qingdao Haier Group Holdings (BVI) Ltd. and CCT Telecom Holdings Ltd. (Haier Electronics Group 2005b: 31).

[137] Illustration bases on Haier interviews, company material and secondary literature. It does not present ownership structures, full range of Haier departments, corporate functions and sales departments of other overseas markets except USA and Western Europe.

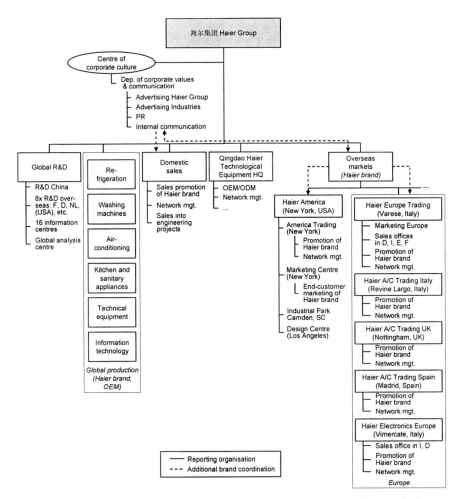

Fig. 5-9. Haier global brand organisation in December 2005 (own illustration)

The department 企业价值观统一处 ('corporate values & communication') is in charge of execution and control of any corporate values, and the internal and external voice of the group. This includes PR activities as well as corporate and product advertising. In weekly meetings, Haier Group's chairman, president and vice presidents define and adapt communication guidelines, including strict and identical brand guidelines, and brand control mechanisms for all domestic sales. OgilvyOne Worldwide Group account director from Beijing Zhang Ying (2006) said that this brand management structure is said to be one of the best in class practices among Chinese companies. Only Lenovo and TCL would have similar sophisticated organisation structures.

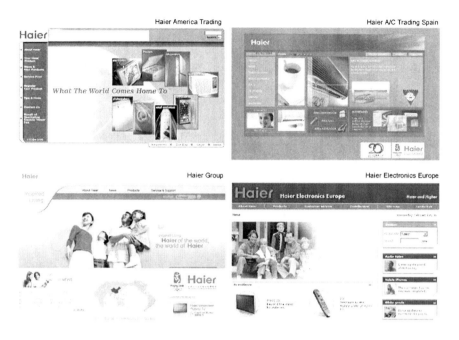

Fig. 5-10. Haier's localised company websites in February 2006 (own screenshots)

Whereas domestic brand management may be sophisticated and conducted at the top management level, Haier manager Liu Zhanjie (2005) admitted that in international markets, the Haier brand approach can vary, since Haier overseas sales centres could manage the brand, and adequate distribution channels and marketing execution very independently. He said that they typically align their brand approach towards their specific market requirements such as local competitors and local consumers. He stressed that they do not have to report every detail to CEO Zhang; he would care about the performance rather than about the method. As a consequence of decentralisation, Haier Group nowadays has a pretty differentiated and localised brand appearance across the markets in the US, WE and China. Whereas the Haier logo remains nearly identical, corporate colours and designs are not standardised, as seen in figure 5-10.[138] With the sponsorship of the 2008 Beijing Olympic Games, it may however become necessary to align and standardise the brand approach at least in terms of brand visuals

---

[138] See also sections 'brand communication' and 'brand distribution' for localised marketing activities.

and slogans, in order to create global spillover effects instead of consumer confusion and brand dilution.[139]

In addition, it is to note that figure 5-9 reveals a pretty complex sales and marketing organisation within the region Western Europe. Whereas in the US the unit 'Haier America' is responsible for all functions and sells the full product portfolio under one roof, Haier had established a bunch of different sales offices in Western Europe: Haier Europe Trading is based in Italy, has four regional offices in Italy, Germany, France and Spain and sells Haier white goods into Europe. Haier Electronics Europe is in charge for Haier audio-video and mobile phones and set up regional offices in Germany and Italy (Wurm 2005). Haier A/C Trading sells Haier air-conditioners through separate subsidiaries in Spain, Italy and the UK (Haier Europe 2006). As a result, it remains non-transparent which subsidiary, for instance, is responsible for supra-regional distribution channels and potential cross-border brand communication activities. It is assumed that 'Haier European Trading' may be in charge of such key-accounts and brand building activities, since the unit was Haier's first office and is thus probably considered its main office in Western Europe. Another possibility would be that its sales offices in the countries are in charge for those key-accounts that are headquartered in the same home country, e.g. France for *Carrefour*, and Germany for *Metro Group*.

To discuss reasons for such a complex organisation structure in Western Europe, one possible reason might be the lack of experienced Haier managers and loyal sales partners, as Haier had found in Michael Jemal for the US market. Jemal is considered a Haier role model: energetic, reliable and, as loyal to CEO Zhang, with significant management autonomy. It is told that Jemal started the Haier office in the US with seventeen people "in an almost all-American team, with only the accountant being sent from China" in the 1990s (Yi/Ye 2003: 209; similar Ling 2005: 99). When asked, if he [Jemal] does not suffer from communication problems to Zhang because of language barriers, he answered: "I can honestly say that, even though I do not speak Chinese, there is no such language barrier. We both [Zhang and me] want the same for one another, and that is to make Haier company and the Haier brand grow" (Jemal quoted in Yi/Ye 2003: 208).

Based on the experience with Jemal, CEO Zhang has also tried to hire local managers for the local markets in Western Europe (e.g., Yi/Ye 2003: 12, 190). For instance, Italian Frams Jamry became the first general man-

---

[139] Starting in December 2006, Haier seems to implement the suggested approach and aligns websites. Haier Electronics Europe since appears in a more similar design to Haier Group.

ager of Haier Europe Trading (Yi/Ye 2003: 199), and Italian Paolo Mainardi leads Haier Electronics Europe since 2004 (HBI Online Press Center 2004). But, CEO Zhang still seems to worry about putting Haier's European business in fully local hands. By end of 2005, he still relies on Chinese employees in key positions: Chinese Sun Shubao, for instance, is marketing manager of the European Division at Haier Europe Trading and contact person for Germany's MediaSaturn Holding (Stremme 2005). Maybe, the new general manager of Sales & Marketing at Haier Europe Trading, the German Kurt Weiss, who has been appointed in 2005 (HBI Online Press Center 2005), will be able to win full credit of CEO Zhang? Figure 5-11 sums up Haier's way of international brand management across all discussed nine sub-sections:

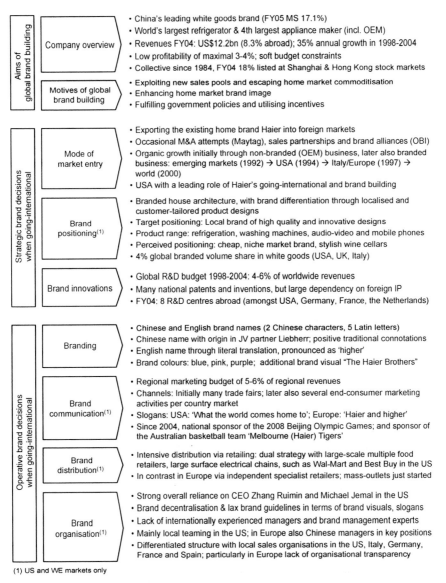

Aims of global brand building	Company overview	• China's leading white goods brand (FY05 MS 17.1%) • World's largest refrigerator & 4th largest appliance maker (incl. OEM) • Revenues FY04: US$12.2bn (8.3% abroad); 35% annual growth in 1998-2004 • Low profitability of maximal 3-4%; soft budget constraints • Collective since 1984, FY04 18% listed at Shanghai & Hong Kong stock markets
	Motives of global brand building	• Exploiting new sales pools and escaping home market commoditisation • Enhancing home market brand image • Fulfilling government policies and utilising incentives
Strategic brand decisions when going-international	Mode of market entry	• Exporting the existing home brand Haier into foreign markets • Occasional M&A attempts (Maytag), sales partnerships and brand alliances (OBI) • Organic growth initially through non-branded (OEM) business, later also branded business: emerging markets (1992) → USA (1994) → Italy/Europe (1997) → world (2000) • USA with a leading role of Haier's going-international and brand building
	Brand positioning[1]	• Branded house architecture, with brand differentiation through localised and customer-tailored product designs • Target positioning: Local brand of high quality and innovative designs • Product range: refrigeration, washing machines, audio-video and mobile phones • Perceived positioning: cheap, niche market brand, stylish wine cellars • 4% global branded volume share in white goods (USA, UK, Italy)
	Brand innovations	• Global R&D budget 1998-2004: 4-6% of worldwide revenues • Many national patents and inventions, but large dependency on foreign IP • FY04: 8 R&D centres abroad (amongst USA, Germany, France, the Netherlands)
Operative brand decisions when going-international	Branding	• Chinese and English brand names (2 Chinese characters, 5 Latin letters) • Chinese name with origin in JV partner Liebherr; positive traditional connotations • English name through literal translation, pronounced as 'higher' • Brand colours: blue, pink, purple; additional brand visual "The Haier Brothers"
	Brand communication[1]	• Regional marketing budget of 5-6% of regional revenues • Channels: Initially many trade fairs; later also several end-consumer marketing activities per country market • Slogans: USA: 'What the world comes home to'; Europe: 'Haier and higher' • Since 2004, national sponsor of the 2008 Beijing Olympic Games; and sponsor of the Australian basketball team 'Melbourne (Haier) Tigers'
	Brand distribution[1]	• Intensive distribution via retailing: dual strategy with large-scale multiple food retailers, large surface electrical chains, such as Wal-Mart and Best Buy in the US • In contrast in Europe via independent specialist retailers; mass-outlets just started
	Brand organisation[1]	• Strong overall reliance on CEO Zhang Ruimin and Michael Jemal in the US • Brand decentralisation & lax brand guidelines in terms of brand visuals, slogans • Lack of internationally experienced managers and brand management experts • Mainly local teaming in the US; in Europe also Chinese managers in key positions • Differentiated structure with local sales organisations in the US, Italy, Germany, France and Spain; particularly in Europe lack of organisational transparency

(1) US and WE markets only

Fig. 5-11. Haier's way of international brand management (own summary)

5.2.2 Case study 2: TCL 集团 Corporation

Aims of global brand building

Company overview

TCL 集团 Corporation was founded with headquarters in Huizhou, Guangdong province in 1981 as a state-owned company making audio-tapes. Based on the establishment of two Sino-foreign joint ventures with Hong Kong investors, TCL Cooperation first became famous in China for its fixed-line telephones since 1989, and later for its televisions and mobile phones (box 5-2). By 2006, TCL Cooperation is one of China's most well-known conglomerates, and *TCL* is one of China's top leading brands, offering also a broad range of other audio-video (A/V) products, white goods, PCs and electrical equipment. In particular since the end 1990s, TCL Corporation has rapidly grown by 36% each year (figure 5-12). According to own figures, they achieved worldwide revenues of US$6.69bn in 2004 thereof 15% abroad, and a market share of 21%[140] for TV sets in China in 2005 (Sun 2006).[141] TCL Corporation has two companies each listed in Shenzhen and Hong Kong stock exchange market. They cover TCL Corporation's both core segments and 62% of worldwide revenues in 2004. TCL Multimedia Corporation Holdings Ltd. includes the core segment television, plus PC and other A/V businesses. TCL Communication Technology Holdings Ltd. includes the core segment mobile phones.

TCL Corporation has also expanded largely into overseas markets. They ranked among the top three brands in emerging markets such as Vietnam, the Philippines, Chile and Argentina with double-digit market share in 2004 (TMC 2005b: 15). After joint ventures with French Thomson for TV sets (TCL-Thomson-Electronics 'TTE') and French Alcatel for mobile phones (TCL-Alcatel Mobile Phones 'TAMP') in 2004, TCL Corporation is since present with sales facilities in more than 50 countries. They also run 14 TV plants (e.g., in Poland, Vietnam, Mexico) and six R&D centres (e.g., in the USA, Germany, France), employing about 40,000 people worldwide. Moreover, the joint venture 'TTE' made TCL Corporation to the world's largest manufacturer of TV sets, competing globally with *Sony, Panasonic, Samsung, Philips* and *LG*. According to own figures, TTE achieved a global market share of 9.15% in 2005 (company data as

---

[140] TCL and Rowa brand. See also section 'brand positioning' for details.

[141] Although both core segments and the majority of TCL Corporation's revenues are publicly-listed, treat overall data with care; they are "based on statistical criteria" (TCL Corporation 2006).

given by Sun 2006).[142] TTE corporate communication director Stacey Sun evaluated TCL Corporation's overall core competences. She particularly underlined TTE's customer insights into the Chinese television market and TTE's efficient global supply chain management (figure 5-13).

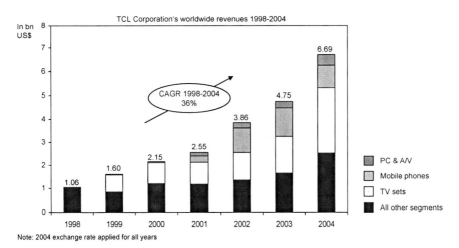

Fig. 5-12. TCL Corporation's worldwide revenues in bn US$ 1998-2004 (company data)[143]

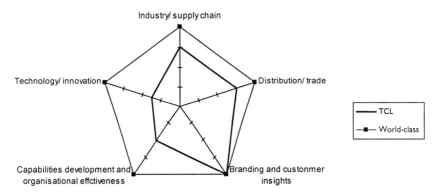

Fig. 5-13. TCL Corporation's perceived core competences on a scale from 1 (basic industry level) to 5 (world-class level) (estimation of Sun 2006)

---

[142] Figure seems to be realistic, if comparing and extrapolating it with Euromonitor data as given for 2003 (Euromonitor 2006). See also chapter 5.1 section TV & video.

TCL was established in 1981 manufacturing audiotapes with headquarters in Huizhou, Guangdong province. In 1982, the joint venture 'TTK Household Electronic Appliance Co. Ltd.' was founded with investors from Hong Kong, and Li Dongsheng, today's chairman and president of TCL Group, joint the company. After some success, a second sino-foreign joint venture 'Telephone Co. Ltd.' was founded in 1985, starting manufacturing fixed-line telephones. Since 1989 TCL telephones got famous and rank first among telephone makers in terms of sales volume in China establishing TCL as a recognised brand name. An audio R&D department was launched in 1992, focusing on product development and production efficiencies. Around the same time TCL began to develop a national distribution system, with the first branch in Shanghai and later on also in Harbin, Xian, Wuhan and Chengdu. As the Chinese government had stopped issuing manufacturing permits, TCL encountered difficulties to enter the promising TV business in the beginning 1990s. TCL was forced to search for strategic partners and finally acquired a company that already owned a TV manufacturing permit. In 1992, TCL launched its first TCL-branded big-screen colour TV sets and has grown rapidly since.

From 1993-1997, TCL diversified business onto further consumer electronics and electrical components. In 1993, TCL went IPO at Shenzhen stock market. TCL was listed at one of the 300 key state-owned enterprises ratified by the state Economy and Trade Commission and the People's Bank of China. In 1996, Li Dongsheng became chairman and president of TCL Group. From 1997-2001, TCL entered several fields of the information technology. They established TCL-GVC Computer Technology Co. Ltd. with Taiwan GVC Computer Company, launched Ejiajia.net on the internet and build up the mobile phone business as TCL's second core segment by 2001. To support expansion plans, TCL went IPO at Hong Kong stock exchange market in 1999, and Li announced the aim to create a world-class Chinese enterprise.

In 2001, price competition broke out among TV makers and TCL intensified overseas business. Besides, TCL began to focus diversification onto household appliances such as air-cons, refrigerators, washing machines and small appliances. In 2003, TCL also acquired ROWA TV brand and set up Guangzhou Digital ROWA Technology Company. Since then, TCL is addressing the domestic TV market by a two-brand strategy, TCL brand for the mid-to high end and ROWA as the second tier brand name.

Box 5-2. TCL's corporate history and domestic growth (own summary)[144]

The short-term corporate aim of TCL Corporation is to fully complete their post-merger integrations with the former parts of Thomson and Alcatel. The goal is to turn around the money loosing mobile phone segment, and to achieve full profitability in each regional TV market by end of

---

[143] Figures base on company data as given by Stacey Sun and by TCL corporate investor relation websites (TCT, TMC). See appendix 5 for original data, and appendix 1 for exchange rates.

[144] Compare to corporate websites and Harvard Case Study on TCL Multimedia (Khanna et al. 2005). For Rowa acquisition see Lehua caidian [Rowa] (2006).

2006.[145] In the long-term run, TCL Corporation targets to close the gap to the world-class level by becoming itself a globally known and internationally competitive *TCL* brand for televisions and mobile phones (TCL Corporation 2002; Sun 2006; TMC 2006a: 16). TCL international CFO Yan announced in November 2003: "We are determined to become the Chinese Sony or Samsung" (in Einhorn et al. 2003; similar in Economist 2005a).

Motives of global brand building

TCL Corporation's chairman and president Li Dongsheng explained in an interview in 2002 that TCL had started thinking of brand building the first time during the Asian financial crisis in the end of 1990s. "At this point", he explained, "we had an opportunity to build our competitive advantage at a time when the Chinese economy was still financially stable and growing amidst the turmoil that was affecting the rest of Asia. Branding was an essential part of building our competitive advantage. [...] It becomes a reason why your product is chosen over another company's product. [...] We became one of the first companies to engage an advertising consultancy in China to advise us on branding concepts, to give training courses to management on branding and to redesign our logo" (Li quoted in Gilmore/Dumont 2003: 91-92).

The impulse to an international brand was then given in 2000, when Li after having participated in Shanghai Fortune Forum, an event attended by CEOs from all over the world, realised that TCL would only survive the market if becoming a world-class enterprise with a significant role on the international business platform (Gilmore/Dumont 2003: 91-92). At this time, a price competition among domestic TV makers broke out and industry profit margins had been shrinking rapidly; TCL Multimedia had a decrease of 16% in net profit in 2000 and of 32% in 2001 (TMC 2001: 12; TMC 2002: 4). As a consequence, TCL Corporation formulated a new competitive strategy called "developing the best products, providing the best services and creating the best brand name" and set up a working team for "strengthening international competitiveness" (TCL Corporation 2006). TTE communication director Stacey Sun (2006) stressed that the main motive of TCL's going-international has been to explore new sales pools in order to develop themselves. She said that TCL has already been everywhere in China and is in contrast to multinational competitors also very familiar with the Chinese tier 2, tier 3 and farer rural areas from early days on. In addition, she underlined that TCL has been among the top 5 players for TV sets, mobile phones, and computer business for several years.

---

[145] TMC and TCT with negative profitability, overall profitability thus assumed as quite narrow (TCT 2006a; TMC 2006a).

When in 2002 German Schneider Electronics announced bankruptcy, TCL took the opportunity and accelerate its entry into Western European markets. Similar to that, when French Thomson and Alcatel offered parts of their business for a good price in 2004, TCL bought them. "The chance to purchase a truly global colour-television company just doesn't come along every day," president Li said (quoted in Chandler et al. 2004), "we looked at the risks, but it seemed to me that this was a unique opportunity." Stacey Sun (2006) added that TCL could buy the Thomson TV part for a good price because it had loosing money for many years and Thomson was going to spin it off: "A good developing brand would have had cost a huge amount of money." The Chinese government had strongly supported the overseas acquisitions with bank loans, deduction of taxes and other special policies, said Stacey Sun, "showing that a Chinese company getting stronger in the world market, this is good for them, too" (see also TMC 2006b: year 2004). An industry observer even argued that the Thomson acquisition was mainly driven by political reasons, rather than by business economics; the Chinese government could show national pride and president Li could enhance his reputation by leading an international instead of a national firm (personal communication).

Whereas TCL Corporation is up to now promoting its own *TCL* brand in domestic and emerging markets, Stacey Sun (2006) said that they plan to expand the TCL brand in the matured markets in the long-term run, too: "Today, TTE promotes three major brands. Three brands in different markets are not easy and cannot be a permanent way. The TCL brand is the only brand we own ourselves, we do not have to pay fees to our own brand. […] Thus, TCL brand will be our own global future brand." TCL Corporation currently exploits developed markets primary by licensing the overseas brands *Thomson, RCA* and *Alcatel*. The aim is to profit and learn from the already established brands, their distribution networks and local market experience. They should build a valuable basis when TCL will start launching its TCL brand within the next years in the developed markets. Stacey Sun (2006) explained that TCL plans to start with the two big businesses: TV sets and mobile phones, and will launch the other products in a second phase. Manager Yuan (quoted in Khanna et al. 2005: 11) summed up TCL Corporation's motives of a global brand building: "We want to create value in consumer products, sell high margin products at the high end, reduce costs by increasing sales volume and run an efficient supply chain."

Strategic brand decisions when going-international

Market entry mode

According to TCL Corporation's memory, overseas business was initiated in 1998, when "the package agreement on authorized export seller's credit line of RMB2bn [US$242m] was signed between [the] Import and Export Bank of China and TCL, which provided TCL with great financial support in exploring the overseas market and enhancing its competitiveness" (TCL Corporation 2006). In the beginning, TCL focused sales into emerging markets in Asia and to some OEM business in South Africa, Russia and Middle East (Khanna et al. 2005: 8). Compare to table 5-13:

Year	Country	Brand mode	Institutional mode	Name	Initial products
1993	Hong Kong	Own brand	Greenfield	TCL Electronics Hong Kong Ltd.	Telephones, TV
1996	Hong Kong	Own brand	M&A	Hong Kong Luk's Enterprise	TV
1998	Vietnam	Own brand	M&A	Hong Kong Luk's Enterprise	TV
2001	Malaysia	Own brand	Majority JV	Sales Office	TV
2001	Indonesia	Own brand	Majority JV	Sales Office	TV
2001	Middle East	Own brand, OEM	Majority JV	Middle East Sales Office	TV
2001	Russia	Own brand, OEM	Greenfield (Alliance)	Sales Office	TV
2001	USA, Japan, Korea	OEM	Greenfield (JV)	Strategic OEM Business Unit, Great Wall Cybertech	TV
2002	Germany	Brand acquisition	M&A	Schneider Electronics	TV
2002	USA	Brand acquisition	M&A	Go.Video Corporation	TV, DVD, MP3
2004	Europe, North America	Brand licence	Majority JV	TCL-Thomson-Electronics	TV
2004	Worldwide	Brand licence	Majority JV	TCL-Alcatel	Mobile phones
2006	F, I, E, B	Brand alliance	Greenfield	Distribution through Carrefour	TV

Table 5-13. TCL's mode of market entry until 2006 (own illustration of major steps)[146]

In 2001, TCL managers then began talking to potential partners in Korea, Japan and the USA (Khanna et al. 2005: 8-9). They decided to enter the US market by OEM business: "TCL managers were aware that Konka had 'failed miserably' in its attempts to sell directly into the United States, selling as an OEM was both a way to enter the US market and a way to upgrade TCL skills through forced compliance with legal and consumer protection measures" (Khanna et al. 2005: 9). In Europe, TCL and its low cost manufactures run against the anti-dumping laws. Shi Wanwen, TCL

---

[146] Table refers to proven FDIs. It does not include countries which have been entered by pure export business. See Schütte et al. (2004: 142-150) for details about TCL entering Vietnam.

Multimedia president, remembered: "We tried to enter the European market in 1989, but antidumping policies basically kept us out. [...] We did try to sell through agents there, but had no brand name or price advantage. [...] We chose to go around these barriers through mergers and acquisitions" (quoted in Khanna et al. 2005: 9).

TCL's first acquisitions was in 2002, when they suddenly got the offer to purchase the bankrupt Schneider electronic company, Germany's seventh largest TV maker, for US$8m from the German company's insolvency administrator. Since the local government did not want the plants to close and to create unemployment, TCL considered the price low. Moreover, they expected to profit from Schneider's assets and brands in the market (Khanna et al. 2005: 9). The acquisition included Schneider brand names *Schneider* and *Dual*, their technology patents, distribution networks, inventory, and three production lines in Türkheim, Germany. Shortly afterwards the new subsidiary started making TCL televisions under Schneider brand label. Even though most parts had been manufactured in China in advance, they could be labelled by 'Made in Germany' stickers (Bartsch 2005; TMC 2006b: year 2002). President Li named the Schneider acquisition a big step forward, similar to the Japanese CE makers decades ago, when, for instance, Sanyo bought US hi-fi icon Fisher (Consumer Electronics 2002).

Based on the Schneider acquisition Li revised TCL's overseas expansion strategy and set further M&As as a central corporate target (TMC 2003: 17; BCG/Wharton School 2005: 16). "What I try to ensure, first, is that these investor companies are leading players in their industries. Second, they should have a similar corporate culture to ours at TCL so as to minimize culture clashes and other problems that will arise from working together. And third, I try to ensure that these partners can somehow add value to TCL, whether in terms of products, technology or markets. [...] Co-operating with multinational firms will bring synergies and integrate our resources. It will be a win-win for both parties" (Li in Gilmore/Dumont 2003: 98; similar in EIU 2005: 19). In 2003, TCL invested US$5m and acquired Go.Video, an American distributor for video products with annual sales of US$200m, starting selling TCL-manufactured TV sets under Go.Video brand name in the US market shortly afterwards. (Khanna et al. 2005: 9) Anh, former CEO of Go.Video and managing director of TCL Overseas Holdings Ltd., gave reasons and said that for TCL it has been too late to introduce a new brand into the US market. He estimated it would have cost US$300m a year to promote a new brand name (Einhorn et al. 2003).

Nowadays, about 4 years later, TTE communication director Stacey Sun (2006) tries to avoid talking about Schneider and Go.Video, both rather seem to be eliminated from corporate memory: "Schneider was a try. It was some years ago. Schneider was TCL's first move. I cannot say it has been successful. It was shutting down and business stopped. But the brand still exists. The Thomson acquisition in 2004 was the real move on globalisation." Discussing reasons why the Schneider deal failed, experts agree that TCL had made false estimations. Though they had been able to improve the manufacturing site by a better cost efficiency, they had to realise quickly that the brand itself was already old-fashioned and did not sell well (Sun 2006). In addition, industry observers found TCL Corporation's overall weak German market know-how, non-transparent corporate business organisations and their replacements of local managers by Chinese managers as major reasons of failure (Schumacher/Schaudwet 2004; Bartsch 2005: 53-54). See also box 5-3:

Professor Zhou Dongsheng from Shanghai CEIBS commented TCL's business failure with Schneider in an interview as follows: "There is one story about TCL and Li Dongsheng. Although Schneider became bankrupt in May 2002, Li Dongsheng was impressed by the factory's cleanliness and the discipline of staff. He agreed on the acquisition and decided to keep all employees and the German manager in duty. Then, some weeks later, it is said that he tried to call the German manager on a Saturday afternoon and could not reach him, as Germans are not used to work on weekends. 'How does it come that my manager is not 24 hours on duty? When I have a problem, I would like to talk to him immediately!' Li Dongsheng had argued. As a consequence, he replaced the German manager by a loyal Chinese who is available 24 hours. In the end, the Schneider operation failed. If you ask me, the exchange of management was the major reason. It is necessary to localise the business according the slogan 'In Rome you have to do it like the Romans do'."

Box 5-3. Professor Zhou's comment on the Schneider failure (Zhou 2005)

However, despite of the unsatisfying Schneider experience TCL Corporation has continued its international expansion strategy by acquiring money loosing business. In 2004, TCL invested US$560m and found a TV and DVD joint venture with French Thomson and shortly afterwards for US$65m a joint venture with French Alcatel for mobile phones (Chandler et al. 2004; Taube 2005: 4). Both brands are considered world leaders, but were not able to manufacture the respective business segments in a profitable way. Thomson, for instance, lost US$56m on TV sets in 2003 (Economist 2003a). The establishment of TCL-Thomson-Electronics Corporation (TTE) with headquarters in Shenzhen made TCL the owner of the world's largest TV manufacture (Frankfurter Allgemeine Zeitung 2003). President Li said, "We are very excited about our strategic alliance with Thomson. The merger is a major initiative in our global business expansion that brings TCL to a new era. This strategic alliance fulfils our objective of being one of the top five players in multimedia electronic devices in the global marketplace, setting solid foundations in competing with international rivals. Thomson is an ideal partner for us. The rapid growth of our TV business in emerging markets together with Thomson's state-of-the-art technologies and unrivalled R&D capabilities will enhance our product mix, increase the market share of our products in the high-end segments, raise resource allocation efficiency, and sharpen our competitive edge in the international marketplace" (TTE 2003: 2). The new company has capacity to ship more than 18 million TV sets, 6 million more than anyone else (Chandler et al. 2004). Thomson Corporation initially got a stake of 33%, but after some organisational restructuring TTE became a wholly-owned subsidiary of TCL Multimedia and Thomson a minority shareholder of the group (e.g., TMC 2006a: 3)

The acquisition of the Thomson part included TV manufacturing sites in Mexico, Thailand and Poland, R&D centres in Germany, Singapore and the USA, sales and marketing networks and about 9,000 employees around the world. In contrast to the Schneider acquisition, it is to note that the Thomson acquisition does not involve ownership transfers of the established Thomson brands (*Thomson* in Europe and *RCA* in North America). They are still owned by Thomson Corporation (TTE 2003: 4; BCG 2006b: 16). Stacey Sun (2006) explained that TCL Corporation has signed a 20 years agreement with Thomson Cooperation including two main aspects. Firstly, TCL has to pay licence fees whenever certain products sales are made under Thomson brand label. And secondly, TCL is bound to conduct some advertising and promotion activities on the marketing side. After the 20 years, Stacey Sun explained, there are not yet any arrangements between TCL Corporation and Thomson Corporation.

A same contract is valid with Alcatel Corporation. Whenever there are sales on Alcatel branded mobile phones, TCL has to pay license fees during the next 20 years. Initially, TCL-Alcatel Mobile Phones (TAMP) was set up as a joint venture with TCL holding 55% and Alcatel 45% shares. The joint venture had the right to use Alcatel's global GSM/GPRS handset business, 600 Alcatel researchers, their patents and distribution networks in 50 countries (TCT 2004a: 4). When end of 2004, the joint venture had not been able to turnaround the business and made further losses of US$36.6m, selling around 6 million handsets instead of the envisioned 20 million, Alcatel Corporation decided to leave the joint venture and fully sold it to TCL Corporation in exchange for a 5% stake in TCL Communication. In addition, Alcatel paid US$27m as a kind of compensation, since the new wholly-owned subsidiary 'T&A' is not more allowed using former Alcatel patents (Bremner/Roberts 2005; EIU 2005: 21; Mobile2day 2005).

Whereas the Economist (2003a) had reported in 2003 that "Mr. Li believes he is creating something new: 'the first Chinese consumer multinational with significant presence in all major markets'. And he promises confidently that the [Thomson] joint venture will make a profit in its first year", Li could not make true his promises. By beginning of 2006, both acquisitions televisions and mobile phones are still struggling profitability. The target is delayed to end of 2006. TTE made operating loss of US$103m in the European and North American markets, T&A a total operating loss of US$207m in 2005 (TCT 2006a: 8; TMC 2006a: 12). Language barriers, the lack of incentive mechanisms and enormous operating costs in the European factories are named as the areas of improvements (Feng 2005). It is also argued that TCL Corporation may have misjudged its power to turnaround the losses of the businesses they had acquired (Financial Times 2005: 22).

TTE communication director Stacey Sun (2006) however remains optimistic and is confident that the combination of both strengths of TCL and Thomson will finally result in a significant business success. Asking her if TCL Corporation would conduct same difficult acquisitions again, she said that for a traditional Chinese company like TCL which do not have much experience in the global markets, M&A is the favourite approach. It is faster than building an own brand: "We do not have to start with zero. We have a very good beginning; we can start with a complete team and network and a famous brand in the market. And then eventually, we are going to have a lot of experience and we gain a lot of insights from our team, and eventually we get our own brand in the world market" (similar president Li in BCG/Wharton School 2005: 16).

Maybe faster than even Stacey Sun herself had expected, TCL Corporation has leveraged its European experience and went on their second step of globalisation in March 2006, when TCL signed an agreement with Carrefour, the number one retailer in Europe and 2nd largest retailer in the world, to sell TCL-branded TV sets in Carrefour stores in France, Italy, Spain and Belgium (TTE 2006). As the decision to launch *TCL* brand in developed markets is a very recent move, it is not yet clear to what extend it will affect the whole TCL expansion strategy and thus strategic and operative brand management decisions. However, it can most likely be assumed that Carrefour is a first try, like Schneider had been for the phase of M&A, and will carefully be regarded by TCL's management before taking on further steps.

It is also to note that though TCL Corporation is expanding branded business in Europe and in the US, and though president Li insisted that TCL is not an OEM enterprise (Gilmore/Dumont 2003: 95), TCL also targets emerging markets and new customers by OEM business for both TV sets and mobile phones. By end of 2005, the segment emerging markets/OEM made up around 16% of TCL's worldwide TV revenues, Europe/North America made up 46% and the home market China 38% (see also TCT 2005b; TMC 2006a: 7).

Brand positioning

TCL Corporation is present in the market with a variety of different brands and brand positioning due to its M&A histories. Figure 5-14 gives a short overview about TCL's worldwide brand portfolio. As shown, TCL Corporation uses its corporate brand name *TCL* for selling products in China and into emerging markets. TCL brand is positioned in the mid to high-end market and enjoys an image of trust and reliability particularly in the home market China (Ding/Zheng 2005: 124; Sun 2006). Although Li argued in 2003 that he perceives TCL's brand image too much product-focused and that it is necessary to develop a brand of more people- and human-related image similar to those of Samsung's 'Everyone is invited' or Sony's 'Go create', which can support a clear brand character across the whole product range from TV sets, mobile phones and refrigerators (Gilmore/Dumont 2003: 96-97), TCL may have come closer to this goal by 2006. The corporate slogan is *'Digital Delights.* 数字家园，快乐无限', and the brand leads the Chinese TV market with 18% market share (Huang/Du 2005: 15, company material).[147]

In addition to *TCL* brand, TCL Corporation sells TV sets under *ROWA* brand in China. ROWA had been acquired by TCL in 2003 and is TCL's second tier brand name. It is mainly marketed in rural areas as a mid-quality television label enjoying 3% market share in 2005. The acquired American Go.Video is available in the Chinese and in the US market. Whereas Go.Video achieved 2.2% volume shares in video products in the USA, it does not play a certain role in China so far (Euromonitor 2006). TCL particularly sells MP3 and MP4 players under Go.Video brand name (Sun 2006, corporate websites). See table 5-14 for volume shares.

---

[147] See section 'brand communication'.

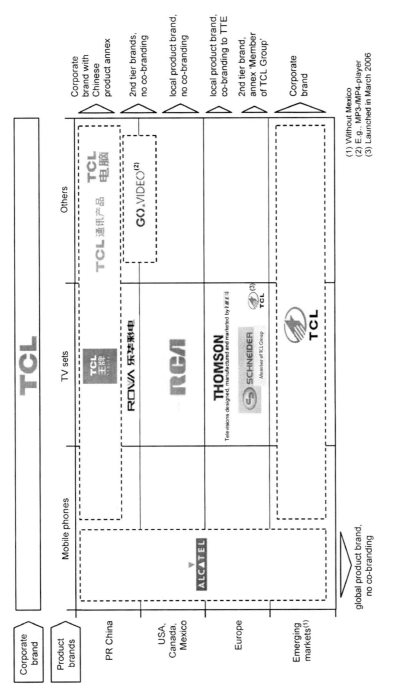

Fig. 5-14. TCL Group's brand portfolio in April 2006 (own illustration)

	Germany	France	Spain	Italy	UK	USA
Thomson	4.2	11.2	<1.0	<1.0	<1.0	--
Schneider	<1.0	<1.0	<1.0	<1.0	<1.0	--
RCA	--	--	--	--	--	4.5
Go.Video	--	--	--	--	--	2.2

Table 5-14. TCL Corporation's brand shares in TV & video in the USh and Western Europe in % of retail volume in 2003 (Euromonitor 2006)

In contrast to the domestic and emerging markets, where TCL functions as an umbrella brand across the total product portfolio, TCL Corporation follows a multi-product-brand strategy in the developed markets so far (Wirtschaftswoche 2004): Licensed Alcatel brand is a standardised global mobile phone brand across all operating country markets. As Alcatel brand has not been profitable for years, it is mainly known for niche products and achieved less than 5% global market share in 2005 (e.g., Bloomberg.com 2005). In the TV industry, TCL Corporation markets three different brand labels. First, there is the *Thomson* brand. It is particularly respected among French consumers for its good quality products at even more competitive prices (table 5-14, Euromonitor 2006), and enjoys a stable market share of around 5.3% in Europe (Sun 2006). The second brand label is *Schneider*. In contrast to *Thomson* brand, *Schneider* brand cannot rely on a strong customer base. Originally a German-imaged TV brand, it is rather perceived as outdated nowadays and does not sell well. TCL thus markets *Schneider* as the second tier brand name to *Thomson* in Europe by 2006.

TCL's third TV brand is *RCA* which is mainly market in the USA. Stacey Sun (2006) explained that *RCA*, the abbreviation of Radio Corporation of America, is a former US-brand which had glorious histories in the 1960s, as they had manufactured world's first colour TV sets (see also Khanna et al. 2005: 1). *RCA* is therefore perceived as quite old-fashioned and is mainly bought by older and traditional Americans with long-term product experience. As Vincent Yan, CFO of TCL Thomson Electronics, put it: "We thought we could sell RCA as a premium brand, but in fact it had already deteriorated into pretty much a low-end brand" (Yan quoted in EIU 2005: 21). Since RCA however obtains stable market shares of around 9% in North America according to own figures,[148] TCL announced a mar-

---

[148] Compare to table 5-4. The market share of 9% refers to the year 2005, includes Canada and exclusively focuses on TV sets. Moreover, it is also a value market share instead of a volume share as given in table 5-4. The market share of 9% may thus be realistic.

keting revitalisation programme in 2005. By promoting a younger and more stylish brand design for RCA, it is the aim to keep the brand vivid and to shift the brand image in order to establish brand attractiveness for younger and new customer segments (TMC 2005c: 12).

In the long-term run, Stacey Sun (2006) explained that TCL is heading for a lean brand architecture with *TCL* as the one and only brand name for all its mobile phones and televisions. The goal is to establish a brand image of quality and high-end. As already started in March 2006 with product launches in selected Carrefour stores in Western Europe, the local TV brands *Thomson*, *RCA* and *Schneider* shall be challenged and later replaced by the *TCL* brand (Sun 2006). Whereas it sounds like a promising strategy in the first place, it is not yet estimated to what extend such brand transfers might cause cannibalisation effects, brand value disruptions and overall reductions of TCL market shares in Western Europe and in the US. Particularly due to the recent RCA brand revitalisation program, it is assumed that a brand transfer of *RCA* to *TCL* brand will be started later than sooner. In Western Europe, however, brand migrations from *Thomson* and *Schneider* brand towards *TCL* brand are more likely in the next years. First and small co-brandings to *TCL* and *TTE* are already in place and could be considered a first transition step. However, it remains unclear why *Thomson* brand is co-branded with TTE instead of *TCL*. TTE has not yet functioned as a brand name so far; and *TCL* is announced to become the future global brand and not TTE. Moreover, since Stacey Sun (2006) insisted that European consumers do not know that *Thomson* brand is operated by a Chinese company TTE or TCL, theoretical spill-over effects of brand awareness and brand images from *Thomson* to *TTE* or *TCL* brand are assumed narrow. Prerequisite of such brand transfers would be the creation of some brand awareness for the *TCL* brand and to explain the European consumers what *TCL* brand is and stands for.[149]

Brand innovations

TTE communication director Stacey Sun (2006) explained that in contrast to Western consumers, Chinese consumers are keener on new product models and would base confidence in a brand on the number of new releases provided into the market. TCL has thus constantly invested in consumer insights and product developments (similar Li in Gilmore/Dumont 2003: 93). For instance in 2005, TCL launched 51 *TCL* branded mobile phone models and 15 *Alcatel* branded models (TCT 2006a: 15). TCL's biggest customer highlight had been a mobile phone model encrusted with jewels which became an immediate best-seller. Guo, vice-president for

---

[149] Compare to section 'brand communication'.

corporate strategy, explained that in China handsets are more and more about fashion and style, since everyone's quality is good and comparable (Einhorn et al. 2003).

TCL Corporation has six R&D centres around the world by 2006, namely in Shenzhen, Wuxi, Singapore, France, Germany and the US. The centres work globally and develop new products for all TCL brands including *TCL, ROWA, Thomson, RCA, Schneider* and *Alcatel* brand. Depending on the local customer needs, R&D results can be country-specific, but there are also innovations which are marketed identically across all countries under different TCL brand names, such as the flat screen panel LCD (Sun 2006). However, Stacey Sun had to admit that technology and innovation itself are not the strengths of TCL Corporation: "Most technology is coming from Western sites. We are trying to learn from the multinational companies. We are just followers." In the last 20 years, she explained, Chinese companies had realised that R&D is important, but they need time to catch up. Within the traditional technologies like televisions the Chinese level is relatively poor: "We are already backwards. We have many national patents, but not yet patens in overseas markets". She sees particular chances for Chinese branded companies in the new technologies such as in mobile phones, IT and computers.

Since standard consumer electronic technology such as LCD is quiet open to everyone and can be licensed from the patent holding company, TCL perceives the own technology lack not as business critical so far. They have rather focused on improving their manufacturing and their supply chain management. Li explained: "Compared to some players, TCL is not the leader in brand and technology, so how can we achieve a big market share? Our great advantage lies in production efficiency -- the speed and the cost at which we can make products. Our products have a good price-performance ratio, which is a big advantage for our manufacturing capability. We should make full use of our manufacturing and supply-chain advantage to gain a position in the market" (in BCG/Wharton School 2005: 15-16). Besides, TCL has also set up several partnerships with foreign leading firms in order to absorb promising technology and know-how over the years. By 2006, TCL is collaborating with LG.Philips for flat panel technology, with Texas Instruments for chips and with Microsoft, Sun, Qualcomm, Intel and Motorola Freescale for telecommunication technology. Since end of 2004 TCL has also established a memorandum of understanding with Toshiba for refrigerators and washing machines (TCT 2004b: 16; TCL Corporation 2006; TMC 2006b).

However, for the long-term run, TCL Corporation has already realised that own intellectual property may be a necessary basis for a successful global brand building. Vincent Yan, managing director of TCL Multimedia said: "No Chinese company is ready to build a global brand. You need technology and products. Just spending money on ads without good products doesn't make sense" (quoted in Economist 2005a). Absorbing patents, technology and know-how has thus been one reason of TCL's takeovers of Alcatel and Thomson. For instance, the Alcatel merger has included 600 advanced R&D professionals (TCT 2004b: 10). See also table 5-15:

	2001	2002	2003	2004	2005
# R&D employees	46	191	322	522	850

Table 5-15. R&D employees at TCT 2001-2005 (TCT 2004b: 9; TCT 2005a: 12)

Due to post-merger integrations and profit losses, investments in R&D have however been limited (Gilmore/Dumont 2003: 95-96; Sun 2006). In 2003 TCL spent around 3% of their worldwide sales on R&D, till 2008 the budget shall be increased to 5% (Einhorn et al. 2003; also Sun 2006). As a result of small budgets, for instance, TCL Communication Technology (TCT) found a R&D joint venture 'JDRC' with two other industry players which focus on mobile phones and other electronic, telecommunication and information technology. According to Fei, CEO of TCL Communication Technology, it is the aim to pool R&D expertise and to share capital resources in order to create a balance of both strengthening product developments and managing costs. In April 2006, TCT increased its share in the joint venture to 46% (TCT 2006b).

Operative brand decisions when going-international

Branding
TCL's corporate brand name can be traced back to TCL's early days, when they set up a Sino-foreign joint venture with Hong Kong investors to manufacture fixed-line telephones in 1985. The name of the joint venture was 'Telephone Communication Limited' and TCL its abbreviation (Gilmore/Dumont 2003: 89-90; Sun 2006). As TCL got famous with the fixed-line telephones and has been number one in this category in China for more than 10 years, it was worth to keep the name (Sun 2006). As a result, *TCL* was registered as the Corporation's trademark in 1986 (TCL Corporation 2006). TCL's brand colours include red, white and black, and the name is written in bold capitalised letters. As the name *TCL* is short, easy to pronounce also in the West and thus regarded as easy to remember, TCL Corporation has also used the name when they entered foreign mar-

kets, combined with a logo visual as seen in figure 5-15. Since 1999, TCL trademark is therefore also registered in the US, Japan and several emerging markets. In Western Europe, however, it seems to be unprotected so far (WIPO 2006). When asking Stacey Sun, if TCL Corporation had never thought of a Chinese brand name instead of or in addition to the three Latin letters, she replied that in China a name does not have to be Chinese, as long as it is easy to remember. However, she had to admit that in rural areas, tier 3 and below cities, TCL is using the brand name *TCL* 王牌 'wangpai' ('King Brand') instead, "as the farmers cannot remember TCL alone" (Sun 2006). *TCL* 王牌 was originally launched as a sub-brand for TCL's high-end TV sets in 1992, before the brand has developed itself and established itself as *TCL*王牌 for the full product range in the countryside (Sun 2006). Figure 5-15 sums up TCL's path to a global brand name:

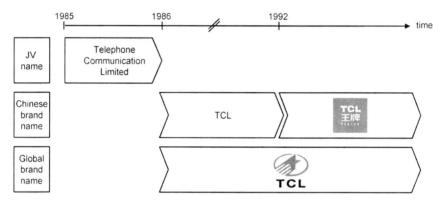

Fig. 5-15. TCL's path to a global brand name 1985-2006 (own illustration)

Brand communication

In China, TCL Corporation has strongly promoted its *TCL* brand across all communication and distribution channels since the early 1990s. President Li explained that TCL Corporation is an atypical state-controlled enterprise, since no state capital has been invested in the company, nor TCL has had state-assigned projects for the market. He said that they have rather conducted its own research and market exploration instead, and has therefore made own plans how to promote and sell the products into the market (Gilmore/Dumont 2003: 92). The brand communication has included classical advertising and sales promotions as well as sponsoring and direct-marketing (Sun 2006). The marketing budget has thereby been quite different over the years. TTE communication director Stacey Sun (2006) explained that in China TCL has invested more in the beginning to establish the brand, whereas they could rely on a leading market position and significant brand equity nowadays. The national marketing spending has however increased over the last one to two years due to accelerating media channel prices. She estimated an overall average marketing budget of 3-5% of TCL's worldwide revenues, although the budget is adjusted in the overseas markets to their respective country needs. Besides these local needs, Stacey Sun underlined that TCL also has to take in account their current situation of operating losses when planning marketing budgets: "We have to invest, although we are on critical business due to post-merger integrations. We have to move on. If we do not invest a reasonable amount, we won't survive the market. However, we cannot spend millions as the Samsungs and Sonys did when they have entered the overseas markets."

As a result, *TCL* brand enjoys almost narrow brand awareness and brand image among end-consumers in Europe and in the US so far. TCL has participated in several fairs and retailer shows such as the IFA in Berlin and the Consumer Electronics Show (CES) in Las Vegas, but end-consumers have rather exclusively been addressed by the local product brands *Thomson, RCA, Schneider* and *Alcatel*. Stacey Sun gave reasons and said that consumers generally do not care and want to know who is manufacturing a brand. They would rather choose the brand if it is trustworthy and if they are aware of the brand during the purchase decision process. Since 2004, however, TCL Corporation has revised its approach. They seem to prepare the launch of their own *TCL* brand in the global markets and started sponsoring the golf tournament at Sanya on Hainan Island, China. TCL has been sponsoring the tournament the third year in row by 2006 (figure 5-16).

When asking Stacey Sun (2006) why TCL had decided on a golf sponsorship, she explained that the image of golf perfectly fits to the brand image of *TCL*. Though golf is a quite new sport in the Chinese market and not yet popular, it refers to the high-end class and high-income consumers. In addition, she said, the sponsorship helps to build up the *TCL* brand on the global markets, since the tournament belongs to the European tour and has been a live broadcast in Europe and in the US. When asking Stacey Sun if TCL had also thought about a sponsorship into the Olympic Games 2008, she said: "I think TCL's branding centre is working on it since a long time. TCL will be involved in a certain part. But I am not yet sure what they will do." As the sponsorships for audio-video is already occupied by the *Panasonic* brand and *Samsung* is sponsoring wireless communication and *Lenovo* computer IT equipment, it is to be doubted if there is still space left to position *TCL* brand in the front light of the Olympic

Games, particularly, as TCL Corporation's budget is limited due to critical business reasons. Maybe the Chinese government will support promoting the Chinese brand *TCL* during the Games instead?

Fig. 5-16. TCL's golf sponsorship in 2006 (pictures taken from corporate websites)

Brand distribution

According to TTE communication director Stacey Sun (2006), TCL Corporation is proud to have the most effective and extensive marketing network in China and also wide market coverage globally. According to own figures, TCL Corporation enjoys country coverage of 80% through 23[150] local sales offices in Europe and 10,000 point of sales in North America. See also appendix 7. TCL organises its distribution very locally due to M&A histories and their established local relationship networks. Common distribution partners of the local brands *Thomson, RCA, Schneider* and *Alcatel* are Carrefour, Wal-Mart and several professional consumer electronics chain stores. Although Stacey Sun said that the distribution channels

---

[150] France, Portugal, Spain, Italy, Belgium, Luxembourg, the Netherlands, Germany, Czech Republic, Austria, Slovakia, Hungary, Greece, Bulgaria, Romania, Moldova, Ukraine, Poland, Belarus, Denmark, Sweden, Finland, and Norway.

are quite different across the European country markets, as the region is complex and performance challenging, it may be apparent that TCL targets mass-markets and thus chose an intensive distribution approach through large volume retailers.

When TCL launched for the first time its TCL-branded TV sets into Europe in March 2006, they decided on the distribution channel *Carrefour*. Fei, vice president of TTE Europe Business Centre and Strategic OEM Business Centre, explained the decision. He said that a sales partnership with Carrefour is the best way for TCL brand to enter an increasingly competitive European market, as the European TV market is not only highly competitive, but also very mature and saturated with major presences of every leading television company. Moreover, he considered Carrefour the right partner due to its large sales network and customer profile which he believes is a good match for TCL's product line: "Thus, for a company like TCL which never had its own branded TVs sold in Europe, a sales partnership is not only a new innovation, but also a necessity, for entering Europe" (quoted in TTE 2006).

As TCL Corporation aims to build a worldwide high-end, classical *TCL* brand, it has however to be questioned if the decision on the distribution channel Carrefour is able to support this long-term goal. Carrefour is a hypermarket offering grocery and non-grocery items. It is generally known for its own private labels and mass-marketing good quality by reasonable prices. A true high-end brand image might be better implemented by volume-orientated but professional electronic chains such as *MediaMarket* or *Saturn* in Germany. They typically comprise a trade-off between sales volume, speed, market coverage and brand building. Especially with TCL's backing through *Thomson* brand's relationships into these distribution channels (own store checks, Stremme 2005), one have to pose the question if TCL Corporation has not yet talked to these chains, or if they have disagreed with a listing for some reasons.

Brand organisation
TCL corporate history and their brand organisation are strongly interlinked with Li Dongsheng who was one of TCL's founders in 1982 and has led TCL Cooperation since 1997 (Gilmore/Dumont 2003: 89; Khanna et al. 2005: 3). Industry observers characterised him as very ambitious and dynamic person. He is known for aggressive marketing, a relentless focus on cost control, and quick decision-making (Einhorn et al. 2003; Chandler et al. 2004). Li himself explained that he has mainly learnt his leadership abilities on the job and learning by doing. He admitted that Chinese entrepreneurs in his position primarily have to rely on own experiences rather than on knowledge that they have acquired at school or in some other

places before they came to work (BCG/Wharton School 2005: 15). Li's personality is thus also the reason why TCL Cooperation, though officially a state-owned company, is said to be far more entrepreneurial than other Chinese companies with global ambitions. Ho, president and CEO of Sampo Group, a Taiwanese consumer-electronics maker and a TCL rival said: "Li may have heavy government backing – the city of Huizhou is the biggest shareholder in TCL – but he still runs the company more like a start-up" (Einhorn et al. 2003). Li persuaded Chinese authorities to let him re-invent TCL Corporation with respect to more market-orientation, and Khanna et al. (2005: 5) concluded TCL had become "privatised" in 1997.

By end of 2004, 62% of TCL's worldwide revenues were publicly-listed at stock markets and the Huizhou government's stake in TCL Multimedia went down to 25.22%.[151] (Khanna et al. 2005: 5) Kroeber, editor of the Beijing-based China Economic Quarterly, commented that TCL is the first large and competitive Chinese corporation in which the national government has allowed state ownership to fall below 50%. He called TCL a lab rat in an experiment in what he calls "stealth privatization". If Li can prove his claim that smaller state ownership means faster growth and fatter profits, he argued, government "regulators may cut other Chinese companies loose as well" (quoted in Chandler et al. 2004; similar Ling 2005: 145).

By 2006, TCL's corporate structure is complex. They operate seven business units: TV sets (TTE), mobile phones (TCT), digital, home appliances, electric, electronics & components and others. Figure 5-17 is thus a simplification of reality and focuses on brand related structures with respect to US and Western European markets.[152] Brand management particularly takes place in the 'Corporate brand management centre' and in the units TTE and TCT (Sun 2006). TTE has five regional business centres (RBC): China, North America, emerging markets, Europe and strategic OEM. In China, TTE is equivalent with TCL, and TTE therefore has to coordinate marketing and promotional activities strongly with the corporate centre. The corporate centre is in charge of all branding and PR issues which are related to the corporate image. This includes key brand messages, print & TV advertising, and guidelines of visual identity (colours, logo) etc. In contrast, brand issues of *Thomson* and *RCA* brand have to be

---

[151] Besides, the general public owns 38.45%, managers and staff 25.01% and strategic partners such as Philips and Toshiba 11.32% of TCL Multimedia. (Khanna et al. 2005: 5)

[152] Illustration bases on interview with Stacey Sun, company data, and corporate websites. It does not present ownership structures, full range of TCL departments, corporate functions and sales departments of other overseas markets except USA and Western Europe. See also appendix 6 and 7.

aligned with Thomson Corporation. Same is true for *Alcatel* branded mobile phones. The parent companies still own the brands and are thus in charge of any branding decisions such as brand positioning, slogans and brand visuals: "We do only the marketing side" (Sun 2006). As a result, the local *TCL* brands appear very differently. See figure 5-18 for the websites of the product brands as an example. Since the *Schneider* brand is managed by TCL themselves, its website is optically already pretty close to *TCL* 王牌. In 2004 *Schneider* brand activities were re-defined and integrated in the RBC Europe. *Schneider* and *Thomson* branded TV sets are since then both manufactured in the Poland plant (TMC 2005b: 10; Sun 2006).

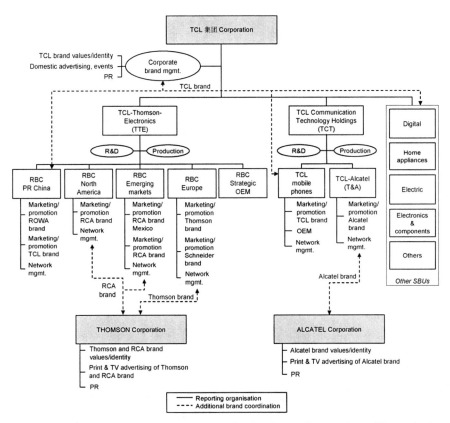

Fig. 5-17. TCL Corp.'s global brand organisation in April 2006 (own illustration)

Besides post-merger integrations in terms of operative brand management issues (Khanna et al. 2005: 12), TTE as well as TCT are also still working on the integration of the former management teams. By 2006,

TCL-Thomson Electronics is managed by an international, multi-cultural team, led by executives coming from both partners. The CEO had been nominated by TCL, while the president was from Thomson (TTE 2003: 3). Further, in 2005 Robert Hu became executive chairman, and Didier Trutt and Alastair Campbell became directors of TCL Multimedia (TMC 2005a: 4).

Fig. 5-18. Websites of TCL's product brands in April 2006 (own screenshots)

In contrast, TCT is particularly led by a Chinese management team; Li is chairman of the group and Dr. Liu Fei is appointed CEO since 2005. Whereas, for instance, the Financial Times (2005: 22) wrote that TCL and Thomson are rumoured to be struggling to get along and the co-operation may be hindered by disagreements within the management team, TCL considers these disagreements as typical for post-merger integrations: "We do not deny that cultural differences exist between the two but these differences do not affect our business operations. Everyone is committed to improving the profitability of TTE and in particular to enhancing the profitability of the North American and European business."

Though some difficulties may be in place, it is to note that particularly TTE seems to work on an effective communication mechanism and a company of international culture. All management levels are required to learn English and to use English as corporate language. Even though other market sources criticised their language capabilities (e.g., Feng 2005), own personal communication confirmed positive results for TTE. Probably, the personal of TCT may be farer behind. Much more interesting than "usual" post-merger integration problems, may be to ask how TCL is going to adapt its global brand organisation in near future, when they sell both TCL branded and foreign branded TV sets into the global markets. Who will be in charge of the local brand building and how are they going to be coordinated with domestic targets in China? As TCL started with branded televisions in Carrefour stores in France, Italy, Spain and Belgium in March 2006 already (TTE 2006), it is expected that TTE's marketing and promotion department of the RBC Europe will get the responsibility in order to leverage local market know-how and brand management expertise. On the other hand, the department may then have to adjust its priorities from a one-brand to a two-brand strategy with single ownership, and may therefore need to renegotiate with Thomson Corporation. Who is served first *Thomson* or *TCL* brand? Since the employees of RBC Europe are mainly former Thomson employees, the employees may be reluctant to support a brand transfer from *Thomson* to *TCL* brand, and may need support from China to learn about TCL brand values and brand positioning.

Figure 5-19 sums up TCL Corporation's style of international brand management across the discussed nine sub-sections.

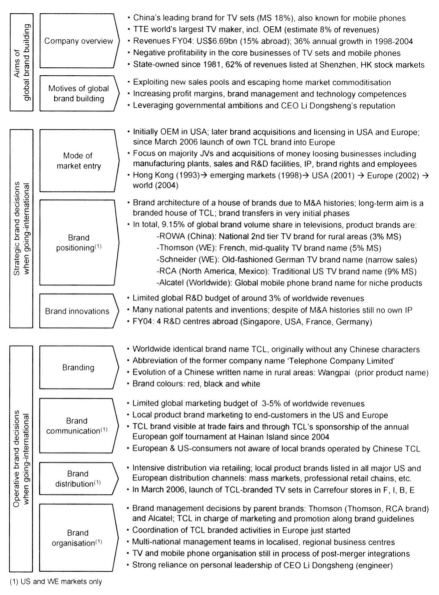

Fig. 5-19. TCL's way of international brand management (own summary)

5.2.3 Case study 3: 海信集团 Hisense Group

Aims of global brand building

Company overview

海信集团 Hisense Group's predecessor was founded in 1969 by Qingdao city governmental authorities. Initial order was to manufacture radio receivers and to develop black & white TV sets for the Chinese market (Hisense Group 2003). Over the years Hisense Group has advanced its technologies and become a large conglomerate (see box 5-4). Hisense Group grew on average 22% each year between 1998 and 2004 (figure 5-20) and became China's number four in televisions (5.5% market share in 2003), number seven in air-conditioners with a market leadership in inverter air-conditioners (around 60% market share in 2004) (Huatongren Shichang Xinxiu [All China Marketing Research] 2004; Euromonitor 2006). According to own figures, Hisense Group gained worldwide revenues of US$3.3bn in 2004 of which more than 15% were made abroad (BCG 2006c: 13; Hisense Group 2006c).[153] In 2005, *Hisense* 海信 brand was also awarded as the 'Most Favoured China Brand' by CCTV, and in 2006 Hisense was honoured the "2006 Export brand" by China Chamber of Commerce for Import and Export of Machinery and Electronic Products (CCCME) (Hisense Group 2006a). According to Hisense (2006b), its corporate strengths in the domestic market are technology, equipment, quality, and branding. Hisense brand manager Wang Ruiji evaluated Hisense Group's strengths compared to the world-class level as seen in figure 5-21.

Hisense Group is considered a typical state-owned company with a listing at the Shanghai stock exchange market to fund growth. The publicly-listed entity is 'Hisense Electric Co., Ltd' and includes the core segment TV sets and since 2001 also digital refrigerators. The entity achieved revenues of US$907m and a net profit margin of 2.43% in 2004 (Qingdao Haixin Dianqi [Hisense Electric] 2005).[154] Since only 28% of Hisense Group revenues are listed till end of 2004, overall figures on profitability

---

[153] Treat figures with care; only 28% of total revenues are publicly-listed at Shanghai stock market.

[154] In 2005 Hisense Electric gained revenues of US$1.26bn. This is an increase of 36% compared to year 2004. Net profit margin also improved to 4.01% (Qingdao Haixin Dianqi [Hisense Electric] 2006). Since 2005 figures for Hisense as a whole are not yet available, it cannot be confirmed whether other Hisense industries met the target of 24% annual growth till 2010 as well or not. Compare to figure 5-50. Treat figures with care; Shanghai stock exchange is said to not require strict publication rules (e.g., Hirn 2005: 129-130).

can only be estimated. It is safe to assume that Hisense Group's overall profitability is lower than the published figure of the entity (Gerke 2006). It is also safe to assume that in case of difficulties, Hisense will receive strong backing from the local government in Qingdao in terms of soft budget constraints (Ling 2005: 139).

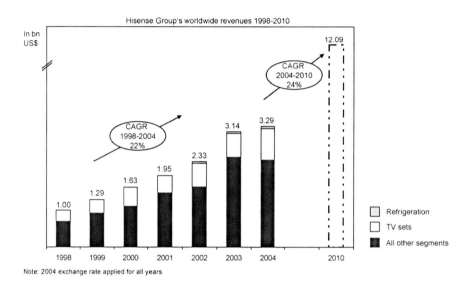

Fig. 5-20. Hisense's worldwide revenues in bn US$ 1998-2010 (company data)[155]

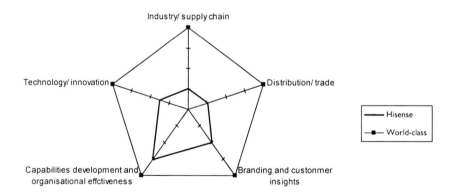

Fig. 5-21. Hisense Group's perceived core competences on a scale from 1 (basic industry level) to 5 (world-class level) (estimation of Wang 2005)

Hisense's history can be traced back to 1969. At this time Qingdao governmental authorities found the state-owned 'Number Two Radio Factory' with thirty employees and a facility area of 1,000 square metres. Initial order was to manufacture radio receivers and to develop black & white TV sets for the Chinese market. First output was a 14inch vacuum tube television in the early 1970s and the technical innovation from manual to mechanical production. By 1975 Hisense developed the transistor television and became a designated TV maker by the Ministry of Machinery and Electronics and the Electronic Industrial Bureau of Shandong Province. In 1979, Qingdao municipal government merged Number Two Radio Factory with three other local factories and established 'Qingdao General Television Factory'. It became one of the largest TV makers in Shandong province. Encouraged by the industrial policy of import substitution as well as being granted more autonomy, Qingdao General Television Factory addressed the demand for colour televisions in the 1980s and agreed with Japan's Matsushita (Panasonic brand) to receive a transfer of equipment and technology. The developed 'Qingdao Brand Colour Television' became popular shortly afterwards.

In 1992, Li Dezhen, then General Manager of Hisense, was appointed to the Electronic Instrument Bureau of Qingdao City as chief director. Zhou Houjian, 35-years-old, became Hisense's new president. Zhou implemented large management reforms and launched the diversification approach of "developing without solely relying on television and engaging in, but not being confined by electronics". The company merged with several provincial companies, was reshuffled across different administrative regions by transfer of state-owned assets and conversions into shareholding ownerships, and purchased further technology from Matsushita to produce wide-screen colour televisions. Finally in 1994, the new organisation was renamed into 'Hisense Group'.

In 1995, Hisense became a world class state-level technology centre for large screen colour TV sets and was selected by the Shandong government as one of the twelve big groups it would support in 1997. In April 1997 Hisense Electric Co., Ltd. went IPO at Shanghai stock exchange market and raised US$50.5m. In 1997 Hisense also found its first trans-provincial operation, a joint-venture with Huari Company Guiyang, in order to distribute Hisense branded products more quickly into Chinese South-Western provinces. Until 1998 Hisense acquired ten loss-making companies with total assets of US$362m.

In 2000 Zhou Houjian retired from the presidency and became chairman of Hisense Group. Yu Shuming became new president. Hisense moved its Qingdao headquarters in the new Hisense Tower and got the official license to manufacture mobile phones in 2005. As a result of Zhou's diversification strategy, the group has broadened its product portfolio into air-conditioners, refrigerators, computers and several non-manufacturing markets such as real estate and retailing. In September 2005, Hisense Air-conditioners bought a 26.43% stake in the crisis-ridden Chinese electronic company Kelon for US$111m and became largest shareholder. The reason of investment seems to be, besides a strengthening in Hisense's position in South China and white goods, the support from Kelon's listing at the Hong Kong stock market for an own overseas IPO until 2009.

Box 5-4. Hisense's corporate history and domestic growth (own summary)[156]

In the world market, Hisense Group is primary presented in emerging markets and through OEM business by 2006. It has 20 subsidiaries (one in the USA and one in Europe), employing more than 10,000 people worldwide. They have 13 global production bases with local sites in South Africa, Hungary, Algeria, Iran and Pakistan and sell more than 10 million TV sets and 3 million air-conditioners each year in more than 40 countries (BCG 2006c: 13). Though Hisense is still considered in the fledging stages in the developed markets, Hisense was honoured with the '2006 Brand Export' award by the China Chamber of Commerce for Import and Export of Machinery and Electronic Products in April 2006. Hisense also attracts global attention due to its strong government support, rapid growth and future ambitions: "We will make Hisense a famous brand in one hundred years" (chairman Zhou quoted in Ling 2005: 140). Besides an international brand name, Hisense also aims for a giant in the world's electronic and information industry and total revenues of RMB100bn by 2010 which is around US$12bn according to 2004 exchange rates. Key segments shall be flat panel TV sets and 3C digital industry.[157] The share of computers and mobile phones shall account for one-third of total revenues; revenues of 3C industry shall reach RMB5bn or US$600m by 2007. In order to fund its ambitions, Hisense plans to go IPO at an overseas stock market before 2009 (see particularly 'Longhu Plan' in Hisense Group 2004; Ling 2005: 134; Hisense Group 2006b: 13; Shenzhen Daily 2006).

Motives of global brand building
Hisense Group's decision to target overseas markets and to develop *Hisense* into an international brand name is described in Hisense's chronicle as follows: "In October 1996, a price war broke out between China's television enterprises, which reduced product prices to unreasonably low levels in order to win the fierce competition. Facing the situation, then Hisense president, Zhou, solemnly announced in the People's Hall of Qingdao that Hisense would not follow suit. Rather, he said, Hisense would win the market by its high technology, fine-quality products and excellent service to the customers. The company was aiming to be an internationally recognized brand on the world market as well as its domestic market" (Hisense Group 2003).

---

[155] Figures base on Hisense Electric Co., Ltd. annual reports 2000-2004 and Hisense Group internet websites (2003; 2006b). See appendix 1 for exchange rates. Treat figures with care.

[156] Summary bases on Ling (2005), Shenzhen Daily (2005b; 2006) and corporate websites.

[157] 3C stands for Consumer electronics and domestic appliances, Computers, and Communications.

Prices of colour TV sets fell by over 80% from 1996 to 2001 (Ling 2005: 134). According to Yi/Ye (2003: 229), Hisense's net profit margin was around 0.47% at this time. Chang Kaixun, president of Hisense Cooperation, confirmed that it has been a question of survival. If Hisense could not be strong overseas, they would die. There has been no choice, but to try (Goodman 2004). CEO Zhou also mentioned the increasing competition from multinational companies in China as a motive of going-international. He said that Chinese firms must take advantage of the opportunity to grow while there is still space for them to do so. China's low labour costs would be a Chinese company advantage only for a limited time, since multinationals producing in China will enjoy the same advantages soon (Zhishi Jingji [Knowledge Economy] 2002). General brand manager Wang Ruiji (2003: 4-6; 2005) added that the development of a strong brand also gets necessary when a firm likes to promote its own technology. Hisense Group said "through [our] promotion of LCD and PDP TV, Hisense is already a flagship among China's home appliance brands and will thoroughly rip off the negative image of Chinese brand featuring low price and bad quality. Hisense will step into the world arena with a new image" (Hisense Group 2006c).

With respect to developed markets in the US and Western Europe, Wang Ruiji explained that Hisense intends to establish its brand in order to increase corporate profits and competitiveness, while growing the group's worldwide sales volume and scale by traditional OEM (similar Goodman 2004). Major OEM-clients are US-based computer and printer giant Hewlett-Packard, Japan's NEC, and French Carrefour (Shenzhen Daily 2006). Wang Ruiji said that in different country markets the role of OEM sales compared to Hisense branded sales can vary a lot. Hisense Group announced Europe, USA, Middle East, South Africa and ASEAN as its prime target markets. For instance, Hisense's long-term sales pattern for Hisense branded refrigerators should be 50% of revenues achieved in the domestic markets and 50% in overseas markets (Hisense Group 2006c).

Besides it is to note that government intervention has been a constant factor in Hisense's decision-making of going-international and global brand building. By global brands such as *Hisense*, the government may intend to demonstrate China's national power and pride towards developed markets such as the US and Western Europe (Gerke 2006). The dispute on Hisense's brand name registration in Germany can be taken as an indicator. (See section 'brand name' for details.) In addition, Ling (2005: 138-139) found that Hisense has got "favourable terms for the purchase of industrial land, technical assistance, import and export quotas, various subsidies in the forms of low-interest or interest-free loans, reduced taxation and even giveaways". Hisense also runs one of the dedicated world class state-level research centres in order to develop global R&D know-how for the Chinese society: "'Creating Perfection, Serving the Society' is our commitment and our paramount goal for all business activities. We have strong sense of social responsibilities. Rejuvenating national industries and serving the society is a way that we repay the society. [...] An enterprise can only grow larger and stronger and find its value and significance of existence by serving the society" (Hisense Group 2006b).

Strategic brand decisions when going-international

Market entry mode

In 1991 Hisense Group founded Hisense Export & Import Co. Ltd. in Qingdao. The entity got the task to explore the overseas markets and to introduce advanced foreign technologies, production and testing equipment into Hisense Group (Hisense Group 2006c). Some OEM partnerships were established and foreign technology imported into China.[158] When in 1996 Hisense president Zhou announced Hisense's going-international as the new overall corporate strategy, it is said that he realised that the developed markets in the US and Western Europe have extremely high entry barriers, and that Chinese companies such as *Changhong* had struggled to compete in these markets so far. As a result, he decided against these markets to start with and shifted his attention to emerging markets, namely South America and South Africa (Goodman 2004; Ling 2005: 143). See also table 5-16.

When Korea's *Daewoo* was willed to sell its factory in Johannesburg for US$2.3m as a consequences of the Asian crises in 1997, Hisense took its chance and founded its first overseas subsidiary in South Africa as a "bridgehead" for entering foreign markets (Hisense Group 2003). The subsidiary was a 60-40 joint venture with the South African bank *NED* and was named 'Hisense South Africa Development Enterprise (Pty) Ltd.' (Hisense Group 2006c). The factory started producing Hisense branded TV sets in the same year (Hisense Group 2003), while OEM has not been an issue there (Wang 2005). In 2004, Hisense expanded the production base into a capacity of 200,000 colour and black & white TVs, 50,000 DVDs & VCDs and 10,000 hi-fi home theatres for US$4m. Besides manufacture, Hisense South Africa has also become in charge of sales distribution into local African markets and local R&D activities. However, it is said that due to unfamiliarity with the local market and local culture, the business performance in South Africa was disappointing, and Hisense perceived their investment under risk because of deteriorating economic envi-

---

[158] See section 'brand innovations'.

ronment and political uncertainty (Ling 2005: 143). As a consequence and due to the fact that the market in China was stagnating, Hisense was hence pressured to pick up speed for entering further foreign markets such as the markets in the US and WE.

Year	Country	Brand mode	Institutional mode	Name	Initial products
1996	South Africa	Own brand	JV	'Hisense South Africa Development Enterprise'	TV
1997	Hong Kong	Own brand	Greenfield	Sales office 'Hisense Hong Kong'	TV
1999	Brazil	Own brand	Greenfield	Sales office 'Hisense Do Brazil'	TV
2000	USA	OEM (own brand)	Greenfield	Sales office 'Hisense USA Cooperation'	TV
2001	Italy	OEM (own brand)	Greenfield	'Italy Branch Office'	TV
2001	Indonesia	Own brand	Greenfield	Sales office 'Hisense Indonesia'	TV
2002	Japan	OEM (own brand?)	JV	Sales office 'Hisense Sumisho (Japan) Co. Ltd.'	TV
2003	Australia	Own brand	Greenfield	Sales office 'Hisense Australia'	TV
2003	Saudi Arabia	Own brand	Greenfield	'Saudi Arabia Branch Office'	TV
2004	Hungary	OEM (own brand)	JV	Manufacturing plant with Singapore Flextronics	TV
2004	France, Italy, UK	OEM (own brand)	JV	Sales agreement with Singapore Flextronics	TV
2004	Pakistan	Own brand	JV	Manufacturing plant with Pakistan AAA Company	TV, A/C
2004	South Africa	Own brand	Greenfield	Expansion of production base	DVD/VCD, Hifi, TV
2005	Australia	Own brand	Alliance	Sales partner 'TAAC Household Appliance'	TV, A/C
2006	Germany	Own brand	Alliance	Distribution through Saturn electronic chain	TV

Table 5-16. Hisense's mode of market entry until 2006 (own illustration of major steps)[159]

In 2000 Hisense Group invested in the US and founded 'Hisense USA Cooperation' in Los Angeles. The plan has been to sell Hisense branded products into the market in the first place and to establish OEM co-operations in the second place (Wang 2005). Since the newspaper Shenzhen Daily recently reported that "[Hisense] scored a small victory last year [2005] when US retailer Best Buy agreed to sell Hisense brand TV sets in addition to Hisense models bearing its own [Best Buy] brand name" (Shenzhen Daily 2006), it is assumed that contrary to their own strategy, Hisense had very likely started US activities with OEM instead of own branded products. By end of 2005, Hisense USA Corporation also runs a R&D facility that works in collaboration with Qingdao research centre (Hisense USA 2006).

---

[159] Table refers to proven FDIs. Markets entered by pure export business are not included. Information about role and volume of OEM in these markets were not available; it is assumed that the developed markets in the USA, Western Europe and Japan have mainly been penetrated by OEM labels.

Shortly after the establishment of Hisense USA Corporation, Hisense also opened up a trading office in Italy in 2001, in order to explore the Western European markets. It is said that Hisense's branded business started with its participation in the IFA in Berlin, Germany in 2003 (Hisense Group 2005b). In the same year, Hisense Group also assigned an international brand consulting agency to develop a market entry strategy for Hisense branded TV sets in the German market (anonymous interview with the CEO of the agency). The agency found a German TV brand, which enjoyed popularity and an image of quality and innovation, though it struggled with profitability at this time. As *Hisense* brand was unknown in Germany and lacked own distribution networks, the agency recommended Hisense Group to acquire this German firm. The plan was to use the German brand as the TV's external body and Hisense Group's technology and manufacturing capabilities for the interior. According to the agency, Hisense Group denied the proposal, as they did not understand the concept and purpose of this brand strategy: "Hisense decided to establish its own factory in Hungary instead. They keep on making television sets under OEM label and focus on volume, volume, volume. Unfortunately, they cancelled the idea of establishing their own brand in Europe" (own translation). General brand manager Wang Ruiji (2005) explained that there had been two reasons: First, Hisense Group's strategy is defined to enter foreign markets on organic growth rather than through M&As. He said that Hisense has realised that it is too difficult to integrate companies in Europe, as from his point of view, TCL Corporation primary brought themselves into a difficult position, when they acquired French Thomson. Second, after he had researched the German market and some affordable German television brands such as *Grundig* by himself, he found their production lines, technology and brand status as quite old-fashioned and inferior to Hisense's own offerings.

Finally, Hisense Group decided to invest in an own colour TV factory in April 2004. They chose Sarvar in Hungary and the joint venture partner *Flextronics,* who was already running an industrial park there. Flextronics is a Singapore firm that makes products for international electronic brands, which Hisense has already hired to make mobile phones at a plant in Shenzhen (Goodman 2004). The new factory employs 150 people and has a capacity of one million units per year (Hisense Group 2006b). Flextronics and Hisense agreed to target France, Italy and the UK in the first place. As expected by the international brand consulting agency, Hisense branded products play a minor role in the manufacture: only 150,000 of the one million units are planned to be branded under Hisense label in 2005 (Goodman 2004; China Daily 2006). Hisense brand manager Wang Ruiji (2005) admitted that OEM business had always played an important role in

Western Europe and other developed markets. However, he is not willed to provide more details. In 2005 Hisense Group announced that they are going to open up a second TV factory in France soon (Hisense Group 2005c), probably as well with focus on OEM?

While one can argue if an acquisition of an established brand name – old-fashioned or not – is the right market entry strategy for Hisense Group in Western Europe and the US, their decision on the no-brand strategy OEM is probably further away from their goal of establishing *Hisense* as a global brand of high quality and innovation.[160] However, recently in August 2006, first few Hisense branded LCD televisions have been introduced into the German market through the electronic chain *Saturn* which belongs to the German *Metro Group* (own store checks). Did Hisense thus finally utilise its relationships to Metro Group from the Chinese market to win a listing in their Western European chain stores? Is Hisense now going to switch to the market entry mode of brand alliances to enter US and WE markets? It is assumed that both brand alliances with foreign brands and M&A would possibly satisfy Hisense Group's brand aims in a better way than pure OEM, and would also overcome the lack in foreign distribution networks and the risk of false investments (compare to comments of Ling 2005: 143-145).

Brand positioning

In China, Hisense intends to position itself in the high-quality segments of standard and flat panel TV, mobile phones and other consumer electronics markets. They claim a strategy of "developing high technology, producing high-quality products, providing high-level services" (Ling 2005: 141). However, compared to the leading global TV brands such as *Sony, Samsung, Philips* and *LG, Hisense* may is perceived as a mid-quality brand and a local player rather than a worldwide competitor. In their Chinese home province Shandong, *Hisense* brand enjoys a market share of more than 40% in colour TV sets and air-conditioners, while already in the neighbouring province Jiangsu they only achieved a market share of 8.5% in 2004 (Ling 2005: 138; Nanjing Caijing Daxue Pinpai Yanjiu Zhongxin [Nanjing Finance and Economics University Brand Research Center] 2005). In total China they achieved a volume share of 5.5% and worldwide a volume share of 1.0% in 2003 (Euromonitor 2006).

Even though *Hisense* may still is considered a middle-sized player and local Chinese brand by 2006, Hisense Group seems very ambitious. Brand manager Wang Ruiji (2005) explained that they care much about brand identity and brand positioning. He himself already wrote a theoretical text

---

[160] See section 'brand positioning' for details.

book about the interactions between corporate and product brand identi-
ties. He focused his theses on the Chinese market and described *Hisense*'s
overall brand identity by the slogan "有爱，科技也动情！" (‚With love,
technology carries emotion!') (own translation of Wang et al. 2003: 4). He
wrote that Hisense Group had implemented this corporate brand identity
by single product values: refrigerators are digital, televisions protect the
environment, air-conditioners are convertible, and mobile phones base on
CDMA technology (Wang et al. 2003: 3-24, 189).

While one can argue if these attributes are brand values from a Western
marketing perspective, Hisense Group has also used the famous Chinese
TV star and master of ceremonies 许戈辉 ('Xu Gehui') as a testimonial to
enhance brand awareness and brand image in China. Xu Gehui is one of
the most favoured masters of ceremonies on the Chinese TV since the mid-
1990s and moderated shows such as "In front of stars" (original:
名人面对面). In 2005, Xu Gehui became Hisense's spokesperson and
promoted their products by the slogan '名人选名品。全球的海信' ('Famous people choose famous products. The world of Hisense') (own translations of Haixin [Hisense] 2005: 1). See the advertisement in figure 5-22
left-hand side as an example.

Fig. 5-22. Advertisements of Hisense brand in China in 2005-2006 (taken from
Haixin [Hisense] 2005: 18, Chinese commercial magazines)

Very recently, in October 2006, Hisense Group also begun to promote its global competence to the Chinese consumers, similar as Haier Group is used to do. Hisense advertisements now include symbols of international cities such as the Paris Eiffel Tour, and the certificate that Hisense Group was awarded "Best of China CE products" by American *TWICE* (This Week In Consumer Electronics). TWICE is a business-trade newspaper for retailers of consumer electronics, computers, telephones, software, and similar products (company websites). See advertisement in figure 5-22 right-hand side.

Despite of these domestic marketing campaigns, Wang Ruiji (2005) however admitted that in China *Hisense*'s unique selling proposition towards foreign brands rather bases on a combination of both: stronger service and distribution networks across all Chinese provinces, and similar product offerings in terms of qualities, product features and technologies. Outside China, he explained, particularly in the US and WE markets, Hisense Group cannot rely on such distribution advantages. The Boston Consulting Group (2006c: 13) therefore certified *Hisense* an image of "stylish consumer products, which provide very good value for an affordable price". An US-customer having evaluated *Hisense* TV sets confirmed: "For the price, this was the best TV we could find and really love it!" (Hisense Group 2006b). A sales person of the German electronic chain *Saturn* added in August 2006 that the Hisense LCD televisions, which they recently started carrying on their shelves, cost between €900 and €1,200, and are thus the cheapest LCD offers in the store (own store check). The fact that *Hisense* may compete on price in the US and WE markets may also be confirmed by the following statement of Wang Ruiji (2005). He said that Hisense Group does not adapt their branded products with respect to local consumer needs for the US and WE markets, except the local market requirements such as different voltages. A reason may be that Hisense Group aims to fully utilise their large scale and low-cost manufacturing bases, and their networks to high volume and low-cost components suppliers, in order to achieve leadership position in price (BCG 2006c: 13).

In terms of available Hisense branded products in the developed markets, Hisense started with a full line of television sets ranging from standard colour sets to both Flat Screen and Plasma Display Panels in the US in 2000. In 2004 Hisense launched their digital cable televisions and also their CDMA handsets, while announcing to expand to refrigerators and air-conditioners in the near future too (Hisense Group 2006c; Hisense USA 2006). Though quite present in the market, market research reveals that Hisense brand has less than 0.1% market share for video products in the USA in 2003 (Euromonitor 2006). In Western Europe, an industry observer published that from 2002 to 2003 Hisense sold 2,300 TV sets under

OEM label (Goodman 2004) and branded business has not started before 2003 (Hisense Group 2005c). Managing director of Germany's leading consumer electronics chain *MediaSaturn* Holding Steffen Stremme (2005) confirmed that *Hisense* brand is not yet playing a role in the German and Western European market so far. However, The Boston Consulting Group (2006c: 13) published in a report that "Hisense has the best-selling brand of flat-panel TV sets in France, where its products are being distributed through major retail chains such as Carrefour." Though a strong statement, it could not be confirmed through other sources in France and Europe so far.

Brand innovations

Hisense brand manager Wang Ruiji (2005) explained that Hisense's brand approach has been to win customers by quality and innovation. He said: "The English word 'brand' only consists of one word, whereas in Chinese 'brand' means 品牌 'pinpai'. 品 addresses the product and its quality. 牌 symbolises its reputation and impression in the market. Hisense is going to use the 品 to get the 牌" (own translation). As a result Hisense Group has concentrated on improving quality, customer understanding and technology over the years (Ling 2005: 140). In 1995 and 1998 Hisense Electronic, Hisense Computer and Hisense Air-conditioner passed the ISO9001 and launched a zero-complaint production process (Hisense Group 2003). To gather information about customer needs, Wang Ruiji named three sources in China: First, there is Hisense's own experience in the market; some engineers had been working for Hisense more than 10 years. Second, Hisense's relationship and distribution networks would provide customer requirements directly out of the market. And third, Hisense would receive market statistics from third parties, particularly from the National Statistic Bureau. When asking him, how Hisense knows what consumers in the US and Western European markets require, he answered that Hisense Group primarily relies on their distribution partners and their experiences in the market. Moreover, Hisense regularly gets statistics from the market research agency *GfK* indicating which products Hisense had sold in which regions and countries.

In terms of technology, Hisense Group has much been guided by the Qingdao municipal government: In the 1970s they ordered radio receivers and black & white televisions, in the 1980s they demanded colour TV sets and, since Hisense was announced one of the world class state-level technology centres in China in 1995, the development of large screen colour TV sets became priority (Hisense Group 2003). Ling (2005: 134-135, 140) found that Hisense had spent nearly 5% of its total revenues on R&D from 1993 to 1998, and has pursued an '80:20 strategy' under which 80 per cent of the company's capital and technological resources are used in high-end products such as digital TV and the remainder in low-end products. Wang Ruiji (2005) added that the R&D budget was around 4% in 2005. Probably the largest investment over the years has been the CDMA mobile phone technology. It is said that the first-phase construction alone had cost US$48.3m and the purchase of the advanced technology equipment and production site from Hitachi and Qualcomm further US$9.7m (Ling 2005: 137). By end of 2005, the state-level technology centre integrates all Hisense R&D facilities of its different entities, including TV, digital refrigerators, computers, and mobile phones. The centre enjoys a good reputation as a "special zone" where 140 postgraduates and other talents enjoy favourable treatment (Ling 2005: 141). Besides the centre in Qingdao, Hisense also runs R&D facilities in the USA and South Africa (Hisense USA 2006).

With respect to government and customer requirements, Hisense is known for a continuous stream of new products to the marketplace (Ling 2005: 135). In 2002 for example, they produced their first 42 inch 16:9 PDP, which can receive high-definition digital signals. However, chairman Zhou admitted in 2004: "We are at least ten years behind Japanese companies in terms of technology, production processes and organisational capability. Our existing technical resources are far from being able to support our long-term development. To catch up, we must make significant efforts in technical processes; after all, technology is the determinant factor in the competition" (Zhou quoted in Jingji Cankao Bao [Economic Reference] 2004; translation of Ling 2005: 141). Since Hisense Group has been aware of their inferior technology, they have historically purchased technology from global players. These are Matsushita (standard colour and widescreen colour televisions), NEC (colour televisions), Toshiba (wide-screen colour televisions), Sanyo (conversion air-conditioning), Lucent (large-scale program exchangers), and Hitachi and Qualcomm (CDMA mobile phone) (Ling 2005: 135-140; Hisense Group 2006b).

In the summer of 2005, however, Hisense Group celebrated its own technology peak. For the first time they achieved a Chinese intellectual property by inventing a digital media processing chip called 'HiView' for colour TV sets (Xin yingxiao [New Marketing] 2005). Hisense Group (2006b) announced "that they cracked the core technology barrier embarrassing China colour TV industry for years [...] structure design and key arithmetic of the chip had reached world advanced level. [...] it will serve as a replacement of the foreign counterparts [...] the national chip will make its debut in China's colour TV industry with 75m annual output." The Qingdao government awarded the R&D team with US$250,000 and several senior Chinese officials including Wen Jiabao, Zeng Qinghong,

Huangju, Wu Guanzheng, Li Changchun made their congratulations (Hisense Group 2006b).

Even though government authorities honoured the new possession of Chinese intellectual property, it is to comment that Hisense Group has done a catch up with global TV standards rather than created something new or unique. Furthermore, Hisense still remains very dependent on other foreign advanced technologies. For instance, Hisense is still collaborating with Lucent, Intel and Ligent Photonics to integrate the 3C digital industries which they had announced as one of their future core businesses (see 'Longhu Plan' in Hisense Group 2006b: 13). Finally, it is noted that a R&D budget of 4-5% is quite low compared to a global industry standard of around 7-8% and might not be sufficient to catch up further in the future.[161]

Operative brand decisions when going-international

Branding

海信 ('haixin') *Hisense* brand name was chosen in 1993, shortly after Zhou Houjian was appointed chief director of 'Qingdao General Television Factory' and revised the corporate strategy. Up to this time all state-owned companies were named after their local city or region like Qingdao (Wang 2005). Since the government had required to internationalise and to modernise the enterprise, it is said that Zhou had changed the brand name to Hisense in order to establish a basis for nationwide instead of provincial consumer awareness (Ling 2005: 129). Hisense brand manager Wang Ruiji (2005) said that a general engineer proposed the English name Hisense because of its positive connotations. *Hisense* combines the two words 'high' and 'sense', symbolising that Hisense stands for 'high quality' and 'high consciousness of technology' (also Hisense Group 2005a). After having decided on the *Hisense* name, they had translated it into Chinese and came up with the two characters 海信 (pronounced 'haixin'). 海 means "hundreds of rivers to the sea" and broadened mind. 信 reflects "unlimited trust" and trustworthiness (Hisense Group 2005a).

Hisense Group finally registered both, the Chinese name 海信 and the English name *Hisense*, as its official corporate names and decided to use it as the umbrella brand name for its products (Hisense Group 2003). Wang Ruiji guessed that the Chinese characters will likely disappear in 10 to 15 years and that the English *Hisense* will become the only global brand name of Hisense Group. Hisense trademark is written in turquoise-green bold

---

[161] The global industry standard bases on the R&D budget of the two major players Samsung (6.82%) and Sony (7.6%) (annual reports 2005). See also hypotheses in chapter 4.

letters, partly combined with yellow-orange colours, and black Chinese letters, as seen in the logo in figure 5-23.

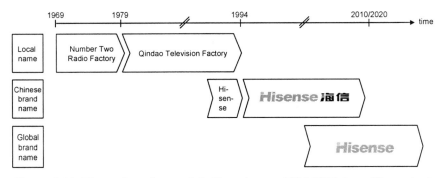

Figure 5-23. Hisense's path to a global brand name 1985-2020 (own illustration)

Although having registered the English *Hisense* brand name in the domestic market in the 1990s, Hisense Group faced strong intellectual property barriers when trying to for register the name in the European markets
in 2002. Hisense had to find out that the trademark was already owned by
German Bosch-Siemens Home Appliances Group (BSH), being different
from the Chinese Hisense only by the capital 'S' (China Daily 2004a).
Siemens had registered a bunch of 'Hi-xx' trademarks in Germany and in
the European Union since 1985, including 'HiCom', 'HiGraph', 'HiCor',
'HiConect', 'HiNet' and in 1999 also 'HiSense' as a sub-brand for their
automatic dishwashers (Gerke 2006; WIPO 2006). Jiangsu Bosch and
Siemens Home Appliances president Roland Gerke (2006) explained that
BSH felt up to terminate the sub-brand and offered Hisense to purchase
'HiSense' trademark for US$12.6m in September 2003 (China Daily
2004a). As Hisense Group was not showing interest in the offer, BSH
raised the price to US$54.6m in February 2004. Since Hisense still denied
the offer, they temporarily started using the newly registered trademark
'Hsense' for entering the European markets (Liu 2005: 35). When in 2004
Hisense Group participated in the IFA in Berlin and promoted its products
under 'Hisense' brand name, the conflict accelerated. BSH sued Hisense
Group for violation of its 'HiSense' trademark and the case was heading
for trial in Cologne.

The dispute was exaggerated all across Chinese media and was a subject
at "every inappropriate meeting" with German, US and European political
representatives at this time (Gerke 2006). BSH was accused to fear competition from China, violating Chinese intellectual property rights and having

set the trade barriers consciously. For instance, the Chinese Beijing Review reported in 2005: "Hisense countered with claims that Bosch-Siemens had unfairly appropriated its time-honoured name and sought to appeal to German authorities to invalidate Siemens' claim" (EMFIS online 2005; Liu 2005: 34; Wang 2005). Roland Gerke (2006) commented that in the end BSH was neither willed to risk their Chinese business and their good brand reputation because of a minor sub-brand nor willed to be subject to the Chinese government and their political power. In March 2005, after about four years of dispute, both parties signed a joint-statement in Beijing that BSH would withdraw its lawsuit in Germany, while Hisense Group would withdraw its application for '*Bosch*' trademark in China.[162] According to Beijing Review, BSH had also agreed to sell the trademark rights on 'HiSense' to Hisense Group for less than US$670,000 (EMFIS online 2005). By 2006 Hisense Group has protected Hisense brand name not only in Germany and across Europe, but learnt their lessons and registered the trademark also in 40 further countries worldwide (WIPO 2006).

Brand communication

Hisense brand manager Wang Ruiji (2005) explained that Hisense Group is very conservative in terms of advertising spending, since they do not want to bother their customers. Hisense rather intends to convince customers by high product quality and customer service. Consequently, the domestic marketing budget is quite low and estimated to 2.5-4.0% of Hisense's total revenues. Whereas in China the budget is primary used for corporate advertising, media spending and channel promotion, Wang Ruiji explained that the budget is primarily used to establish distribution networks and to convince sales partners in overseas markets. The international marketing budget is estimated to 1.5-3.0% of Hisense's total revenues. Major overseas sales events are so far the annual participation in Germany's IFA exhibition in Berlin since 2003 and the Consumer Electronics Show in Las Vegas, USA in 2006 (Hisense Group 2005c; Shenzhen Daily 2006).

Wang Ruiji emphasised that there has been no Hisense branded end-consumer advertising in the USA and Western Europe. As a result, Hisense scored an unaided brand awareness of 1% in the consumer survey as conducted in October 2006 in Germany (chap 3). However, Hisense runs English corporate internet websites which promote Hisense Group by

---

[162] It was not possible to clarify when, why and how Hisense Group had applied for 'Bosch博世' trademark in China. It is assumed that they had applied for a product category in which BSH is not interested in, as it is beyond their brand approach, e.g., TV sets and mobile phones.

the slogan "Technology with love, innovate your life" in November 2005. See figure 5-24 left-hand side. The website of Hisense USA, in contrast, uses the slogan "High Quality, High Style ... Hisense" in October 2006. In addition, Hisense Group launched a global brand communication approach called 'Hisense Anyview' in 2004 in order "to give its high quality and innovative PDP and flat screen TV an own characteristic and personality worldwide" (Wang 2005; Hisense Group 2006b). See figure 5-24 right-hand side. Sales partners, domestic consumers and OEM clients are assumed to be the major target audiences of both brand building activities.

When asking Wang Ruiji for reasons, why Hisense is not a sponsor in the 2008 Beijing Olympic Games, particularly, since the Olympic sailing competition takes place in Hisense Group's hometown Qingdao, he answered: "Even though we are not going to participate in an official sponsorship, the Qingdao government is eager to promote us during the sailing competitions. [...] We think that after all Hisense will be capable to establish some worldwide brand awareness during the Games" (own translation).

Figure 5-24. Hisense's global brand communication in November 2005 (pictures taken from corporate websites)

Brand distribution

In China, Hisense branded products are widely distributed through 35,000 retail stores and through more than 20,000 independent and exclusive dealers (Wang 2005). In developed markets Hisense is also going to target mass-market consumers and planned to approach an intensive distribution through large volume retailers. Hisense general brand manager Wang Ruiji (2005) explained that distribution channels and sales partners however have to be managed differently than in China due to their dual strategy of both: OEM and Hisense branded business in US and WE markets. When asked where a consumer could buy Hisense branded products in Western Europe, he declared *Carrefour* as one of the most important points of sale: "Where Carrefour is, there are also Hisense products" (own translation). Whereas it did not become explicit, if he had meant Hisense branded products or Hisense manufactured products (OEM) by 'Hisense products', he said that the most difficult part of going-international is to convince sales partners of either ways: "Crucial is that the sales partners recognise Hisense as a top brand and that we can make money together" (own translation). Wang Ruiji thus described the relationship to Carrefour as a "profit cooperation". They would not do any co-branding activities. Hisense simply provides information material about its products and Carrefour promotes the products in all stores. A similar arrangement is assumed with German electronic chain *Saturn* which sold as a promotional offer around five Hisense branded LCD television sets per store in August 2006 (own store checks).

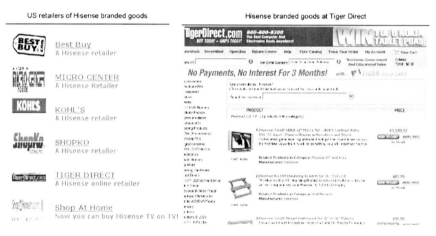

Fig. 5-25. Hisense branded goods in the US market in February 2006 (own screenshots from corporate websites)

In the US, Hisense offered its branded products via three distribution channels by February 2006 (Hisense USA 2006): First, Hisense branded products are sold in the retail stores *Micro Centre*, *Kohl's*, *Shopko* and since 2005 in *BestBuy* (Shenzhen Daily 2006); second, they are sold via television shopping on the TV-show 'Shop at home'; and third, they can be purchased online in the internet at the consumer electronics shop *Tiger Direct*. When searching for Hisense products at www.tigerdirect.com on 21

February 2006, one Hisense 43" plasma TV set and two types of wall mounts had been available as seen as in figure 5-25.

In order to win more global retailers such as Carrefour, Saturn and Best Buy, Hisense invited 100 international dealers to a global customer conference to Qingdao in 2003 titled "Our Hisense. Common Future." In 2004, Hisense repeated the event during the festivals of Hisense's 35th anniversary. According to own figures, 600 dealers from 30 countries and regions participated in the conference (Hisense Group 2006b). However, when evaluating Hisense's OEM business and their sales at Carrefour, Saturn, BestBuy and Tiger Direct, one can conclude that Hisense's branded business is still in its very fledging stages in the US and Western Europe. It will be interesting, if and to what extent Hisense will be increase its branded share in future.

Brand organisation
Hisense Group is a state-owned company. Though reorganised by then president and today's chairman of the group Zhou Houjian along the slogan "the capital market should be viewed in the eyes of capitalists" in 1992 and partly listed at Shanghai stock market since 1997 (Hisense Group 2003), Hisense brand manager Wang Ruiji (2005) admitted that contributions to the Chinese economy and the local government have mainly driven the organisation and behaviour of the Group (similar Ling 2005: 144). He said that the government supports Hisense by funding, land and international relationship networks; in return they expect healthy corporate growth, corporate governance and money for the country. Ling (2005: 139) found that in Qingdao, Hisense is thus characterised as less aggressive and more conservative compared to the also Qingdao-based company Haier Group. Hisense typically avoids investment and financial risks, and is against fighting for market shares at the expense of efficiency.[163] The attitude is stressed by corporate slogans like 'Safety before profitability', 'Never damage the credit structure for higher profit', 'Never overstock even if it means missing market opportunities', 'Never over-invest even if it means missing investment opportunities', and it is also the reason why Ling (2005: 140) found that financial targets account for 80% of the overall evaluation of every Hisense manager, including annual pay, bonus and promotion. It is said that to control these targets and to implement the overall conservative attitude in Hisense Group, Zhou Houjian and Yu Shuming have led the company with a strong hand (Goodman 2004). Since

---

[163] Compare to the remarks in the section 'brand positioning': Hisense does not adapt their products to local consumer needs in the US and WE markets in order to fully utilise their large-scale and low cost manufacture advantages.

2000 Zhou is chairman of the group and focuses on Hisense Group's long-term strategies, while Yu is president and manages the daily business (Hisense Group 2003; Ling 2005: 133).

By end of 2005, Hisense Group is a complex conglomerate including more than eight industries organised along a functional structure. Figure 5-26 is thus a simplification of reality and focuses on brand related structures with respect to US and Western European markets:[164]

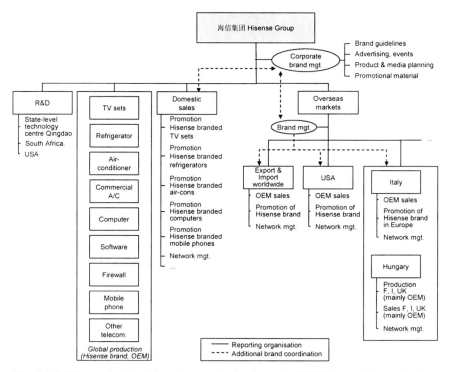

Fig. 5-26. Hisense's global brand organisation in end of 2005 (own illustration)

Brand management particularly takes place in the department 'Corporate brand management' which directly reports to the president of the group. Chief of this department is Wang Ruiji. He (2005) explained that his department includes in total 18 employees. Besides overall development and control of Hisense brand guidelines in terms of brand logo, brand colours and advertising execution (see examples in figure 5-27), the de-

---

[164] Illustration bases on interview with Wang Ruiji, company data, and corporate websites. It does not present ownership structures, full range of Hisense departments, corporate functions and sales departments of other overseas markets except USA and Western Europe.

partment has three subdivisions 'Advertising & media', 'Product & media planning' and 'Promotional material'. Wang Ruiji said that they usually get information input from the industry entities and give back instructions for promotions to the sales department. He said that they also work together with the global branding team in order to align marketing activities and brand positioning.

Fig. 5-27. Hisense's guidelines on brand logo and colours in 2005 (Haixin [Hisense] 2005: 3-4)

The global branding team works under the division 'Overseas markets'. They are in charge for the whole international business, including import & export, OEM and branded Hisense goods (Wang 2005). Whereas in the US 'Hisense USA Corporation' is in charge of OEM and branded sales, it is not clear how responsibilities are shared between the European sales office in Italy, the manufacturing and sales base in Hungary and the division 'Import & Export Worldwide'. Since OEM production is huge in Hungary, it is assumed that Hisense branded goods are most likely managed by the office in Italy. In addition, it is assumed that the division 'Import & Export Worldwide' is not in charge of Western European markets, but of sales into foreign markets which are not covered by own local sales offices.

Wang Rujin (2005) explained that most employees dealing with overseas markets are based in Qingdao. For the US and Italian sales offices he estimated a workforce of maximal 20 employees each. When asked, if Chinese or local people are working in these offices, he answered: "Of course Chinese! [...] But we also employ some local people. They are necessary in order to provide local market knowledge" (own translation). In practice, the Chinese employees may primarily be in charge of transferring and communicating local needs into the research centre in Qingdao, while the host-country employees deal with local distributors and clients. Hisense Group's preference for Chinese managers in local subsidiaries is also confirmed by the story published in the Washington Post as seen in box 5-5.

Figure 5-28 sums up Hisense Group's style of international brand management across the discussed nine sub-sections.

"Wu Yongliang arrived in April with a suitcase full of instant noodles, a bad case of jet lag and a mind overwhelmed by his mission -- to somehow turn Hisense, a Chinese television maker still owned by the Communist Party government, into a brand as recognized as Samsung or Sony. Other than a week-long trip to Korea, he had never been outside China. He spoke no Hungarian and minimal English. He could not pronounce the name of the village where he was to live, its entrance sign looming like a daily taunt – Ostffyass-zonya. The thought of transforming an empty factory into Hisense's first European beachhead filled him with anxiety. 'I thought: Here, there is nothing. We need everything,' he said. 'There is only darkness, emptiness. We don't know how to do this.' [...]

Wu, 34, was raised in the northern Chinese province of Shandong. Fresh out of graduate school, Hisense dispatched him to the remote northwestern province of Gansu, one of China's poorest areas, and a new venue for the company. In less than two years, Wu locked up one-fourth of the market, prove of his ability to build a new business in frontier conditions. Hisense then dispatched him to one of its most lucrative markets, Zhejiang province, a fast developing coastal region south of Shanghai. He revelled in his life in the provincial capital, Hangzhou, famed for its lake dotted with pagodas. When the chairman tapped him for the Hungary post, he demurred. He had a wife and a 2-year-old son and preferred to stay home. But in China today, career ambitions usually trump family concerns. Wu ultimately travelled to Sarvar alone and resides here in a three-story manor house with four Hisense technicians and two company sales agents. Despite the tennis court, the crystal chandelier and the marble bird bath in the garden, their lifestyle seems more frat boy than corporate titan. Empty beer bottles line the kitchen walls. Laundry dries on racks in the sun porch. Wu's bedroom is bare save for four flat-panel televisions and pants flopped over the door of a wardrobe. His office is set up in the foyer, naked telephone wires and printer cables snaking along red carpet. Wu still struggles with his alien surroundings, his Hungarian vocabulary now expanded to three compact phrases: 'thank you,' 'no' and 'The bill, please.' He is flummoxed by the paprika and potatoes in the local diet. He dislikes bread. 'We prefer to buy rice and cook ourselves,' he said. [...] 'We are famous in Europe now' , perhaps getting ahead of himself. 'Our customers know us.'"

Box 5-5. Indicator of Hisense Group's management philosophy in overseas markets (transcript from Goodman 2004)

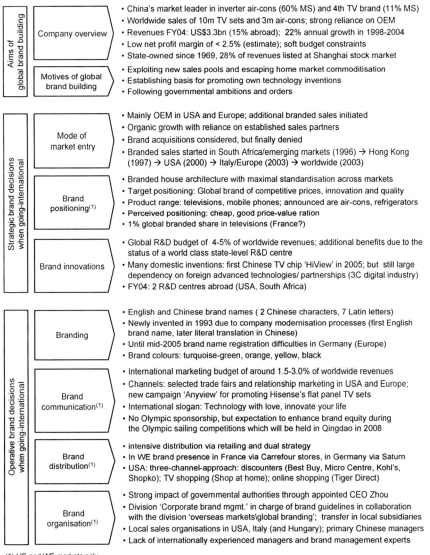

Aims of global brand building	Company overview	• China's market leader in inverter air-cons (60% MS) and 4th TV brand (11% MS) • Worldwide sales of 10m TV sets and 3m air-cons; strong reliance on OEM • Revenues FY04: US$3.3bn (15% abroad); 22% annual growth in 1998-2004 • Low net profit margin of < 2.5% (estimate); soft budget constraints • State-owned since 1969, 28% of revenues listed at Shanghai stock market
	Motives of global brand building	• Exploiting new sales pools and escaping home market commoditisation • Establishing basis for promoting own technology inventions • Following governmental ambitions and orders
Strategic brand decisions when going-international	Mode of market entry	• Mainly OEM in USA and Europe; additional branded sales initiated • Organic growth with reliance on established sales partners • Brand acquisitions considered, but finally denied • Branded sales started in South Africa/emerging markets (1996) → Hong Kong (1997) → USA (2000) → Italy/Europe (2003) → worldwide (2003)
	Brand positioning(1)	• Branded house architecture with maximal standardisation across markets • Target positioning: Global brand of competitive prices, innovation and quality • Product range: televisions, mobile phones; announced are air-cons, refrigerators • Perceived positioning: cheap, good price-value ration • 1% global branded share in televisions (France?)
	Brand innovations	• Global R&D budget of 4-5% of worldwide revenues; additional benefits due to the status of a world class state-level R&D centre • Many domestic inventions: first Chinese TV chip 'HiView' in 2005; but still large dependency on foreign advanced technologies/ partnerships (3C digital industry) • FY04: 2 R&D centres abroad (USA, South Africa)
Operative brand decisions when going-international	Branding	• English and Chinese brand names (2 Chinese characters, 7 Latin letters) • Newly invented in 1993 due to company modernisation processes (first English brand name, later literal translation in Chinese) • Until mid-2005 brand name registration difficulties in Germany (Europe) • Brand colours: turquoise-green, orange, yellow, black
	Brand communication(1)	• International marketing budget of around 1.5-3.0% of worldwide revenues • Channels: selected trade fairs and relationship marketing in USA and Europe; new campaign 'Anyview' for promoting Hisense's flat panel TV sets • International slogan: Technology with love, innovate your life • No Olympic sponsorship, but expectation to enhance brand equity during the Olympic sailing competitions which will be held in Qingdao in 2008
	Brand distribution(1)	• intensive distribution via retailing and dual strategy • In WE brand presence in France via Carrefour stores, in Germany via Saturn • USA: three-channel-approach: discounters (Best Buy, Micro Centre, Kohl's, Shopko); TV shopping (Shop at home); online shopping (Tiger Direct)
	Brand organisation(1)	• Strong impact of governmental authorities through appointed CEO Zhou • Division 'Corporate brand mgmt.' in charge of brand guidelines in collaboration with the division 'overseas markets\global branding'; transfer in local subsidiaries • Local sales organisations in USA, Italy (and Hungary); primary Chinese managers • Lack of internationally experienced managers and brand management experts

(1) US and WE markets only

Fig. 5-28. Hisense's way of international brand management (own summary)

5.2.4 Case study 4: Lenovo Group联想集团

Aims of global brand building

Company overview

Lenovo Group's predecessor was founded in Beijing in 1984 by Liu Chuanzhi and ten other computer scientists as an enterprise of the Computing Institute of the Chinese Academy of Sciences *lenovo* (CAS) (Lu 2000: 64-65).[165] In the first years Lenovo was a small distributor of imported foreign-branded computers, then the company started producing its self-branded desktops in 1990 and since then evolved into China's leading computer firm (box 5-6). In 1997 the brand 联想 ('lianxiang') became China's top selling PC desktop brand. By 2006 the brand holds the market leadership and over 25% market share in China for more than eight consecutive years plus some brand presence in Asia, competing against brands such as *Dell, HP* and *Toshiba* (IDC sources). Over the years Lenovo has also diversified into other PC products such as portables, workstations, and servers, as well as into mobile phones and digital entertainment products (Lenovo Group 2006c).

Due to the fact that Lenovo spun off its foreign-branded distribution business, which accounted for a third of their revenues, as a new listed company at Hong Kong Stock Exchange in 2001, annual growth rates were moderate with 12% in 1998-2004 (figure 5-29). Lenovo Group itself is already listed at Hong Kong Stock Exchange since 1994, and gained total revenues of US$2.9bn in 2004, over 90% thereof in China (Quelch/Knoop 2006: 18). In 2000 Lenovo Group announced to aim at a total revenue of US$10bn by 2005 and to become one of *Fortune Global 500* companies by 2010 at latest. Since 2003 they have also wanted to become a global leading brand and to generate 25% of their revenues in overseas markets by 2006 (Chen et al. 2001; Khermouch et al. 2003; Pan 2005).

In May 2005 Lenovo already came closer to these goals, when they acquired IBM's PC Division for US$1.75bn, including their global brands *ThinkPad* (portables) and *ThinkCentre* (desktops) (Lenovo Group 2005b). The acquisition made the Lenovo Group into the world's third largest PC vendor, with around US$13bn in annual revenue, 60% thereof abroad, and products serving enterprises and consumers in more than 160 countries (appendix 8 and 9). Lenovo's new executive headquarters moved from

---

[165] See section 'market entry' and 'brand organisation' for ownership and organisation models. Lenovo has been neither a typical state-owned enterprise nor a collective or private enterprise.

Beijing to Purchase, New York with principal operations in Beijing and Raleigh, North Carolina, and an enterprise sales organisation worldwide, including sales headquarters in New York, Paris, Beijing and Sydney. The company operates six manufacturing sites in China and India, and runs nine R&D centres in different countries, employing more than 19,000 people (Lenovo Group 2006c).

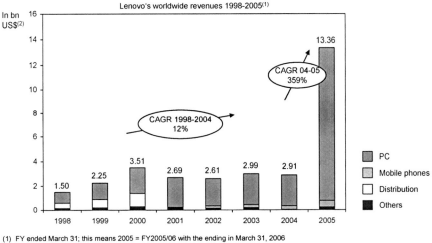

(1) FY ended March 31; this means 2005 = FY2005/06 with the ending in March 31, 2006
(2) Original company data in HK$; 2005 exchange rate applied for all years

Fig. 5-29. Lenovo Group's worldwide revenues 1998-2005 in US$bn (own illustration of Legend 2002; Lenovo Group 2005a, 2006d)

According to Meng Yutian (2006), Lenovo Group's senior supervisor of brand management in Beijing, the new group's advantages lie in technology innovation and a strong combination of both consumer PC retailing and b2b-client handling. She evaluated Lenovo's corporate strengths compared to world-class level as seen in figure 5-30. She admitted that Dell has a more efficient supply-chain which is to be challenged by their ongoing post-merger integrations with IBM PCs. Lenovo is also implementing a new global brand strategy to match its new worldwide reach. Lenovo's priority is to maintain and extend the brand equities of the brands *Lenovo*, *ThinkPad*, *ThinkCentre*, and *Lianxiang* in all major markets worldwide (Lenovo Group 2006d, 2006e; Meng 2006; Zhang 2006).

In 1984 Liu Chuanzhi, a computer scientist who became an administrative manager in the Computing Institute of the Chinese Academy of Sciences (CAS) in Beijing, was given US$24,000 to found a company, in order to commercialise the Institute's research results and to fund their ongoing research costs. Liu and ten like-minded colleagues founded the New Technology Development Company (NTD) based on the principle 'state-owned, but not government-run'. They started operations in a small bungalow given by the Institute for free. In the first two years, NTD was a pure distributor of computer and non-computer products, by acquiring them from large domestic distributors and state-owned importing companies, and selling them to government agencies and large SOEs.

Since almost all PC operating systems were in English at this time, and only few Chinese people could speak English, Liu realised that the language barrier was the bottleneck of PC development in China and decided to start his own product development by translating the English into a Chinese operating system. In 1985, the NTD invented the 'Lianxiang Chinese Character Card', which was designed to be inserted in PC motherboards. The technology was successfully rolled out in1987 by bundling with the imported PCs from *AST* and *HP*. A year later the Card was famous in China and accounted for one third of the company's total revenues. The invention was also awarded with the highest National Science-Technology Progress Award by the Chinese government in 1988.

In 1990 the company formed the new 'Legend Group Company' with Liu as their president, and started to introduce self-branded computers into China. By 1992 Legend was a designated computer manufacturing base of the Chinese government, and decided to consolidate all PC-related business in a new PC business unit. Liu appointed Yang Yuanqing, then 29 years old, as the unit's general manager. To fund further growth, Legend went IPO at the Hong Kong Stock Exchange in 1994. Three years later Legend became China's top selling PC brand, partly because of their competitive price, partly by PC personalistion. They also started expanding on portables, workstations, servers, and later digital entertainment products. In 1999, China's Ministry of Information Industries placed Legend at the top of its annual list of China's top 100 electronics companies.

In 2000, Legend became a constituent stock of the Hang Seng Index in Hong Kong, and decided to fully focus on their self-branded business. Though their third-party distribution business still accounted for a third of Legend's total revenues in 2000, they spun it off as a new listed company 'China Digital' in Hong Kong in 2001. At the meantime, Liu established a new unit, the 'Venture Capital Investment Unit', to provide start-up financing and management experience for high-tech companies operating in Beijing's Zhongguancun area. Liu stepped down as president and became chairman to devote more time to the new unit. He promoted Yang Yuanqing as the new president and CEO of Legend Group. As a part of their 3C-approach, Legend diversified into mobile phones in 2002.

In 2003, Legend announced their international ambitions and building of a global brand. They changed their name from *Legend* to *Lenovo* in 2003/04. Lenovo became an Olympic Worldwide Partner in 2004, and a few months later Lenovo and IBM announced an agreement by which Lenovo would acquire IBM's PC Division. The M&A closed on May 1, 2005, and Liu stepped aside. William J. Amelio was appointed CEO and president of the new Lenovo Group. Yang Yuanqing became chairman.

Box 5-6. Lenovo's corporate history and domestic growth (own summary)[166]

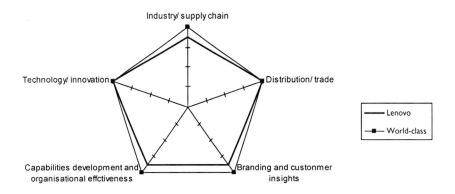

Figure 5-30. Lenovo Group's perceived core competences on a scale from 1 (basic industry level) to 5 (world-class level) (estimation of Meng 2006)

Motives of global brand building

It has been reported that Lenovo's predecessor, Legend, has considered a global brand building in 2000 for the first time, when they announced the aim to become a *Fortune Global 500* by 2010 at latest and to increase revenues from US$3bn to US$10bn until 2005 (Chen et al. 2001: 9). At this time founder and then Legend's president, Liu Chuanzhi, worried about two external threats that might oust Legend from its leadership in the Chinese market. The internet was reshaping the world, forcing old economy companies to rethink their business models. Rapidly growing internet portals and business-to-business e-commerce start-ups were attracting large venture capital funding and going-public. Although China lagged a few years behind developed countries in terms of internet usage, it was forecasted that by 2003, 34 million Mainland Chinese were expected to have access to the internet (Forrester research quoted in Chen et al. 2001: 1). Even traditionally slow, bureaucratic Chinese government agencies were also moving online, accelerated by a highly publicised campaign by the central government. In addition, China's accession into the WTO in 2001 was close, and Liu expected increased global competition. Legend could not longer count on local player advantages such as government imposed tariffs and quotas on imports, or restrictions on foreign companies' ownership rights, investments and, access to distribution channels (Chen et al. 2001: 12). Legend also had to deal with the rise of other Chinese manu-

---

[166] Based on Lu (2000), Chen et al. (2001), Gold et al. (2001), Access Asia (2002), Gilmore and Dumont (2003), Chuanzi and Chandler (2004), Pan (2005), Wharton School (2005b), Zhu (2005), and Lenovo Group (2006c).

facturing giants, such as the appliance maker Haier, introducing their own branded PCs (Quelch/Knoop 2006: 4).

Given Legend's extraordinary performance in the past few years, "Liu wondered whether now was the appropriate time for radical changes" (Chen et al. 2001: 1). To actively address both threats, he saw two divergent strategies: globalisation or localisation (Wharton School 2004). If Legend chose globalisation, they would specialise in one or several product categories in order to develop a global brand like the American IT giants: *Intel, Microsoft, Cisco* and *Dell*. If they chose the path of localisation, they would widen their national business scope and would expand from one product line to multiple product lines, and from PC manufacturing towards service, in order to become China's most famous brand not only for computers but also for IT services. Reflecting the Chinese market situation in 2000, Legend management decided on localisation and to stay in China for the next three to five years (Chen et al. 2001: 9). They concluded that they were not strong enough to deploy resources overseas in order to become a global brand. Although their market share of 30% outdistanced their nearest domestic rival's 10% market share (IDC sources), they assumed that both threats, the internet and China's WTO accession, would require Legend's full efforts in their home market. Of particular concern was *Dell*'s introduction of their direct-selling business model in China, which allowed customers to place their orders over the internet and by phone (Quelch/Knoop 2006: 4). In the words of Mary Ma, the group's CFO: "The biggest challenge we face is competition that includes brands from overseas and here in China" (quoted in Huang 2001). Instead of going-international, they decided on the clear objective to dominate not only the domestic PC market but to diversify within China (Wharton School 2004).

Despite of these market initiatives, Legend faced increased competition in China in 2003 (Pan 2005: 11-12). Dell's market share rose to 6.9% as reported by Gartner, which meant that in relative terms Dell was growing faster than Legend, and that Dell was successfully implementing their direct-sales model in China, as they had already done elsewhere in the world. In addition, the PC market in China's larger cities showed signs of saturation, and Legend was forced to seek additional business opportunities in smaller and medium cities, in non-PC segments, and in international markets. CEO Yang Yuanqing explained: "Although our business focus is still on China, expanding into the international market is an inevitable path with the globalization of the IT industry and for Legend's self-development. That is why we must take a proactive action in our preparation" (quoted in Legend 2003b). The Economist (2001) reported "Ultimately, Mr Liu concedes that even the Chinese market will have limits.

Then Legend will have to become a true multinational and a global brand" (similar Chuanzhi/Chandler 2004).[167]

Strategic brand decisions when going-international

Market entry mode

Although CEO Yang announced Legend's going-international and global brand aims in 2003, the company had already been in touch with foreign markets many years ago. This happened when in the late 1980s Legend's predecessor, the New Technology Development Company (NTD), had the ultimate company goal "to develop, manufacture, and market its own computer systems" (Lu 2000: 75). Because the NTD was not directly owned by the Ministry of Electronic Industries (MEI), which regulated the electronics industry and owned most of the larger electronics companies in China, they were not granted a PC manufacturing license, and could only distribute foreign-branded PCs instead (Chen et al. 2001: 3). Not giving up their initial aim, they finally decided to go abroad and chose Hong Kong as their base of operation. Hong Kong had been under British rules since the 19th century and was used by many foreign multinationals as a springboard to tap the growing Chinese market. In addition, Hong Kong was a major financial centre in Asia with well-developed financial markets and many large lending institutions (Chen et al. 2001: 3). The management designed a three-step and multi-year overseas expansion plan (Lu 2000: 75): First, the NTD would form a trading company in Hong Kong. Second, it would build an industrial base that integrated R&D, manufacturing and market-ing. And third, it would establish itself as a major company by going-public on the Hong Kong Exchange Market.

According to the plan, in 1988, the NTD formed the equity joint venture 香港联想 'Legend Hong Kong Technology Inc.' with Daw, a small Hong Kong based trading company, and China Technology Transfer Company (CITC), which was jointly owned by the Bank of China, China Resources, and two other well-connected mainland firms (Lu 2000: 76; Chen et al. 2001: 3). Liu Chuanzhi, then NTD's general manager, described the joint venture as "the Blind carrying the Lame" (quoted in Chen et al. 2001: 3), meaning that the NTD had strong R&D capabilities but was blind to the in-ternational market place due to lack of experience. Daw, though their per-sonnel was very experienced in international marketing, fluent in English and familiar with local customs and culture, did not have any R&D capa-

---

[167] Note that brand aims that were formulated after the IBM deal in 2005 are dis-cussed within the section 'brand positioning' due to story telling reasons of the case.

bility and lacked financial resources. However, it is reported that Daw was one of the first authorised distributors for IBM PCs in Hong Kong and China, and the NTD had been doing business with Daw for two years at this time (Lu 2000: 76). CITC was brought on board due to its deep financial pockets and international legal expertise. Further, Liu had personal connections within the company. Liu's father was chairman and general manager of one of the major shareholders of CITC, the China Patent Agent (H.K.) Ltd., who would also guarantee the joint venture's initial transactions with loans. In the first year of operation, more than 60% of total revenues were generated from the Chinese Mainland market, mainly through the distribution channels of the NTD (Lu 2000: 77-78).

While the trading and distribution business grew quickly and became very profitable, Legend Hong Kong continued to look for opportunities to expand into computer manufacturing as their second step of overseas expansion. In 1988, just four months after their founding, they acquired 80% of a small owner-managed motherboard manufacturing company in Hong Kong, Quantum Design International (QDI) (Lu 2000: 78).[168] A market observer thus concluded: "the company [Legend] had combined the two steps of globalisation and industrialisation (backward integration into manufacturing) in one stroke" (Lu 2000: 64). In 1989, the company sent its first self-made products to the CeBit in Hannover, Germany, one of the largest computer shows in Europe. Legend aggressively marketed their QDI-branded motherboards by a low price strategy. Liu compared this price strategy to "selling Mao-tai [the premier white liquor in China] at the price of Er-guo-tou [a bargain liquor]" (quoted in Chen et al. 2001: 4). The products' high performance and low price immediately won orders for several thousand units per months. But back at home, the company had to realise that QDI's existing plant capabilities were insufficient to fulfil the orders, and that "the market was lost" (Lu 2000: 80). After some breathtaking crises, the company finally managed to ship a steady volume of 3,500 motherboards a month by end of 1989 (Lu 2000: 81).

In 1990 they incorporated 'Legend Group Company', and formed a second R&D centre in Hong Kong, besides that in Beijing (Lu 2000: 84). In 1993, in order to keep up with the latest trends in the PC technology, they also opened up a R&D centre in California's Silicon Valley (Pan 2005: 6). Even though the participation in the CeBit learnt Legend some international market lessons, their products, in particular their first self-developed

---

[168] The motherboard is the heart of a computer system. Once a motherboard and other add-on cards are developed, system integration is the next step. Inline with its complexity, motherboards and add-on cards are low-margin products, whereas computer systems promise high margins.

PC based on an Intel 80286 microprocessor, made an impression on the Chinese government and the MEI, who finally awarded Legend with a national PC manufacturing license (Chen et al. 2001: 4). The group started to introduce its own Legend-branded computers in China in 1990. Although Legend Hong Kong had initially developed the PC for international markets, they found that it was too difficult to establish a new brand into the international consumer market. They continued to focus on marketing *QDI*-branded motherboards and add-on cards instead (Lu 2000: 88), and established 21 sales offices throughout the world according to own figures (Legend 1995; QDI 2004).[169] In 1994, Legend fulfilled their third step of overseas expansion and went IPO at the Hong Kong Stock Exchange (Lu 2000: 92).[170] They also bought 70% of the shares of the Hong Kong-based 'Valence Holding' in order to enter the semiconductor business (Lu 2000: 99).[171]

Despite of those Hong Kong businesses, Legend kept it focus on the Chinese market. Due to falling *QDI*-motherboard sales, revenues from overseas also remained relatively small and accounted for 5-7% of its output by 2003/2004 (Khermouch et al. 2003; Zhu 2005: 159, appendix 10). As a consequence, market observers reported that Legend prepared for its 'real' international expansion with the announcement to transfer their English brand name from *Legend* to *Lenovo* in 2003 (e.g., Meng 2006; Quelch/Knoop 2006: 5). In 2004 they also re-branded their English corporate name to 'Lenovo Group Limited', while the Chinese names remained unchanged.[172] Although the new *Lenovo* brand was unknown to all markets, it has rapidly made headlines around the world since. In 2004, Lenovo Group became an Olympic Worldwide Partner for the 2006 Torino Winter Games and 2008 Beijing Summer Games.[173] A few months later in December 2004, Lenovo and IBM announced an agreement by which Lenovo Group would acquire IBM's PC Division. Despite of interventions of the US congress initiated by a trio of high-ranking Republican members of the House of Representatives, fearing "the deal could threaten the US

---

[169] These were located in USA (5), Canada (3), UK, France, Germany, the Netherlands, Denmark, Spain, Austria, Sweden, Australia (2), Singapore, Malaysia, and Taiwan.

[170] Initial shareholders after IPO were as follows: Beijing Legend Group (38.8%), CITC (2.2), Daw, divided into its individual owners Lui Tam Ping (12.0), Ng Lai Yick (12.0), Cheung Nap Kai (4.2), Cheng Kwok (2.6), and other individuals (1.2), Feng Ming Investment (2.0), and the public (25.0) (Lu 2000: 93).

[171] By 2004, around 4% of Legend's total revenues were generated by contracted manufacturing, tendency decreasing (Datamonitor 2005f: 14).

[172] See section 'branding' for details on this brand transfer.

[173] See section 'brand communication' for details on this sponsorship.

security interests and help the transfer of US military-related technologies to China" (Chan/Guo 2005), the M&A deal was finally closed on May 1, 2005. The new Lenovo became the third largest computing company in the world after Dell and HP, and thus a new international IT competitor (Lenovo Group 2006c). Further, the acquisition allowed Lenovo to move quickly into the international marketplace: the expanded firm claimed customers and businesses in more than 160 countries (Quelch/Knoop 2006: 6). Yang Yuanqing, then chairman of the new Lenovo, stated "[…] the transaction […] constitutes a new era of the international PC industry" (Lenovo Group 2005b).

Lenovo paid US$1.75bn for the acquisition, US$650m thereof in cash, up to US$600m in common stock, and an assumed US$500m in IBM liabilities (Lenovo Group 2005b). As a part of the agreement, IBM continued to own a share of the new Lenovo Group of 18.9%. The Chinese government owned 46% of the new entity through Legend Holdings. In 2005 private investors (mostly private equity firms, including Texas Pacific Group, General Atlantic LLC and Newbridge Capital LLC) took about 10%, leaving IBM with 13.2%, the original founders with 14.7%, and the public with 34.7%. The Chinese Academy of Sciences held a 27.3% share as passive investor with no board seats (Lenovo Group 2005b, 2006c; Quelch/Knoop 2006: 5).

For IBM, this deal was considered an opportunity to shed an unprofitable operation and concentrate on consulting services and middleware solutions, as historically the division has frequently dipped into the red. For instance, in 2003, IBM lost over US$100m in this division (Datamonitor 2005f: 19). Deepak Advani, an IBM veteran who became Lenovo's chief marketing officer (CMO), explained the IBM rationale: "We had to decide what the right long-term play for IBM was. PCs were more and more at the fringe, with IBM moving more and more into services. A potential acquisition by Lenovo was an option, as was spinning out the division to a private equity firm. IBM and Lenovo decided to do the deal." Three years prior, Liu Chuanzhi explained, IBM had approached Lenovo for a potential similar transaction, which Lenovo had declined as "there was too much risk" (quoted in Chuanzhi/Chandler 2004). But then, he said, about a year ago, "we made a firm commitment to go global, […] and we came to see the IBM's offer in a different light". Lenovo management forecast synergies of US$200m, particularly to be realised in supply-chain management and manufacturing (Hamm 2005). Since they worried about loosing customers, they worked out an agreement that would allow Lenovo to continue the IBM brand, to keep the IBM salespeople, and even to keep the top executive of IBM as CEO. "IBM has all the things we need. This deal brings us market share, management know-how, technology, and international reach" (Liu quoted in Chuanzhi/Chandler 2004).

More specifically, the deal involved the purchase of IBM's well-established product brands *ThinkPad* (portables) and *ThinkCentre* (desktops), and gained the right to use the *IBM* brand on these products for up to five years (Lenovo Group 2005b). A fair estimate for the purchased brand value may be considered at US$415m, an amount which is equal to the brand value *IBM* lost in 2005 according to *Interbrand* statistics (2005: 90).[174] In return, Lenovo promised not to compete with IBM's services and consulting groups. IBM would continue to provide global support for the computers for five years, including warranty services, leasing and financing arrangements (Lenovo Group 2006c). Moreover, Lenovo took ownership of IBM's R&D centres in Japan and North Carolina and its *ThinkPad* factory in Shenzhen, and thus became the employer of 10,000 former IBM employees (Lenovo Group 2005a: 7; BCG 2006b: 17). Of that number, over 40% already worked in China and fewer than 25% worked in the US. Some 2,000 were members of sales teams. Lenovo also had access to IBM's 30,000-member enterprise sales team and ongoing support from partner and channel management programs. The new Lenovo headquarters moved from Beijing, China to Purchase, New York, not far from IBM's corporate headquarters (FAZ.net 2004; Lenovo Group 2006c).

Though announced as a "strategic alliance" (Lenovo Group 2006c), a JP Morgan analyst said about the Lenovo-IBM PC division merger: "The market consensus is quite negative about the deal as the major problem with the PC market is tight margins and cutthroat competition" (quoted in Chan/Guo 2005). Others argued that Lenovo had paid too much: "IBM's business was $680.2 million at the end of last June. This looks worst when compared to the $1.75 billion Lenovo paid for it" (Feng 2005). Michael Dell was even more categorical: "It won't work" (quoted in London 2005); "When was the last time you saw a successful acquisition or merger in the computer industry?" (quoted in Hamm/Engardia 2004). In the first half of 2006, Lenovo had the debut of their first Lenovo-branded computers outside of China into the US, Europe and India (Liu 2006). The product launch and the fact that the group managed to ensure operational profitability already in the first year might be taken as a first indicator for a

---

[174] Roll (2006: 20-21) estimated the added brand value at US$488m. This higher value is due to a different calculation approach and calculation inaccuracies. Roll based his estimate on IBM's brand contribution of 39% to the overall market capitalisation in 2002. Since the acquisition took place in 2004, he mixed up annual data from 2002 and 2004, and ignored that the IBM brand had made own developments during that years.

smooth transition (Lenovo Group 2006d: 18; Meng 2006, appendix 11). However, their global market shares have been struggling throughout 2005 and 2006, and also Chairman Yang Yuanqing admitted in September 2006 that it would take at least three years to return to strong profitability (Reuters 2006).

Table 5-17 sums up Lenovo's major market entry steps into international markets. See the next section for Lenovo's new brand positioning and recent market shares.

Year	Country	Brand mode	Institutional mode	Name	Initial products
1988	Hong Kong	Foreign brands	JV	Legend Hong Kong	PCs
1988	Hong Kong	Brand acquisition	M&A	Quantum Design International	Motherboards
1990	Hong Kong	Own brand	Greenfield	R&D centre, Hong Kong	PC products
1993	USA	Own brand	Greenfield	R&D centre, Silicon Valley	PC products
1994	Hong Kong	Not-branded	Majority JV	Valence Semiconductor Design	PC semiconductor products
until 1997	Worldwide (14 countries)	Own brand (QDI)	Greenfield	21 sales offices	Motherboards
2005	Worldwide (160 countries)	Brand acquisition	M&A	IBM PC division	PCs
2006	Worldwide	Own brand (lenovo)	Greenfield	Distribution of Lenovo 3000 series	PCs

Table 5-17. Lenovo's mode of market entry until 2006 (own illustration of major steps)[175]

Brand positioning

Meng Yutian (2006), senior supervisor of brand management department in Beijing, explained that the brand positioning of today's Lenovo is not as simple as probably expected. As the figure 5-31 shows, Lenovo deals with several different brands by 2006: *Lenovo, Lianxiang, QDI,* and after the acquisition of IBM PCs also the brands *ThinkPad, ThinkCentre, IBM* and *Lenovo 3000 series.* They all comprise different brand equities across different regional markets.

In China, Lenovo is particularly known by its Chinese brand name 联想 ('lianxiang'). *Lianxiang* is China's leading PC brand. It accounted for more than one-third of the Chinese PC market in 2005 as reported by IDC, and enjoys high brand awareness of more than 90% (Sino.com.cn 2003b). In contrast, the English name *Lenovo* has gained little brand recognition among Chinese end-consumers so far. If it has gained any brand recogni-

---

[175] Major steps focus on Lenovo's FDIs; they do not include branding and brand communication activities. For reference see in particular Lu (2000), Chen et al. (2001), Pan (2005), Quelch and Knoop (2006).

tion, then among consumers of China's tier 1 and tier 2 cities, and among IT decision makers (Meng 2006; Momentum Market Intelligence 2006). *Lianxiang* PCs are known for their user-friendly, tailor-made designs and customised solutions for various customer needs, mainly targeting home users and SMEs. 'Lenovo Lianxiang' also features a broad and expanding product line including mobile phones, servers, peripherals and digital entertainment products for the Chinese market (Lenovo Group 2006c). In addition to *Lianxiang*, Lenovo also markets its well-established *QDI* motherboard brand into China and into other world markets through its subsidiary in Hong Kong. While *Lianxiang* is an end-consumer brand, *QDI* may be known among PC makers as a b2b-brand. By 2004 *QDI*-brand is one of the world's largest and leading motherboard brands, accounting for 10-15% of the global market share according to own figures (Legend 1995; QDI 2004).

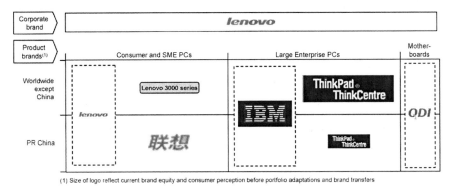

(1) Size of logo reflect current brand equity and consumer perception before portfolio adaptations and brand transfers

Fig. 5-31. Lenovo Group's brand portfolio in January 2006 (own illustration)[176]

Beyond the QDI brand, Lenovo was little known outside Asia, when they acquired IBM PCs in May 2005. The new enlarged company therefore had the opportunity and challenge to build an international brand from scratch, while making the most out of the well-established global brands *ThinkPad* and *ThinkCentre* and the right to use *IBM* logo on these products for up to five years (Lenovo Group 2005b; Quelch/Knoop 2006). The only major overlap of *Lenovo* and *IBM* brands, though a welcome one, was seen in their underlying brand value propositions. CMO Advani said: "The two companies had similar values with a focus on meritocracy. [...] Since Lenovo had in part modelled itself after HP and IBM. Customer focus, in-

---

[176] Illustration refers to the brand equities as given at the time of IBM acquisition, and after launch of Lenovo 3000 series. See section 'branding' for details on the brand transfers as part of the merger.

novation and trustworthiness were shared values" (quoted in Quelch/Knoop 2006: 7). The new *Lenovo* brand should therefore focus on selling product innovation at a premium level. Market share should matter less than providing innovation and customer service to those customers who appreciated it and were prepared to pay for it (Li 2005). To differentiate Lenovo from other competitors such as *Sony* and *Apple* who focus on innovation too, Advani explained: "We have a very efficient base in China, along with a 5% after-tax profit and global infrastructure. Unlike the competition we feel we have the ability to combine efficiency *and* innovation. That is what Lenovo is all about and it's what we've set down in our mission statement: *We put more innovation in the hands of more people so they can do more amazing things"* (quoted in Quelch/Knoop 2006: 10).

Beyond innovation, the complementary offers of *Lenovo* and *IBM* brands should become a key message to deliver to customers. A Lenovo executive explained: "What Lenovo brings to the table is the best from East and West. From the original Lenovo we have the understanding of emerging markets, excellent efficiency and a focus on long-term strategy. From IBM we have deep insights into worldwide markets and best practices from western companies. So we view Lenovo as a new world type of company, the kind Friedman talks about in his book *The World is Flat"* (quoted in Quelch/Knoop 2006: 8). In addition, Lenovo's focus had been on SME and home users through retail channel management, whereas IBM had long targeted large enterprise customers on a b2b-basis (table 5-18). "On paper this was pretty much a match made in heaven," Advani recalled. "We had complementary products and client bases, and practically no channel conflict. We could use the broad product portfolio we sell in China and use global distribution and take products around the world" (quoted in Quelch/Knoop 2006: 6-7).[177]

	Lenovo (% sales)	IBM (% sales)
Product type	85% desktop	60% portable
Client base	80% small business and consumers	57% large enterprise and mid-market
Coverage	Mostly China	Strong around the world, but relatively weak in China

Table 5-18. Lenovo and IBM complementarities (taken from Quelch/Knoop 2006: 7)

---

[177] See also appendix 8 for a before and after comparison of the product and revenue mix.

A major issue of the new brand positioning was the necessity to deal with *ThinkPad*, which was such considered a great sub-brand that Lenovo was reluctant to lose it. Besides, it was central to the value of the IBM deal with US$10bn in annual revenue and around 5% market share in each major market around the globe (IDC sources). The *ThinkPad* was consistently ranked as the undisputed premium-brand leader in the global PC industry, and synonym for an ultimate and indestructible business tool empowering success and prestige (Quelch/Knoop 2006: 23).

There was uncertainty about how ThinkPad's existing customers, who typically demand the highest quality products and services, would react to the new Chinese ownership arrangement and possible brand transfers. Since IBM is one of the most trusted brands around the world and has a series of strategic relationships that the new company could build on, Advani underlined: "we had a priceless gem of a brand. We also had the right to use the IBM logo for five years. We wanted to leverage that asset. Having the IBM stamp of approval on the notebook is serving as a very good bridge, because they're thinking that IBM trusts this company enough with its logo and if IBM is doing systems support, then I'm going to give these guys a shot" (Quelch/Knoop 2006: 8). In addition, Advani confirmed that Lenovo would not use the *Think*-family brands on existing Lenovo products. He said: "Some executives argued, 'Let's take the retail products Lenovo sells in China, label them ThinkPad and take them around the world,' and I said absolutely not. I am not going to take a product that has not been built from the ground up as a ThinkPad, put the ThinkPad name on it, and sell it as ThinkPad. That would be the best way to destroy the ThinkPad franchise. You don't build great brands simply through advertising and marketing, but by understanding your brand essence and value proposition and communicating it in a clear and compelling way. If you communicate something that is not authentic, it will backfire. [...] We have been very disciplined about everything that goes into the ThinkPad to make sure that it fits that essence" (Quelch/Knoop 2006: 10).

Finally, after having evaluated several scenarios for Lenovo's future brand architecture, Lenovo decided on a "synergy approach", a hybrid model whereby *Lenovo* will be marketed as the corporate umbrella and parent brand, and *Think* as the "hero" sub-brand (Quelch/Knoop 2006: 9). The corporate brand approach was attractive, since companies using it were moving up on the annual brand ranking as conducted by *Interbrand*. For example, *Samsung* had recently overtaken *Sony*, a clear sign in Lenovo's mind that corporate brands could be used to rapidly build brand equity (Quelch/Knoop 2006: 9). The rationale behind the hero sub-brand was that the *Think* should enhance *Lenovo* with some positive brand spill-over effects and its brand personality (Meng 2006). The brand architecture would require combined and balanced investments to build both the *Lenovo* and *Think* brands.

In addition, Lenovo expected that during the transition period their PC competitors would surely try to dislodge their loyal customers. A particular concern for the Western markets was China's quite poor image of country of origin and its negative connotations of the Chinese government (Quelch/Knoop 2006: 7-9). As a part of the strategy to disprove this image, Lenovo developed the new branded product line 'Lenovo 3000 series' and debut them into the world markets in February 2006. The series featured new desktop and portable models specifically designed to provide worry-free computing to the SME market segment. They are also planned to target PC home users in future (Bartsch 2005; Lenovo Group 2006c). 'Lenovo 3000' is positioned "as a smart lifestyle choice" (Quelch/Knoop 2006: 23), including brand value propositions like great price-value ratio, stylish design, and worry-free multimedia excitement. While *ThinkPad* and *ThinkCentre* products were priced at a slight premium to the competition, the 3000 would be priced equal to rival products from brands such as *Dell, HP, Acer, Gateway,* and *Fujitsu-Siemens* (Bartsch 2005; Quelch/Knoop 2006: 12).[178] For instance in Germany, the 'Lenovo 3000 J' desktops was launched at a price of €555 in April 2006, while the Think-Centre A60 cost €599.[179] By November 2006, Lenovo offered three notebook lines in Germany, the 3000 C (€600-800), the 3000 N (€800-1,000), and the 3000 V (€1,400). Though the ThinkPad R series was available for €700-800, other ThinkPad series were priced at €1,300-1,800 (Lenovo websites; German ads).

While it is not yet clear by the end of 2006, if and to what extent Lenovo 3000 has been accepted in the markets as Lenovo's second product line brand, Lenovo conducted a brand-related survey in January 2006 in order to gather first data on *Lenovo's* overall brand equity. The survey was conducted among IT decision makers in China, the US, Germany, Japan and India, half *ThinkPad*-customers, half non-customers (Momentum Market Intelligence 2006, appendix 12). The results showed that the IT decision makers in China, Japan and India had greater awareness of the Lenovo/IBM deal than those in the US and Germany. In the US, Japan and China *ThinkPad* customers were significantly more likely aware of the fact than non-customers. With respect to *Lenovo* brand, brand familiarity was low in all surveyed countries except China. 75% of IT decision makers in Germany reported that they were unfamiliar with *Lenovo* brand. However, in October 2006, an unrepresentative online survey certified *Lenovo* an un-

---

[178] See section 'brand innovations' for further details on Lenovo 3000 series.
[179] Both came with 512 MB memory, 160 GB hard drive.

aided brand awareness of 29% among 82 Germans. Therewith they became the best known Chinese brand in Germany, ahead of the 'oldies' *Haier* and *Tsingdao* brand (own research, chap 'China's country-of-origin').

But, in terms of market shares, it is to note that Lenovo lost significant shares throughout 2005 and 2006 (table 5-19, Reuters 2006). While before the IBM acquisition the combined share was 8.1%, Lenovo only obtained 6.4% in Q1 2006. To make and retain Lenovo successful will therefore largely depend on the extent global PC users will trust into the new *Lenovo* and *Think* brands in future, and to what extent new Lenovo can satisfy their brand value propositions.

	1Q 2004	4Q 2004	1Q 2005	2Q 2005	3Q 2005	Q1 2006
Lenovo global, combined shares	7.4%	8.1%	7.1%	7.5%	7.7%	6.4%
Lenovo global, before acquisition	1.9%	2.4%	2.1%			
IBM global, before acquisition	5.5%	5.7%	5.0%			
Lenovo China	28.8%	32.1%	29.6%	33.8%	34.5%	31.3%

Table 5-19. Lenovo and IBM market shares before and after acquisition Q1 2004-Q1 2006 in % PC shipments (based on IDC sources)

Brand innovations

While IBM is considered one of the most innovative companies in the world in terms of PC technologies and designs (e.g., McGregor 2006), Lenovo's market success in China primarily based on strong customer orientation and computer personalisation. Li Qin, executive vice president of Legend, once explained: "Our differentiating strategy was reflected in both product positioning and product design. In the product positioning area, we tried to differentiate our products based on functions, instead of core technology, since there was really no significance in the core technology for PCs by the late 1990's. As for product design, our engineers tried very hard to take ergonomics and local consumer preferences into consideration" (Chen et al. 2001: 7). In addition, Legend was known in China for their extensive service networks including 6 regional technical service centres and 500 maintenance outlets, a 24-hour hotline and on-site service. Further, they were the first computer manufacturer to commit to a 3-year service guarantee in China (Access Asia 2002: 41).

In terms of product inventions, they became known in the 1985/86 by the 'Lianxiang Chinese Character Card', which translated the computer's English operating system into Chinese language and therewith empowered China to benefit from computing systems. Although state-owned companies such as 'Founder Electronics' were explicitly founded in 1986 in order to carry out the government's "Chinese Character Processing" project, the Lianxiang Card set the industry standard. As the technology was hardware-based and the Card was inserted into PC motherboards, it did not occupy much of the then costly hard-disc space and was not that easy to pirate in comparison to software-based Chinese language solutions (Chen et al. 2001). In 1990 Legend developed their first PC based on an Intel 80286 microprocessor, and pioneered the fast growing segment of home users and small enterprise users by the 'Legend 1+1' home PCs in 1992 (Lenovo Group 2006c). Legend 1+1' was sold at a retail price of RMB 3,000, which was a very competitive price, since at this time most of the PCs were sold to corporate enterprises at an average price of RMB 10,000 (Pan 2005: 6). Another example for Legend's customer orientation was their internet solutions and internet PCs. In 1997 Lenovo agreed with Microsoft to manufacture the set top boxes for Microsoft's Venus Project in China. The boxes allowed for access to the internet via TV sets and bypassed the lack of home-owned PCs in China. In 1999 Legend launched their Tianxi PC which included a specially designed keyboard that offered a 'one-touch-to-the-net' access to user specified internet sites, e-mail, and service and support menus. To promote the PC, Legend was offering a full year of free internet access in cooperation with China Telecom. The Tianxi also came with a handwriting pad that enabled users to enter Chinese language characters when composing emails (Access Asia 2002: 34-35; Lenovo Group 2006c). As different users have different needs in surfing the net, Legend later launched four product series, namely Tianhui, Future Pioneer, Tianlu and Tianle. Tianhui is specially designed for children; Future Pioneer for high school students; Tianlu for adult and Tianle for middle-aged and elderly (Access Asia 2002: 45-46). In 2002 Legend marked their beginning in the 3C era. As a part of their strategy, they entered the mobile phone segment and initiated the IGRS Working Group, in cooperation with a few large companies and the Chinese Ministry of the Information Industry, to promote the formation of the industrial standard (Lenovo Group 2006c).

Despite of these achievements, it is to note that Lenovo was criticised by some market observers to lack a detailed development blueprint and to be too short-sighted (e.g., Beijing Review 2006). Larry H.P. Lang, economist with the Chinese University of Hong Kong, explained that Lenovo's internet operation lost over US$25m after the failure of the one-year cooperation with 'Yestock Information Technology'. Moreover, their joint venture with America Online closed with a loss after two years due to respective internal problems. Lenovo's IT service business, though growing, profitable and attractive in terms of brand image building, was suddenly stopped and sold to 'AsiaInfo Holdings' in July 2004 for US$36m because of their inability to reach their preset goals in a short-time frame.

In addition, there is evidence that Lenovo was reluctant to invest in R&D. They usually spent around 1-2% of their revenues on R&D, in their financial year 2000/2001 even only 0.09% (Access Asia 2002: 40), an amount which can be considered very low and unusual for a high-tech company. In comparison, IBM and HP spend around 5-6% of their revenue on R&D. However Dell used to be short on R&D spending too and spent around 2% in 2003 (Park/Burrows 2003). Lang commented: "Lenovo took research and development lightly. It believed marketing was the priority and underestimated the importance of technology. This mentality didn't change until 2004, when it put 200 million yuan [US$24m] into R&D, but that still accounted for less than 1.2 percent of the total turnover that year. Compared with Huawei Technologies and Haier Group, Lenovo's R&D assets fell far behind. Huawei pours no less than 10 percent of its total turnover each year into R&D, while Haier spends no less than 5 percent" (quoted in Beijing Review 2006). Finally, Access Asia (2002: 40) reported that Legend closed several co-operations with international computer vendors to obtain the most advanced technology.

However, when Legend decided to enter overseas markets in 2003, it is reported that the management considered the needs of foreign markets quite different to those in China and that they could not simply transfer their products sold in China (Pan 2005: 10). Lenovo's CFO Mary Ma said that the group had therefore approved a plan to spend at least one billion RMB (US$121m) a year on product development (Perez 2003). In FY 2003/2004, this would have been 4.1% of Lenovo's total revenues. Given this lack in R&D, one can also argue that the acquisition of IBM PCs in 2005 was in particular attractive to Lenovo due to their R&D capabilities (Liu 2006). Lenovo took ownership not only of the IBM research centres in Yamato near Tokyo, Japan and Raleigh, North Carolina, USA but also of 2,000 international patents and of hundreds of IBM experienced scientists and researchers, who have produced some of the world's most important advances in PC technology (BCG 2006b; Lenovo Group 2006c). In November 2006, Lenovo had 1,700 scientists and engineers, of which 1,200 are in Beijing, China, and the rest in Japan and the US. According to Richard Cheston, executive director of Lenovo's research facility in Raleigh, the three teams are highly complementary. The US team is specialised in software and architecture design, the team in Japan is strong in hardware and notebooks, and the Chinese team includes experts in designing personalised consumer products (Liu 2006).

In 2005, the first product created by combined efforts of the three R&D teams was launched into the market, the new wide screen ThinkPad Z60. As reported by Quelch and Knoop (2006: 11), "the product team was challenged to make something appealing that anyone who owned a ThinkPad would want to upgrade to" and that would in particular disprove some customers' worries that Lenovo would "mess up the ThinkPad". Though a significant risk, the design team finally chose a titanium cover, which is a major departure from the traditional black of the ThinkPad. "Titanium delivered a real benefit to customers— protection. And it looked beautiful," CMO Advani explained. "That's the way it was received in the marketplace. Fortune magazine did a story that said, 'All told, Lenovo's stewardship of this brand is off to a good start, with perhaps the best ThinkPad yet.'" *Fortune* also acknowledged that Lenovo made the "legendary" keyboard even better (Lewis 2005). Lenovo took the media credit as a compliment: "We made clear we're not going to mess it up—we showed we could make products that were true to the ThinkPad brand essence and even improve upon it," Advani said (quoted in Quelch/Knoop 2006: 11).

In February 2006, Lenovo also made the debut of their first Lenovo-branded computers into the international market place, the 'Lenovo 3000 series', including several models of desktops and portables (Lenovo Group 2006d: 18). To create the product line, Lenovo did extensive market research in the first place. Lenovo staff talked to over 4,000 customers face-to-face and surfaced three main concerns towards the global PC market (Quelch/Knoop 2006: 9): innovation would slow down, quality would suffer, and service and support would be outsourced overseas. To address and neutralise the last point, it is reported that Lenovo structured the original deal to include ongoing worldwide service and support from IBM via its existing global service infrastructure. Regarding the first two concerns, Lenovo hoped to reassure customers that innovation and quality would not decrease but might actually increase because the new firm would be solely PC focused. In terms of branding, it is reported that some managers wanted to give these new products a sub-brand name like other PC sub-brands such as *Presario* or *Vario* (Quelch/Knoop 2006: 12). A number was finally chosen so as to not detract from the Lenovo name.

The new 'Lenovo 3000 family' was targeted at the small business market. Lenovo research among SMEs in Germany, Japan, the UK and the US revealed that these customers perceived quality, reliability, and durability as key. Due to small staffs, they also valued simplicity and easy, open dealings with PC vendors, and a competitive price. CMO Advani explained that price as the selling factor was not an option, since any perception of Lenovo as a company from China providing cheap products (US$359-499) might devalue the Lenovo corporate brand, and could also damage the premium *ThinkPad* brand by negative spillover effects. To address the other consumer needs, Lenovo planned to ensure that the 3000 series had a unique, distinctive and attractive design to build brand awareness. Each PC also came with a set of tools called "LenovoCare" providing "worry-free computing." The marketing campaign for Lenovo 3000 reinforced the notion that small business owners wanted to "worry about [their] business, not [their] PC" (Quelch/Knoop 2006: 12-13). See also section 'brand communication' for ad samples.

Operative brand decisions when going-international

Branding

The origin of Lenovo's Chinese brand name联想 ('lianxiang') can be traced back to 1985, when the NTD invented the "Lianxiang Chinese Character Card", in Chinese 联想式汉卡 ('lianxiang shihan ka') (Lenovo Group 2006c). An important feature of this technology was 联想 ('lianxiang') which means 'association'. The association feature enabled the PC system to prompt Chinese characters which could be used to form expressions and phrases with the character input. Chen (2001: 2) explained, when a user wanted to write 中国 'zhongguo' (China) and typed the character 中 'zhong' (centre), the system would immediately offer 国 'guo' (country), amongst others, each with its own number, which the user could type to complete the input of the whole expression. The feature offered associations for most everyday phrases and saved tremendous Chinese character input time. Due to its comfort, the Lianxiang Card became famous in China within one year, and was awarded with the highest National Science-Technology Progress Award by the Chinese government in 1988 (Lenovo Group 2006c).

To capitalise on the brand recognition generated by the Lianxiang Card, the NTD decided on联想 *'Lianxiang'* as their Chinese brand name in June 1988, when they opened up 香港联想 'Lianxiang Hong Kong'. In 1989 the NTD also changed their corporate name in China to 北京联想 'Beijing Lianxiang' and later to联想集团 'Lianxiang Group' in 1990 (Chen et al. 2001: 2; Lenovo Group 2006c). As a part of their Hong Kong strategy they also chose *Legend* as their English corporate name which is a direct transliteration of 'Lianxiang' (Zhu 2005: 166, annual reports). According to market observers, the English name *Legend* became not known among Chinese consumers, rather they referred to the 'Lianxiang' brand only (Lu 2000; Sino.com.cn 2003a).

When in 2003 the group started preparing the brand for a worldwide launch, they abandoned the English brand name *Legend* and re-named it into *Lenovo*. CEO Yang explained: "To further develop our brand and make it more consistent with our long-term strategic vision, last year we initiated a comprehensive reassessment of our brand strategy, eventually deciding to adopt a single brand structure. Since our original English brand name 'Legend' has already been registered by businesses in many countries, we started to change our logo from 'Legend' to 'lenovo' from April this year" (Legend 2003a: 7). Legend manager Zhang Guisen added (in an interview with Sino.com.cn 2003b) that they had also evaluated a brand transfer to the *QDI* brand. But, as the brand is only known for motherboards, they found the brand is not promising for computers and mobile phones. He explained that they finally developed the English name *Lenovo* together with a foreign brand agency. The name was considered easy to pronounce in many languages and available for brand registration in all major markets in America, Europe and South East Asia (Sino.com.cn 2003b; Quelch/Knoop 2006: 5).

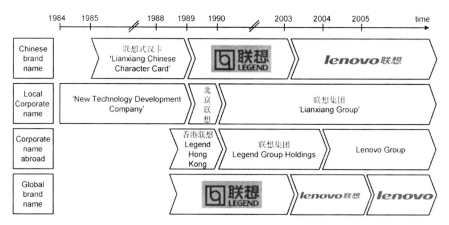

Fig. 5-32. Lenovo's path to a global brand name 1984-2006 (own illustration)

Lenovo was derived from 'Le-' for *Legend* and '-novo', the Latin word for 'new', reflecting the spirit of innovation as the company's core competence. As CEO Yang expressed, the new *Lenovo* brand was designed to represent "an innovative Legend" (Legend 2003a: 7). In terms of brand colours, the new brand logo 'Lenovo 联想' kept the blue Legend colour and is written in blue bold italic letters. A year later in 2004, the company adopted 'Lenovo Group' also as the group's official English name (Lenovo Group 2006c). Starting in 2005 when Lenovo became a Worldwide Olympic Partner and announced to acquire IBM PCs, they finally abandoned the two Chinese characters 联想 as a part of their global brand name (Lenovo Group 2005a). As a result of this branding history, market observers nowadays distinguish three periods: the computer technology period, the *Legend* period and the *Lenovo* period (e.g., Sino.com.cn 2003a; Yu 2006: 52-54). See also the illustration in figure 5-32.

With the acquisition of the IBM PC division in May 2005 probably a fourth branding period of Lenovo has just started. Since the acquisition allows them to use the *IBM* logo for up to five years on the *Think*-family products, they recently implemented a global brand transfer of *IBM Think-Pad* and *IBM ThinkCentre*. "The research showed that in many customers' minds the IBM and ThinkPad brands were hard to separate," Mark McNeilly, Lenovo's director for branding and marketing strategy explained. "They really were linked together" (quoted in Quelch/Knoop 2006: 6). In Western countries the challenge would therefore be to eliminate the *IBM* logo from the *Think*-family brands while retaining their brand equity and market shares. Meng Yutian (2006) said the challenge would be different in China and in some other emerging markets. She explained that Chinese consumers would not be aware of the product brand *ThinkPad* but of the corporate brand *IBM*, and would typically name their computer "the IBM notebook" or "my IBM". Therefore, the goal in China and similar countries would rather be to build a new *ThinkPad* brand by transferring *IBM*'s brand equities and interlinking it to *Lenovo* brand: "We cannot get rid off it [the IBM brand] immediately. We have to leverage it." According to Meng Yutian (2006), the ultimate branding for all markets would finally be an independent *ThinkPad* and *ThinkCentre* logo with a tagline to the corporate brand *Lenovo*.

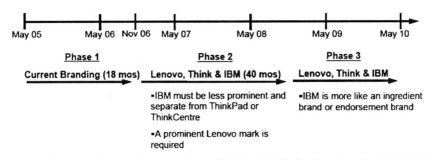

Fig. 5-33. Brand transfer schedule of IBM Think-family brands 2005-2010 (company material as taken from Quelch/Knoop 2006: 17)

In terms of time schedule, Lenovo management set up the brand transfer as shown in figure 5-33. In the first phase till November 2006, all branding should remain unchanged. In phase two, from November 2006 till end of 2008, IBM's prominence should be reduced with the pace Lenovo's prominence would increase. In phase three starting in 2009, IBM branding should become small and should function as an endorsement or ingredient brand (see also Beijing Ribao [Beijing Daily Newspaper] 2005).

In terms of product branding, Lenovo successfully stepped into phase two in October 2006, as seen in figure 5-34 left-hand side, when they put a small *Lenovo* logo on the ThinkPad T60 notebook (IT.com.cn 2006). In terms of brand advertising, it is note that Lenovo already started communicating the tagline 'ThinkPad. A product of Lenovo' in June 2005 in Germany, within the TV spot promoting ThinkPad's 'bionic finger' (German TV channels, Dickie et al. 2005). Figure 5-34 right-hand side shows that the tagline 'ThinkPad. A product of Lenovo' is also used in the Chinese market place. See also next section for Lenovo's brand communication including ad samples.

Fig. 5-34. Examples of Lenovo's brand transfer of ThinkPad brand (taken from IT.com.cn 2006 and Lenovo websites)

Brand communication

Prior to Lenovo's going-international, it is reported that Lenovo's predecessor, Legend, started to invest in advertising and other brand communication activities in 2001, when competition became fiercer in China. According to an estimate given by Pan (2005: 9), Legend spent a total of US$12.2m on advertising in 2002, US$6.8m thereof on the home PC segment. Many famous stars, amongst them, Zhang Ziyi served as spokespersons. Given no other advertising spending, this would have equal to a share of 0.47% of total revenue in FY 2002/03. In comparison, competitor Dell spent about double the amount on advertising in China in the same year. In 2003 and 2004, Lenovo have increased their budgets and have spent around 1.0-1.2% of their total revenue on advertising (Huang/Du 2005: 429). Although one can consider the budget as quite low for a company who perceives their values as customer orientation and marketing, it is to note that besides advertising, Legend has also built their brand through online offers, strong distribution networks and product promotions such as the PC including an one-year free internet access (Meng 2006). In addition, the group was regularly present at the world's largest computer fairs since 1990, and was engaged in several national sports sponsorships. Among others, the company sponsored the Chinese national women's soccer team in 1999, and two years later Beijing's successful bid to host the 2008 Olympic Games. Known slogans in China were 'Every day, we are improving' and 'As legend becomes closer to you, technology comes closer to you' (Gilmore/Dumont 2003: 147; Yang 2005: 133).

Thinking globally, Lenovo also became the first Chinese company to join the Olympic Partner Program in March 2004, the International Olympic Committee's (IOC) highest marketing programme. 'Engaging the world' was the slogan Lenovo used at its signing ceremony (Quelch/Knoop 2006: 5). As a worldwide sponsor with the IOC, the group will be the exclusive supplier of computing equipment and services, such as desktops, portables, servers and desktop printers, and will be funding in support of the 2006 Winter Games in Torino, Italy and the 2008 Summer Games in Beijing, China (Lenovo Group 2006c; Meng 2006). Lenovo paid a price of admission of US$80m which was considered a significant investment for a company with sales of around $US3bn at this time (Quelch/Knoop 2006: 5). Although Lenovo will be able to benefit from using the Olympic logo for marketing and promotions and have access to exclusive worldwide marketing opportunities, Quelch and Knoop (2006: 5) noted that the company would have to spend at least twice the amount of the sponsorship cost on advertising to leverage the investment. These advertising expenses would be spread over five years, and the company expected that about half of the sponsorship costs are to be paid back through products and services.

In 2005, Lenovo spent a total of US$250m on worldwide marketing, with over 80% of it on television and print advertising, and the remainder being allocated to the internet, outdoor and other media (Quelch/Knoop 2006: 12). In the US, Dell's marketing spending reached US$460m (nearly 20 times more than Lenovo), followed by HP with US$130m. In Japan, Dell spent US$110m (nearly 10 times more than Lenovo) followed by NEC at US$26m. Dell also led in spending on advertising in the UK and Germany, while HP dominated in France, Brazil, India, and Mexico. According to Quelch and Knoop (2006: 12), in many major markets Lenovo's gap to their key competitors in share of voice was at least 1:3. Taking this weakness into account, Lenovo planned a US$100m campaign to factor in Lenovo's sponsorship of the 2006 Winter Olympic Games and the Summer Olympic Games in Beijing. The campaign was orchestrated by IBM's former advertising team at Ogilvy & Mather. The initial plan incorporated online ads, television, and print (Quelch/Knoop 2006: 12). The overall slogan was "New World. New Thinking", addressing Lenovo as a supplier of innovation and as a new world enterprise (Lenovo Group 2006e: 41).

Fig. 5-35. Impressions from Lenovo at 2006 Torino Olympic Winter Games (own illustration)

While originally Lenovo targeted the Olympic sponsorship to help to introduce the *Lenovo* brand around the globe (Lenovo Group 2006c; Meng 2006), the 2006 Torino Winter Games became a crucial platform to showcase their capabilities after the IBM deal. Furthermore, the deal itself had brought Lenovo considerable public visibility and brand awareness (Quelch/Knoop 2006: 8). In terms of product supply, the new Lenovo supported the Winter Games in Torino with 5,000 desktop PCs, 350 servers and 1,000 notebook computers. Lenovo also hosted seven internet i.lounges for use by Olympic athletes, visitors, and journalists (Lenovo Group 2006f). In terms of brand communication, a number of product marketing activities in China were centred on the Olympic Games by joining in with other Olympic sponsors like Visa International and Coca-Cola (Li 2005; Lenovo Group 2006d: 19). See figure 5-35 for impressions on Lenovo's Olympic sponsorship.

In addition, Lenovo set up a three phase plan which embodied the Olympic Games as a milestone. Phase one was planned to establish trust and continuity, phase two to strengthen *ThinkPad* and establish *Lenovo*, and phase three to accelerate *Lenovo* brand (Lenovo Group 2006b: 19). As part of phase one, the company ran a global advertising campaign from May to September 2005, where every ad signed off with the product brand *ThinkPad* instead of *IBM* or *Lenovo*. The objective was to maintain Think-Pad sales momentum, which meant reassuring customers that little had changed since the acquisition (Saal 2005; Quelch/Knoop 2006: 10). The second phase included the campaign "ThinkPad Unleashed". It was scheduled to run on TV during the Torino Olympics Opening Ceremony on February 10, 2006. The message was that Lenovo was not just maintaining the status quo but making the ThinkPad even better, doing things that IBM could not have done or would never have done (Quelch/Knoop 2006: 10). Phase two also included ads to debut the Lenovo logo and the 'Lenovo 3000 series' as seen in figure 5-36.

Beyond global marketing initiatives, CMO Advani explained that Lenovo also tried to find creative ways to address consumers in their respective country markets. For instance, in India, they placed a Lenovo monitor on a very popular game show on television, India's version of 'Who wants to be a Millionaire'. The show ran at prime time three times a week for six months and was hosted by one of the top Indian movie stars. A 50,000 rupees question on the show asked players to name the company that is formed out the combination of the English word 'legend' and the Latin word 'new' (Quelch/Knoop 2006: 12).

Another example was the marketing campaign surrounding the Football World Cup in Germany in June 2006 (figure 5-37). Lenovo's campaign was endorsed by the footballer of the year Ronaldinho and was run in 20 countries, including Europe, Latin America and China (Lenovo Group 2006a: 7). For the US market, Lenovo also became Official PC Partner of the National Basketball Association (NBA) in 2006 (Lenovo Group 2006b: 19-20)

Although all these marketing activities have definitively resulted in some brand awareness building for *Lenovo* brand, CMO Advani admitted that a more difficult part would now be ahead with phase three: "The next step is to give the brand meaning and have it stand for something unique that customers care about. Moving consumers to consider and prefer the brand is what we need to work on next" (quoted in Quelch/Knoop 2006: 12).

Fig. 5-36. 'Lenovo 3000' print ads as debuted in 2006 (German version taken from Die Zeit, 23.03.2006, US-version from Quelch/Knoop 2006: 26)

Fig. 5-37. Ronaldinho as Lenovo's spokesperson during 2006 Football World Cup hosted in Germany (Chinese version taken from The Economic Observer, 10.07.2006; German version from Die Zeit, 01.06.2006)

Brand distribution

With the acquisition of IBM PCs in May 2005, Lenovo Group became present in more than 160 countries by their *Think*-family brands. They are mainly distributed by certified sales agencies and distribution partners (Meng 2006). CEO Amelio explained in 2006: "We are absolutely committed to our channel partners for serving our transaction customers and for fulfilment of our large enterprise customers. At the same time, we will continue to provide end-users who prefer to buy directly with the means to do so" (Lenovo Group 2006d: 15). According to Lenovo websites, this included *Think* direct-sales at Lenovo internet websites and direct-sales via business partner's online shops.

In contrast to *Think*-family brands, the key distribution channels of Lenovo-branded computers are retail stores and internet online-sales (Meng 2006). In China, Lenovo targets large volume sales through its integrated distribution strategy which combines retail, channel distribution and direct-to-customer models (online and telephone sales), and allows Lenovo to cover various consumer segments (Pan 2005: 5; Lenovo Group 2006c). The strategy includes an extensive network with 18 sales regions, comprising 108 grids and more than 4,000 retail shops across the country, penetrating also deeply into the township villages. They also ran more than 130 Lenovo "1+1 Specialty Shops" (Access Asia 2002: 40). For the international markets, it may be the goal to copy the national distribution model over the next couple of years (Lenovo Group 2006d; Meng 2006). So far, Lenovo-branded products are available in the US, Europe and India (Liu 2006). To align with their brand positioning, they started with contracting computer specialised resellers to target the focused segment of SMEs. In March of 2006, Lenovo also launched their 'Lenovo Partner Network', their new business partner program. The Network shall position Lenovo partners as the primary route to market Lenovo-branded computers to SMEs worldwide. In addition, it shall provide them with new tools and solutions to address the unique requirements of the SME market. In the US, in addition to close relationships with specialised resellers, Lenovo is reaching out to the SME audience at selected Office Depot and Best Buy stores in 2006 (Lenovo Group 2006d: 13). In all targeted markets Lenovo-branded PCs are also available online, e.g., at www.buylenovo.de. Similar to the Dell approach, the online channel seems to emerge as a major Lenovo channel to reach several consumer segments and several geographic markets worldwide by relatively low investments. However, storage, delivery, after-sales and b2b-services for Think-family products will still remain business-crucial. How Lenovo therefore is going to distribute their products after the IBM crew of 30,000 salespersons have left in May 2010 remains challenging. See also next section 'brand organisation' for current bonds to IBM Corporation.

Brand organisation

Prior to the IBM deal, the founder Liu Chuanzhi and follower Yang Yuan-qing have built up the organisation structure of the company. Although the NTD was official founded as a state-owned enterprise in 1984, Liu enjoyed large autonomy from the Chinese government starting from the founding of the company. In the 1990s, Legend described their organisational form as "a new type of state-owned enterprise that emerged from China economic reform, particularly the reform of the science and technology system" (Lu 2000: 63). More specifically, they adopted an organisation that based on the principle of 'state-owned, non government run', with a balance of state ownership on the one hand and managerial autonomies in finance, personnel, planning and management on the other hand. The organisational model was also compared to 'one academy, two systems', which is addressing the symbiosis between the system of scientific research and technology commercialisation under one organisational roof of the Chinese Academy of Sciences (Lu 2000: 64). Beyond this organisational model, Liu had a simple approach. Since Legend has been listed at Hong Kong Stock Exchange in 1994, he acted with the basis that "Legend is accountable only to shareholders, with the transparency that this would suggest" (Economist 2001). Distributing HP-branded computers into

China for more than a decade, Liu also took HP as his teacher and role model in the PC business. An employee described that Liu had a very strong entrepreneurial and innovative spirit, and that this spirit became an important part of the company's corporate culture (Gilmore/Dumont 2003: 139).

The era of Yang Yuanqing started in 1994 when Legend consolidated all PC-related segments in one PC business unit, and Yang, then 29 years old, became the unit's general manager. Yang joined Legend in 1988 after obtaining a master degree in computer science from the elite University of Science and Technology. Recalling his appointment as a "risky decision", Liu later noted, "I did not really have any other choice. Most of the senior managers of the company were older than 50 and did not have much experience working in a market environment, not to mention a rapidly changing industry like the PC industry" (Chen et al. 2001: 5). Under the new structure Yang was responsible for purchasing, manufacturing and marketing of all PC products, and was granted flexibility in determining new product launches, channel selection, and pricing strategies based on market conditions.

As Access Asia (2002: 42) reported, Legend removed the label of 'state-owned' in January 2000, when they became a joint-stock holding company. Legend was the second enterprise in Beijing's Zhongguancun (China's Silicon Valley) to undergo this kind of property right restructuring. The first was the 'Stone Company', another of China's leading IT firms at the time, which reorganised through a management buyout. Under the equity-restructuring plan, a 35% equity share of Legend was distributed to Legend employees. Of that amount, Legend's original founders got 35%, the around 100 employees who had worked at Legend since 1988 got a 20% share, and the remainder of 45% were distributed among key players in China's computer and software industry. The equity holding were freely traded in order to avoid the possibility of a hostile takeover. In 2001 with the termination of Legend's foreign-branded distribution business, Liu stepped aside as president and became chairman of Legend Group. He appointed Yang as the new president and CEO of the group. To better fit to the competitive and fast changing market environments and to prepare for Legend's going-international, Yang finally simplified the organisation structure with respect to core businesses and efficiency targets in 2003.[180] Pan (2005: 10) commented that "the top management at Legend really understood that the road to capturing the international markets was an uphill one".

---

[180] See appendix 13 for Lenovo Group's organisation structure 2003-2005. See Chen et al. (2001: 23-26) for prior organisation structures.

With the acquisition of IBM PCs in May 2005 and starting post-merger integrations, the management team changed. While it is reported that in the beginning Chinese Lenovo wanted to keep the leadership (Bartsch 2005), Liu, then in his 60s, finally left the operational business and became non-executive director. Yang, 40 years old, stepped aside as president and became chairman of new Lenovo Group. Instead, half of the company's top jobs went to executives of American, Australian, European, and Indian origin (London 2005). Amongst them, Steve Ward from IBM became the first president and CEO of the new Lenovo Group. He was replaced by Bill Amelio from Dell in December 2005 (Quelch/Knoop 2006: 7). Moreover, English became the company's working language, and the headquarters were moved to New York, USA, which may have disappointed many Chinese people. Marc Fischer, chief of Lenovo Germany, explained that Lenovo wanted to be perceived as an international company not as a Chinese company (Bartsch 2005). Finally, Chinese executives only kept the responsibility for finance, technology, the Chinese market, and mobile phones (see appendix 14 for an illustration of the whole management team).

For Lenovo brand management, Deepak Advani from India became chief marketing officer (CMO). Previously, Advani worked with IBM for 12 years and in the end was the vice president of marketing for IBM's PC division. Advani holds a master degree in computer engineering and an MBA from the Wharton School of the University in Pennsylvania (Lenovo Group 2006c). In comparison to prior brand organisations and to other Chinese branded companies (Gilmore/Dumont 2003), it is to note that the establishment of a CMO can be considered a unique move. It may reflect IBM's strong influence within the organisation on the one hand, and the importance of brand management for new Lenovo's business success on the other hand. CMO Advani recalled: "[...] one of the first questions I asked Yang was, 'As chief marketing officer, do you have some ideas on a preferred branding strategy or am I free to start with a clean slate and craft a new branding strategy based on market research and our best judgment?' And I will always remember this. He said, 'You are the CMO and you do the market research, and we as a company will do what you recommend,' which was terrific" (Wharton School 2005a; Quelch/Knoop 2006: 8).

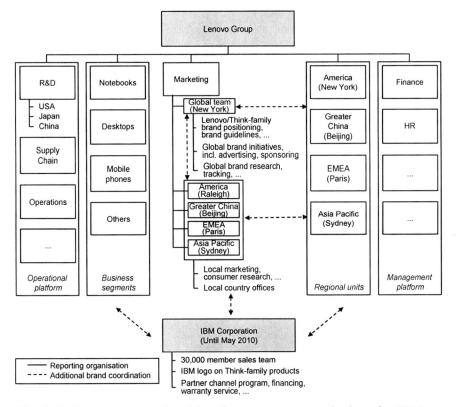

Fig. 5-38. Lenovo's international brand management organisation after IBM acquisition (own illustration of first findings)[181]

Asking Zhang Ying (2006), part of Lenovo's Ogilvy & Mather team in Beijing, further details on Lenovo Group's new brand organisation, she revealed that Lenovo's marketing would be organised by regions, similar to the approach of the overall company organisation (figure 5-38). Greater China would thereby be separated from the other markets due to the unbalanced brand equities of *Lenovo* brand. CMO Advani added that there were global marketing teams in New York and Raleigh (Wharton School 2005a). The teams are supposed to be responsible for global brand and marketing activities such as global research, definition and control of brand value propositions, brand guidelines, brand and ad tracking, and global marketing initiatives, including the Olympic sponsorship and the

---

[181] The illustration is a simplification of reality and focuses on brand-related units. Due to ongoing post-merger integrations, the author can also not guarantee correctness in all details.

World Cup.[182] In addition, Advani said that he also could rely on marketing teams in the EMEA headquarters (Europe, the Middle East, and Africa) in Paris, France, in the Asian headquarters in Sydney, Australia and Beijing, China. There are also localised marketing teams at country level. Advani explained: "These teams work to understand what the trends are in a given country, what the real met and unmet needs are of the target customer and what the best way is for us to communicate our value proposition. [...] Though old Lenovo did not have a lot of international experience [...] there are many lessons we can apply from China and the other emerging markets" (quoted in Wharton School 2005a). In addition, Lenovo's advertising company, Ogilvy & Mather, supports Lenovo at the global and country level. The company also planned to set up an Indian headquarter in October 2005 (Liu 2005).

Although Lenovo's new organisation may appear promising, market observers remained concerned that the potential for cultural and operational clashes between IBM veterans and Chinese nationals might still be present (Feng 2005; Quelch/Knoop 2006: 7). Lenovo, they argued, would still resemble a Chinese state-owned enterprise in terms of company culture. The new organisation would also be more complex and need to serve many more geographical markets. For instance, the 12-hour time difference between Beijing and the US east coast caused some strain and demanded working via conference calls around the clock, while the original Lenovo team was used to meeting together to solve problems. However, Meng Yutian (2006) was satisfied and said that the integration went smoothly so far. CMO Advani gave reasons and recalled a meeting, where Yang demanded the top executives to work together: "The key message was to trust the other person. Because we all came from different backgrounds, we had to respect each other's position. Always remember that the real competitor is outside. And be ready to compromise. Even if you think that your decision is grounded in 'better business' logic or facts, you should be willing to compromise if that makes more sense" (quoted in Quelch/Knoop 2006: 7).

Figure 5-39 sums up Lenovo's way of international brand management across all discussed nine sub-sections. Since Lenovo/IBM post-merger integrations are still ongoing and many activities were therefore confidential or in a transition process, it is emphasised that the summary is due to accessible data by November 2006.

---

[182] Assumption base on details of section 'brand communication' and on details given Zhang Ying (2006), and by Quelch and Knoop (2006).

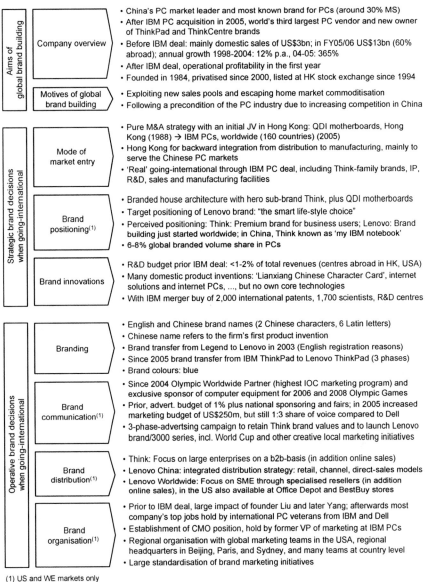

Aims of global brand building	Company overview	• China's PC market leader and most known brand for PCs (around 30% MS) • After IBM PC acquisition in 2005, world's third largest PC vendor and new owner of ThinkPad and ThinkCentre brands • Before IBM deal: mainly domestic sales of US$3bn; in FY05/06 US$13bn (60% abroad); annual growth 1998-2004: 12% p.a., 04-05: 365% • After IBM deal, operational profitability in the first year • Founded in 1984, privatised since 2000, listed at HK stock exchange since 1994
	Motives of global brand building	• Exploiting new sales pools and escaping home market commoditisation • Following a precondition of the PC industry due to increasing competition in China
Strategic brand decisions when going-international	Mode of market entry	• Pure M&A strategy with an initial JV in Hong Kong: QDI motherboards, Hong Kong (1988) → IBM PCs, worldwide (160 countries) (2005) • Hong Kong for backward integration from distribution to manufacturing, mainly to serve the Chinese PC markets • 'Real' going-international through IBM PC deal, including Think-family brands, IP, R&D, sales and manufacturing facilities
	Brand positioning[1]	• Branded house architecture with hero sub-brand Think, plus QDI motherboards • Target positioning of Lenovo brand: "the smart life-style choice" • Perceived positioning: Think: Premium brand for business users; Lenovo: Brand building just started worldwide; in China, Think known as 'my IBM notebook' • 6-8% global branded volume share in PCs
	Brand innovations	• R&D budget prior IBM deal: <1-2% of total revenues (centres abroad in HK, USA) • Many domestic product inventions: 'Lianxiang Chinese Character Card', internet solutions and internet PCs, ..., but no own core technologies • With IBM merger buy of 2,000 international patents, 1,700 scientists, R&D centres
Operative brand decisions when going-international	Branding	• English and Chinese brand names (2 Chinese characters, 6 Latin letters) • Chinese name refers to the firm's first product invention • Brand transfer from Legend to Lenovo in 2003 (English registration reasons) • Since 2005 brand transfer from IBM ThinkPad to Lenovo ThinkPad (3 phases) • Brand colours: blue
	Brand communication[1]	• Since 2004 Olympic Worldwide Partner (highest IOC marketing program) and exclusive sponsor of computer equipment for 2006 and 2008 Olympic Games • Prior, advert. budget of 1% plus national sponsoring and fairs; in 2005 increased marketing budget of US$250m, but still 1:3 share of voice compared to Dell • 3-phase-advertising campaign to retain Think brand values and to launch Lenovo brand/3000 series, incl. World Cup and other creative local marketing initiatives
	Brand distribution[1]	• Think: Focus on large enterprises on a b2b-basis (in addition online sales) • Lenovo China: integrated distribution strategy: retail, channel, direct-sales models • Lenovo Worldwide: Focus on SME through specialised resellers (in addition online sales), in the US also available at Office Depot and BestBuy stores
	Brand organisation[1]	• Prior to IBM deal, large impact of founder Liu and later Yang; afterwards most company's top jobs hold by international PC veterans from IBM and Dell • Establishment of CMO position, hold by former VP of marketing at IBM PCs • Regional organisation with global marketing teams in the USA, regional headquarters in Beijing, Paris, and Sydney, and many teams at country level • Large standardisation of brand marketing initiatives

(1) US and WE markets only

Fig. 5-39. Lenovo's way of international brand management (own summary)

6 The Chinese way of international brand management

Having presented the way of international brand management for each individual company, Haier, TCL, Hisense and Lenovo, separately, the rationale of the following chapter is now to identify similarities and differences among these four cases and to test them against the formulated hypotheses of chapter 4. To what extent can the hypotheses be confirmed by the four cases? What are reasons why a hypothesis may or may not be confirmed? What did these Chinese branded companies decide differently in comparison to companies from Japan and South Korea? Can we identify a Chinese way of international brand management among the four cases? To what extent may this way be generalised across and beyond the industry? To answer these questions, the chapter starts with cross-case comparisons of the four investigated cases, structured in the same sub-sections as applied in the individual case narratives. In the second section the findings are tested against the formulated hypotheses. The chapter closes with the integration of all prior findings in the descriptive model, presenting the Chinese way of international brand management.

6.1 Cross-case comparisons

6.1.1 Aims of global brand building

Company overview
Before analysing Haier, TCL, Hisense and Lenovo with respect to international brand management issues, table 6-1 starts with a comparison of the companies' key financials. They are considered the basis of any international brand strategy, and enable a short overview about the four firms' status quo. As the table shows, in 2004, Haier was the largest company in terms of revenue with US$12.3bn, while TCL gained US$6.7bn, Hisense US$3.3bn and Lenovo US$2.9bn. All had double-digit annual growth rates in 1998-2004, although Lenovo grew quite moderate by 12% per year. Since all four companies were founded in the early 1980s, except for

Hisense, which was founded in 1969, the reason for Lenovo's 'underper-formance' cannot refer to an unequal starting point, but lies in the fact that Lenovo refocused themselves towards their core competence of 'PCs' and terminated their foreign-branded distribution business in 2003/04. In contrast, Haier, TCL and Hisense continued to diversify in many related and non-related industries, and besides grew through self-branded business as well as through foreign-branded OEM. In particular Haier grew largely through OEM and emerged as a large conglomerate covering white goods, black goods, PCs, mobile phones, retailing, real estate, financials, travel service, and medicine. Although Hisense seems to have followed a similar growth path as Haier, they are said to be less aggressive and more conservative with respect to investments, financial risks and fighting for market shares at the expense of efficiency (Ling 2005: 139). Since all four companies gained relatively small revenue shares abroad until 2004, TCL and Hisense both 15%, Haier 8%, and Lenovo under 5%, one can further conclude that corporate growth was mainly based on the Chinese growing market at this time.

	Haier	TCL	Hisense	Lenovo
Revenues FY04 *(FY05)* in US$bn	12.3	6.7	3.3	2.9 *(13.4)*
CAGR 1998-2004 *(2004-2005)*	35%	36%	22%	12% *(365%)*
Revenue share gained abroad FY04 *(FY05)*	8.3%	15%	15%	<5% *(>60%)*
Revenue share publicly-listed FY04	18%	62%	28%	100%
Profitability compared to industry pears	low	negative	low	moderate

Table 6-1. Comparison of key financials of Haier, TCL, Hisense and Lenovo in 2004/2005 (details as presented in case narratives)

Moreover, in all cases profitability was quite low and seemed not to be a major corporate issue by 2004. Probably due to soft budget constraints guaranteed by the Chinese government, particularly the state-owned company Hisense did not have to worry about profitability. Also Haier, a collective-owned enterprise, could enjoy strong support from the Qingdao municipal government. Maybe only TCL and Lenovo, who were officially founded as state-owned enterprises, but were considered privatised by the end 1990s, were not able to rely on government funding in a broader sense.

TCL was considered a governmental experiment of "stealth privatization" (Chandler et al. 2004), and is still struggling with post-merger integrations with Alcatel and Thomson. Lenovo may not have been perceived as important as a Haier, TCL, or as a Founder Electronics, who was the state-owned rival of Lenovo in the Chinese PC market. Although Lenovo acquired IBM PCs, they managed to do so with continued operational profitability.

The role of the government for the respective companies may also be indicated by the publicly-listed revenue share: The higher the revenue share, the lower the supposed impact of the government on the company. By 2004 Haier was supposed to be highly impacted by the government, as only 18% were listed in Hong Kong stock exchange. Hisense, although public with 28% of total revenue, was listed at Shanghai stock exchange which is said to be not so strict with its publication rules compared to overseas exchange markets (e.g., Hirn 2005: 129-130). In contrast, TCL and Lenovo seemed to be quite independent from the government by 2004. TCL was publicly-listed with 62% at Shenzhen and Hong Kong, and Lenovo was entirely listed at the Hong Kong stock exchange.

While it is assumed that Haier, TCL and Hisense developed similar to previous years throughout 2005, Lenovo did a huge jump of 365% revenue growth by acquiring IBM PCs in May 2005. Lenovo has grown to a company of a similar size to Haier Group, although they are much more focused in terms of product portfolio (self-branded PC products and mobile phones only), relatively independent from the Chinese government (100% publicly listed and headquartered in New York), and with a large presence in the international market place (7 times as much as Haier, and 4 times as much as TCL and Hisense in terms of revenue share gained abroad). However, despite of the IBM PC deal, Lenovo is still small in comparison to *Fortune Global 500* companies, such as IBM, Dell, Sony and Samsung, and was not amongst the 2005 ranking (Fortune 2005).

Regarding their perceived core competences, figure 6-1 reveals that the four investigated companies Haier, TCL, Hisense and Lenovo evaluated themselves quite differently. While Haier and Lenovo named innovation in terms of customer-tailored product designs and efficiency as their core competence and estimated their firm's overall level close to world-class, TCL and Hisense acknowledged both strengths and weaknesses. TCL perceived themselves strong in consumer insights especially in the Chinese TV market, but admitted that they would lack own core technologies in terms of international patents and organisational effectiveness due to ongoing post-merger integrations. In contrast, Hisense evaluated its internal organisation as a core competence, but perceived distribution/trade, technology/innovation and their supply chain as quite weak. Taking into account the details of the case narratives, one could argue about the respective core competences and if company externals would have estimated them in a similar way. Especially in the case of Haier, one might argue that it is overrated, since they only play a global role in the industry of white goods. And in this industry they can be considered second or third tier due to some deficits in advanced production processes, quality standards and own technology competences.

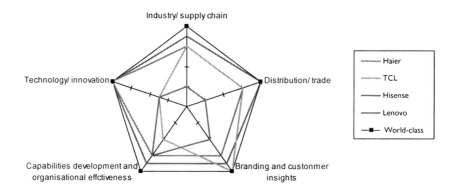

Fig. 6-1. Comparison of perceived core competences as estimated by company representatives in 2005/2006 on a scale from 1 (basic industry level) to 5 (world-class level) (details as presented in case narratives)

Motives of global brand building

Comparing the four companies with respect to their future corporate aims, they all announced to want to become a leading giant in their respective industry and a global brand name. Haier and Lenovo were most precise. Both aim to become a *Fortune Global 500* before 2010 and a globally fa-mous brand. TCL aims to become profitable and an internationally known brand for televisions and mobile phones. Hisense aims to become a giant in the world's electronic and information industry and to gain revenues of US$12bn by 2010, which will not make them to a *Fortune Global 500*.

The motives behind these corporate aims also appear quite similar (table 6-2). All four companies started planning to enter foreign markets and to build a global brand at the end of the 1990s and early 2000s. At this time, they all suffered from decreasing profit margins due to price wars and in-creased domestic competition. Moreover, all four companies perceived China's entry into the WTO in 2001 as a close event that would accelerate global competition in China. In addition, Haier and Hisense feared that their low-cost advantages would be limited in time and would be negated by multinationals producing in China in near future. Lenovo also perceived that additional global competition arrived through the direct-sales models via the internet.

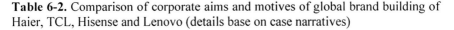

	Haier	TCL	Hisense	Lenovo
Corporate aims	• Fortune Global 500 • Global famous brand	• Internationally known brand for televisions and mobile phones; • Profitability	• Giant in the world's electronic and information industry	• Fortune Global 500 • Global famous brand
Motives of global brand building	• Exploiting new sales pools • Escaping home market commoditisation • Enhancing brand image in China • Fulfilling government policies and utilising incentives	• Exploiting new sales pools • Escaping home market commoditisation • Enhancing brand management and technology competences • Increasing profit margins • Leveraging government and personal CEO ambitions	• Exploiting new sales pools • Escaping home market commoditisation • Establishing basis for promoting own technology inventions • Following government orders and ambitions	• Exploiting new sales pools • Escaping home market commoditisation • Following a pre-condition of the PC industry due to increasing competition in China
Brand role models	GE, Sony	Sony, Samsung	Haier	HP, Dell

Table 6-2. Comparison of corporate aims and motives of global brand building of Haier, TCL, Hisense and Lenovo (details base on case narratives)

Since all four companies were also very well known brands in China and enjoyed strong market leadership positions in their respective industries across both urban and rural areas, they did not perceive enough room for further growth in China. They wanted to exploit new sales pools in overseas markets in order to escape the home market commoditisation. Haier is China's white good leader with around 17% market share, TCL is China's TV leader with 18% market share, Lenovo is the undisputed market leader in PCs with more than 30% market share, and even Hisense is number four in China's television market (5.5% market share) and number one in inverter air-conditioners with 60% market shares. TCL and Hisense additionally aimed at increasing their competitiveness by reducing costs due to larger volumes, by a more efficient supply-chain and, though a minor goal, by gaining higher profit margins in overseas markets. Lenovo even regarded global presence and a global brand as a precondition to survive the PC market on the long run. Hisense also found a strong brand name crucial as a platform to promote own technology. Further, it becomes evident that all four companies have followed certain brand role models. Haier referred to GE, Sony and Nike. TCL explicitly named to follow

Sony and Samsung. Lenovo took HP and Dell as their role model. In the case of Hisense, one could think that they took Haier as their brand role model, since many brand details appeared quite alike. For instance, they just started to use their going-international to enhance *Hisense* brand in the Chinese market.

Beyond the economic reasons, it becomes evident that the more government-impacted companies Haier, TCL and Hisense also aimed for a global brand building because of national and political motives. In particular Haier's international initiatives were largely supported by Chinese local and central governments. It was said that Haier has placed the bid for acquiring US-Maytag mainly to gain international attention. One could also argue that Haier has primarily used their status of a 'national champion' and 'China's most global and prominent brand' to enhance brand equity among Chinese consumers in the home market. It was also said that TCL has decided on the mergers with French Thomson and Alcatel in order to demonstrate China's national power towards the West, and to satisfy TCL CEO's personal ambitions. Since TCL is still struggling with the acquisitions in terms of business economics, the accusations may be justified. A similar thing is true for Hisense, where local and central Chinese governments had pressured Bosch-Siemens to sell their registered brand name 'HiSense'. In contrast, Lenovo seemed not to be accused for political motives. Possibly, CEO Yang had also followed personal reasons when having acquired IBM PCs, but, as the management team changed towards a foreign leadership and the headquarters were moved to New York, the Chinese government might struggle to sell the deal in terms of an increase of national pride towards the West. However, in terms of establishing a global brand in the world's marketplace and to increase the number of Chinese firms among the ranking of *Fortune Global 500*, Lenovo may now be the closest candidate and ahead of the national champion Haier.

6.1.2 Strategic brand decisions when going-international

Market entry mode

Although all four companies, Haier, TCL, Hisense and Lenovo, announced that they wanted to go international and to build a global brand in the late 1990s and early 2000s, they already got in touch with international markets a decade earlier. As the figure 6-2 reveals, Haier started their international path with OEM into emerging markets, while Lenovo was somehow forced into Hong Kong to integrate backwards from distributing foreign-branded PCs into self-branded PC manufacturing. In contrast, TCL and Hisense immediately started with branded business into emerging markets.

Hong Kong seemed to play quite a role in their early days, although it is not emphasised in their company histories. They probably had, similar to Lenovo, some personal relationships and government backing for a market entry into Hong Kong.

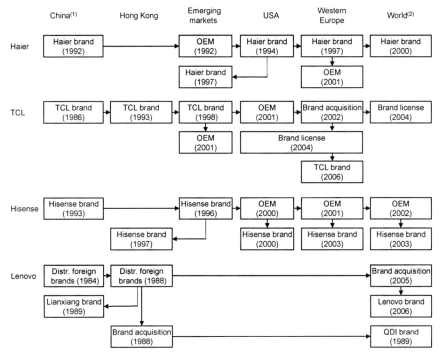

(1) Year 'China' refers to the creation of the brand name as given in the case section 'branding'; all other years refer to first market entry
(2) or remaining markets

Fig. 6-2. Comparison of the brand mode of market entry until 2005/06 (details as presented in case narratives and proven by FDI)

In addition, the figure shows that Haier, TCL and Hisense geographically expanded by a step-by-step approach, starting with emerging markets particularly in the region of South East Asia, entering then the US market, followed by Western Europe and finally by the remaining markets, such as emerging markets in Eastern Europe or Japan or Australia. On average they entered a new market region every two years, and thereby took advantage of both OEM and self-branded business. However, particularly for Haier it becomes evident that the US market played an exceptional role (also Liu/Li 2002). Haier explicitly excluded OEM investments there, as they got brand advice from their distributor and US-national Michael Jemal. Within Western Europe all four companies show a tendency to have entered the region through the countries of Italy and France,[183] while the German market was often entered at later stage, as it is considered very competitive and challenging.

Further, it is to remark that TCL switched their brand mode of market entry in 2000. Since the geographical expansion of the own brand took very much time, they speeded up the market entries into Western Europe and the US with respect to televisions through brand acquisitions (*Schneider*, *Go.Video*) and brand licenses (*Thomson, RCA*). TCL also entered the global mobile phone market by licensing *Alcatel* brand. TCL planned to fully transfer the acquired brands into their own brand *TCL* at a later stage, and started with launching TCL-branded televisions into Western Europe in 2006. In contrast to Haier, TCL and Hisense, Lenovo focused their core business PCs much longer on the Chinese markets and entered the world markets by a quite sudden and impressive cue in 2005, when the acquired IBM PCs including the worldwide well-established brands, *IBM ThinkPad* and *IBM ThinkCentre*. Prior to the deal, Lenovo only gained some international experience by their lower prioritised QDI-branded motherboard segment, which they had also acquired by brand acquisition. In addition to the *Think*-family brands, Lenovo entered the world markets with their Lenovo-branded PCs in 2006, starting with the markets of the USA, Europe and India.

It is to note that both TCL and Lenovo acquired branded companies to enter the US and Western European markets which had struggled with operational profitability. More precisely, although market observers argued that Lenovo paid too much for IBM PCs (Feng 2005), there is evidence that the foreign companies approached the Chinese counterparts and offered the respective units at a lower price level in order to get rid off them. TCL conducted four M&As and paid an initial total of US$626m, including established sales organisations, R&D and manufacturing facilities, experienced employees, and some brand ownership rights. In contrast, Lenovo only conducted one M&A and paid an initial price of US$1.75bn, including similar benefits and full brand ownership rights and 2,000 international patents.[184] Comparing both totals, Lenovo's investment was 2.8

---

[183] Haier started with Germany, the Netherlands and Italy, but finally set up their European sales office in Italy and purchased a manufacturing facility there. Hisense started with Italy by founding a sales office. TCL, although they started with Germany, later focused on France and Italy. And finally, even Lenovo, who entered all major markets at the same time, chose Paris for their headquarters in Europe.

[184] The acquisition of QDI motherboards is not counted as a second M&A because it was not acquired to accelerate market entries into the US and WE markets,

times higher than those of TCL. One could therefore conclude that Lenovo bought a company of a better shape, more valuable facilities, and more powerful intangible assets such as the international patents, employees' know-how, client databases, and the brands' equity.

Brand positioning

Based on the different modes of market entry, the brand architectures and the degree of international brand standardisation are quite different among the four cases, Haier, TCL, Hisense and Lenovo in the US and WE markets by early 2006. While Haier and Hisense conducted a corporate brand approach ('branded house'), TCL followed a multi-product-brand strategy ('house of brands'), and Lenovo marketed its corporate brand in addition to the acquired family-brand *Think* ('branded house with hero sub-brand'). Both Lenovo brands as well as the *Hisense* brand seem to be marketed with maximal brand standardisation in order to realise economies of scales and global spillover effects. Due to their corporate brand aims, TCL also planned to target a branded house with maximal standardisation as their future brand scenario. For Hisense, TCL and Lenovo, whose key industries are TV & audio and PCs, a standardised global brand approach seems to be the right decision, as competition globalises and a global brand name is often considered an industry prerequisite. In contrast, in the case of Haier, whose core industry is white goods, it is to note that industry peers and competitive rivals, amongst them *Electrolux* and *Whirlpool*, typically do not follow the approach of maximal brand standardisation, but market several localised and regional brands instead. As Haier seems to have realised this industry character, they planned to market their *Haier* brand as a local brand in every country market by customer-made product designs and localised marketing initiatives, while keeping the branding identical. Further, Haier placed a bid to acquire US-brand *Maytag* in 2005, an attempt that would also have switched Haier's brand architecture to a more multi-product-brand portfolio at this time.

In terms of brand value propositions, all four companies were reported to rely on strong distribution networks, reliable after-sales services and a brand image of innovative product personalisation and trustworthiness in China. Probably only Hisense's brand image was limited to Shandong province. Accordingly, when starting entering US and WE markets, all four companies targeted to establish a similar brand image abroad (table 6-3).

---

but was conducted to enable the company to start with PC manufacturing for the Chinese market.

Further, all four companies announced that they wanted to negate China's poor country image and wanted to prevent their corporate brands from being marketed at a cheap price. However, as the case narratives reveal, *Haier*, *Hisense*, and probably also the recently launched *TCL* brand are all sold at lower price levels, and mainly perceived as cheap buys, possibly also associated with low quality and cheap technology. The only exception so far seems to be Lenovo. Lenovo actively markets their self-branded desktops and portables as "a smart life-style choice" comprising a competitive price-value ratio and stylish designs combined with emotional values of worry-free computing, multimedia excitement and good customer service, including warranties and financing (Quelch/Knoop 2006). Due to their current marketing efforts, Lenovo may become the first Chinese corporate brand name that is able to achieve their set brand value propositions and a sophisticated brand image.

		Haier	TCL	Hisense	Lenovo
Internal brand perspective	Brand architecture	Branded house	House of brands	Branded house	Branded house with hero sub-brand
	Degree of international brand standardisation	Product differentiation	Full product differentiation	Maximal standardisation	Maximal standardisation
	Targeted positioning of the corporate brand in US and WE markets	Local brand of high quality and innovative, customer-tailored product designs	Global brand of quality, high-end and classic	Global brand of competitive prices, quality and innovation	"The smart life-style choice"
	Offered product portfolio in US and WE markets	Refrigerators, washing machines, audio-video, mobile phones	Televisions, mobile phones	Televisions, mobile phones, air-conditioners[2], refrigerators[2]	PCs
External brand perspective	Perceived positioning of the corporate brand in US and WE markets	Cheap, niche market brand, stylish wine cellars	n/a (assumption: cheap)	Cheap, good price-value ratio	n/a (assumption: clever brand)
	Global branded volume share of core business	White goods: 4%[1]	Televisions: 9%	Televisions: 1%	PCs: 6-8%
	Major markets of branded sales	USA, UK, Italy	France, Germany, USA, Canada	France[2]	USA, Germany, UK, Japan, India, ... (worldwide)

(1) 2003   (2) Announced

Table 6-3. Comparison of the internal and external brand perspective of Haier, TCL, Hisense and Lenovo in US and WE markets in 2005/2006 (details as presented in case narratives)

The fact that price must not be the only selling argument is also confirmed by the brands' market shares in US and WE markets, especially as given in volume shares. While *TCL* and *Lenovo* brands are too young in these markets to show any results as launched in 2006, *Hisense* and *Haier* brand struggle with visibility. *Hisense* brand holds narrow market shares in the US and WE markets, and if any, then at Carrefour retails stores in France. Due to stronger market positions in several emerging markets, Hisense accounts in total for around 1% global volume shares in branded televisions. The case of Haier might be considered worse. Despite of more than 10 years of market presence in the US, *Haier* brand holds around 1% volume share in large kitchen appliances and 6.5% in refrigeration. *Haier* brand is particularly known for niche products and low priced standard-sized refrigerators. In Western Europe, *Haier* brand enjoys some brand awareness and holds minor volume shares in Italy and the UK, where they account for around 1% in large kitchen appliances. Worldwide, due to their leading market position in China, *Haier* brand however holds a volume share of around 4%. Besides the value proposition 'price', another reason for this relatively poor performance may also lie in the product portfolio itself. Both Haier and Hisense started with their core industries, respectively refrigerators and televisions, but with increasing speed, they also started launching their other product categories: white goods, black goods, mobile phones, and air-conditioners. Probably, they should have focused on building some brand equity for one product category first?

In contrast, TCL postponed the product launch labelled by their own brand, and started with marketing their acquired brands in the US and WE markets. Those had the advantage to already enjoy some brand equity, although not always favourable. *Thomson* brand enjoys 11% market share in TV & audio in France and 4% in Germany. *RCA* brand holds 5% market share and *Go.Video* 2% in the US. *Schneider* brand is perceived poorly in all markets and holds narrow market share. Further, TCL became the largest manufacturer of TV sets due this M&A history and jumped to more than 9% of the global volume share in branded televisions. Similar to Haier and Hisense, TCL also did not focus on one product category when entering US and WE markets. Shortly after the merger with Thomson televisions, TCL acquired Alcatel mobile phones and started marketing its second product category into the world markets since. *Alcatel* is perceived as a niche-market brand which is not ranked amongst the world's top 5 mobile phone vendors.

In contrast to TCL, Lenovo acquired only one foreign brand so far, the brand family *Think*, and focused on PCs only. Similar to *Alcatel* brand, *Think* is already present in all major world markets, but in contrast, it is a significant market player with around 5% global PC volume share, and is considered the premium brand for enterprise customers. Moreover, Lenovo can use IBM's logo, sales agents and customer service for the *Think* products for five years, which will provide them some credibility. Finally and again in contrast to TCL, Lenovo also did not wait to launch their self-branded computers into the same world markets. Instead, Lenovo leveraged the public visibility and brand awareness that the IBM deal had brought, and started their Lenovo-branded computers within less than one year. The IBM deal made Lenovo to the world's third largest PC vendor with a global branded volume share of 6-8%.

Overall, in terms of brand positioning, Lenovo therefore appears to own the strongest and most promising brands compared to the brand portfolio of Haier, Hisense and TCL. The underlying factors might be the high degree of international brand standardisation and its distinct brand value proposition. However, this statement might be argued about, as prior to the IBM deal *Haier* was usually named the most known Chinese brand. Lenovo has not yet emancipated itself from IBM and struggles with decreasing market shares. Moreover, TCL may be considered first, as they account for a slightly higher global market share when adding up all individual brand shares (table 6-3). On the other hand, TCL does not own the more promising brands themselves, but is licensing them, and thus planned to transfer them towards the *TCL* brand in future. This might diminish some of the current brand equity.

Brand innovations

According to their brand positioning in China, it becomes evident that all four companies, Haier, TCL, Hisense and Lenovo, focused their R&D efforts on personalised product innovations for the Chinese consumer market. Haier is proud to develop 1.2 new products every day and to offer the smallest freezer and a set of different stylish wine-cellars. TCL launched more than 50 different TCL-branded mobile phones into the Chinese market in 2005, amongst them, a mobile phone model encrusted with jewels. Hisense is known for a continuous stream of new products in the Chinese market, primarily developed due to the orders of the Qingdao municipal government. And Lenovo served different Chinese consumer groups with localised and personalised product inventions that empowered them to access computer systems and the internet. As a result, Haier, TCL and Hisense, those backgrounds lie in manufacturing, perceive their advantage in terms of brand innovations in innovation speed, supply chain management and manufacturing efficiency. In contrast, Lenovo, who has origins in distributing foreign branded PCs, perceives their advantages in marketing of their custom-tailored product designs.

Acknowledging that foreign consumers may demand different products and designs than Chinese consumers, all four companies established R&D centres in major overseas markets. As table 6-4 shows, all four companies run R&D centres in the US, a move that can be evaluated as aligned with their mode of market entry, where the USA plays a significant role as well. In addition to these, Haier and TCL have R&D centres in Western Europe, particularly in Germany and France. Hisense also runs a R&D centre in South Africa to research consumer needs of emerging markets, and Lenovo used to run a R&D centre in Hong Kong. Haier's leading position in terms of numbers of centres may be due to Haier's brand positioning and due the fact that the industry of white goods requires more local adaptations.

	Haier	TCL	Hisense	Lenovo[1]
R&D 1998-2004 in % of revenue	4-6%	~3%	4-5%	1-2%
R&D centres abroad FY2004	USA, Canada, Japan (2), South Korea, France, Germany, the Netherlands	Singapore, USA, France, Germany	USA, South Africa	USA, Hong Kong

(1) Before IBM deal

Table 6-4. Comparison of key R&D data of Haier, TCL, Hisense and Lenovo in 2004/2005 (details as presented in case narratives)

As a consequence of the focus on customer-orientated product inventions, all four companies were used to lack own core technologies awarded with international patents. When starting to enter markets in the US and Western Europe, they therefore were forced to buy or license those from foreign companies. Moreover, all four companies, though pretending to be high-tech firms, seemed to have limited internal R&D budgets to catch up with foreign rivals. Lenovo spent 1-2% of their revenues on R&D in 1998-2004, TCL 3%, Hisense 4-5% and Haier 4-6% (table 6-4). On the one hand one could argue that Haier's R&D share is not low in comparison to industry peers of the white goods industry. For instance, Electrolux only spends around 2% of total revenues on R&D (company websites). On the other hand, one has to remark that Haier is a large conglomerate that also serves R&D efforts in black goods, PCs and mobile phones. In these industries Haier's spending appears quite low. Samsung and Sony spend around 7-8% of total revenues on R&D, and IBM and HP spend around 5-6% (Park/Burrows 2003, company websites). Comparing the four Chinese R&D budgets with each other, it may be surprising that the more government-impacted enterprises, Haier and Hisense, spent relatively more on R&D than the more privately run companies, TCL and Lenovo. A reason may be that Haier and Hisense enjoyed external incentives from the Chinese government in terms of funding, fixed assets and access to well-educated researchers that had increased the internal share too.

Despite of the R&D initiatives by the government, all four companies admitted that they also tried to address the lack of own technologies though external partnerships with foreign leading firms. Haier originated through a joint venture with German Liebherr, where they absorbed advanced technologies and know-how in refrigeration. Haier also runs a set of partnerships in the high-tech sector, including Microsoft, LG, Philips, Toshiba, Lucent Technologies, Ericsson, Fujitsu and Hitachi. Hisense collaborates with Lucent, Intel and Ligent Photonics to integrate 3C digital industries. In addition to partnerships, the more privately run companies TCL and Lenovo recently accelerated their speed towards the ownership of international patents through M&As. TCL acquired the R&D capacities and some hundred researchers of Thomson televisions and Alcatel mobile phones. Lenovo acquired IBM PCs, including 2,000 international patents, hundreds of scientists and engineers, and research facilities in the US and Japan.

Since TCL admitted not to have gained international patents through the M&As (Sun 2006), Lenovo seems to be the only company with international patents among the investigated four Chinese firms by early 2006. Moreover, Lenovo's latest brand innovations of 'Lenovo 3000' and the new 'ThinkPad Z60' seem to have potential to compete successfully against its industry peers Dell and HP at the global stage. On the other hand, Haier is well-prepared to continue competing in the global industry of white goods due to their customised product designs. They should probably focus more on this industry, and skip R&D investments in televisions, PCs and mobile phones, where global competitors may be too far ahead.

6.1.3 Operative brand decisions when going-international

Branding
Comparing the four cases, Haier, TCL, Hisense and Lenovo with respect to branding, the most evident similarity is that they all distinguish brand naming in China from brand naming in foreign markets, while keeping their brand visuals quite identical. In China they all use a brand name written in Chinese characters, whereas in foreign markets the brand name sounds English and is composed of Latin letters. *Haier* is 海尔 ('haier'),

TCL is 王牌 ('wangpai'), *Hisense* is 海信 ('haixin'), and *Lenovo* is 联想 ('lianxiang'). Typically, all four Chinese brand names are composed of two Chinese characters. In terms of translations, Haier and Hisense brand names sound in the Chinese and in the English version quite alike and are literal translations, while TCL and Lenovo use completely different names.

Interestingly and unusual for the traditional Chinese way of name seeking, *TCL* is an abbreviation of the former company name 'Telephone Company Limited'. Since it implies no meaning, it is not surprising that in China *Wangpai* later emerged as TCL's Chinese standard brand name, even though it was originally a product name. In contrast to the abbreviation TCL, *Wangpai* is composed of Chinese characters and means 'King brand'. Contrary to *TCL* and *Wangpai*, *Lenovo* is quite a young name, while the Chinese version of *Lianxiang* is already more than 15 years in place. *Lianxiang* means 'association', a meaning which has positive connotations and which, similar to *Wangpai*, also originated with a product name, the 'Lianxiang Chinese Character Card'. The English name *Lenovo* comprises also a meaning, but a different one and was therefore chosen by creative translation. 'Le' refers to Lenovo's former English name 'Legend', and 'novo' shall associate with new and innovation.

In contrast to Lenovo and TCL, Haier and Hisense seem to have followed the rules of traditional Chinese name seeking in more detail. The two Chinese characters of 'haier' have positive connotations in both pronunciation and writing. The written Chinese name means 'a lot of sons', and spoken it can also mean 'brothers'. Both meanings are associated with happiness, family, and wealth according to Chinese traditions. However, the brand name was not freely chosen, but has origins in Haier's histories. It refers to Haier's initial joint venture partner Liebherr from Germany, whose name is written in Chinese 利勃海尔 ('Libohaier'). Haier's English name is a literal translation of the pinyin-transcription and is supposed to associate with 'higher'. In the case of Hisense, it is reported that they first chose the English name Hisense, and later literally translated it into *Haixin* Chinese characters (Wang 2005b). The Chinese characters mean 'unlimited trust'. The English name is composed of 'high' and 'sense' and shall symbolise that Hisense stands for 'high quality' and 'high consciousness of technology'. In contrast to the Haier, TCL and Lenovo brand names, neither Hisense's English nor Chinese name seem to have origins in Hisense's company history. See also table 6-5.

When starting to enter US and WE markets in the 2000s, Hisense and Lenovo had difficulties to launch their English name, while TCL and Haier proceed smoothly. The reason was that both names *Hisense* and Lenovo's former brand name *Legend* were already registered by other companies in many major markets. While Lenovo accepted the fact and changed the name from *Legend* to *Lenovo*, a transfer that probably also led to a more appealing brand name, Hisense did not want to switch its name. Supported by the Chinese government they finally pressured Siemens-Bosch, who owned the name at this time, to sell the brand rights to Hisense. Despite of these learnings, it is surprising that *Haier* and *TCL* brand names are still not yet registered in all major markets. Probably, since intellectual property rights were not as strict in China as in Western markets, the four investigated companies may not have been used to brand registration processes, and have not yet realised that the availability of the brand name for registration is a prerequisite for a brand's going-international.

	Haier	TCL	Hisense	Lenovo
English name	Haier	TCL	Hisense	Lenovo
Chinese name	海尔 ('haier')	王牌 ('wangpai')	海信 ('haixin')	联想 ('lianxiang')
Reasons of name choice	• Origin in JV partner Liebherr • Positive meaning of 'lots of sons' and 'brothers' • English name through literal translation	• Origin in a former company's name abbreviation: TCL • Chinese name refers to a product name • Positive meaning of 'king brand'	• English name associates with 'high' and 'sense' • Chinese name through literal translation • Positive meaning of 'unlimited trust'	• Chinese name refers to a product name: 'association' • English name through creative translation • Associates with the firm's former name and 'new/innovation'

Table 6-5. Comparison of Haier's, TCL's, Hisense's and Lenovo's corporate brand naming (details as presented in case narratives)

Evaluating the choice of the four English brand names from a Western perspective, *Haier*, *TCL*, *Hisense* and *Lenovo* sound all quite non-Chinese. The *TCL* brand name may have difficulties in consumer recognition similar to the Chinese market, since it is an abbreviation without a distinctive meaning towards the product category or brand value proposition. In terms of brand colours, the four investigated companies do not reveal a preference, if one, then towards the colour of blue which has positive connotations in both Chinese and Western societies according to brand theory. Blue is said to be associated with high quality and sincerity (Yang 2005: 119). Haier's brand colours include blue, pink and purple. TCL's brand colours are red, white and black. Hisense's main colour is a turquoise-green, partly combined with yellow-orange colours, and black Chinese letters on the brand logo. Lenovo's brand colour is blue. Except Haier, none of the other three companies seem to leverage brand visuals besides their brand logo. Haier launched their 'Haier Brothers' in the mid-1980s in

China and later also into the overseas markets. The Haier Brothers are visible as a symbol on the front of all Haier-branded products. The brand visual comprises two boys, a German and a Chinese boy, symbolising the fact that Haier started their business in cooperation with the German company Liebherr. Moreover, it transports the meaning of the brand name in the sense of 'brothers'.

Due to M&A histories, one finally has to note that both Lenovo and TCL have some challenging brand transfers ahead. While Lenovo has already started to transfer *IBM ThinkPad* to *Lenovo ThinkPad*, brand transfers from *Schneider, Thomson, RCA* or *Alcatel* brand towards *TCL* brand are future scenarios. Since brand transfers are costly and risky, and particularly TCL is not experienced in brand transfers, Haier and Hisense have the advantage that they can proceed with their branding as usual and can fully concentrate on other brand building aspects instead.

Brand communication

Another important brand building aspect is brand communication. Comparing the marketing budgets of the four companies, Haier, TCL, Hisense and Lenovo, with respect to overseas markets, it becomes evident that they are all quite small. Haier deals with a marketing budget of around 5-6% of the regional sales in the respective regional markets. TCL has a worldwide budget of 3-5% including the marketing activities in China. Hisense has an international budget of around 1.5-3.0% of their total revenues. While Haier, TCL and Hisense, are therefore supposed to deal with tens of million of US-dollars in the US and WE markets, Lenovo probably had the largest global marketing budget of US$250m in 2005. In addition, Lenovo supplied the 2006 Torino Olympic Games with a large amount of computers. On the other hand, when comparing Lenovo's marketing spending with industry peers such as Dell and HP or with company benchmarks such as South Korea's Samsung, the budget appears rather small. Dell and HP spend up to 20 times more on marketing in each major country market. For instance in the US, Dell spent US$450m on marketing in 2005 which is almost double the size of Lenovo's global marketing budget (Quelch/Knoop 2006). Samsung spends around US$3bn a year on global marketing, which is 12 times the budget of Lenovo (company websites).

Comparing the brand communication activities the four Chinese companies usually spend their international budgets, one can identify two main channels. The first channel addresses distributors and resellers, and played quite a role to build a basis of brand awareness in the companies' early years of going-international. The respective channels were namely worldwide trade fairs and reseller events organised in their home market in China. The Consumer Electronics Show (CES) in Las Vegas, USA, and the IFA exhibition in Berlin, Germany were the most often attended trade shows for black goods. In contrast, Lenovo primarily focused on participating in the computer fair CeBit in Hannover, Germany. While TCL, Hisense and Lenovo seemed to limit their participation on key fairs, it becomes evident that Haier attended a whole set of fairs, varying in terms of size, industry focus and country scope. For instance, Haier regularly participated in the Cologne Appliance Exhibition, Germany, Milan's Expo-Comfort Fair, Italy, the Electrical Retailing Show and the Exhibition for Hotel Consumables and Daily Necessities in London, UK, the House Wares Show and the Kitchen/Bath Industry Show in the US. Since Haier's revenue basis originates with OEM, the participation into these fairs might also have been a focus to contracting new OEM clients instead of promoting their own branded products to resellers. Similar reasons might be true for Hisense's brand communication approach.

The second main channel of brand communication into US and Western European markets which one can identify among the four cases is sports sponsoring. As the four cases show, sports sponsoring has in particular gained importance with the decision to build a global brand in the late 1990s and early 2000s, and with the decision that Beijing will host the 2008 Olympic Summer Games. Since January 2004 Haier sponsors the Australian basketball team 'Melbourne (Haier) Tigers', and in August 2005 Haier became a national sponsor of the 2008 Beijing Olympic Games in the category of white goods. TCL started sponsoring the annual golf tournament at Sanya on Hainan Island, China in 2004. The tournament belongs to the European golf tour and has a live broadcast in Europe and in the US.

While Hisense has not invested significantly in sports sponsoring so far, Lenovo may be the company with the largest investments. Lenovo was engaged in several national sports sponsorships, among them the Chinese national women's soccer team in 1999 and Beijing's bid to host the 2008 Olympic Games. Further, they became the first Chinese company to join the Olympic Partner Program in March 2004, the International Olympic Committee's (IOC) highest marketing programme. As a worldwide sponsor with the IOC, the group would be the exclusive supplier of computing equipment and services and funding for the 2006 Winter Games in Torino, Italy and the 2008 Summer Games in Beijing, China. Lenovo ran a marketing campaign featuring the Football World Cup in Germany in 2006 endorsed by the football star Ronaldinho. Lenovo also became an official partner of the American National Basketball Association (NBA) in 2006.

Interestingly, though TCL and Hisense are in contrast to Haier and Lenovo no official sponsors of the 2008 Beijing Olympic Games, all four companies expect positive effects on their global brand building during the

Games. Since Lenovo is sponsor in the highest IOC category, and was already a sponsor in Torino, Italy, they may benefit from the Olympic sponsorship most. On the other hand, the highest category is also the most expensive category. In comparison, Haier will spend less money, but will probably gain less brand building effects, especially at the global stage. Although one can argue whether TCL and Hisense might be able to build any brand equity during the Games without a sponsorship at all, national brand effects may be possible under the condition that the Chinese local and central governments will promote both brands.

Comparing the four companies and their brand communication activities in terms of quality and brand impact in the US and WE markets, it is surprising that Haier and Hisense had initially launched their self-branded goods without creating a momentum at the targeted end-consumers, the mass-markets. Although one could argue that such marketing would be expensive, and that at least Haier has conducted some initiatives in different European countries after the initial product launch, they seemed to lack an overall marketing approach in the first place. Haier wanted to do marketing in a localised way, but in Europe all marketing activities had appeared as rather sporadic, uncoordinated and cheap. Maybe in the US, Haier's approach had been more advanced, as they decided on fewer, but cleverer marketing activities such as advertising on luggage carts at New York's JFK airport. In contrast, although Hisense-branded goods are available in the US and in Germany, Hisense has not invested in any mass marketing so far, except some English corporate websites. However, these websites are out of date and not designed in an appealing style. For instance, when accessing the websites in early 2006 most information was updated the last time in 2002/2003.

In contrast, TCL and Lenovo decided to start with end-consumer marketing before their initial product launch took place. TCL started sponsoring the golf tournament in 2004, two years in advance to their product launch in Europe in 2006. Further, TCL runs global websites that are interlinked to the websites of the product brands and are partly carrying taglines such as 'Schneider. Member of the TCL Group'. Lenovo decided on the Olympic Sponsorship in 2004 and leveraged the media attention that the Games in Torino in 2006 and the IBM deal in 2005 had brought, to debut their Lenovo-branded products. Moreover, Lenovo decided on a more globalised and integrated marketing approach instead of Haier's brand localising. All major Lenovo marketing initiatives, including websites, were standardised and addressed several regional markets at the same time, probably generating some positive spillover effects across countries.

As a result, one has to acknowledge that Lenovo became known in all major markets in quite a short-time frame. For instance in Germany,

Lenovo became the most famous Chinese brand name with an unaided brand awareness of 29% according to the consumer survey as conducted in October 2006 (chap 3). Haier scored a similar high at 27% of unaided brand awareness. TCL scored 7% and Hisense scored expectedly low at 1% of unaided brand awareness. Taking into account that the relatively high scores of *Haier* and *TCL* brands in the German market may not have originated with their own marketing initiatives, one has to question which other external channels might have created this brand attention. There is only one possibility: public media. This assumption is supported by the fact that the country of China and Chinese companies were recently often a subject across the media in Germany, and were regularly discussed with respect to production shifts and low labour cost advantages. Furthermore, there is evidence that the company of Haier was often mentioned in the reports with reference to China's 'national champion'.

	Haier	TCL	Hisense	Lenovo
Global marketing budget in US$ million FY 2004	50-60[1]	30-50[1]	7-15[1]	250[2]
Major communication channels in US and WE markets[3]	• Many trade fairs • Sponsor of the Melbourne Tigers • National sponsor of the Beijing 2008 Olympics • Several small and localised initiatives	• Selected trade fairs • Sponsor of the European golf tournament at Hainan Island • Product brand promotions	• Selected trade fairs	• Selected trade fairs • Worldwide Partner of Torino 2006 and Beijing 2008 Olympics • Spokesperson Ronaldinho during 2006 World Cup • Sponsor of the NBA
Unaided brand awareness[3] in Germany, Oct 2006	27%	7%	1%	29%

(1) Own estimate: global marketing budget = share of total marketing budget x share of revenues abroad x total revenues
(2) FY2005/06   (3) Corporate brand only

Table 6-6. Comparison of key brand communication data of Haier, TCL, Hisense and Lenovo until 2006 (details as presented in case narratives)

Despite of this media attention, it remains questionable whether public media can create favourable brand images too. Actively conducted marketing initiatives, as conducted by companies such as Lenovo, may achieve more sophisticated results that correspond to the targeted brand value propositions in a better way. However, it is to note that none of the four investigated corporate brands, including *Lenovo* brand, have achieved these brand image or brand loyalty results outside China so far (compare to table 6-3). All four companies have to address this task in their future brand communication initiatives. Table 6-6 sums up the cross-case comparison with respect to the companies' key brand communication data.

Brand distribution

Besides brand communication, the decision on the 'right' brand distribution channels can also have impact on brand equities, such as the unaided brand awareness. Which channels did the four companies, Haier, TCL, Hisense and Lenovo choose to enter US and WE markets? Do they fit to the brands' value propositions? As table 6-7 shows, one can identify two contrary tendencies in terms of horizontal channel selection, intensive distribution and selective distribution. In terms of vertical channel selection, all four companies decided on retail distribution by early 2006, while Lenovo and Hisense additional chose some direct-sale business models.

	Haier	TCL	Hisense	Lenovo
Target consumer segments	Mass-markets	Mass-markets	Mass-markets	SMEs
Horizontal channel selection	Intensive distribution	Intensive distribution	Intensive distribution	Selective distribution
Vertical channel selection	Retail	Retail	Retail, direct-sale	Retail, direct-sale
Dual strategy	Yes	Possibly	Yes	No
Type of key retailers	Large-scale multiple food retailer, large surface electrical chains, independent resellers	Large-scale multiple food retailer	Large-scale multiple food retailer	Computer specialised resellers
Key retailers	Wal-Mart, Best Buy	Carrefour	Carrefour, Best Buy, Saturn	--

Table 6-7. Comparison of distribution approach of Haier, TCL, Hisense and Lenovo into US and WE markets in early 2006 (details base on case narratives)

Hisense, TCL and Haier belong to the first group of intensive distribution approach. They target mass-markets and approach retail chains that support large volume sales and sales of different product categories, such as white goods, black goods, mobile phones and air-conditioners. Key resellers are large-scale multiple food retailers such as Wal-Mart and Carrefour, and large surface electrical retailers such as Best Buy and Saturn. While Haier is not listed at Carrefour, Haier's most important branded sales channel is Wal-Mart for the US. Haier is also available at Lowe's, Best Buy, Home Depot, Office Depot, Target, Fortunoff, Menards, Bed bath & Beyond, BJ's, Fry's, ABC, BrandsMart and in over 7,000 independent stores, although it remains unclear whether these chains run exclusively Haier-branded goods or also OEM labels ('dual strategy'). Further, Haier approached every distributor and reseller to determine whether they were willing to sell Haier-branded goods into Western Europe. Initially it seemed that these were especially some specialised resellers, but by early 2006 Haier has also conducted few promotional offers at the large surface electrical chain, MediaSaturn, and was cooperating with Germany's do-it-yourself chain, OBI.

Similar to Haier, Hisense has also approached several volume-orientated distribution channels at the same time. In Western Europe, Hisense is listed at Carrefour retail stores, although it remains again unclear whether they do not conduct a dual strategy. Besides, Hisense ran some promotional offers at the large surface electrical chain, Saturn, in Germany in 2006. In the US, the Hisense brand is sold across three channels: at retail stores, including Micro Centre, Kohl's, Shopko and Best Buy, at the TV-show 'Shop at home', and online in the internet at the consumer electronics shop, Tiger Direct. Since TCL-branded goods were recently launched into Western Europe in 2006 and are not yet available in the US at all, they are only available at one distribution channel so far, Carrefour. A dual strategy might be possible due to TCL history.

In contrast, Lenovo-branded computers have neither been available at Wal-Mart, Carrefour, Best-Buy and Saturn retail stores, nor has Lenovo performed a dual strategy. Lenovo seemed to be more focused so far, and has not targeted the mass-markets in the US and Western Europe, but according to their announcement, have been targeting the segment of small- and medium-sized enterprise users (SMEs). Further, Lenovo has aimed to establish a brand premium by offering consumer services including financing and a long warranty among others. Since neither the target group buys computers at large-scale multiple food retailers, nor are these shops able to support advanced consumer services, these might be the reasons why Lenovo-branded goods are not available at Wal-Mart or Carrefour. Instead, Lenovo computers are primarily available in hundreds of specialised computer shops in both, the US and in WE markets. In addition, as the sale is not exclusive and restricted to their target group, all Lenovo computers are also available online in the internet for any possible consumer segment. Similar is true for their *Think* family PCs. They are available online in the internet and through certified PC agencies in order to provide large enterprises the best consumer service possible.

As a result, when comparing how the distribution channel fits the brands' value propositions and target groups, Lenovo seems to rank first. On the one hand, Haier and Hisense appear too unfocused. On the other hand, mass markets, dual strategy and many different channels fit to their overall volume strategy, but may not be able to transport the targeted brand image of a brand of quality and innovation. Large-scale multiple food retailers, e.g. Wal-Mart and Carrefour, tend to position the brands as pure price discount offers, a brand positioning which all four companies explicitly wanted to prevent. The same is true for any branded promotional offers at Best Buy and Saturn, although these chains may be a good choice when obtaining a permanent listing that allows them to offer several branded products at different price levels at the same time. In terms of TCL, one therefore has to ask why TCL had chosen Carrefour to enter the WE market and had not leveraged their supposed well-established relationships to the electrical chains such as Saturn and MediaMarkt. Since TCL is the only company of the four investigated firms, who already enjoys listings at these chains due to their acquired product brands *Schneider, Thomson, RCA* and *Alcatel,* it should be significantly easier to get listed with its *TCL* brand there in future too.

Brand organisation
Since every international brand strategy finally starts with the management team and its organisation creating and implementing it, the last section of the cross-case analysis investigates the brand organisation of the four companies, Haier, TCL, Hisense and Lenovo. As the case narratives reveal, all four organisations had a strong organisational base with their founders and with a few company leaders. Typically for Chinese organisations, none of those had been educated in brand management or marketing, but used to be technocrats or computer scientists. Haier's CEO Zhang Ruimin was originally an economic engineer and a former bureaucrat of the Qingdao municipal government. TCL's president and chairman Li Dongsheng used to be an engineer and was one of TCL's founders in 1982. Hisense's chairman Zhou Houjian studied electricity at Shandong University and joined the company in 1982. Lenovo was founded by Liu Chuanzhi, a computer scientist, in 1984. He was followed as the company's CEO and president by Yang Yuanqing, who also used to be a computer scientist and who had joined the company in 1988.

While Haier and TCL are still led by their initial presidents Zhang and respectively Li, Hisense is led in its second generation by Yu Shuming as president. Lenovo is led in its third generation of presidency, after they acquired IBM PCs and established a new management team with US-American Steve Ward, as their CEO and president. Yang Yuanqing became chairman of new Lenovo, even though Yang is still quite young in terms of age. While he is around 40 years old, the three leaders of the other Chinese companies are already in their 60s or even older.

Yang's younger age may therefore be taken as a proxy for Lenovo's organisational flexibility and openness towards new management principles. Further, Lenovo seems to be relatively independent from the Chinese government. Combining these aspects, they may be reasons why Lenovo's organisation structure and brand management organisation look quite different since its third generation of presidency, compared to those of the companies of Haier, TCL and Hisense. Although all four companies were running designated corporate brand management units at the time of the IBM deal, Lenovo additionally moved their headquarters from Beijing to New York, and changed its organisation structure towards an integrated structure separated by the regions 'Greater China', 'Americas', 'EMEA', which is Europe, Middle East and Africa, and 'Asia Pacific'. Further, due to their new global brand reach, they established the position of a chief marketing officer (CMO) who became responsible for all markets, including China and the overseas markets. While the regions became in charge of sales, promotional activities, and local marketing, they also established global marketing teams in the US to conduct globally standardised product design, brand positioning, brand communication, brand control, and market research. According to brand theory, one can thus categorise Lenovo's brand organisation structure as an "integrated mixture" of regional and product-orientation (Berndt et al. 2003: 278-279).

Taking into account that Lenovo was under 100% Chinese leadership and gained more than 95% of their sales in the Chinese market before the IBM deal, the change towards an integrated organisation structure with a geocentric perspective can be considered quite an innovative and large move, especially for a Chinese originated company. In the new Lenovo organisation the region 'Greater China' became only one of four regional markets, though China still remains the largest single country market.

In contrast, Haier and Hisense seem to represent the more typical Chinese organisations. Both are quite ethnocentrically orientated, meaning that they focus their business on the home market China and tend to regard international sales as adjunct to the domestic business. By early 2006, both companies therefore run differentiated organisation structures that separate the home market 'China' from the 'overseas markets'. Major marketing and brand management decisions take place in a corporate brand management department in the Chinese headquarters, which is responsible for brand guidelines, advertising, and PR. Whereas Hisense usually runs little brand communication initiatives in US and WE markets and thus has little implementation need, Haier targets to localise their brand towards the markets specific consumer needs. Further, the US market seems to play a leading role with respect to Haier's international sales. Due to these two aspects, one could argue that Haier's brand organisation might tend to be polycentric or regional-centric.

In the case of TCL, the organisation structure may appear as more complex due to their multi-product-brand approach. *TCL*-branded televisions are sold in China and emerging markets, *Thomson* (and *Schneider*) brand in Europe, and *RCA* in North America. Separated from the industry of televisions, *TCL*-brand mobile phones are managed in China and *Alcatel* mobile phones in the rest of the world markets. On the one hand, since the organisation seems to be primarily separated by its products and brands rather than regions, one could name the organisation structure "a product-orientated structure" according to brand theory (Berndt et al. 2003: 273). On the other hand, since TCL's home market China still accounts for the major part of their total revenues, and since *TCL* brand was very recently introduced in Western Europe, one could also assume that TCL's organisation may be managed in a quite ethnocentric way. The assumption may be supported by the fact that TCL is also not responsible for the brand management of its product brands *Thomson*, *RCA*, and *Alcatel*, as they are still owned by the parent companies. While Thomson and Alcatel thus continue to decide on all brand building elements, TCL focuses on implementing sales promotions and local marketing initiatives through their local subsidiaries.

Based on these organisation structures, the degree of centralisation is different among the four companies, as conducted in the US and WE markets. Haier is strongly decentralised due to their approach to localise brand value propositions and marketing initiatives. Since the US market and their country manager Michael Jemal have always been reported as crucial for Haier's international sales, it would not be surprising, if the US organisation, Haier America, and their respective marketing team would emerge as the designated lead-country for brand management in developed markets. In contrast, Hisense's and Lenovo's brand organisations seem to apply a much higher degree of international brand standardisation. Although Hisense's international branded sales are quite small in volumes compared to Lenovo's sales, Hisense has already agreed on strict brand guidelines in terms of brand colours, brand visuals and brand slogans. Lenovo is also very strict with respect to brand communication and brand value propositions. In the case of TCL, the degree of brand standardisation so far remains unclear, since they just recently introduced TCL-branded televisions in Western Europe. While TCL's foreign-owned product brands are managed by large decentralisation due their brand license agreements, it is supposed that due to TCL's corporate brand aims the degree of its international brand standardisation will be rather high.

Comparing all four companies with respect to the origin and experience level of their management teams, it becomes evident that Hisense tends to employ mostly Chinese nationals. They employ them in leading positions in both markets, in China as in-country nationals and in overseas markets as expats. There is evidence that these Chinese nationals had also gained little experience with US and WE markets before they were sent in the countries. In contrast, Haier and TCL plan to leverage local know-how in their foreign subsidiaries. Haier America is said to be run by an almost American team under the leadership of US-American Michael Jemal. Also in Western Europe several managing positions of the Haier subsidiaries are held by in-country nationals, although they seemed to be supported by Chinese managers too. While it seems that Haier initially made positive experiences with in-country nationals and wanted to extend this approach onto other markets, it was the other way round in the case of TCL. They were accused to part from German managers and German staff after their acquisition of Schneider. Since many experts thought that this was a major issue of M&A failure, TCL seemed to have learnt from the Schneider experience and kept hundreds of local managers and employees after the merger with Thomson and Alcatel. More precisely, the board of TTE, the television unit of TCL, since then also includes several directors from France. Also they started using English as their corporate language.

Although one could describe TCL's management team as more multinational and more internationally experienced compared to a typical Chinese company, Lenovo did a much larger step towards an international team. As a part of the IBM deal, Lenovo kept the former IBM PC senior executive and US-national Steve Ward, and appointed him to be Lenovo's new CEO and president.[185] Former president, Chinese Yang Yuanqing, stepped aside and became chairman of the new Lenovo Group. Furthermore, half of the company's top jobs went to executives of American, Australian, European, and Indian origin. All of them previously worked for IBM PCs or Dell. The position of the CMO went to Deepak Advani from India who had previously worked with IBM for 12 years and in the end was vice president of marketing for IBM's PC division. Finally, English became the company's working language, and they had an almost 24 hour working day due to time differences between New York and Beijing. There is evidence that at the local level Lenovo also kept the majority of the former IBM employees and tried to find additional in-country nationals to support the *Lenovo* brand building.

---

[185] He was replaced by Bill Amelio from Dell in 2005.

	Haier	TCL	Hisense	Lenovo
Type of organisation structure	Differentiated	Product-orientated	Differentiated	Integrated mixture
Degree of international brand organisation	Ethnocentric	Regional-centric	Ethnocentric	Geocentric
Degree of centralisation[1]	Low	n/a (assumption: high)	High	High
Origin of local management team	Large share of in-nationals	Large share of in-nationals	Low share of in-nationals	Large share of in-nationals
Origin of top management team	Chinese nationals	Chinese nationals and few foreigners	Chinese nationals	Majority foreigners
Level of market experience[2]	Moderate	Moderate	Low	High

(1) Corporate brand only; US and WE markets only   (2) US and WE markets only

Table 6-8. Comparison of key brand organisation characteristics of Haier, TCL, Hisense and Lenovo with focus on US and WE markets by early 2006 (details base on case narratives)

Overall, in terms of brand organisation, one could therefore conclude that Lenovo has the most brand-orientated, sophisticated and international-ised brand organisation and the most experienced management teams with respect to US and WE markets among the four investigated companies (table 6-8). This statement may however be due to the fact that Lenovo's or-ganisation is the most transparent organisation, while for instance Haier's organisation is very complex and non-transparent. Haier has a bunch of different subsidiaries in Western Europe where it remains unclear which tasks are fulfilled by whom in which department and in which country. Further, all three companies of Haier, Hisense and TCL have the problem that they are large conglomerates that include several different branded and non-branded industries, of which only a part is publicly-listed at inter-national stock exchange markets. The other part typically remains non-transparent and is thus hard to analyse. Finally, it is to note that, even though these three do not get best marks within these nine sub-sections of cross-case analysis, all four brand management organisations can be con-sidered as advanced in comparison to the typical Chinese state-owned en-terprise (Zhang 2006). There is evidence that all four companies also use international consulting and brand agencies to receive external support and to compensate their potential lack of internal brand building and interna-tional market know-how.

6.2 Test of hypotheses

After having identified similarities and differences among the four companies Haier, TCL, Hisense and Lenovo by cross-case comparisons in the last chapter, the following chapter will test these findings against the hypotheses described in chapter 4. The rational is to investigate if and to what extent the hypotheses described the way of international brand management of these four Chinese companies. Further, if a hypothesis can be not confirmed for a certain company, to determine the specific reasons why.

6.2.1 Aims of global brand building

H1: Under the current conditions, Chinese branded companies have two main motives of global brand building and entering US and WE markets. First, they aim to use brand building as an additional channel to increase their sales by entering new growth markets. And second, they aim to enlarge their corporate size to fulfil the target, set by the Chinese government, to establish Chinese brands as significant global players as a prove of China's economic and political power in the world economy.

As the cross-case comparisons have shown, all four companies, Haier, TCL, Hisense and Lenovo, named the search for new sales pools in US and WE markets as their major motive of going-international. Further, they all aim to become a global famous brand and a giant in their respective industry. It becomes evident that they particularly refer to sales volume (e.g., *Fortune Global 500*) and global volume shares when describing an industry giant. Profit and higher price levels are minor corporate brand aims. Unlike Western branded companies, shareholder value also does not seem to be a key driving motive. However, one can argue that Lenovo is an exception. On the one hand, Lenovo continued to market the *Think*-family brand at a price premium, and announced to target the segment of SME users with their self-branded PCs, who may be willing to pay a price premium due to additional consumer services. On the other hand, there is evidence that the *Lenovo* brand is not priced at a higher level than its major competitive brands. Rather, it is planned to expand the brand's scope on consumer mass-market in the future as well. Overall, one can therefore conclude that all four cases, including Lenovo, entered the US and WE markets in order to increase sales in the first place. The first motive is therewith confirmed for all four companies.

Regarding the second motive, the analysis has shown that Haier, Hisense and TCL had been very much impacted by the Chinese government at all stages of their going-international. However, in the case of Lenovo, the analysis could not prove any political motives. The second motive is therefore only confirmed for Haier, TCL and Hisense, and not for Lenovo.

6.2.2 Strategic brand decisions when going-international

H2: Under the given conditions and not interfered by legal brand regulations, Chinese branded companies decide on a global standardised brand approach and a brand architecture of a branded house with very limited adaptations in branding and brand values across all operating country markets.

The analysis has shown that all four companies had decided on a brand architecture of a branded house. While Haier, Hisense and Lenovo have already established a branded house, TCL has currently a multi-product-brand portfolio due to M&A histories, but aims to transfer them into a branded house in future too. Further, all companies follow a high degree of brand standardisation when marketing their corporate brand. Their brand value propositions are quite identical across all country markets. Their branding only differs in the sense that the Chinese market requires a brand name written in Chinese characters in addition to the name written in Latin letters. Although one might argue that Haier is rather differentiated due to their aim to adapt the *Haier* brand with respect to local consumer needs, the analysis has revealed that adaptations in brand value propositions and branding were rather few. Instead, Haier planned to concentrate its brand by adapting brand communication initiatives and brand innovations in terms of personalised product models and localised designs. This hypothesis is therewith confirmed for all four companies.

H3: Given that Chinese branded companies lack own innovations, advanced technologies and international patents, they promote their brands globally as 'clever brands', positioning them as a brand of quality, me-too technology and low price, while being perceived advanced to pure discount goods.

The brand positioning of 'clever brands' implies that price must not be the major selling argument, but should enhance other functional and emotional brand values. As the analysis has revealed, only Lenovo seems to satisfy this requirement, since they position themselves as 'a smart life-style choice'. Particularly, their consumer service in terms of warranties and financing, similar to those of the *Think*-family brands, might evolve as a real unique selling proposition. In contrast, Haier, TCL and Hisense seem to lack a distinguished brand positioning and an integrated brand strategy. They aim for a brand image of quality and technology, which is rather not differentiating. Further, the external market perspective among Western consumers has shown that they are primarily perceived as niche products and a cheap buy. This hypothesis could therefore not be confirmed for Haier, TCL and Hisense, but it is confirmed for Lenovo.

H4: Given that own innovations and own international IP are regarded as crucial for a long-term brand success globally, Chinese branded companies invest heavily in R&D in order to catch up with the global market players (dependent on the industry, a R&D budget of at least 7-8% of total revenues may become necessary to catch up).

The cross-case comparisons have shown that all four companies had originally lacked own technology innovations and international patents. Acknowledging that own innovations may become crucial in order to ensure future competitiveness, all four companies have increased their R&D budgets, invested in R&D partnerships with foreign companies, and started acquiring foreign capacities and know-how. However, as the analysis has also revealed, the companies were rather reluctant to increase the budgets to the hypothesised share. Haier had the largest R&D spending with a maximum of 6% of its total revenues. Although one could argue that the more state-impacted companies may have been supported with additional funding from the government, the R&D efforts seemed not to have resulted in any significant Chinese-owned IP so far. Maybe Lenovo is the only company, who could enhance their R&D to a globally competitive level, after they had acquired IBM PCs and had obtained 2,000 international patents as a part of the deal. On the other hand, it is to remark that Haier would not have needed larger R&D budgets, if they had focused their efforts on the industry of white goods. With a R&D budget of up to 6% they would have been ahead of any major white goods competitor and should have been able to apply for international patents. Overall, the hypothesis is confirmed for Lenovo. It could not be confirmed for Haier, TCL and Hisense.

H5: Given that Chinese branded companies target a global standardised brand approach in all stages of their going-international in US and WE markets, they decide on geographical brand extension as their mode of

*market entry. Given that there are external market forces, unplanned mar-
ket opportunities, or political reasons which are considered more crucial
to business, Chinese branded companies decide on brand acquisitions
combined with brand transfers at a later stage.*

Analysing the market entries of the four companies, Haier, TCL, Hisense
and Lenovo, into the US and WE markets, one could identify two different
paths. Haier and Hisense chose the geographical brand extension as their
mode of market entry, combined with the non-brand approach of OEM
business. They expanded quite slowly in terms of timing and on a market-
by-market process. Moreover, they tried to leverage sales partners with
whom they had already worked together in China. Haier approached Wal-
Mart and OBI; Hisense approached Carrefour. In contrast, TCL and
Lenovo mainly decided on brand acquisitions and brand licensing instead,
in order to speed up and to enter several markets simultaneously. In addition, the going-international of all four companies revealed a large influence from unplanned market opportunities, external market forces, and political motives, rather than a clear international market strategy. Haier
entered the US market, because Michael Jemal convinced the Haier management. TCL acquired the business-losing companies Schneider, Thomson and Alcatel, because they were available at a low price. The Chinese
government seemed to have pushed the deals in order to show national
power towards the West. Hisense initially entered South Africa, since the
former Daewoo factory was suffering from the Asian crisis. In the case of
Lenovo, IBM approached the firm, as they wanted to part from their PC
business which suffered from low profitability. Further, Lenovo admitted
that a global brand presence would be necessary as a prerequisite to survive the fast changing global PC market. The hypothesis is therewith confirmed for all four companies.

6.2.3 Operative brand decisions when going-international

*H6: Given H1-H5, Chinese brand companies introduce their global stan-
dardised brand approach in the US and WE markets by a unique and powerful, but cost-clever brand execution, including excellence in branding,
brand communication and brand distribution (dependent on the industry
and foreign market, a marketing budget of around 20% of total revenues
may become necessary in the first three years).*

The analysis of the international marketing budgets has shown that Haier,
Hisense and TCL have not yet invested heavily in end-consumer market-

ing in US and WE markets so far. Their typical budget was at around US$50m, in the case of Hisense even lower at around US$10m. Moreover, they were used to split the budget across products in the case of TCL and across markets in terms of Haier. Although some local marketing initiates of Haier may be considered as unique, their impact was rather low. In contrast, the analysis has proven that Lenovo has decided on a unique and powerful, but cost-clever brand execution with excellence in all three areas. They spent US$250m on their international marketing, after they had acquired IBM PCs. As the analysis has revealed, Lenovo invested in both global standardised marketing initiatives, such as the Olympic Partnership Program for the 2006 and 2008 Olympics, as well as in cross-border and more localised marketing initiatives, such as the product placement at India's TV show 'Who wants to be a Millionaire'. Since the Lenovo budget is still small compared to their competitors' spending and Samsung's benchmark, one could name Lenovo's brand approach also 'cost-clever'. Overall, the hypothesis is therewith confirmed for Lenovo, while it cannot be confirmed for Haier, TCL and Hisense.

H6a: Chinese branded companies choose a global standardised brand name that does not sound Chinese and does not include Chinese characters in the US and WE markets.

Due to their brand aims, all four companies have chosen a global standardised brand name. Haier is Haier, TCL is TCL, Hisense is Hisense and Lenovo is Lenovo. Although all four companies in addition use Chinese written brand names in China, none of the four companies use any Chinese characters as a part of their brand naming abroad. Moreover, one can say that all four names do not sound Chinese, and could theoretically be originated with any country besides China. The hypothesis is therewith confirmed for all four companies.

H6b: Chinese branded companies decide on one or two sponsorships in large scale events, amongst them the 2008 Beijing Olympic Games, in order to establish global brand awareness and to build brand image in US and WE markets.

The analysis has revealed that sport sponsoring, and especially those of larger scale events, is one of the key communication channels among the three companies, Haier, TCL, and Lenovo. Haier became national sponsor of the 2008 Beijing Olympic Games. TCL became sponsor of the European golf tournament at Hainan Island, China. And Lenovo became worldwide partner and exclusive PC sponsor of the 2006 and 2008 Olympic Games, PC sponsor of the US-NBA, and features the 2006 Football World Cup in Germany with an international marketing campaign endorsed by the football star Ronaldinho. Only Hisense had not invested in any large-scale sports sponsoring so far, although they expect that their brand will benefit from the 2008 Beijing Olympic Games anyway, because the sailing competition is going to be held in Hisense's home town Qingdao. When arguing about the reasons, one could think that Hisense is a small company in terms of revenues that have difficulties to afford such an investment. One could also think that Hisense is in its fledging stages in terms of branded business and still prioritises non-branded, OEM expansion into US and WE markets. They will probably decide on sports sponsorships at a later stage of their going-international. This hypothesis is therefore confirmed for Haier, TCL and Lenovo.

H6c: Chinese branded companies decide on distribution channels of large consumer reach and brand fit. In the area of electrical appliances, they therefore decide to take the electronics chains MediaMarkt and Saturn for WE markets. Given that speed of market entry is more crucial to business, they chose Carrefour and Wal-Mart as their favourite initial distribution partners in US and WE markets.

In terms of distribution channel selection the analysis has shown that the electronics chains MediaMarkt and Saturn seemed not to be the favoured distribution channels. Instead, Haier, Hisense and TCL, who aimed for intensive distribution and volume sales in the US and WE markets, have rather decided on large-scale multiple food retailers such as Wal-Mart and Carrefour in the first place. However, it seemed that Haier and Hisense also had a few promotional offers at Saturn, although they have not yet obtained a permanent listing. Further, both companies are listed at Best Buy, which may be considered the American version of MediaMarkt and Saturn for the US market. It became evident that the issue of brand fit was rather not a key decision factor when selecting those distribution channels, but large volumes and large reach were. Since Haier and Hisense have entered the global markets on a country-by-country approach, and Haier's negotiations with Wal-Mart appeared quite time-consuming, the aspect of speed could also have been a key motive to select those channels. Finally, it remains unclear, why at least TCL had not shown more interest in distribution-related brand fit. They could have had pushed more intensively for a listing at MediaMarkt and Saturn, as their product brands *Schneider*, *Thomson* and *Alcatel* were already sold at these stores for years. In contrast, in the case of Lenovo, brand fit seemed to have been a key issue, but they did not decide to take MediaMarkt and Saturn as their key resellers either. Since they target SME users, who are likely not to shop their PCs at large surface electrical chains, but at computer specialised resellers, they chose those resellers combined with direct-sale via the internet as their major distribution channels. As a result, the hypothesis cannot be confirmed for all four investigate companies.

H7: Given H1-H6, Chinese branded companies establish a corporate brand department which is in charge of aligning, steering and controlling all brand management decisions across all world markets. Given that Western and Chinese markets demand different marketing qualities, sales & marketing of the region "US and WE markets" is organisationally separated from the region "China".

The case narratives and the analysis have shown that all four companies established a designated corporate brand management department. Haier's department is called 'Department of corporate values & communication', and is in charge of any Haier-branded advertising, PR and internal communication. TCL runs a corporate brand management department which is responsible for all branding and PR issues that are related to the corporate image, including brand messages, print & TV advertising, and guidelines of visual identity. Hisense has a similar centre which is also in charge of promotional material and product-media planning. Lenovo established the position of a chief marketing officer (CMO) as a part of its post-merger integrations with IBM PCs. The CMO is in charge of all worldwide markets and is supported by global and local marketing teams. Further, all four companies seemed to have acknowledged that overseas markets may require different marketing efforts. Despite of differences in their overall organisation structure, they all have separated the function of sales & marketing in China from sales & marketing in overseas markets. As the case narratives have shown, all four companies also distinguish in some way between sales & marketing in Europe from sales & marketing in the US market. The hypothesis is therewith confirmed for all four companies.

H8: Given that Chinese branded companies lack Western market knowledge and experienced brand managers, they seek for external support to run the corporate brand department and the sales & marketing unit "US and WE markets".

As the cross-case comparison has shown, all four companies, Haier, TCL, Hisense and Lenovo, have received external brand support from international consultancies. However, it seems that only Lenovo's corporate brand department has been led by a marketing expert and non-Chinese national so far. Deepak Advani is from India and became chief marketing officer (CMO) after Lenovo acquired IBM PCs. Advani is an experienced marketing veteran from the IBM PC division. In contrast, the corporate brand department at Haier, TCL and Hisense seemed to be led by a Chinese national whose international marketing experience might be questioned. With respect to the sales & marketing units in the US and WE markets, the analysis has shown that Haier, TCL and Lenovo employ a large share of in-national managers and staff, whereas Hisense mainly relies on Chinese nationals. Overall, the final hypothesis can therefore be confirmed for Lenovo, and partly for Haier and TCL. The final hypothesis cannot be confirmed for Hisense.

6.3 Development of a descriptive model

Summing up the findings of the cross-case comparisons and the test of hypotheses, one can identify several brand-related similarities and differences among the four companies, Haier, TCL, Hisense and Lenovo, entering US and WE markets.

Similarities
With respect to similarities, all four companies have shown that they understood global brand building as a tool to generate larger sales. Price premiums, larger profits and larger shareholder value were minor decision factors. Further, their global brand building was accelerated by the fact that China's accession to the WTO increased global competition in their home market China. They realised that their low labour cost advantages were not eternal, and that they have to globalise and to build a powerful brand name to survive the Chinese market in the long-term run.

Furthermore, the analysis has shown that all four companies decided on a branded house architecture as their long-term aim. This architecture was considered attractive, since companies using it were moving up on the annual brand rankings as conducted by *Interbrand*. Other decision factors were the possibility to expand the product portfolio onto several different industries, while enjoying spillover effects and lower marketing costs. Thus, the four investigated companies also decided on higher degrees of brand standardisation in corporate branding and brand value propositions, while addressing different consumer needs by localised product models. It has become evident that all four companies wanted to address China's poor country-of-origin within their corporate brand strategy actively. They targeted to be perceived as a brand of higher quality, technology, design and service instead of a pure discount good.

Since none of the four companies had invented own core technologies, they all have tried to absorb foreign IP and know-how through partnerships, joint-ventures and M&A over the years. Moreover, it could be proven that they, though increasing their budgets, still tended to invest in smaller numbers compared to their global competitors by 2004. They also often missed a clear and focused R&D strategy.

Analysing the mode of market entry, one could also conclude that all four companies lacked a clear international market plan (China Daily 2005b). Their market entry decisions were strongly impacted by external market and political factors. One could therefore argue that foreign companies and managers, who had approached the Chinese companies to enter their foreign markets, were finally responsible for the fact that Chinese brands had appeared at the global stage. Further, their process of market entry often relied on established relationships from the Chinese market. Lenovo chose Hong Kong as their first overseas base partly due to Chinese family bonds. Hisense invested in a joint venture in Savar, Hungary, because they had already worked together with the joint venture partner Flextronics in China. Haier, TCL and Hisense also decided to take international retailers such as Wal-Mart, Carrefour, and the Metro Group as their key distribution partners, which were already selling their branded goods in China.

In addition, it became evident that all four companies tended to chose modes of market entries and brand strategies which implied lower amounts of investment. On the one hand, TCL and Lenovo acquired branded business units which suffered from profitability and were therefore available at lower price levels. On the other hand, Haier and Hisense decided on smaller brand communication budgets that were hardly sufficient to create a momentum for their self-branded goods, and to persuade Western end-consumers that the brands were of better quality than their prejudice. However, since China has won the right to host the 2008 Beijing Olympic Games, one could identify more brand building efforts among all four investigated companies. For instance, they started investing in different larger scale sports sponsorships, amongst them the 2008 Beijing Olympic Games themselves.

Further, the analysis has shown that in terms of brand naming, all four companies have chosen a non-Chinese sounding brand name to enter overseas markets. Since the majority of Chinese consumers still require a brand name written in Chinese characters, transliteration was the most often applied method of translation to retain a certain similarity. It became also evident that all names were either originated with the company history or due to the Chinese traditional way of name seeking.

Finally, it seemed that all four companies have acknowledged the importance and role of brand management for their business success within their organisation structure. They all have established a corporate brand management department which is in charge of aligning, steering and controlling all corporate brand-related decisions. Further, they all have separated sales & marketing in China from sales & marketing in overseas market due to unequal brand equity. Admitting that they lack own marketing and brand management competences, they all have also obtained external support from international brand consultancies.

Differences
However, discussing differences and which ways of international brand management may appear alike, one could group the four cases in three types. Type I would include Lenovo. Type II would consist of the case of TCL. And type III would include Haier and Hisense. As the analysis has revealed, there are many good reasons to categorise Lenovo's global brand approach as the most advanced, most integrated and most powerful approach compared to those of the other three companies. Lenovo have set clear brand aims, which were implemented in a coherent system of strategic and operative brand measures. For instance, Lenovo corporate brand was positioned close to the recommended approach of a 'clever brand' and was introduced in the overseas market by a powerful momentum, generated by the IBM deal and its 2006 Olympic sponsorship. With the acquisition of IBM PCs, Lenovo also established themselves as one of the major PC players in the world over night, enhancing their brand value through the premium brand *Think*. Lenovo can today be considered as one of the world's leaders in PC brand innovation and PC market experience, employing globally experienced brand and executive managers at all layers of their organisation.

While the grouping of Lenovo in a separated type I is therefore well-defined, the grouping of TCL in type II, and Haier and Hisense into type III may not be clear. Haier and Hisense appear very alike in their brand management decisions, because both companies decided to have the same way of market entry into the US and WE markets. They both chose a branded house architecture and the mode of geographical brand extension at all stages of their going-international. Further, they entered the markets by the same country-by-country path: China – emerging markets – USA – Western Europe (Italy) – other world markets. While TCL and Lenovo focused on one or two core industries when entering the US and WE markets, Haier and Hisense both tried to introduce their complete product portfolio, including white goods, black goods, mobile phones, computers, and air-conditioners, within a short-time frame. Besides branded sales, both companies also heavily expanded through non-branded OEM business as a dual strategy. Despite of their international brand ambitions, Haier and Hisense are also still organised and managed with a strong China-focus. They both have established a differentiated organisation structure and are still led by an exclusively Chinese national top management team. Finally, one could get the impression that both companies have primary utilised their international market presence to enhance their brand image and market position in their home market China.

One could argue that Haier's international brand position is much more advanced than those of Hisense, and that Haier should therefore be grouped with TCL into type II. Haier holds 4% global branded market share in their core business, TCL around 9% and Hisense only 1%. However, if analysing the reasons why Haier and TCL are more internationally present than Hisense, it becomes evident that this is not due to their similarity of brand management decisions, but due to their aggressiveness and quality of execution of the chosen brand decisions in the market. The cases of Haier and TCL differ largely with respect to mode of market entry, brand portfolio and brand organisation. TCL acquired a foreign branded company and chose a multi-product-brand portfolio as their mid-term brand strategy. They re-organised their businesses with respect to regions and its product brands in the regions. Since they target a branded house architecture in the long-term, they have challenging brand transfers ahead. Since Haier and TCL are larger in China with respect to corporate size and market positions than Hisense, both aspects may be key reasons why they could outperform Hisense at the global stage. They were supported by larger funding and were able to choose more powerful strategies, so that they finally obtained larger market experience and larger branded shares in a shorter time-frame (Liu/Li 2002: 705).

In summary, in terms of brand management decisions, Haier's and Hisense's way have been very alike (type III). They decided on a strong corporate brand and the mode of geographical brand extension at all stages of their going-international. Despite of international ambitions, their business focus is their home market China. In contrast, TCL decided on several licensing agreements of ailing brands, and is regionally orientated (type II). Lenovo decided on one powerful brand acquisition and the world as their total relevant market (type I).

The descriptive model
Comparing the identified types I, II and III from a broader perspective, one could think that the underlying and dominating factor of the grouping is the autonomy from the Chinese government. Since initially all four companies had been state-owned or collective-owned enterprises, their pure

category of ownership may be not sufficient for a characterisation. A better proxy of autonomy could be the share of total revenue publicly-listed at international stock exchange markets. Another valuable proxy could be profitability and its importance for the company. Or, a proxy could be the intensity of global competition that a company had to deal with in the Chinese market. The larger the autonomy from the Chinese government, the less a company could rely on soft budget constraints and government funding. Instead, the company was forced to reorganise themselves towards free-market principles. They aimed for profitability and a listing at international stock markets to earn funding. They were also more open to try out new management principles such as brand building, and opened up their organisations for foreigners and international experts to absorb advanced marketing competence. As result, the more autonomy the company had from the Chinese government, the better the quality of their global brand management. They achieved larger branded shares in the US and WE markets and gained significant global brand equity in terms of brand value, brand image and brand awareness in a shorter time frame.

Testing the cause-and-effect-chain by the three types, one could find the following supportive arguments:

Type I: Large autonomy and high brand management quality
Although initially a state-owned enterprise, Lenovo enjoyed large autonomy since the founding of the company in 1984. Since they had not been able to obtain a PC manufacturing licence from the Chinese government until 1990, they were forced to go abroad and entered Hong Kong. Since 1994 Lenovo is fully listed at the Hong Kong stock exchange market and has tried to be as transparent to their shareholders as possible. Since 2000 Lenovo's main concern has been Dell's launch of the direct-sale business model in the Chinese market. To stay competitive, Lenovo finally chose the world as their relevant market and internationalised their organisation by powerful investments. They became a worldwide Olympic partner and acquired IBM PCs. Their headquarters were moved to New York, an US-America became their president and CEO, and they established the position of a chief marketing officer. Within one year, Lenovo became a significant market player, a recognised brand name and owner of the premium brand *Think*. It seems that Lenovo was willing to change towards an organisation where long-term brand building enjoys priority over short-term orientated volume targets.

Type II: Middle autonomy and middle brand management quality
TCL, initially a state-owned company, was partly liberalised from the Chinese government by president Li's personal efforts. TCL has since been

regarded as an experiment in order to test private company ownership be-haviour. TCL is listed with two companies in Shenzhen and Hong Kong stock exchange market, covering 62% of their total revenues. Further, TCL decided that a global market entry on a country-by-country basis would take them too long to survive the changing and competitive consumer elec-tronics market. They acquired several foreign branded business units and opened up their organisation for foreign influence and free-market princi-ples. However, their foreign investments were rather moderate and unfo-cused. They did not include the purchase of premium brands, but brand li-censing rights of mid-quality brands. They also did not focus on one brand or one market, but purchased several regional brand names of different in-dustries. The Chinese government also seemed to have accelerated M&A due to political motives. As a result, TCL has been struggling with profit-ability since, and is required to transfer their set of different brands to their corporate brand in future. Although TCL holds a significant total of branded volume shares, the fulfilment of their global brand aims are future scenarios.

Type III: Low autonomy and low brand management quality
Haier and Hisense are largely impacted by the Chinese government, and can be considered typical large collective-owned and state-owned enter-prises. They seemed not to have ever been concerned about profitability due to soft budget constraints and other government support, particularly from the municipal government in Qingdao. Further, both companies are very intransparent and complex, since less than 20% of their revenues are publicly-listed at an international stock exchange market. In terms of branded sales, Haier and Hisense strongly rely on their home market China. Their brand initiatives in US and WE markets could be described as adjunct to domestic sales, and were supported by very small investments and a combination of OEM and branded business. Since global brand management was thus not their priority, its quality was rather poor, al-though Haier could enhance their marketing in the US by the single efforts of their country manager Jemal.

Synthesis
Figure 6-3 illustrates the described cause-and-effect chain, which can be summed up by the phrase of 'the autonomy from the Chinese government has impact on the firm's global brand management quality'. In the figure, the x-axis therefore presents the autonomy from the Chinese government, while the y-axis presents the quality of the global brand management. As the figure reveals, the correlation is not exclusive. There can be company examples that have low autonomy, but high quality in global brand man-

agement. There can also be Chinese companies that enjoy high autonomy from the Chinese government, but perform poorly in global brand management. One could suppose small private enterprises which have established a promising brand name in China, but do not have the critical mass, funding and personnel to take their brand global.

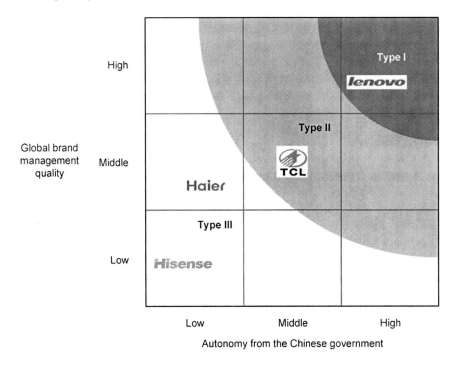

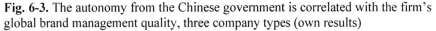

Autonomy from the Chinese government

Fig. 6-3. The autonomy from the Chinese government is correlated with the firm's global brand management quality, three company types (own results)

The identified correlation may also be supported by the following train of thought: The Chinese government had announced Chinese global brand building as one of their major government aims (chap 'Government policies of outward investment and global brand building'). To support the Chinese companies, they established the China Brand Name Promotion Committee. Even though one might suppose that the more support a firm gets from the Committee, the better has to be the firm's quality of global brand management, one can in general doubt this effect. It might be that in China, where government support is generally regarded as positive (e.g., Sun 2006), the policies may initiate corporate brand building and may lead to a priority change towards it. Organisation structures may be reorganised to get a brand management department, and regular brand value reports may be established and discussed on every meeting. This was also the case at Haier and Hisense. However, though the relevance of brand management may be increased by the government policies, there is no evidence that the quality of brand management itself has automatically improved, at least in the short-term. The performance of a brand will still be limited by the managers' capabilities, experiences and priorities, and by the quality of the support of the China Brand Name Promotion Committee. It seems that the changes implemented through these government policies have so far been fairly superficial, since there has only been a change of organisation structures and commitment to brand building, but no additional knowledge about brand management and brand building has been acquired by the relevant Chinese managers.

China-specifics

Discussing whether the government initiatives are a China-specific or are conducted in similar ways in other countries too, one probably has to say that it is a China-specific. Of course, the Japanese and South Korean companies Sony and Samsung had also got support from their governments when they went abroad, and also US and European governments have always been supportive if a national company wanted to invest globally. However, the dimensions and qualities seem to be different in China. The central Chinese government has enormous reserves of foreign exchange. One could suppose that, if the government is willing to fund the going-international of a Chinese branded company and wants to increase its global brand management quality, they should be able to afford it and will eventually purchase lacking competences from foreign multinationals. Besides the central government, in China the local governments are also very important. While the central government follows national interests and approves large foreign direct investments, the provincial and municipal governments care more about single company cases. This might be due to the fact that the Chinese provinces stay in huge national competition. There are statistics and rankings that officially prove that *Haier* and *Hisense* are brands from Qingdao, Shandong province, while *TCL* brand is from Guangdong, and *Lenovo* brand is from Beijing (e.g., Huatongren Shichang Xinxiu [All China Marketing Research] 2004; Huang/Du 2005; Wang 2005a).

Beyond the government initiatives, another China-specific may be China's huge market size. When comparing Chinese companies' global brand building with those of the companies from Japan and South Korea, it becomes evident that Chinese companies were immediately noticed at the global stage, although they had not yet gained any significant sales in US and WE markets. For instance, Haier gains its 4% branded market share mainly through its branded sales in China and in emerging markets. A similar thing is true for China Mobile. Although China Mobile was ranked as the world's fourth most powerful brand by Millward Brown in 2005, they obtained this rank not because of its international relevance, but because of its immense domestic market power of over 240 million subscribers in China (chap 3.1.1.2, CRIENGLISH.com 2006).

On the other hand, China's huge market size combined with China's open door policy has led to an enormous global competition in China. No foreign brand and large multinational dares strategise without taking China into consideration. Therefore, Chinese branded companies had always been concerned about their home market positions, while the markets in Japan and South Korea appeared as quite stable. Although all four investigated Chinese companies were market leaders in their respective industries, they could thus not fully focus on their going-international. Since Chinese consumers have often regarded foreign brands as superior to Chinese brands, Chinese companies were also forced to go abroad to retain competitiveness and to satisfy the increasing Chinese consumer demands. The motives of Japanese and South Korean companies had probably been different. They mainly went globally in order to achieve a critical volume, similar to the companies from smaller countries in Western Europe, such as Switzerland (e.g., Meffert 1986). Further, it is to note that the challenge for Chinese companies to build a famous brand might have increased these days. Compared to the time when Sony and Samsung went globally in the 1960s and 1980s, competition nowadays moves faster and is more globalised.

Looking in the future, one can assume that Chinese companies will learn fast and will improve their global brand management quality quickly. Lenovo, in this study acknowledged with the most advanced quality of global brand management, might be outperformed in future by a 'type 0'. Type 0 would have larger communication budgets, would have developed own Chinese IP and would enjoy a distinct brand image, similar to those of Samsung, Sony, Nike or Apple. Since Chinese branded companies just started to go international, one has to admit that Haier and TCL have been the Chinese pioneers in the global markets and suffered from many trial & error. Hisense was less straight-forward and followed the Haier role model. Lenovo is the most recent Chinese branded company that has entered the global stage. They have definitively benefited and learnt from the Haier and TCL experiences. The next generation of Chinese branded companies will probably take Lenovo as their benchmark and role model. One could assume, if Lenovo can prove the Chinese government that more autonomy pays off, they will reduce their impact on more companies in future too (Ling 2005: 145).

7 Summary and future research

The study has integrated the three topics of Chinese companies, going-international and brand management, an integration which is a new field of research. Since China, Chinese companies and Chinese brands gain large public media attention and are often topic at meetings in US and Western European companies, thus the findings of the study are relevant for many different audiences. Because Chinese companies traditionally have a talent to demonstrate strengths and to hide weaknesses (e.g., Bartsch 2005: 54), this study wants to contribute to transparency. The study has shown that there is not one Chinese market and not one way of Chinese brand management. The study has also shown that it is neither true that Chinese companies are unable to perform brand management, nor that Chinese brands will overstock the US and WE markets in the short-term.

The study has identified three different types of Chinese global brand management. Type I includes companies that are highly independent form the Chinese government and have demonstrated a high quality in their brand management in US and WE markets. They prioritise long-term brand building as a key corporate goal and implement it by a coherent system of strategic and operative brand measures. They are willing to support their global brand building by larger investments and are open for re-organisations towards a global market orientation and international management teams. As a result they hold leading global market positions, and achieve significant brand equity in US and WE markets in a short-time frame. In this study, type I is represented by Lenovo.

Companies of type II enjoy moderate autonomy from the Chinese government and have shown a middle quality of brand management in US and WE markets. Their way of global brand management is characterised by moderate, but unfocused and uncoordinated investments. Although global brand building is a major corporate aim and they are willing to re-organise their company towards modern management principles and global market orientation, their decisions are often impacted by political motives and conducted on a basis of trial & error. As a result companies of type II hold significant branded shares in the global market, but have not yet built brand equity for their corporate Chinese brand. In this study, type II is represented by TCL.

Finally, companies of type III have little autonomy from the Chinese government and have shown low quality in brand management in US and WE markets. They are typical Chinese state-owned or collective-owned companies. Although they are ranked with branded market shares in global market statistics, their country focus is on China. They mainly employ Chinese nationals and are rather reluctant to take the risks of modern management principles. They regard brand management as an additional way to increase short-term orientated volume targets in US and WE markets. They therefore try to expand the brand's scope onto as many industries and products as possible, often combining branded sales by dual strategies and OEM. As a result they enjoy low brand equity in US and WE markets and typically struggle with China's poor country image. In this study, type III is represented by Haier and Hisense.

In addition to these three types of global brand management, the study has identified the huge size of the Chinese market combined with China's open door policy as a China-specific factor. Since China started their modernisation process in 1978, thousands of foreign multinationals has been attracted by the potential of 1.3bn customers and has entered the Chinese market place. Chinese companies were forced to reorganise themselves towards free-market and modern management principles including brand building in order to survive the market. While Chinese brands copied Western marketing approaches in the beginning, nowadays several Chinese brands have emerged as equal competitors. They can enjoy a large consumer base in China, and are even known in the world markets, although they might not have yet gained any significant market share. However, as the study has revealed, powerful Chinese branded companies are so far rare in international markets. Lenovo is probably the first company which can emerge as an internationally famous brand name.

Taking into account that the research method of case studies implies some limits, the findings of this study need to be tested and proven by future research. The study investigated four different cases, Haier, TCL, Hisense and Lenovo, which had been chosen by the researcher by "theoretical sampling" (Glaser/Strauss 1967). Although there had been strong indications that allowed integrating the findings in a descriptive model and identifying three types of global brand management, the results still remain hypotheses. Future research is necessary to generalise the findings beyond the four cases. These can be studies on further Chinese household appliances and consumer electronics brands such as *SVA*, *Midea*, *Gree*, *Chunlan*, *Skyworth*, *Konka*, and *Galanz*. These can also be studies on other industries such as automotive (e.g., *SAIC*, *Brilliance*, *Nanjing Automobile*), beverages and food (e.g., *Tsingdao* beer), or textiles (e.g., *Erdos*) (BCG 2006c; Jing 2006; Sedan 2006). Further, one could argue that the identified company differences in mode of market entry, brand architecture and brand organisation may be system-inherent. Case studies do not aim to be representative but want to address typical, differentiating and interesting aspects (Yin 1994). Therefore, future research is also necessary to eliminate this potential source of error.

In addition, it would be interesting to gather more information about the brand equity of Chinese brands in US and WE markets. While this study investigated the Chinese brands from a company perspective, a consumer perspective would be a next logical step. In this study, the researcher already started with a short online survey among 82 end-consumers in Germany. Since it is not representative, it needs to be extended onto larger numbers in future. Further, the survey should be extended onto more country markets in Western Europe and in the US.

Generalising the study's findings, one can say that on the one hand Chinese branded companies have advantages in low cost manufacturing, supply chain, and assembling, on the other hand they lack competences in R&D, IP and advanced marketing techniques. Chinese branded companies therefore typically rely on fast production-cycles and competitive prices. They focus on marketing custom-made product designs, while they understand brand management as another opportunity to push products in the market and to make larger sales in a shorter time frame. They typically choose a branded house architecture combined with high degrees of brand standardisation in brand value propositions and branding. They typically lack thoroughly planned market entry and brand strategies in US and WE markets, and are reluctant to support their global brand building by larger investments. If there is any brand communication to end-consumers in US and WE markets, they tend to decide on larger scale sports sponsorships, in particular on the 2008 Beijing Olympic Games. Their brand names are typically globalised and do not sound Chinese. Due to the large presence of multinationals in China, Chinese branded companies got used to foreign sales cultures and basic Western consumer needs. They have also been able to establish relationships to global distribution partners, such as Wal-Mart and Carrefour. Finally, the Chinese government started to strongly support Chinese branded companies to take their brands global. Although the quality of the support could so far be questioned, this will probably change in future. Chinese people and Chinese companies usually learn quickly. And since Lenovo has so far succeeded at the global brand stage, other Chinese branded companies may be as motivated as never before to follow their path.

Appendix

Appendix 1. Applied exchange rates

	€/US$	RMB/US$	HK$/US$
1984		2,79	
1985		3,20	
1986		3,71	
1987		3,72	
1988		3,72	
1989		4,72	
1990		5,23	
1991		5,40	
1992		5,84	
1993		5,81	
1994		8,44	
1995		8,32	
1996		8,33	
1997		8,31	
1998		8,28	7,7465
1999		8,28	7,7710
2000		8,28	7,7992
2001	1,12867	8,28	7,7968
2002	0,95393	8,28	7,7977
2003	0,79637	8,27	7,7648
2004	0,73292	8,27	7,7760
2005	0,84441	8,07	7,7530

Source: OANDA.com, RMB/US$ 1984-2002 transcript from Yi/Ye 2003: 241

Appendix 2. Interview guideline – Example TCL Corporation

Sandra Bell, 宁夏路 353 弄 30 号 502 室, 上海 200063, 手机: 13761060233, 电话: 021-62452377

RESEARCH APPROACH
Doctoral thesis written by Sandra Bell,
University of Duisburg-Essen, Germany; Shanghai Fudan University, Management School

Working title of thesis:

International brand management of Chinese companies. Five case studies on the Chinese household appliances and consumer electronic industry entering US- and European markets.

中国公司的国际品牌管理。五个中国国内家用电器和电子消费品公司如何进入欧美国家成熟市场的个案研究。

Research question:

How do Chinese branded companies enter developed markets such as the USA and Europe with respect to brand management decisions?

(What are reasons behind? What does the decision making process look like?)

Objectives and milestones:

- Understand history and status quo of Chinese brands and Chinese branded companies in the domestic market.

   National brand champions, role of brands for Chinese consumers, brand management organisation, impact of intellectual property rights etc.

- Discuss the market entry strategy into developed markets in Europe and the USA of selected household appliances and consumer electronics companies such as Lenovo, Haier, Hisense, Konka, and TCL.

   Reasons, market entry mode, brand management decisions (e.g., own brand versus OEM)

Research methodology:

- Interviews with company, market and industry experts
- Case studies of Lenovo, Haier, TCL, Konka and Hisense with focus on their international brand management decisions

Guideline of questions – Interview with TCL representatives:

1 COMPANY AND BRAND OVERVIEW

- Characterise TCL's position in domestic and in developed markets such as USA and Europe: product range, sales figures, market shares, corporate structure, location of production, R&D and marketing sites, etc.
- Evaluate TCL's following competences on a scale from 1 to 5, with 1 basic industry level and 5 international top level:
   - Technology/innovation
   - Industry/supply chain

- 2 -

- o Distribution/ trade
- o Branding and consumer insights
- o Capabilities development and organizational effectiveness
- Describe the development of TCL's international business, including OEM.

2 BRAND BUILDING

- Describe TCL's historical decisions on corporate names and product names?
- What are TCL brand values? What does differentiate TCL from its competitors?
- What are your most important marketing communication channels in China and why?
- How much does TCL spend on marketing/brand building per year, in % of annual sales?
- Do you use same channels and budgets in the USA and Europe?
- Why should an US/ European consumer buy a TCL product?
- Did TCL think of sponsoring the Olympic Games Beijing 2008?

3 INTERNATIONAL BRAND ORGANISATION

- How does TCL organise its brand management internally? Who is responsible? Which departments exist? How does the organisational structure look like?
- Who is in charge of foreign markets like USA and Europe? Especially for marketing/branding issues?
- How does TCL do market research and satisfy consumer needs of Chinese and overseas customers?
- Describe the strategy how TCL enters developed markets.
- Describe TCL's current presence in the developed markets in Europe and the USA: number of staff, departments, brand awareness scores, market position, distribution channels etc.

4 FUTURE AIMS

- What do you expect from TCL by 2020? Brand position in China and globally?
- What do you expect from Chinese companies and Chinese brands overall? Who will be global brand by 2010, by 2020?

Guideline of questions – Interview with TCL representatives – Chinese:

1 公司和品牌历史

- 请简单介绍一下 TCL 在国内和国外的现状：产品范围，销售额，市场份额，公司结构，产品生产地，研发部门和营销场所等。
- 对于下列几点特性，请您对TCL在国际市场的实力，用1-5的分值给出评价。1分：《一般的实力》、5分：《在国际市场具有最强实力》：

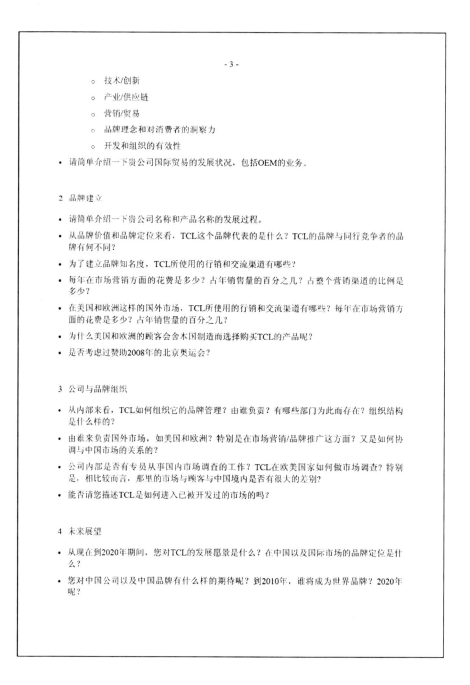

- 3 -

  o 技术/创新

  o 产业/供应链

  o 营销/贸易

  o 品牌理念和对消费者的洞察力

  o 开发和组织的有效性

- 请简单介绍一下贵公司国际贸易的发展状况，包括OEM的业务。

2 品牌建立

- 请简单介绍一下贵公司名称和产品名称的发展过程。

- 从品牌价值和品牌定位来看，TCL这个品牌代表的是什么？TCL的品牌与同行竞争者的品牌有何不同？

- 为了建立品牌知名度，TCL所使用的行销和交流渠道有哪些？

- 每年在市场营销方面的花费是多少？占年销售量的百分之几？占整个营销渠道的比例是多少？

- 在美国和欧洲这样的国外市场，TCL所使用的行销和交流渠道有哪些？每年在市场营销方面的花费是多少？占年销售量的百分之几？

- 为什么美国和欧洲的顾客会舍本国制造而选择购买TCL的产品呢？

- 是否考虑过赞助2008年的北京奥运会？

3 公司与品牌组织

- 从内部来看，TCL如何组织它的品牌管理？由谁负责？有哪些部门为此而存在？组织结构是什么样的？

- 由谁来负责国外市场，如美国和欧洲？特别是在市场营销/品牌推广这方面？又是如何协调与中国市场的关系的？

- 公司内部是否有专员从事国内市场调查的工作？TCL在欧美国家如何做市场调查？特别是，相比较而言，那里的市场与顾客与中国境内是否有很大的差别？

- 能否请您描述TCL是如何进入已被开发过的市场的吗？

4 未来展望

- 从现在到2020年期间，您对TCL的发展愿景是什么？在中国以及国际市场的品牌定位是什么？

- 您对中国公司以及中国品牌有什么样的期待呢？到2010年，谁将成为世界品牌？2020年呢？

Appendix 3. Details on emerging Chinese consumer brands in 2005/2006

Yue-Sai 羽西 cosmetics

Yue-Sai is China's most famous cosmetic brand with a strong market position and around US$47.7m sales in 2003. The brand is sold in around 800 department stores in China's 240 biggest cities, competing against global brands such as *Shiseido* and *Lancôme*. The brand's identity bases on the personality of Chinese-American founder Yue-Sai Kan (e.g., Ballhaus 2005: 34), who established the cosmetic company in 1992 as a result of "[her] frustrations at not being able to find cosmetics that suited her Asian skin tone and facial features" (Gilmore/Dumont 2003: 195). It is said that the person Yue-Sai Kan is known by up to 95% of the Chinese population (Gilmore/Dumont 2003: 196), since she hosted the weekly TV programme 'One World' on CCTV in 1986 (Rousseau 2000). After a joint venture with French cosmetics giant *Coty* in 1996, the Chinese brand Yue-Sai belongs to French *L'Oréal* since January 2004 (L'Oréal 2004).

GOME 国美 consumer electronics chain

The founder Huang Guangyu of *GOME* started from scratch in the beginning of the 1990s. At this time 18 years old, he wanted to make money and rented "a market stall in Beijing hawking cheap plastic appliances" (Roberts et al. 2004). By 2006, GOME is China's top consumer electronics chain, with US$1.5bn in revenue in 2004 and over 200 stores, planning to open 800 to 1,000 outlets nationwide till 2008 (Liu 2005). Although GOME enjoys brand recognition similar to the US-electronic chains Circuit City or Best Buy in the USA, it continuously has to compete against the Chinese peers *Suning* 苏宁 (US$1.1bn revenues in 2004) and *Yongle* 永乐 (US$1.0bn) very strongly. The reasons are that customer loyalty is poor, brand communication is considered similar, and that "in most big electronics retail outlets, vendors design their own sales counters, display their own brands and even pay for their own sales staff on the floor" (China Chain Store & Franchise Association 2005).

Meng Niu 蒙牛 dairy

The company *Meng Niu* 蒙牛 dairy was founded in 1999 by three former employees of China's largest state-owned dairy in Inner Mongolia. The company has grown to China's largest liquid milk producer within 5 years and achieved around 26% market share by volume against international giants like *Nestlé* and the local peers *Yili* 伊利 and *Bright Daily* 光明 in 2005. It is said that Meng Niu has managed its growth particularly by strong marketing capabilities, as they have focused most of its resources on marketing and promotion from early stages on. For instance, Meng Niu sponsored the 'Super-Girl' contest on television or the Chinese astronauts when they went into the space the first time in Chinese history (ABN-AMRO 2005: 16-17).

Wahaha 娃哈哈 beverages

Wahaha is China's largest soft drink manufacturer. While 20 years ago Wahaha was a small shop selling stationary goods, ice-cream and beverages to a middle school in Hangzhou, they nowadays emerged to a large company of total annual revenue at US$1.7bn. The company was founded by Zong Qinghou who was a retired teacher. Since 1990 the company is named Wahaha, a name that sounds like children's laughing. Besides soft drinks, Wahaha also sells snacks, ice-cream and since 2002 also children's clothes. In China Wahaha is as famous as Coca-Cola in the US or in Europe (Ding/Zheng 2005; Schramm/Spiller 2006; Wirtschaftswoche 2006).

Appendix 4. Haier marketing chain process model v.4 (comp material, 3 pages)

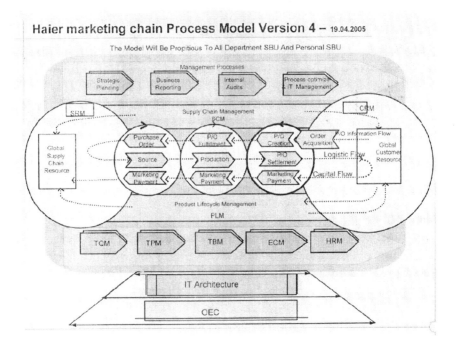

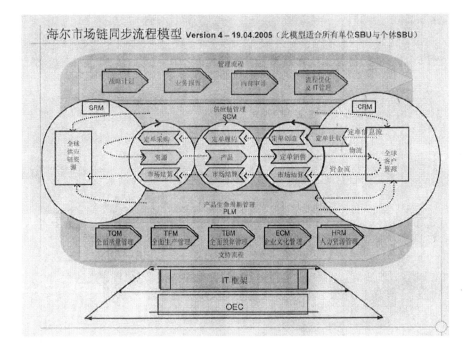

Appendix 5. TCL Corporation revenues 1998-2004 (company material)

Performance−Revenues (1998 − 2004)

Revenues in 2004 rose to RMB 55.3 billion

By RMB 100million

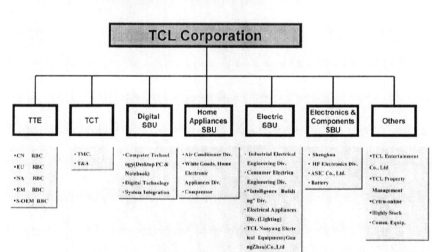

Appendix 6. TCL Corporation organisation structure (company material)

Appendix 7. TCL Corp's distribution network (company material, 2 pages)

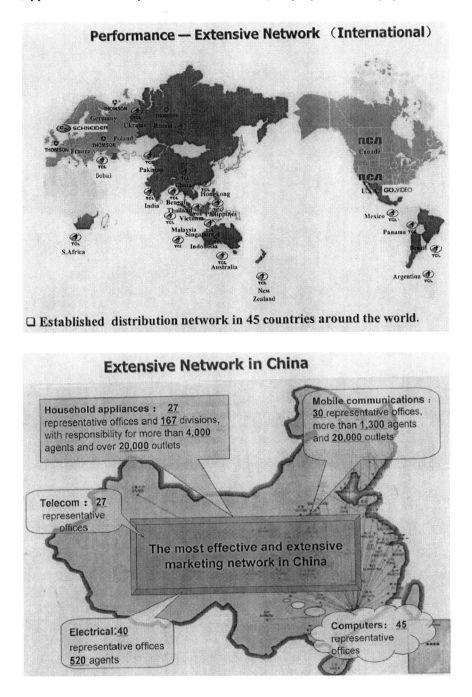

Appendix 8. IBM and Lenovo revenue distributions before acquisition, early 2004 (company material as taken from Quelch/Knoop 2006: 18)

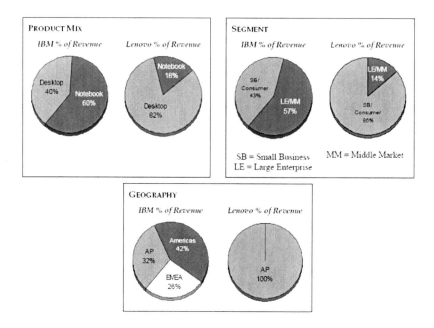

Appendix 9. IBM and Lenovo revenue distributions after acquisition, spring 2005 (taken from Quelch/Knoop 2006: 18)

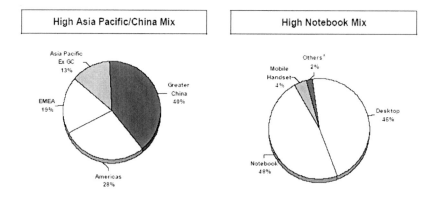

Appendix 10. Legend's operational results 1999-2000 (company data as published by Access Asia 2002: 44)

Table 2.11   LEGEND: OPERATIONAL RESULTS, FIRST HALF 1999 - FIRST HALF
2000

HK$ million

	1999 Turnover	1999 Profit (loss)	2000 Turnover	2000 Profit (loss)
Product divisions				
Legend PC & other access devices	3,618.6	161.5	7,795.9	323.6
Motherboards	440.2	(24.1)	539.8	47.8
Internet services	na	na	59.4	(47.0)
Foreign brand distribution	2,503.8	40.7	3,459.7	75.0
Systems integration	542.0	(5.7)	900.4	4.8
Others	228.7	1.2	335.2	34.4
Geographical markets				
People's Republic of China	6,795.8	186.5	12,445.1	370.3
Asia Pacific (excluding PRC)	99.7	(7.9)	208.0	19.2
North America	131.8	2.5	154.5	24.0
Europe	306.0	(7.4)	282.7	25.2
TOTAL	7,333.4	173.6	13,090.3	438.7

Source: Access Asia from company accounts

Appendix 11. Lenovo operating profit by region, FY 2005/2006 (taken from Lenovo Group 2006g: 5)

Geography Summary (excluding restructuring charges in 4Q)

	Turnover HK$ mn			Segment Operating Profit HK$ mn			Segment Operating Profit Margin		
	3Q	4Q	FY	3Q	4Q	FY	3Q	4Q	FY
GC	11,453	8,411	37,998	744	402	2,176	6.5%	4.8%	5.7%
Americas	8,948	7,361	30,900	196	(252)	408	2.2%	(3.4%)	1.3%
EMEA	6,992	5,147	21,615	14	(87)	(101)	0.2%	(1.7%)	(0.5%)
AP (ex GC)	3,672	3,459	13,038	(139)	62	(8)	(3.8%)	1.8%	(0.1%)
Total	31,066	24,378	103,551	815	125	2,476	2.6%	0.5%	2.4%

Appendix 12. Lenovo logo evaluation research, January 2006 (Momentum Market Intelligence 2006)

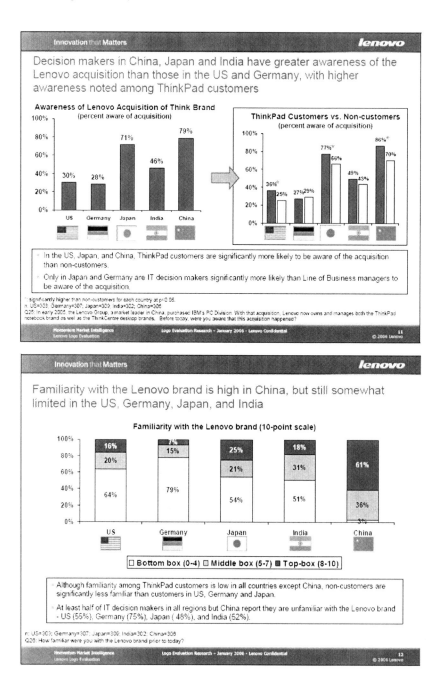

Appendix 13. Lenovo Group's organisation structure 2003-2005 (taken from Lenovo Group 2004: 26)

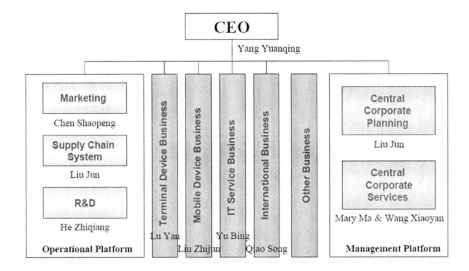

Appendix 14. New Lenovo Group's management team as in place by November 2006 (Lenovo Group 2006c)

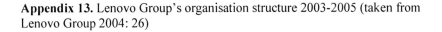

List of abbreviations

3C	Consumer electronics and domestic appliances, Computers, and Communication
3G	The third generation
A/C	Air-conditioning
A/V	Audio and video
ADAC	Allgemeiner Deutscher Automobil Club
ASEAN	Association of South-East Asian Nations
AQSIQ	General Administration of Quality Supervision, Inspection and Quarantine of the People's Republic of China
b2b	business to business
BOCOG	Beijing Organizing Committee of the Olympic Games
BCG	The Boston Consulting Group
BSH	Bosch and Siemens Home Appliances
c2c	consumer to consumer
CAGR	Compound average growth rate
CAS	Chinese Academy of Sciences
CCFA	China Chain Store & Franchise Association
CCT	China Construction Telecommunication Company
CCTV	China Central Television
CDMA	Code division multiple access
CEIBS	China European International Business School (Shanghai)
CEO	Chief executive officer
CFO	Chief financial officer
CES	Consumer Electronics Show (Las Vegas)
CFO	Chief financial officer
CITC	China Technology Transfer Company
CITIC	China International Trust and Investment Corporation
COGS	Costs of goods sold
COO	Country-of-origin

CMO	Chief marketing officer
CNOOC	China National Offshore Oil Corporation
CNPC	China National Petroleum Corporation
CRT	Cathode ray tube
CSA	Conseil Supérieur de l'Audiovisuel
EIU	Economist Intelligence Unit
EMC	Electromagnetic compatibility
EMFIS	Emphasising Emerging Markets
EPRG	Ethnocentric, polycentric, regional-centric, geocentric
FAW	First Automotive Works
FDI	Foreign Direct Investment
FIFA	International Federation of Football Association
FMCG	Fast moving consumer goods
FY	Financial year
G&A	General and administration
GATT	General Agreement on Tariffs and Trade
GDP	Gross domestic product
GE	General Electrics
GPRS	General Packet Radio Service
GM	General Motors
GS	Geprüfte Sicherheit
GSM	Global system for mobile communication
IFA	Internationale Funkausstellung (Berlin)
IAA	International Automobil-Ausstellung (Frankfurt)
IP	International patents
IPO	Initial public offering
IPR	Intellectual property rights
JV	Joint venture
LCD	Liquid Crystal Display
MBA	Master of Business Administration
M&A	Merger and acquisition
MEI	Ministry of Electronic Industries
MNC	Multi-national company
MOFCOM	Ministry of Commerce of the People's Republic of China
MS	Market share
n/a	Not announced
NAFTA	North America Free Trade Agreement

NDRC	National Development and Reform Commission
NTD	New Technology Development Company
OEM	Original equipment manufacturer
PDP	Plasma display panel
P&G	Procter & Gamble
QDI	Quantum Design International
R&D	Research and development
RBC	Regional Business Centre
RCA	Radio Corporation of America
SAFE	State Administration of Foreign Exchange
SAIC	Shanghai Automotive Industry Company
SG&A	Selling, general & administration
SME	Small & medium enterprises
SBU	Strategic business unit
T&A	TCL & Alcatel Corporation
TAMP	TCL-Alcatel Mobile Phones Corporation
TCL	Telephone Communication Limited
TCT	TCL Communication Technology Corporation
TMC	TCL Multimedia Corporation
TNC	Transnational corporation
TTE	TCL-Thomson-Electronics Corporation
UNCTAD	United Nations Conference on Trade and Development
VCD	Video Compact Disc
VDE	Verband der Elektrotechnik Elektronik Informationstechnik
VW	Volkswagen
WE	Western Europe
WIPO	World Intellectual Property Organization
WTO	World Trade Organisation

Glossary of Chinese terms

Chinese	Pinyin	English
阿里巴巴	alibaba	Alibaba.com
百炼	bailian	Shanghai Bailian
宝高	baogao	Blocko
宝马	baoma	BMW
博世	boshi	Bosch
长	chang	Long
长虹	changhong	Changhong
第一汽车	diyi qiche	First Automotive Works
电	dian	Electricity
电脑	diannao	Computer
飞	fei	Flying
飞鸽	feige	Flying pigeon
格兰	gelan	Galanz
国	guo	Country
国美	guomei	GOME
关系	guanxi	Personal relationships
海	hai	Sea; a lots of
海尔	haier	Haier
孩儿	haier	Child, son, brother
海信	haixin	Hisense
虹	hong	Rainbow
红塔山	hongtashan	Hongtashan
华为技术	huawei jishu	Huawei Technologies
集团	jituan	Group, corporation
金	jin	Gold
金狮	jinshi	Golden lion
久	jiu	A long time
康佳	kangjia	Konka

Chinese	Pinyin	English
可口可乐	kekou kele	Coca-Cola
克莱斯勒	kelai sile	Chrysler
李宁	lining	Li-Ning
联想	lianxiang	Association (Lenovo)
面子	mianzi	Face
美的	meide	Midea
蒙牛	mengniu	Mengniu
名人面对面	mingren mian dui mian	Face to face with stars
名人选名品。	mingren xuan mingpin.	Famous people choose
全球的海信	quanqiu de haixin	famous products. The world of Hisense
脑	nao	Brain
牌	pai	Plate, shop sign
品	pin	Product, quality
品牌	pinpai	Brand
琴岛利勃海尔	qindao libo haier	Qindao-Liebherr
琴岛青岛海尔	qindao qingdao haier	Qindao Qingdao Haier
企业价值观 统一处	qiye jiashiguan tongyichu	Department of corporate values & communication
上海星巴克 咖啡馆	shanghai xingbake kafei guan	Shanghai Xinbake Coffee Bar
数字家园, 快乐无限	shuzi jiayuan, kuaile wuxian	Digital home, pleasure without limits
苏宁	suning	Suning
淘宝	taobao	Taobao.com
娃哈哈	wahaha	Wahaha
万达奴	wandanu	Wandanu
王牌	wangpai	King Brand
五粮液	wuliangye	Wuliangye
西门子	ximenzi	Siemens
信	xin	Trust
星巴克	xinbake	Starbucks
友爱, 科技地动情!	youai, keji de dongqing!	With love, technology carries emotion!
永	yong	Forever

Chinese	Pinyin	English
永久	yongjiu	Always and forever
玉兰油	yulan you	Olay
羽西	yuesai (Cantonese)	Yue-Sai
中	zhong	Centre
中国	zhongguo	China
中国移动	zhongguo yidong	China Mobile
通信	tongxin	

References

Access Asia (2002) Made in China: China's leading brands 2001. Shanghai London

Aaker DA (1991) Managing brand equity: Capitalizing on the value of a brand name. Free Press, New York

Aaker DA (2002) Building strong brands. Free Press et al, London

Aaker DA (2004) Brand portfolio strategy: Creating relevance, differentiation, energy, leverage, and clarity. Free Press, New York et al

Aaker DA, Joachimsthaler E (2000) Brand leadership. Free Press, New York

Aaker DA, Joachimsthaler E (2001) Brand leadership: Die Strategie für Siegermarken (in German). Financial Times Deutschland et al, München et al

Aaker JL (1995) Brand personality: Conceptualization, measurement and underlying psychological mechanism. Ann Arbor

ABN-AMRO (2005) China Mengniu Dairy, analyst report, Shanghai

Absatzwirtschaft (2000) Miele und Cie: Diese Marke speichert Leistungsgeschichte (in German). 43 (Sondernummer Oktober 2000): 36–46

Access Asia Ltd (2002) Made in China: China's leading brands 2001. Shanghai London

ACNielsen (2005) Mainland Chinese among the world's 3 optimistic. Http://www.acnielsen.com.cn/news.asp?newsID=96, release order 13/10/2005

ADAC (2005) Das erste chinesische Auto im ADAC-Crashtest: Test 09/2005 (in German). Http://www.adac.de/Tests/Crash_Tests/jiangling_landwind/default.asp, release order 14/09/2005

Adler NJ (2002) International dimensions of organisational behaviour, 3rd edn. South-Western College Pub, Cincinnati Ohio

Agarwal S, Ramaswami SN (1992) Choice of foreign market entry mode: Impact of ownership, location and internationalization factors. Journal of International Business Studies 23 (1): 1–27

Ahlert D (1981) Vertragliche Vertriebssysteme zwischen Industrie und Handel (in German). Gabler, Wiesbaden

Ahlert D (1996) Distributionspolitik (in German), 3rd edn. Schäffer-Poeschel, Stuttgart et al

Ahmed SA, d'Astous A (1995) Comparison of country-of-origin effects on household and organizational buyers' product perceptions. European Journal of Marketing 29 (3): 35–51

Alexander N, Doherty AM (2004) International market entry: Management competencies and environmental influences. European Retail Digest 42: 14–19

Alon I (ed) (2003) Chinese culture, organizational behaviour, and international business management. Praeger, Westport

Alonzo V (1994) The wide world of sports marketing. Incentive 168 (5): 44

Ambler T (2004) Doing business in China, 2nd edn. Routledge, London et al

Amine LS, Chao MCH, Arnold MJ (2005) Executive insights – Exploring the practical effects of country of origin, animosity, and price-quality issues: Two case studies of Taiwan and Acer in China. Journal of International Marketing 13 (2): 114–150

Andresen T, Esch FR (2001) Messung der Markenstärke durch den Markeneisberg (in German). In: Esch FR (ed) Moderne Markenführung, 3rd edn. Gabler, Wiesbaden, pp 1081–1103

AQSIQ (2006) Mingpian zhanlüe [Brand strategy] (in Chinese). Http://www.aqsiq.gov.cn/cms/template/channel_all.html?cid=38, release order 03/10/2006

Arnold D (1992) Modernes Markenmanagement (in German). Ueberreuter, Wien

Ash RF (1993) Agricultural policy under the impact of reforms. In: Kueh YY, Ash RF (eds) Economic trends in Chinese agriculture. Clarendon Press, Oxford, pp 11–45

Aslam MM (2006) Are you selling the right colour? A cross cultural review of colour as a marketing cue. Journal of Marketing Communications 12 (1): 15–30

Ayala J, Lai R (1996) China's consumer market: A huge opportunity to fail? McKinsey Quarterly 3: 56–71

Backhaus K (2003) Industriegütermarketing (in German), 7th edn. Vahlen, München

Backhaus K, Büschken J, Voeth M (2003a) Internationales Marketing (in German), 5th edn. Schäffer-Poeschel, Stuttgart

Backhaus K, Erichson B, Plinke W, Weiber R (2003b) Multivariate Analysemethoden (in German), 10th edn. Springer, Berlin et al

Bain (ed) (2004) China goes West – Eine Chance für die deutsche Wirtschaft (in German). Kompass, München

Balfour F, Matlack C, Barrett A, Capell K, Roberts D, Wheatley J, Symonds WC, Magnusson P, Brady D (2005) FAKES! Business Week 3919: 54–64

Ballhaus J (2005) Im Land der Marken-Fetischisten (in German). Absatzwirtschaft 5: 30–35

Bamberg G, Coenenberg AG (2004) Betriebswirtschaftliche Entscheidungslehre (in German), 12th edn. Vahlen, München

Barboza D (2005) China seeks known brands to go global. International Harald Tribune 30/06/2005

Bartsch B (2005) Kommt doch (in German). Brand eins 10 (Dec 2005): 48–54

Barwise P, Robertson T (1992) Brand portfolios. European Management Journal 10 (3): 277–285

Bauer E von (2002) Internationale Marketingforschung (in German), 3rd edn. Oldenbourg, München

Baumgarth C (2001) Markenpolitik: Markenwirkung, Markenführung, Markenforschung (in German). Gabler, Wiesbaden

BCG (2003) China: The pursuit of competitive advantage and profitable growth. Boston et al

BCG (2005) Opportunities for action: A new deal for durables. Toronto Munich

BCG (2006a) Beyond the Great Wall: Intellectual property challenges for Chinese companies. Boston et al. (in press)

BCG (2006b) China's global challengers: The strategic implications of outbound M&A. May 2006, Shanghai Beijing

BCG (2006c) The new global challengers: How 100 top companies from rapidly developing economies are changing the world, May 2006, Boston et al

BCG (2006d) Opportunities for action: Cheap is Good (Geiz ist Geil). Boston et al

BCG, Wharton School (2005) Overcoming the challenges in China operations. China Report: Studies in Operations and Strategy, Boston et al

Beebe A, Hew C, Feng YQ, Shi DL (2006) Going global: Prospects and challenges for Chinese companies on the world stage. IBM Institute for Business Value, School of Management at Fudan University, Somers, New York

Beijing Famous Brand Evaluation (2004) Report on values of Chinese brands in 2004. Http://www.mps.com.cn/en3.htm, release order 02/06/2005

Beijing Review (2006) Is China developing an independent technology capability? Http://www.bjreview.com.cn/06-12-e/zm-1.htm, release order 26/11/2006

Beijing Ribao [Beijing Daily Newspaper] (2005) Lianxiang tiqian qi yong IBM pinpai [Lenovo is going to abandon the IBM brand] (in Chinese). Http://www.nbd.com.cn/newShow.asp?D_ID=12022, release order 03/11/2005

Bekmeier-Feuerhahn S (1998) Marktorientierte Markenbewertung: Eine konsumenten- und unternehmensbezogene Betrachtung (in German). Postdoctoral thesis, University of Paderborn

Bell MW et al (1993) China at the threshold of a market economy. IMF occasional paper No. 107, Washington

Berndt R (1995) Marketing 3: Marketing-Management (in German), 2nd edn. Springer, Berlin et al

Berndt R (2005) Marketingstrategie und Marketingpolitik (in German), 4th edn. Springer, Berlin et al

Berndt R, Altobelli CF, Sander M (1997) Internationale Marketing-Politik (in German), Springer, Berlin et al

Berndt R, Altobelli CF, Sander M (2003) Internationales Marketing-Management (in German), 2nd edn. Springer, Berlin et al

Best Buy (2006) Morgan Stanley Global Consumer & Retail Conference. Presentation of Nov 14, 2006

Bettignies HC de (ed) (1996) Business transformation in China. International Thomson Business Press, London et al

Beuermann M (1976) Die Marketingbasis der Hannover Messe (in German). Messe-Nachrichten Hannover Jan: 3–5

Biel AL (2001) Grundlagen zum Markenwertaufbau (in German). In: Esch FR (ed) Moderne Markenführung, 3rd edn. Gabler, Wiesbaden, pp 61–90

Bieling M, Wiechers K (2004) Internationalisierung von Marken (in German). Arbeitspapier No. 35, Institut für Anlagen und Systemtechnologien, Marketing Centrum Münster

Biers D (2001) Taking the fight to the enemy. Far Eastern Economic Review 164 (12): 52–54

Björkman I (1989) Foreign direct investments: An empirical analysis of decision making in seven Finnish firms. Svenska handelshögskolan, Helsingfors

Blackett T, Russell N (1999) What is co-branding? In: Blackett T, Boad B (eds) Co-branding: The science of alliance. Macmillan, Houndsmill et al, pp 1–21

Bloomberg.com (2005) Nokia, Motorola widen market share lead over Samsung (update4). Http://www.bloomberg.com/apps/news?pid=10000080&sid=a8YA r1QfUxDA&refer=asia#, release order 20/07/2006

Blume G (2005) Wird die Welt chinesisch? (in German). Die Zeit 16/06/2005: 21–23

Blume G (2006) Der Pirat wird Erfinder (in German). Die Zeit 24/08/2006: 17–18

BOCOG (2006) The official website of the Beijing 2008 Olympic Games: Games of the XXIX Olympiad. Http://en.beijing2008.com/, release order 12/10/2006

Bolz J (1992) Wettbewerbsorientierte Standardisierung der internationalen Marktbearbeitung (in German). Darmstadt

Brahm LJ (2001) China's century: The awakening of the next economic powerhouse. Wiley Asia, Singapore et al

Brand Agency (2006) Interview. Shanghai (unpublished)

Branigan C (2005) Building brands in China: Companies in the Middle Kingdom are starting to develop their own design language. Business Week Online, release order 22/11/2005

Bremner B, Roberts D (2005) The Chinese Are Coming! Business Week Online, release order 22/11/2005

Brockdorff B (2003) Die Corporate Brand bei Mergers & Acqusitions: Konzeptualisierung und Integrationsentscheidung (in German). Doctoral thesis, University of St Gallen

Brockdorff B, Kernstock J (2001) Brand Integration Management: Erfolgreiche Markenführung bei Mergers & Akquisitions. Thexis 18 (4): 54–60

Bruhn M (1995) Die Rolle der Nicht-Klassiker in der integrierten Kommunikation (in German). In: Tomczak T, Müller F, Müller R (eds) Die Nicht-Klassiker der Unternehmenskommunikation, St Gallen, pp 28–48

Bruhn M (2003) Kommunikationspolitik (in German), 2nd edn. München

Buckley Ebrey P, Liu KC (1996) The Cambridge illustrated history of China (Cambridge illustrated histories). Cambridge University Press, Cambridge

Buckley PJ, Clegg J, Tan H (2004) Knowledge transfer to China: Policy lesson from foreign affiliates. UNCTAD Transnational Corporations 13 (1): 31–72

Bukhari I (1999) Europäisches Brand Management: Entwicklung und Umsetzung erfolgreicher europäischer Marketingkonzepte (in German). Wiesbaden

Burkat R (2006) Interview. Member of the Board, Portelet AG, Shanghai (unpublished)

Burns JP (1987) China's nomenklatura system. Problems of Communism 36: 36–51

Burns JP (2001) Public sector reform and the state: The case of China. Public Administration Quarterly 24 (4): 419–436

Burt T (2002) His name's Bond, and He's been licensed to sell. Financial Times 20/10/2002: 22

Business Week (2004) China's brands on a broader stage. International editions 3907: 92

Business Week Online (2004) The Branding of China Http://search.epnet.com/ login.aspx?direct=true&db=buh&an=15055981, release order 10/11/2004

Buzan T, Buzan B (2002) Das Mind-Map-Buch (in German), 5th edn. Landsberg

Cai KG (1999) Outward foreign direct investments: A novel dimension of China's integration into the regional and global economy. The China Quarterly 160: 857–880

Carter C (1996) Fighting fakes in China: The legal protection of trade marks and brands in the People's Republic of China. Intellectual Property Institute, London

CCFA (2005) IPO to fuel battle between China electronics chains. Http://www.ccfa.org.cn/english/news_show_2005.jsp?id=20292, release order 10/10/2005

Chai JCH (1997) China: Transition to a market economy. Clarendon Press, Oxford

Chai JCH (ed) (2000) The economic development of modern China, Edward Elgar, Cheltenham

Chan AKK (2006) Interview. Professor of Marketing, Hong Kong Baptist University (unpublished)

Chan AKK, Huang YY (1997) Brand naming in China: A linguistic approach. Marketing Intelligence and Planning 15 (5): 227–234

Chan AKK, Huang YY (2001) Chinese brand naming: A linguistic analysis of the names of ten product categories. Journal of Product & Brand Management 10 (2): 103–119

Chan AKK, Huang YY (2003) Shilei zhongguo chanpin pinpai mingcheng de yuyanxue fenxi [Chinese brand naming: a linguistic analysis of the brands of ten product categories] (in Chinese), Nankai Guanli Pinglun [Nankai Business Review] 6 (2): 47–54

Chan S, Guo X (2005) Lenovo: IBM deal on despite challenges. China Daily 28/01/2005: 1

Chandler C, Kim H, Wang A (2004) TV's Mr. Big: Li Dongsheng bought RCA and in the process became the world's largest TV maker. Fortune 09/02/2004: 84

Chang LY, Tam T (2004) The making of Chinese business culture. In: Gomez ET, Xiao X (eds) Chinese enterprise, transnationalism, and identity. Routledge, London, pp 23–38

Chen CJJ (2004) Transforming rural China: How local institutions shape property rights in China. Routledge, Abingdon

Chen H, Qin H, Ye G, Zheng Y (2001) A technology legend in China. Case No. 9-701-052 Harvard Business School, Boston MA

Chen LY (2006) China to seed high-tech export growth. Shanghai Daily 24/12/2006: A18

Chen YG, Penhirin J (2004) Marketing to China's consumers. McKinsey Quarterly 2004 special edition: 62–73

Cheng H, Schweitzer JC (1996) Cultural values reflected in Chinese and U.S. television commercials. Journal of Advertising Research 36 (3): 27–45

Chernatony L de, McDonald M (2003) Creating powerful brands, 3rd edn. Butterworth-Heinemann, Oxford

Child J (1994) Management in China during the age of reform. Cambridge University Press, Cambridge UK

Child J, Lu, Y (eds) (1996) Management issues in China. Routledge, London

Child P (2006) Lessons from a global retailer: An interview with the president of Carrefour China. McKinsey Quarterly special edition: 70–81

China Daily (2004a) High quote blocking Hisense-BSH dispute. Http://www.chinadaily.com.cn/english/doc/2004-09/26/content_377815.htm, release order 26/09/2004

China Daily (2004b) Overseas investments encouraged with loans. Http://english.people.com.cn/200411/04/print20041104_162710.html, release order 04/11/2004

China Daily (2005a) GDP growth mode breeds vicious circle. 01/12/2005: 4

China Daily (2005b) Outward FDI meets challenges, http://service.china.org.cn/link/wcm/Show_Text?info_id=126797&p_qry=hisense, release order 24/04/2005

China Daily (2005c) Strategy to establish renowned Chinese brand. Http://www.chinadaily.com.cn/english/doc/2005-02/16/content_416836.htm, release order 16/02/2005

China Daily (2006) Commercial Hub Planned for Hungary, http://service.china.org.cn/link/wcm/Show_Text?info_id=155507&p_qry=hisense, release order 18/01/2006

China Economic Review (2006) Battle of the brands. 16 (5): 34–40

China-Embassy (2006) Foreign investors eager to move R&D into China. Http://www.china-embassy.org/eng/xw/t232451.htm, release order 23/01/06

China View (2003) People: Zhang Ruimin, http://news.xinhuanet.com/english/2003-05/02/content_855995.htm, release order 28/04/2006

Choi KC (1991) Koreanische Direktinvestitionen in Europa: Insbesondere in der Bundesrepublik Deutschland (in German). Cuvillier, Göttingen

Consumer Electronics (2002) Chinese CE-maker TCL buys Germany's Schneider. Dual 42 (38): N.PAG

Choosin T (1996) Foreign direct investment from the People's Republic of China. In: De Bettignies HC (ed) Business transformation in China. International Thomson Business Press, London et al, pp 85–114

Chou BKP (2005) Implementing reform of appraisal service. China Information XIX (I): 39–65

Chuanzhi L, Chandler C (2004) The man who bought IBM. Fortune U.S. edition 27/12/2004: 44

Cohen P (2004) Book review: 'Brand Warriors China: Creating Sustainable Brand Capital'. Journal of Brand Management 11 (6): 463–466

Confucius (1998) The Analects, bilingual ed. Foreign Language Education and Research Press, Shanghai

Court DC, Leiter MG, Loch MA (1999) Brand leverage: Developing a strong company brand. McKinsey Quarterly 2: 100–110

Credit Suisse (2006) Nokia leads competition in China. Shanghai Daily 24/02/2006: A7

CRIENGLISH.com (2006) China Mobile among global top 100 most powerful brands. Http://en.chinabroadcast.cn/855/2006/04/05/262@71790.htm, release order 05/04/2006

Cullen JB (1999) International Management: A strategic approach. South Western, Cincinnati OH

Czinkota MR, Ronkainen IA (1999) International marketing, reprint of 5th ed. Dryden Press, Fort Worth et al

Daily Times (2003) China PC market overtaking the US. Http://www.dailytimes. com.pk, release order 20/10/2003

Daniels JD, Pitts RA, Tretter MJ (1984) Strategy and structure of U.S. multinationals: An exploratory study. Academy of Management Journal 27 (2): 292–307

d'Astous A, Valence G, Tourville J (2000) Consumer evaluations of multiple sponsorship programmes. In: Wierenga B, Smidts A, Antonides G (eds) Marketing in the New Millenium. Proceedings of the 29th EMAC Conference, Rotterdam, CD-ROM-Version

Datamonitor (2005a) European PCs. Industry profile, Reference code: 0201-0677, New York et al

Datamonitor (2005b) Global household appliances. Industry profile, Reference code 0199-2078, New York et al

Datamonitor (2005c) Global PCs. Industry profile, Reference code: 0199-0677, New York et al

Datamonitor (2005d) Global TV & Video. Industry profile, Reference code 0199-0564, New York et al

Datamonitor (2005e) Household appliances in China. Industry profile, Reference code 0099-2078, New York et al

Datamonitor (2005f) Lenovo Group Limited. Company profile, Reference code 7357, New York et al

Datamonitor (2005g) PCs in China. Industry profile, Reference code: 0099-0677, New York et al

Datamonitor (2005h) PCs in the United States. Industry profile, Reference code: 0072-0677, New York et al

Davies H, Leung TKP, Luk STK, Wong YH (2003) Guanxi and business practices in the People's Republic of China. In: Alon I (ed) Chinese culture, organizational behaviour, and international business management. Praeger, Westport, pp 41–55

Dembinski P, Cook K (1991) The logic of planned economy: The seeds of the collapse. Clarendon Press, Oxford

Deng SL, Dart J (1995) The impact of economic liberalization on marketing practices in the People's Republic of China. European Journal of Marketing 29 (2): 6–22

Deng SL, Dart J (1999) The market orientation of Chinese enterprises during a time of transition. European Journal of Marketing 33 (5/6): 631

Denison DR (2001) Managing organizational change in transition economies. Lawrence Erlbaum Associates, Mahwah NJ

Deresky H (1997) International management: Managing across borders and cultures. Addison Wesley, Reading MA

Dickens M (2004) Enter the dragon. Brand Strategy 186: 34–35

Dickie M, Lau J, London S (2005) IBM loyalty holds the key for Lenovo. In: Financial Times (ed) China goes global. London et al, p 19

Ding X, Zheng Z (2005) Renzhi chengchang yu pinpai zhanlüe [The development of private enterprises and the strategies of famous brands] (in Chinese). Shanghai Sanlian Shudian, Shanghai

Doherty AM (2000) Factors influencing international retailers market entry mode strategy: Qualitative evidence from the UK fashion sector. Journal of Marketing Management 16: 223–245

Dolan KA (2004) Taking it Haier. Forbes 173 (10): 48

Dolan KA, Hardy Q (2002) The challenge from China. Forbes 169 (11): 72–76

Dong LC, Helms MM (2001) Brand name translation model: A case analysis of US brands in China. Journal of Brand Management 9 (2): 99–115

Drees N (1999) Markenbewertung. Markenbewertung und Markenberatung in Deutschland: Ergebnisse einer empirischen Studie und Begriff des Markenwertes und Modelle zur Markenwertermittlung (in German), Erfurter Hefte zum angewandten Marketing No. 6, University of Erfurt

Drysdale P (2000) The implications of China's membership of the WTO for industrial transformation. In: Drysdale P, Song LG (eds) China's entry to the WTO. Routledge, London New York, pp 100–120

Drysdale P, Song LG (eds) (2000) China's entry to the WTO. Routledge, London New York

DTK Computer (2006) Partner (in German). Http://www.dtk.at/atnew/partners.asp, release order 01/10/2006

Du YP (2003) Haier's survival strategy to compete with world giants. Journal of Chinese Economics and Business Studies 1 (2): 259–266

Dyer G (2005) Haier ist bekannteste chinesische Marke (in German). Financial Times Deutschland, http://www.ftd.de/ub/in/20200.html?mode=print, release order 30/08/2005

Economist (2001) Legend in the making. 360 (8239): 64

Economist (2003a) The big picture. 369 (8349): 60

Economist (2003b) "Just do it" Chinese-style. 368 (8335): 59

Economist (2004) Haier's purpose. 370 (8367): 72

Economist (2005a) China's big companies: The struggle of the champions. 374 (8708): 59–61

Economist (2005b) The myth of China Inc. 376 (8442): 53-54

Economist (2006) The cultural what? 20/05/2006: 12

Einhorn B, Kripalani M, Ewing J (2004) Huawei: More than a local hero. Business Week 3903: 180–184

Einhorn B, Roberts D, Matlack C (2003) Bursting out of China. Business Week International editions 3858: 20

EIU (2005) Domestic companies in China: Taking on the competition, London et al

EIU (2006) Online database of country data, release order: July-September 2006

EMFIS online (2005) Chinas HiSense mit massiven Vorwürfen gegen Siemens (in German). Http://www.emfis.com/Index.1+M5d529a8cb37.0.html, release order 25/02/2005

Endmark (2001) Trendstudie: Zuordnung neuer Markennamen zu den jeweiligen Produkten, Dienstleistungen und Unternehmen (in German), Endmark AG, Köln

Esch FR (2004) Strategie und Technik der Markenführung (in German), 2nd edn. Vahlen, München

Esch FR, Andresen T (1997) Messung des Markenwertes (in German). In: Alumni Münster eV, Hauser U (eds): Erfolgreiches Markenmanagement. Gabler, Wiesbaden, pp 11–37

Esch FR, Redler J (2002) Markenallianzen gestalten (in German). In: Esch FR, Tomczak T, Kernstock J, Langner T (eds) Corporate Brand Management. Gabler, Wiesbaden

Esch FR, Tomczak T, Kernstock J, Langner T (2004) Corporate Brand-Management: Marken als Anker strategischer Führung von Unternehmen (in German), 1st edn. Gabler, Wiesbaden

Euromonitor (2006) Global market information database. Http://www.gmid.euromonitor.com, release order July-October 2006

European Retail Digest (2006) A focus on emerging markets. 49: 49–51

Ewing MT, Napoli J, Leyland F, Pitt WA (2002) On the renaissance of Chinese brands. International Journal of Advertising 21: 197–216

Fan LB (2005) 2004 nian, zhongguo guanggao shuju xinliang dian [China's advertising data 2004] (in Chinese). Zhongguo guanggao [China Advertising] 10: 107–111

FAZ.net (2004) Chinesen übernehmen PC-Geschäft von IBM (in German). Http://www.faz.net, release order 08/12/2004

Feige S (1996) Handelsorientierte Markenführung (in German). Peter Lang, Frankfurt a M et al

Feldmann A, BBDO (2005) Chinesen mögen deutsche Marken (in German). VDI Nachrichten 09/12/2005, N.PAG

Feng JH (2005) Into the unknow. Lenovo takes a precarious step forward. Beijing Review 06/01/2005: 38–40

Financial Times (2005) China goes global. London et al

Financial Times Deutschland (2006) Ford holt Hilfe von Finanzberatern (in German). Http://www.ftd.de/karriere_management/koepfe/114472.html, release order 19/09/2006

Fischer S, Eck R, Richter HJ (2004) Was sich gegen Produkt- und Markenpiraterie tun lässt (in German). Harvard Business Manager 3: 47–57

Fließ S (1994) Messeselektion: Entscheidung für Investitionsgüteranbieter (in German). Dt. Univ.-Verlag, Wiesbaden

Fortune (2005) Fortune Global 500 online database. Http://money.cnn.com/magazines/fortune/global500/, release order 25/07/2005

Francis JNP, Lam JPY, Walls J (2002) The impact of linguistic differences on international brand name standardization: A comparison of English and Chinese brand names of Fortune-500 Companies. Journal of International Marketing 10 (1): 98–116

Frank O (2005) Interview im Rahmen der Diplomarbeit 'Chinesisches Branding - Ästhetik chinesischer Unternehmen auf dem deutschen Markt' mit den Gründern von Mandarin Sino Consult (in German). Http://www.mandarin.de, release order 01/10/2006

Frankfurter Allgemeine Zeitung (2003) Thomson und TCL bilden den größten Fernseherproduzenten der Welt. 04/11/2003: 14

French P (2006) Carl Crow: Rules of China. EPWS presentation on 15/02/2006 by Access Asia, Shanghai (unpublished)

Fried MH (1953) Fabric of Chinese society: A study of the social life in a Chinese country seat. Praeger, New York

Fuchs-Heinritz W, Lautmann R, Rammstedt O, Wienold H (eds) (1995) Lexikon der Soziologie (in German), 3rd edn. Westdeutscher Verlag, Opladen

Fukuyama F (1995) Trust: The social vitues and the creation of prosperity. Hamish Hamilton/Penguine, Harmondsworth Middlesex England

Gao P, Woetzel JR, Wu YB (2003) Can Chinese brands make it abroad? McKinsey Quarterly 4: 54–65

Gary R (1990) Lessons from the world's best product developers. The Wall Street Journal 04/04/1990: A12

Gehrmann W (2006) Ehrgeiz in Schlesien (in German). Die Zeit 26/10/2006: 26

Gerke R (2006) Interview, President of Jiangsu Bosch and Siemens Home Appliances Sales Co Ltd, Nanjing (unpublished)

Giesen C, Vougioukas J (2005) Auslandsfieber: Chinas Firmen zahlen oft deutlich zu viel für Übernahmen (in German). Süddeutsche Zeitung 2005: 20

Gilmore F, Dumont S (2003) Brand warriors China: Creating sustainable brand capital. Profile Books, London

Glaser BG, Strauss AL (1967) The discovery of grounded theory: Strategies for qualitative research. Aldine Publ Comp, New York

Göttgens O (2005) Rechnen Sie mit einer Markeninvasion aus dem Reich der Mitte (in German). Absatzwirtschaft Online 23/03/2005: N.PAG

Gold AR, Leibowitz G, Perkins A (2001): A computer Legend in the making. McKinsey Quarterly 3: 73–83

Gold T (1985) After comradeship: Personal relations in China since the cultural revolution. China Quarterly 104: N.PAG

Goldman Sachs (2003) Global Automotives: The Chinese auto industry. Global Equity Research

Goodman PS (2004) Chinese TV Maker Sharpens Focus on Europe. Washington Post France 13/12/2004: A01

Gould SJ, Gupta PB, Grabner-Krauter S (2000) Product placements in movies: A cross-cultural analysis of Austrian, French and American consumers' attitudes toward this emerging, international promotional medium. Journal of Advertising 29 (4): 41–58

Grant A (2006) The new Chinese consumer. McKinsey Quarterly Special edition: 4–5

Gregory JR, Wiechmann JG (2002) Branding across borders: A guide to global brand marketing. McGraw-Hill, Chicago et al

Grill B (2006) Die neuen Kolonialherren (in German). Die Zeit 14/09/2006: 32–33

Grimes A, Doole I (1998) Exploring the relationships between colour and international branding: A cross cultural comparison of the UK and Taiwan. Journal of Marketing Management 14 (7): 799–817

Gu ZM (2002) Haier: Zhongguo de shijie mingpai [Haier: China's worldwide known brand] (in Chinese). Jingji Guanli Chubanshe, Beijing

Guan HP (2004) Interkulturelles Management: Am Beispiel des deutsch-chinesischen Joint Ventures (in German). Kovac, Hamburg

Guojia Tongji Ju [National Bureau of Statistics] (ed) (1998) Zhongguo tongji nianjian 1998 [China Statistical Yearbook 1998] (in Chinese). China Statistics Press, Beijing

Guojia Tongji Ju [National Bureau of Statistics] (ed) (2004) Zhongguo tongji nianjian 2004 [China Statistical Yearbook 2004] (in Chinese). China Statistics Press, Beijing

Guojia Tongji Ju [National Bureau of Statistics] (ed) (2005) Zhongguo tongji nianjian 2005 [China Statistical Yearbook 2005] (in Chinese). China Statistics Press, Beijing

Gupta PB, Gould SJ (1997) Consumers' perceptions of the ethics and acceptability of product placements in movies: Product category and individual differences. Journal of Current Issues & Research in Advertising 19 (1): 37–50

Haase H (2000) Testimonialwerbung (in German). Planung und Analyse 3: 56–60

Haedrich G, Tomczak T (eds) (2003) Strategische Markenführung: Planung und Realisierung von Markenstrategien (in German), 3rd edn. Haupt, Bern et al

Hahn D (1985) PuK: Planung und Kontrolle: Planungs- und Kontrollsysteme, Planungs- und Kontrollrechnung; wertorientierte Controllingkonzepte, 3rd edn. Gabler, Wiesbaden

Haier America (2006) Your ideal product. http://www.haieramerica.com/ideal_product.php, release order 26/01/2006

Haier Electronics Group (2005a) Annual report 2004. Qingdao Bermuda

Haier Electronics Group (2005b) Interim report 2005. Qingdao Bermuda

Haier Europe (2006) Wer wir sind (in German). Http://www.haiereurope.com/ger/company/aboutus.php, release order 26/01/2005

Haier Group (2005a) Corporate profile. Http://www.haier.com/abouthaier/corporateprofile/index.asp, release order 18/01/2005

Haier Group (2005b) Haier's ambition to gain worldwide recognition. Http://www.haier.com/english/news/content.asp?ID=689, release order 04/10/2005

Haier Group (2005c) Sport projects. Http://www.haier.com/abouthaier/SocialContributions/SportsProject.asp, release order 11/12/2005

Haier Group (2006a) Haier worldwide. Http://www.haier.com/abouthaier/Haier-Worldwide/events_eur.asp, release order 26/01/2006

Haier Group (2006b) Milestones 1984-2005. Http://www.haier.com/abouthaier/Milestone/index.asp, release order 26/01/2006

Haier Wenhua Zhongxin [Haier Cultural Centre] (ed) (2005) Haier pinpai zhi lu [The path to Haier brand] (in Chinese). Qingdao Publishing Company, Qingdao

Haixin [Hisense] (2005) Chanpin pinpai zhenghe chuanbo shibie xitong shouce [Handbook on product brand communication and identification system] (in Chinese). 45 pages, Qingdao (unpublished)

Hall RH, Xu W (1990) Research note: Run silent, run deep: Cultural influences on organizations in the Far East. Organizational Studies 11: 569–576

Hamilton GL, Biggart NW (1988) Market, culture and, authority: A comparative analysis of management and organisation in the Far East. American Journal of Sociology 94: S52–S94

Hamm S (2005) East meets West, Big-Time. Business Week 09/05/2005: N.PAG

Hamm S, Engardia P (2004) Big Blue's bold step into China. Business Week 20/12/2004: N.PAG

Hang ZH (2006) Pinpai guanli zhuanti [Brand management] (in Chinese). Seminar presentation at the Management School of Fudan University, Shanghai (unpublished)

Harding H (1987) The rise of the reformers. In: China's second revolution: Reform after Mao, chap 3. Brooking Institutions, Washington DC, pp 40–69, 310–316, reprinted in 2000 in: Chai JCH (ed) The economic development of modern China. Edward Elgar, Cheltenham, pp 3–39

HBI Online Press Center (2004) Haier Electronics Europe startet mit Telekommunikations- und Consumer-Electronic-Produkten in Deutschland (in German). Http://www.hbi.de/clients/Haier/Haier.php, release order 26/01/2006

HBI Online Press Center (2005) Kurt Weiss wird General Manager Vertrieb und Marketing bei Haier Europe Trading (in German). Http://www.hbi.de/clients/Haier/Haier.php, release order 26/01/2006

Heenan DA, Perlmutter HV (1979) Multinational Organization Development. Addison-Wesley, Reading Mass et al

Heise.de (2005) Chinesische Haier Gruppe will europäischen Markt erobern (in German). Http://www.heise.de/newsticker/meldung/57425, release order 12/03/2005

Helm R (1997) Internationale Markteintrittsstrategien: Einflussfaktoren auf die Wahl der optimalen Form des Markteintritts in Exportmärkte (in German). Eul, Lohmar et al

Hemerling J, Hsu H, Lam A (2004) Wholesale distribution changes for a winning China strategy. Opportunities for Action in May 2004, The Boston Consulting Group, Shanghai Hong Kong

Hermanns A (2004) Sponsoring Trends 2004 (in German). BOB Bomlitz Group, Bonn München

Hill W, Fehlbaum R, Ulrich P (1981) Organisationslehre (in German), 3rd edn. Schäffer-Poeschel, Stuttgart

Hirn W (2005) Herausforderung China: Wie der chinesische Aufstieg unser Leben verändert (in German). S Fischer Verlag, Frankfurt a M

Hisense Group (2003) History of Hisense 1969 - 2001: 32 Years of Perseverance and Development. Http://www.hisense.com/english/about/History/index.html, release order 11/12/2005

Hisense Group (2004) Hisense global strategy. Http://www.hisense.com/en/about/about_global_strategy.htm, release order 07/02/2006

Hisense Group (2005a) Hisense culture: Creativity is Life. Http://www.hisense.com/english/about/Culture/index.html, release order 11/12/2005

Hisense Group (2005b) Hisense Shows Itself in IFA. Http://www.hisense.com/english/news/detail.jsp?cont_id=8436, release order 15/02/2006

Hisense Group (2005c) Hisense Shows Itself on IFA 2005 and the EU Strategy is On Horizon. Http://www.hisense.com/english/news/detail.jsp?cont_id=8327, release order 15/02/2006

Hisense Group (2006a) Hisense is given the honor of "2006 Export Brand". Http://www.hisense.com/english/news/detail.jsp?cont_id=8633, release order 17/04/2006

Hisense Group (2006b) Hisense profile. Http://www.hisense.com/en/about/ about_memorabilia.htm, release order 07/02/2006

Hisense Group (2006c) Hisense subsidiaries. Http://www.hisense.com/en/about/ sub_inc/electric.htm, release order 07/02/2006

Hisense USA (2006) About Hisense USA. Http://www.hisenseusa.com/CompanyOverview.asp, release order 07/02/2006

Hofstede GH (1980) Culture's consequences: International differences in work-related values. Sage, Beverly Hills

Holten RH (1985) Marketing and the modernization of China. California Management Review 27 (4): 33–45

Homburg C, Lucas M, Bucerius M (2000) Kundenbindung bei Fusionen und Akquisitionen. Gefahren und Erfolgsfaktoren (in German). Working paper Management Know-how No. M 51, Institut für marktorientierte Unternehmensführung, University of Mannheim

Hoover's online (2006): Report Haier America

Huang F (2001) Legend looks to defend its turf. Http://www.ebnnews.com/story/OEG20011214S0045, release order 13/12/2001

Huang SM, Du GQ (2005) 2005 nian: zhongguo guanggao zhu yingxiao tuiguang qushi baogao No.1 [2005: Report on the promotion trend of China's advertisers No.1] (in Chinese). Social Sciences Academic Press, Beijing

Huang YY, Chan AKK (1997) Chinese brand naming: from general principles to specific rules. International Journal of Advertising (special issue on Advertising in the People's Republic of China) 16 (4): 320–335

Huang YY, Chan AKK (2002) Zhongguo shangpin pinpai mingcheng de guize he tedian [Chinese brand naming: From general principles to specific rules] (in Chinese). Nankai Guanli Pinglun [Nankai Business Review] 5 (1): 68–71

Huatongren Shichang Xinxiu [All China Marketing Research] (2004) Zhongguo shichang nianjian 2005 [China markets yearbook 2005] (in Chinese). Foreign Languages Press, Beijing

Hwang KK (1987) Face and favor: The Chinese power game. American Journal of Sociology 92 (4): N.PAG

IDC (2005) Worldwide PC market: 1Q 05 Review. Framingham MA

IDC (2006) Worldwide PC 2006-2010 forecast update: September 2006, Framingham MA

Institut für Marketing (1996) Ziele und Nutzen von Messebeteiligungen: Zusammenfassung einer empirisch gestützten Untersuchung auf der Grundlage einer Befragung deutscher Aussteller im Auftrag des Ausstellungs- und Messe-Ausschusses der deutschen Wirtschaft eV (AUMA) (in German), Westfälische Wilhelms-University Münster, Köln Bergisch Gladbach

Interbrand (2005) Global brands: Annual report. Economist 08/01/2005: 86–94

IT.com.cn (2006) Qu IBM hua? Thinkpad benxian lianxiang logo [Get rid off IBM? Thinkpad now with Lenovo logo] (in Chinese). Http://www.it.com.cn/f/notebook/0610/26/341097.htm, release order 26/10/2006

Jacobs L, Keown C, Worthley R, Ghymn KI (1991) Cross-cultural colour comparisons: Global marketers beware! International Marketing Review 8 (3): 21–30

Janke K, Weiland H (2005) Neue Marken aus dem Reich der Mitte (in German). Horizont 24/03/2005: 20–21

Jansen SA (2000) Mergers & Acquisitions: Unternehmensakquisitionen und – kooperationen (in German). Gabler, Wiesbaden

Jiang W (2005) China's overseas acquisitions skyrocket. China Daily 11/10/2005: 10

Jiang Y (2004) Bailian Group has grand growth vision. China Business Weekly Online at http://www.chinadaily.net/english/doc/2004-05/25/content_333 625.htm, release order 25/05/2004

Jiang Z (1992) Accelerating reform and opening up. Beijing Review 35: 9–32

Jin B (ed) (2004): Zhongguo qiye jingzhengli baogao [Blue Book of China's enterprises competitiveness] (in Chinese). Social Sciences Academic Press, Beijing

Jing J (2006) SAIC pushes to make its own name in autos. Shanghai Daily 11/04/2006: A1

Jingji Cankao Bao [Economic Reference] (2004) [Hisense established new R&D centre] (in Chinese). 17/05/2004: N.PAG

Joas A, Offerhaus P (2001) Brand equity: Wie die Marke den Unternehmenswert steigern kann (in German). Spektrum 1: 9

Kaas KP (1990) Langfristige Werbewirkung und Brand Equity (in German). Werbeforschung & Praxis 35 (3): 48–52

Kapferer JN (1992) Die Marke - Kapital des Unternehmens (in German). Verlag Moderne Industrie, Landsberg-Lech

Kapferer JN (2004) The new strategic brand management: Creating and sustaining brand equity long term, 3rd edn. Kogan Page, London et al

Kapferer JN (2005) The post-global brand. Journal of Brand Management 12 (5): 319–324

Karmasin H (1993) Produkte als Botschaften (in German). Carl Ueberreuter, Wien

Ke RY (2005) HK to help mainland enterprises go global. China Daily 10-11/09/2005: 12

Keegan WJ (1999) Global marketing management, 6th edn. Prentice-Hall, Upper Saddle River NJ

Keegan WJ, Green MC (2005) Global marketing, 4th intern edn. Pearson Prentice Hall, Upper Saddle River

Keller KL (1993) Conceptualizing, measuring, managing customer-based brand equity. Journal of Marketing 57 (1): 1–22

Keller KL (2001) Brand research imperatives. Journal of Brand Management 9 (1): 4–6

Keller KL (2003) Strategic brand management: Building, measuring and managing brand equity, 2nd edn. Prentice Hall, Upper Saddle River NJ

Kelz A (1989) Die Weltmarke (in German). Schulz-Kirchner, Idstein

Khanna T, Oberholzer-Gee F, Lane D (2005) TCL Multimedia. Case No. 9-705-502 Harvard Business School

Khermouch G, Einhorn B, Roberts D (2003) Breaking in the new game: China's manufactures are building their brands to go global. Business Week 3827: 54

Kieser A, Kubicek H (1992) Organisation, 3rd edn. Berlin New York

King AYC (1991) Kuan-hsi and network building: A sociological interpretation. Daedalus 120: N.PAG

Kirsch Werner (ed) (1997) Beiträge zu einer evolutionären Führungslehre (in German). Schäffer-Poeschel, Stuttgart

Klein JG, Ettenson R, Morris MD (1998) The animosity model of foreign product purchase: An empirical test in the People's Republic of China. Journal of Marketing 62 (January): 89–100

Klein-Bölting U (1989) Die Auswahl internationaler Messe- und Ausstellungsplätze. Eine Marketingentscheidung (in German). Diploma thesis, Institut für Anlagen und Systemtechnologien, Westfälische Wilhelms-University of Münster.

Knudsen TR, Finskud L, Törnblom R, Hogna E (1997) Brand consolidation makes a lot of economic sense. McKinsey Quarterly 34 (4): 189–193

Koeppler K(2000) Strategien erfolgreicher Kommunikation (in German). München Wien

Köhler R (1993) Beiträge zum Marketing-Management (in German), 3rd edn. Schäffer-Poeschel, Stuttgart

Köhler R (1995) Marketing-Organisation (in German). In: Tietz B, Köhler R, Zentes J (eds) Handwörterbuch Marketing, 2nd edn. Schäffer-Poeschel, Stuttgart, pp 1636–1652

Kong QJ (2005) WTO, internationalization and the intellectual property rights regime in China. Marshall Cavendish Acad, Singapore

Kopp M (1972) Hypothesenformulierung in der Absatzforschung (in German). Duncker & Humblot, Berlin

Kotler P, Bliemel F (2001) Marketing-Management: Analyse, Planung und Kontrolle (in German), 10th edn. Schäffer-Poeschel, Stuttgart

Kreutzer RT (1987) Lead-Country-Konzept (in German). Wirtschaftliches Studium 8: 416–419

Kreutzer RT (1989) Markenstrategien im länderübergreifendem Marketing (in German). Markenartikel 11: 569–572

Kreutzer RT, Raffée H (1986) Organisatorische Verankerung als Erfolgsbedingung eines Global-Marketing (in German). Thexis, 2: 10–21

Kricsfalussy A, Semlitsch B (2000) Marketing ist Werttreiber (in German). Absatzwirtschaft 43 (Sondernummer Oktober 2000): 22–34

Kroeber-Riel W (1993) Bildkommunikation (in German). Vahlen, München

Kroeber-Riel W (1993) Konsumentenverhalten (in German), 5th edn. Vahlen, München

Kroeber-Riel W, Esch FR (2004) Strategie und Technik der Werbung: Verhaltenswissenschaftliche Ansätze (in German), 6th edn. Kohlhammer, Stuttgart

Kubicek H (1976) Heuristische Bezugsrahmen und heuristisch angelegte Forschungsdesign als Elemente einer Konstruktionsstrategie empirischer Forschung (in German). Working paper No. 16, Institut für Unternehmensführung, Freie Universität Berlin

Laaksonen OJ (1977) The power structure of Chinese enterprises. International Studies of Management and Organization 7 (1): 71–90

Laaksonen OJ (1984) The management and power structure of Chinese enterprise during and after the Cultural Revolution: With empirical data comparing Chinese and European enterprises. Organization Studies 5 (1): 1–21

Laaksonen OJ (1988) Management in China during and after Mao in enterprises, government and party. Walter de Gruyter, Berlin New York

Laforet S, Saunders J (1994) Managing brand portfolios: How the leaders do it. Journal of Advertising 34 (5): 64–76

Lamnek S (1995a) Qualitative Sozialforschung. Band 1: Methodologie (in German), 3rd edn. Beltz, Weinheim

Lamnek S (1995b) Qualitative Sozialforschung. Band 2: Methoden und Techniken (in German), 3rd edn. Beltz, Weinheim

Lampert SI, Jaffe ED (1996) Country of origin effects on international market entry. Journal of Global Marketing 10 (2): 27–52

Langner T (2003) Integriertes Branding: Baupläne zur Gestaltung erfolgreicher Marken (in German). Deutscher Universitätsverlag, Wiesbaden

Lanzeni ML, Hansakul S (2004) Enterprise reform & stock market in mainland China. Deutsche Bank Research, Frankfurt a M

Lardy N (2002) Integrating China into the global economy. Brookings Institution, Washington DC

Laux H (2003) Entscheidungstheorie (in German), 5th edn. Springer, Berloin et al

Lee C, Green RT (1991) Cross-cultural examination of the Fishbein behavioural intensions model. Journal of International Business Studies 2nd Quarter: 289–305

Lee HW, Liu CH (2006) Determinants of the adjustment of expatriate managers to foreign countries: An empirical study. International Journal of Management 23 (2): 302–311

Legend (1995) Annual report 1994/95. Hong Kong

Legend (2002) Annual report 2001/02. Hong Kong

Legend (2003a) Annual report 2002/03. Hong Kong

Legend (2003b) Legend adopts new logo. Http://www.lenovogrp.com, release order 23/04/2003

Lehua caidian [Rowa] (2006) Dashiji [Memorabilia] (in Chinese), http://www.rowa.com.cn/idex.php?option=com_content&task=view&id=18&Itemid=49, release order 30/04/2006

Lenovo Deutschland (2005) Lenovo schließt die Akquisition der IBM Personal Computing Devision ab (in German). Http://www.lenovo.com/news/de/de/2005/05/050105annc.html, release order 28/06/2005

Lenovo Group (2005a) Annual report 2004/05. Hong Kong

Lenovo Group (2005b) Lenovo schließt die Akquisition der IBM Personal Computing Devision ab (in German). Http://www.lenovo.com/news/de/de/2005/05/050105annc.html, release order 28/06/2005

Lenovo Group (2006a) 2006/07 1Q results. Presentation of 03/08/2006, Hong Kong

Lenovo Group (2006b) 2006/07 interim results. Presentation of 09/11/2006, Hong Kong

Lenovo Group (2006c) About Lenovo. Http://www.lenovo.com/uk/en/, release order 14/11/2006

Lenovo Group (2006d) Annual report 2005/06. Hong Kong

Lenovo Group (2006e) Lenovo China: Corporate branding project proposal of 21/06/2006. Internal ppt-presentation of 61 pages, Beijing (unpublished)

Lenovo Group (2006f) Lenovo: An Olympic partner. Http://www.pc.ibm.com/europe/lenovo/about/olympics.html?uk&cc=uk, release order 14/11/2006

Leung K (1996) The role of beliefs in the Chinese culture. In: Bond MH (ed) The handbook of Chinese Psychology. Oxford University Press, Hong Kong, N.PAG

Levitt T (1983) The globalization of markets. Harvard Business Review 61 (3): 92–102

Lewis P (2005) The new improved notebook. Fortune 31/10/2005: N.PAG

Li WT (2005) Lenovo pins high hopes on Olympics as key to success. China Daily 09/11/2005: 11

Liedtke A (1994) Der Wechsel des Markennames (in German). In: Bruhn M (ed) Handbuch Markenartikel. Teilband II (in German). Schäffer-Poeschel, Stuttgart, pp 791–811

Ling L (2005) China's industrial policies and the global business revolution: The case of the domestic appliance industry. Routledge, Abingdon New York

Link W (1997) Erfolgspotentiale für die Internationalisierung (in German). Wiesbaden

Liu BJ (2005) Lenovo speeds up consolidation with IBM's PC ops. China Daily 03/10/2005: N.PAG

Liu BJ (2006) Global Vision. China Business Weekly 20-26/11/2006: 3

Liu H, Li KQ (2002) Strategic implications of emerging Chinese multinationals: The Haier case study. European Management Journal 20 (6): 699–707

Liu Y (2005) Intellectual barricades. Beijing Review 48 (13): 34–36

Liu ZJ (2005) Interview. Director of Qingdao Haier Medical and Laboratory Instruments Co Ltd, Haier Group, Qingdao

Lo TWC, Lau HF, Lin GS (2001) Problems and prospects of supermarket development in China. International Journal of Retail & Distribution Management 29 (2): 66–75

Lockett M (1988) Culture and the problem of Chinese management. Organization Studies 9: 475–496

London S (2005) A global power made In China - Lenovo: The making of a multinational. Part I. Financial Times 10/11/2005: N.PAG

Lu L (2003) Influences of Confucianism on the market economy of China. In: Alon I (ed) Chinese culture, organizational behaviour, and international business management. Praeger, Westport, pp 27–39

Lu QW (2000) China's leap into the information age: Innovation and organization in the computer industry. Oxford University Press, Oxford et al

Lu XW (2005) Interview. Director of Management School, Fudan University, Shanghai (unpublished)

Luo YD (2000a) Multinational corporations in China: Benefiting from structural transformation. Copenhagen Business School Press, Copenhagen

Luo YD (2000b) Partnering with Chinese firms: Lessons for international managers. Ashgate, Aldershot et al

M+M Planet Retail (2006) E-intelligence on global retail. Http://www.planetretail.net, release order June 2006

Ma HZ (2003) Lifestyle segmentation of Chinese consumers. Sinomonitor International, Beijing et al

Macharzina K (1992) Internationalisierung und Organisation (in German). Zeitschrift für Führung und Organisation 1: 4–11

Macharzina K, Oesterle MJ (1995) Organisation des internationalen Marketing-Managements (in German). In: Hermanns A (ed) Internationales Marketing-Management. Vahlen, München, pp 309–338

Madden N (2001) Chinese brands turn to Western agencies. Ad Age Global 1 (10): 21

Madden N (2004) Wu's aim: Help Li-Ning vault into global sport-apparel biz. Advertising Age 75 (43): 40

Mahatoo WH (1990) Marketing in China. Journal of General Management 15 (Spring): 63–79

Marketing Leadership Council (2000) Marketing organizational trends: Early observations on structural change in the marketing function. Executive inquiry research, Washington London

Markus HR, Kitayama S (1998) Culture and self: implications fro cognition, emotion and motivation. Psychological Review: 224–253

Marx K (1970) Ziben [Capital] (in Chinese). Chinese Foreign Language Publishing House, Beijing

Maslow AH (1964) A theory of human motivation. In: Levitt HJ, Pondey LR (eds) Readings in managerial psychology. University of Chicago Press, Chicago, pp 6–24

Mayrhofer U (2004) International market entry: Does the home country affect entry-mode decisions? Journal of International Marketing 12 (4): 71–96

Mayring P (2003) Qualitative Inhaltsanalyse: Grundlagen und Techniken (in German), 8th edn. Beltz, Weinheim

McEwen WJ (2005a) Battle of the brands among Chinese consumers. Gallup Poll Tuesday Briefing 08/03/2005: 1–4

McEwen WJ (2005b) Chinese Consumers Go High-Tech. Gallup Management Journal Online 03/10/2005: 1–4

McGregor J (2005) One billion customers. Free Press, New York et al

McGregor J (2006) The world's most innovative companies. Business Week 24/04/2006: 63–74

McKinsey (2005) Panel examines China's economy. Http://www.mckinsey.com/ ideas/infocus/china/roundtable/, release order 09/01/2006

Meffert H (1986) Marketing im Spannungsfeld von weltweitem Wettbewerb und nationalen Bedürfnissen (in German). Zeitschrift für Betriebswirtschaft 56: 689–712

Meffert H (1994) Entscheidungsorientierter Ansatz der Markenpolitik (in German). In: Bruhn M (ed) Handbuch Markenartikel: Anforderungen an die Markenpolitik aus Sicht von Wissenschaft und Praxis. Schäffer-Poeschel, Stuttgart, pp 173–197

Meffert H (2000) Marketing: Grundlagen marktorientierter Unternehmensführung (in German), 9th edn. Gabler, Wiesbaden

Meffert H (2002) Eine Frage der Zeit (in German). McK Wissen 1 (3): 118–119

Meffert H, Backhaus K, Becker J (2003) Markenmanagement: Lohnen sich Investitionen in die Marke? Documentation paper No. 161, Wissenschaftliche Gesellschaft für Marketing und Unternehmensführung eV, Münster

Meffert H, Bolz J (1998) Internationales Marketing-Management (in German), 3rs edn. Kohlhammer, Stuttgart et al

Meffert H, Burmann C (1996) Identitätsorientierte Markenführung: Grundlagen für das Management von Markenportfolios. Working paper No. 100, Wissenschaftliche Gesellschaft für Marketing und Unternehmensführung eV, Münster

Meffert H, Burmann C, Koers M (2005) Markenmanagement: Identitätsorientierte Markenführung und praktische Umsetzung (in German). 2nd edn. Gabler, Wiesbaden

Meffert H, Koers, M (2002) Identitätsorientiertes Markencontrolling (in German). In: Meffert H, Burmann C, Koers M (eds) Markenmanagement. Wiesbaden, pp 403–428

Meissner HG (1994) Internationale Markenstrategien (in German). In: Bruhn M (ed) Handbuch Markenartikel. Gabler, Wiesbaden, pp 673–685

Melewar TC, Meadows M, Zheng WQ, Rickards R (2004) The influence of culture on brand building in the Chinese market: A brief insight. Journal of Brand Management 11 (6): 449–461

Meng YT (2006) Interview. Senior Supervisor of Brand Management Department, Lenovo Group, Beijing (unpublished)

Meyer R (1999) Entscheidungstheorie (in German). Gabler, Wiesbaden

Milbank D (1994) Made in America becomes a boast in Europe. The Wall Street Journal 19/01/1994: B1

Millward Brown Optimor (2006) Millward Brown announces a new ranking of the world's most powerful brands. Http://www.insidewpp.com/brandz2/ BRANDZ_Global_Release_03_April_06.pdf, release order 03/04/2006

Mobile2day (2005) Alcatel zieht sich vom Handymarkt zurück (in German). Http://www.mobile2day.de/news/news_details.html?nd_ref=4214, release order 10/05/2006

MOFCOM (2006a) The "Brand Promotion Activity" by Ministry of Commerce initiated in the China Millennium Monument of Beijing. Http://www.ipr. gov.cn/ipr/en/info/Article.jsp?a_no=5905&col_no=99&dir=200606, release order 12/06/2006

MOFCOM (2006b) Brand Promotion formally launched. Http://www.ipr.gov.cn/ ipr/en/info/Article.jsp?a_no=6049&col_no=115&dir=200606, release order 12/06/2006

MOFCOM (2006c) Online database of statistics. Http://english.mofcom.gov.cn, release order August 2006

Momentum Market Intelligence (2006) Logo evaluation research January 2006. In: Quelch J, Knoop CI (2006) Lenovo: Building a global brand. Case No. 9-507-014 Harvard Business School, Boston MA, pp 21–22

Müller M, Turner A (2006) Die chinesische Industriepolitik: Orientierung am Beispiel Japans und Südkoreas? (in German). (in press)

Müller S, Gelbrich K (2004) Interkulturelles Marketing (in German). Vahlen, München

Müller T (2006) Markenaufbau für lokale Unternehmen mühsam (in German). Http://www.fiducia-china.com, release order 17/07/2006

Mure D, Minder R, Muscat S (2006) China setzt Signal gegen Markenpiraten (in German). Financial Times Deutschland at http://www.ftd.de/ub/di/39200. html?mode=print, release order 18/01/2006

Murphy J (2005) Carrefour scoops top spot in study of China retailers. Media Asia 26/08/2005: 6

Mussler D, Mussler S (1995) Markenbewertung in der Praxis: Eine Zwischenbilanz, Teil 1 (in German). Marketing Journal 28 (3): 184–187

Mysan.de (2005) Haier zielt auf ein Wachstum von 60% in 2005 ab (in German). Http://www.mysan.de/article35254.html, relese order 07/11/2005

Nagashima A (1970) A comparison of Japanese and U.S. attitudes toward foreign products. Journal of Marketing 34 (January): 68–74

Nan Z, Belk RW (2004) Chinese consumer readings of global and local advertising appeals. Journal of Advertising 33 (3): 63–76

Nanjing Caijing Daxue Pinpai Yanjiu Zhongxin [Nanjing Finance and Economics University Brand Research Center] (2005) 2004 pinpai toushi (caidian pian) [2004 Brand Searching (colour TV sets)] (in Chinese). Zhong Guo Guang Gao [China Advertising] 11: 84–87

Naughton B (1995) Growing out of the plan: Chinese economy reform 1978-1993. Cambridge University Press, New York

Nayyar PR (1990) Information asymmetries: A source of competitive advantage for diversified service firms. Strategic Management Journal 11 (7): 513–519

Nolan P (2001) China and the Global Economy: National Champions, Industrial Policy and the Big Business Revolution. Palgrave Macmillan

O'Donnell S, Jeong I (2000) Marketing standardization within global industries. International Marketing Review 17 (1): 19–33

Oelsnitz D von der (2000a) Markteintritts-Management; Eine Einführung (in German). In: Oelsnitz D von der (ed) Markteintritts-Management: Probleme, Strategien, Erfahrungen. Schäffer-Poeschel, Stuttgart, pp 1–9

Oelsnitz D von der (ed) (2000b) Markteintritts-Management: Probleme, Strategien, Erfahrungen (in German). Schäffer-Poeschel, Stuttgart

OgilvyOne Worldwide (2006) Anli fenxi haier [Haier case study]. Internal ppt.-presentation, 16 pages, Beijing (unpublished)

Onkvisit S, Shaw JJ (1989) The international dimension of branding: Strategic considerations and decisions. International Marketing Review 6 (3): 22–34

Opper S (1999) Wirtschaftsreform und Beschäftigungswandel in der VR China (in German). Nomos, Baden-Baden

Paine LS (2001a) The Haier Group (A). Case No. 9-398-101 Harvard Business School, Boston MA

Paine LS (2001b) The Haier Group (B). Case No. 9-398-102 Harvard Business School, Boston MA

Paine LS (2001c) The Haier Group (C). Case No. 9-398-162 Harvard Business School, Boston MA

Pan YG (2005) Lenovo: Countering the Dell challenge. Case No. HKU356 Asia Case Research Centre at University of Hong Kong and School of Management at Shanghai Fudan University, Hong Kong

Pan YG, Tse DK (2000) The hierarchical model of market entry modes. Journal of International Business Studies 31 (4): 535–554

Pan YG, Tse DK, Li XL (2003) Evolution of brands in transnational economies: The case of China in 1993-1998. Http://www.globalbrands.org/research/papers.htm, release order 15/09/2006

Papadopoulos NG (1993) What product and country images are and not. In: Papadopoulos NG, Heslop LA (eds) Product-country images. New York et al, pp 3–38

Papendick U (2002) Macht der Marke (in German). Manager Magazin 4: 232–234

Park A, Burrows P (2003) What do you don't know about Dell. Http://www.businessweek.com/print/magazine/content/03_44/b3856001_mz001.htm?chan=gl, release order 03/11/2003

Park HJ (1995) Sponsoring und Werbung im Sport: Eine Longitudinalstudie zur Sportsponsoringwirkung am Beispiel des koreanischen Elektronik-Konzerns Samsung (in German). Doctoral thesis, Publizistik und Kommunikationswissenschaften, Westfälische Wilhems-University Münster

Park SK (1994) Auslandsinvestitionen der Entwicklungsländer als Instrument zur Erschließung europäischer Märkte: Dargestellt am Beispiel koreanischer Unternehmen (in German). Doctoral thesis, Technische Hochschule Aachen

Pausenberger E (1994) Alternative Internationalisierungsstrategien (in German). In: Pausenberger E (ed) Internationalisierung von Unternehmungen: Strategien und Probleme ihrer Umsetzung. Schäffer-Poeschel, Stuttgart, pp 1–30

Peill-Schoeller P (1994) Interkulturelles Management: Synergien im Joint Venture zwischen China und deutschsprachigen Ländern (in German). Berlin

People's Daily Online (2001) Chinese brands ensure quality. Http://english.people. com.cn/english/200103/27/eng20010327_66086.html, release order 14/10/2005

Perez B (2003) Legend changes face as it takes on world: Mainland computer giant has a long haul ahead to make Lenovo a recognized name - especially in the US. South China Morning Post 06/05/2003: N.PAG

Perlitz M (1997) Spektrum kooperativer Internationalisierungsformen (in German). In: Macharzina K, Oesterle MJ (eds) Handbuch Internationales Management. Gabler, Wiesbaden, pp 441–457

Perlitz M, Seger F (2000) Konzepte internationaler Markteintrittsstrategien (in German). In: Oelsnitz D von der (ed) Markteintritt-Management, Schäffer-Poeschel, Stuttgart, pp 89–119

Perlmutter HV, Heenan DA (1974) How multinational should your top managers be? Harvard Business Review (November-December): 121–132

Pinzler P (2006) Das große Zaudern (in German). Die Zeit 24/05/2006: 22

Porter ME (1999) Wettbewerbsstrategie: Methoden zur Analyse von Branchen und Konkurrenten (in German), 10th edn. Frankfurt a M

Priester JR, Petty RE (2003) The Influence of Spokesperson Trustworthiness on Message Elaboration, Attitude Strength, and Advertising Effectiveness. Journal of Consumer Psychology 13 (4): 408–421

Publicis Sasserath (2006) Deutschland und China: Chancen aus der Markenperspektive (in German). Frankfurt

QDI (2004) International Media tour Legend QDI factory in China. Http://www. qdigrp.com/qdisite/eng/award/medtour1.htm, release order 25/11/2006

Qian YY (2000) The process of China's market transition (1978-1998): The evolutionary, historical, and comparative perspectives. Journal of Institutional and Theoretical Economics 156: 151–171

Qingdao Haier Dian Bingxiang [Qingdao Haier Refrigeration] (2006) 2005 nian niandu baogao [Annual report 2005] (in Chinese). Qingdao

Qingdao Haixin Dianqi [Hisense Electric] (2005) 2004 nian niandu baogao [Annual report 2004] (in Chinese). Qingdao

Qingdao Haixin Dianqi [Hisense Electric] (2006) 2005 nian niandu baogao [Annual report 2005] (in Chinese). Qingdao

Quelch JA (1992) The new country managers. McKinsey Quarterly 4: 155–165

Quelch JA, Hoff EJ (1986) Globales Marketing - nach Maß. Harvard Manager 4: 107–110

Quelch JA, Knoop CI (2006) Lenovo: Building a global brand. Case No. 9-507-014 Harvard Business School, Boston MA

Rappoport J (1996) BMW Z3. Advertising Age 24/06/1996: 37

Rautsola P (1988) Die Markt- und Markteintrittsstrategien der multinationalen Unternehmungen (in German). Doctoral thesis, München Ludwig-Maximilian-University

Redding SG, Ng M (1992) The role of face in the organisational perceptions of Chinese managers. Organizational Studies 3: 204–209

Redler J (2003) Management von Markenallianzen: Eine Analyse unter besonderer Berücksichtigung der Urteilsbildung der Konsumenten (in German). Logos-Verlag, Berlin

Remmerbach KU (1988) Markteintrittsentscheidungen: Eine Untersuchung im Rahmen der strategischen Marketingplanung unter besonderer Berücksichtigung des Zeitaspekts (in German). Gabler, Wiesbaden

Remmerbach KU, Walters M (1994) Markenstrategien im europäischen Binnenmarkt (in German). In: Bruhn M (ed) Handbuch Markenartikel. Band 1. Schäffer-Poeschel, Stuttgart, pp 653–672

Reuters (2006) World No.3 PC maker Lenovo's Q2 disappoints. release order: 09/11/2006

Roberts D, Balfour F, Einhorn B, Arndt M, Shari M, Kiley D (2004) China's power brands. Business Week 3907: 77–84

Robertson KR (1987) Recall and recognition effects of brand name imagery. Psychology & Marketing 4 (1): 3–15

Roehrig MF (1994) Foreign joint ventures in contemporary China. St. Martin's Press, New York

Roll M (2006) Asian brand strategy: How Asia builds strong brands. Palgrave Macmillan (UK), New York et al

Root FR (1994) Entry strategies for international markets, rev. and expanded ed., Jossey-Bass, San Francisco

Rosenbush S (2005) Ready for Chinese Merger Mania? Business Week Online

Rossiter JR, Percy L (2001) Aufbau und Pflege von Marken durch klassische Kommunikation (in German). In: Esch FR (ed) Moderne Markenführung, 3rd edn. Gabler, Wiesbaden, pp 523–538

Roth D (2005) China tries to kick the piracy habit. Fortune 151 (1): 56–58

Roth GD (1981) Messen und Ausstellungen verkaufswirksam planen und durchführen (in German). Moderne Industrie, Landsberg/Lech

Rugman AM (1980) A new theory of the multinational enterprise: Internationalization vs. internalization. Columbia Journal of World Business 17 (1): 23–29

Rui HC (2005) Globalisation, transition and development in China. Routledge Curzon, London et al

Rüschen G (1984) Internationale Nestlé-Strategie und –Organisation (in German). In: Meffert H, Wagner H (eds) Internationales Management - Erfahrungen im Auslandsgeschäft. Working paper No. 17 of Wissenschaftliche Gesellschaft für Marketing und Unternehmensführung eV, Münster, pp 47–61

Russo JE, Leclerc F (1994) An eye-fixation analysis of choice processes for consumer nondurables. Journal of Consumer Research 21 (2): 274–290

Saal M (2005) Lenovo läuft sich warm (in German). Horizont 21/07/2005: 12

Sabel H, Weiser C (2000) Dynamik im Marketing (in German), 3rd edn. Gabler, Wiesbaden

Sambharya RB (1996) Foreign experience of top management teams and international diversification strategies of US multinational corporations. Strategic Management Journal 17: 739–746

Samsung (2006) We love sports. Http://www.samsung.com/AboutSAMSUNG/WeLoveSports/index.asp, release order 01/10/2006

Sandler DM, Shani D (1992) Brand Globally but Advertise Locally?: An Empirical Investigation. International Marketing Review 9 (4): 18–32

Sattler H (2001) Markenpolitik (in German). Kohlhammer, Stuttgart et al

Schaffer AR, Rhee JH (2005) Consider cost and strategy when choosing between expatriate and host-national managers. Journal of Business & Management 11 (1): 59–71

Schaffmeister N, Ziegler N (2005) The unloyal brand conscious consumer. Business Forum China 4 (July/August): 58–60

Schanz G (1994) Organisationsgestaltung (in German), 2nd edn. Vahlen, München

Schiele TP (1997) Markenstrategien wachstumsorientierter Unternehmen (in German). Doctoral thesis, University of Mannheim

Schlevogt KA (1999) Inside Chinese organizations: An empirical study of business practices in China, doctoral thesis, University of Oxford

Schmidkonz C (2005) Die „Five Friendlies" für Peking 2008: Ein teuer zu bezahlendes Geschenk (in German). China Standpunkt Nr. 7, Think!Desk China Research & Consulting, München Beijing

Schmitt BH (1995) Language and Visual Imagery: Issues of Corporate Identity in East Asia. Columbia Journal of World Business 30 (4): 28–36

Schmitt BH, Pan YG, Tavassoli NT (1994) Language and consumer memory: The impact of linguistic differences between Chinese and English. Journal of Consumer Research 21 (3): 419–431

Schneider H (1978) Hypothese - Experiment – Theorie (in German), 1st edn. De Gruyter, Berlin New York

Schramm M (2005) Chinas Marken-Dilemma: Zwischen Markenklau und Markenaufbau (in German). China Standpunkt 2, Think!Desk China Research & Consulting, München Beijing

Schramm M, Spiller A (2006) Brand Roll Back. Gefahr für das Brand Management in China (in German). China Essential No. 2, Think!Desk China Research & Consulting, München

Schramm M, Taube M (2006): The Chinese consumer puzzle: Placing branded FMCG in the Chinese market. In: Simon H, Ebel B, Hofer M (eds) Business Development in China. Bonn, pp 11–28 (forthcoming)

Schramm M, Staack T, Taube M (2006) Markenpräferenzen chinesischer Konsumenten: Eine empirische Untersuchung (in German). Zeitschrift für Betriebswirtschaft Sonderheft Asian (Mai 2006): 111–131

Schuiling I, Kapferer JN (2004) Executive insights: Real differences between local and international brands: Strategic implications for international marketers. Journal of International Marketing 12 (4): 97–112

Schumacher H, Schaudwet C (2004) Spur des Scheiterns: Chinas Konzerne und ihre Flops und Fehlinvestitionen in der deutschen Industrie (in German). Wirtschaftswoche 30/09/2004: 54–58

Schurmann F (1971) Ideology and organization in communist China. University of California Press, Berkeley

Schütte H (1998) Consumer behaviour in Asia, New York University Press, New York

Schütte H, Ang SH, Leong SM, Tan CT (2004) Marketing Management - An Asian casebook, Prentice Hall, Singapore et al

Sedan S (2006) China Targets European Auto Market (in German). Http://www.spiegel.de/international/0,1518,440570,00.html, release order 04/10/2006

Seeger A (2001) Die Privatisierung von Staatsunternehmen in der VR China (in German). Shaker, Aachen

Seidler J (1998) Für eine "durchgängige internationale Markenführung" (in German). Markenartikel 60 (3): 12–26

Selinski H, Sperling UA (1995) Marketinginstrument Messe: Arbeitsbuch für Studium und Praxis (in German). Wirtschaftsverlag Bachem, Köln

Sellers P (1994) Pepsi opens a second front. Fortune 08/08/1994: 70–76

Shanghai Daily (2006) China outlines bold program for science. 10/02/2006: 1

Shanghai Tongji Ju [Shanghai Bureau of Statistics] (ed) (2005) Shanghai tongji nianjian 2005 [Shanghai Statistical Yearbook 2005] (in Chinese). Shanghai Statistics Press, Shanghai

Shapiro J (2001) Mao's war against nature: politics and the environment in Revolutionary China. Cambridge University Press, Cambridge New York

Shaw A, Schmitz W, Scott L, Clark DT (2003) The myth of 2.3 billion consumers. Deutsche Bundesbank, New York et al

Shenzhen Daily (2005a) Advertising spending up 20% up to US$17.7b. 26/09/2005: N.PAG

Shenzhen Daily (2005b) Hisense May Transfer Assets to Kelon. Http://www.china.org.cn/english/BAT/145824.htm, release order 18/10/2005

Shenzhen Daily (2006) Hisense Group May Seek Overseas IPO. Http://www.china.org.cn/english/BAT/154484.htm, release order 09/01/2006

Shi L et al (1989) Dangdai zhongguo duiwai jingji hezuo [Contemporary China's foreign economic cooperation] (in Chinese). Contemporary China Press, Beijing

Shi YS (2001) Technological capabilities and international production strategy of firms: The case of foreign direct investment in China. Journal of World Business 36 (2): 184–204

Shirk S (1993) The political logic of economic reform. University of California Press, Berkeley

Sino.com.cn (2003a) Lianxiang pinpai fazhan zhi lu [The path of developing Lianxiang brand] (in Chinese). Http://tech.sina.com.cn/other/2003-06-10/1136196465.shtml, release order 10/06/2003

Sino.com.cn (2003b) Pinpai guancha: Lianxiang jituan liangnian (sannian) mouhua biaoshi [A look into brands: Legend Group's two year (three year) design of Lenovo trademark]. San bufen [Three parts] (in Chinese). Http://tech.sina.com.cn/other/2003-06-11/1942197262.shtml, release order 11/06/2003

Sokianos NP (2006) Produkt- und Konzeptpiraterie erkennen, vorbeugen, abwehren, nutzen, dulden (in German). Gabler, Wiesbaden

Solomon MR, Ashmore RD (1992) The beauty match-up hypothesis: Congruence between types of beauty. Journal of Advertising 21 (4): 23–34

Sony (2006) Sony History. Http://www.sony.net/Fun/SH/, release order 01/10/2006

Specht G (1992) Distributionsmanagement (in German), 2nd edn. Stuttgart et al

Spiegel Online (2005) Gegenwind für Landwind (in German). Http://www.spiegel.de/auto/aktuell/0,1518,374667,00.html, release order 14/09/2005

Staiger B, Friedrich S, Schütte HW (2003) Das große China-Lexikon (in German), 1st edn. Wissenschaftliche Buchgesellschaft, Darmstadt

Stremme S (2005) Interview. Managing Director, Media Saturn Holding GmbH, Ingolstadt (unpublished)

Sun S (2006) Interview. Director Corporate Communication, TTE Corporation, Shenzhen (unpublished)

Swander & Pace (1997) Newsletter. Winter

Swystun J (2006) Email. 04/01/2006 (unpublished)

Swystun J, Burt F, Ly A (2005) The strategy for Chinese brands. Part 1 - The perception challenge. Interbrand, New York

Tam JLM, Tai SHC (1998) Research note: The psychographic segmentation of the female market in Greater China. International Marketing Review 15 (1): 61–77.

Tan JJ, Litschert RJ (1994) Environment-strategy relationship and its performance implications: An empirical study of the Chinese electronics industry. Strategic Management Journal 15 (1): 1–20

Taube M (2003a) China als Ziel deutscher Direktinvestitionen: Gesamtwirtschaftliche Rahmenbedingungen und operative Herausforderungen (in German). In: Nippa M (ed) Markterfolg in China: Erfahrungsberichte und Rahmenbedingungen. Physica, Heidelberg Berlin, pp 29–48

Taube M (2003b) Chinas Rückkehr in die Weltgemeinschaft: Triebkräfte und Widerstände auf dem Weg zu einem "globalen player" (in German).Working paper No. 51, Ostasienwissenschaften, University of Duisburg-Essen

Taube M (2005) Chinas Unternehmen im Kaufrausch (in German). China Standpunkte 3, Think!Desk China Research & Consulting, München Beijing

Taylor A, Zhang DH (2004) Shanghai Auto wants to be the world's next great car company. Fortune 150 (7): 102–110

TCL Corporation (2002) Chairman's speech. Http://www.tcl.com/English/01about/index.htm, release order 23/04/2006

TCL Corporation (2006) TCL memorabilia. Http://www.tcl.com/English/01about/index4.jsp#1980, release order 14/04/2006

TCT (2004a) 3Q 2004 results: Corporate presentation of October 2004. Http://www.tclcom.com/eng/ir/presentations.asp, release order 20/04/2006

TCT (2004b) Listing on HKSK: Corporate presentation of September 2004. Http://www.tclcom.com/eng/ir/presentations.asp, release order 20/04/2006

TCT (2005a) 3Q 2005 results: Corporate presentation of October 2005. Http://www.tclcom.com/eng/ir/presentations.asp, release order 20/04/2006

TCT (2005b) 2004 annual results: Corporate presentation of April 2005. Http://www.tclcom.com/eng/ir/presentations.asp, release order 20/04/2006

TCT (2006a) FY2005 and 1Q2006 Results: Corporate Presentation of 27 April 2006. Http://www.tclcom.com/admin/upload/ir/presentation/ep060427.pdf, release order 08/05/2006

TCT (2006b) Press release of 3 April 2006: Acquisition of an additional 38.58% stake in JDRC. Http://www.tclcom.com/eng/ir/press.asp, release order 20/04/2006

Temporal P (2000) Branding in Asia: The creation, development and management of Asian brands for the global market, rev. edn. Wiley, Singapore et al

Terpstra V (1983) International marketing. 3rd edn. Chicago et al

Think!Desk (2005) Black Box China: Markenpräferenzen und Konsumentenverhalten (in German). München

Thomas MJ, Bureau JM, Saxena N (1995) The relevance of global branding. Journal of Brand Management 2 (5): 299–307

Thometzek E (1995) Die Etablierung und Entwicklung eines Schlüsselbildes: Von der Deklination durch die Medien zur Integration von Produktbotschaften (in German). In: icon Forschung & Consulting (ed) Wechsel, Wandel, Vielfalt - Was hält die Marke aus? Strategien und Konzepte für die Markenführung. 3rd icon-Congreß, Nürnberg, pp 22–36

Tian G (2000) Property rights and the nature of Chinese collective enterprises. Journal of Comparative Economics 28: 247–268

TMC (2001) Annual results 2000. Http://www.tclhk.com/tclhk/admin/upload/ir/presentation/ep050412f.pdf, release order 11/05/2006

TMC (2002) Annual results 2001. Http://www.tclhk.com/tclhk/admin/upload/ir/presentation/ep050412p.pdf, release order:11/05/2006

TMC (2003) Annual results 2002. http://www.tclhk.com/tclhk/admin/upload/ir/presentation/ep050412aa.pdf, release order 11/05/2006

TMC (2005a) 3Q 2005 results: Corporate presentation of 28 October 2005. Http://www.tclhk.com/tclhk/new/eng/ir/presentation.asp, release order 20/04/2006

TMC (2005b) 2004 annual results: Corporate presentation of 18 April 2005. Http://www.tclhk.com/tclhk/new/eng/ir/presentation.asp, release order 20/04/2006

TMC (2005c) TTE Corporation Presentation at CES 2005 (Las Vegas). Http://www.tclhk.com/tclhk/new/eng/ir/presentation.asp, release order 20/04/2006

TMC (2006a) FY2005 and 1Q2006 Results: Corporate Presentation of April 2006. Http://www.tclhk.com/tclhk/admin/upload/ir/presentation/ep060427.pdf, release order 01/05/2006

TMC (2006b) Years in review. Http://www.tclhk.com/tclhk/new/eng/about/event_2004.asp, release order 01/05/2006

Toh SM, DeNisi AS (2005) A local perspective to expatriate success. Academy of Management Executive 19 (1): 132–146

Tomczak T (1992) Forschungsmethoden in der Marketingwissenschaft: Ein Plädoyer für den qualitativen Forschungsansatz (in German). Marketing Zeitschrift für Forschung & Praxis (2): 77–87

Tomczak T, Schögel M, Feige S (2001) Erfolgreiche Markenführung gegenüber dem Handel (in German). In: Esch FR (ed) Moderne Markenführung. Gabler, Wiesbaden, pp 913–937

Tripp C, Jensen TD (1994) The effects of multiple product endorsements by celebrities on consumers' attitudes and intentions. Journal of Consumer Research 20 (4): 535–547

Tse DK (1996) Understanding Chinese people as consumers: past findings and future propositions. In: Bond MH (ed) The handbook of Chinese psychology. Oxford University Press, Hong Kong, N.PAG

Tse DK, Pan YG, Au K (1997) How MNCs choose entry modes and form alliances: the China experience. Journal of International Business Studies 28 (4): 779–805

TTE (2003) TCL and Thomson: Creating a new global leader in the TV industry. Http://www.ttecorp.com/w_news/detail.asp?InfoID=706, release order 02/05/2006

TTE (2006) TCL branded TV enters Europe under new partnership with Carrefour. Http://www.ttecorp.com/w_news/detail.asp?infoid=761, release order 24/04/2006

Tung RL (1982) Chinese industrial reform after Mao. Lexington Books, Lexington MA

Tye MG, Chen PY (2005) Selection of expatriates: Decision-making models used by HR professionals. Human Resource Planning 28 (4): 15–20

UNCTAD (2003) China - An emerging FDI outward investor. E-Brief 04/12/2003, Geneva

UNCTAD (2004) World investment report 2004. New York Geneva

UNCTAD (2005a) Country fact sheet – China. Http://www.unctad.org/Templates/Page.asp?intItemID=2441&lang=1, release order 28/09/2006

UNCTAD (2005b) World investment report 2005. New York Geneva

UNCTAD (2006) Online database on country fact sheets. Http://www.unctad.org/Templates/Page.asp?intItemID=2441&lang=1, release order 28/09/2006

Underwood L (2006) Lessons from China CEOs. EPWS presentation 14/06/2006, American Chamber of Commerce in Shanghai, Shanghai (unpublished)

Underwood L, Wong V (2005) The new Chinese challengers. Insight The Journal of the American Chamber of Commerce in Shanghai October 2005: 19–23

Usunier JC (2000) Marketing across cultures. 3rd edn. Financial Times Prentice Hall, Harlow et al

Valikiotis M, Clifford M, McBeth J (1994) The lure of Asia. Far Eastern Economic Review 157 (5): 32–34

Van Gelder S (2005) The new imperatives for global branding: Strategy, creativity and leadership. Journal of Brand Management 12 (5): 395–404

Voeth M, Wagemann D (2004) Internationale Markenpolitik (in German). In: Bruhn M (ed) Handbuch Markenführung, 2nd edn. Gabler, Wiesbaden

Volkmar JA (2003) Context and control in foreign subsidiaries: Making a case for the host country national manager. Journal of Leadership and Organizational Studies 10 (1): 93–105

Wagnleitner R (2000) Von der Coca-Colonisation zur Sili-Colonisation (in German). Köln

Walder A (1986) Communist neo-traditionalism: work and authority in Chinese industry. University of California Press, Berkeley

Wang J (ed) (2005) Pinpai youshi: 1995-2004 zhongguo pinpai shizhi baogao [Brands have value: Report about Chinese brand values 1995-2004] (in Chinese). Entreprise Management Publishing House, Beijing

Wang RJ (2005) Interview. General Brand Manager, Hisense Group, Qingdao

Wang RJ, Yao Y, Liu W (2003) Chuwei: haixin PBI [Exceed potential: Hisense's PBI] (in Chinese). Entreprise Management Publishing House, Beijing

Wang X, Yin P (2005) More efforts needed for firms to go global. China Daily 29/11/2005: 7

Wehrfritz G (1996) Mao was the best emperor of all time. Newsweek 127 (19): 44

Weiland H (2004) China-Offensive: Die Samsungs von morgen (in German). Horizont 04/11/2004: 16

Weiss CA (1996) Die Wahl internationales Markteintrittsstrategien: Eine transaktionskostenorientierte Analyse (in German). Gabler, Wiesbaden

Welge MK (1980) Management in deutschen multinationalen Unternehmungen: Ergebnisse einer empirischen Untersuchung (in German). Stuttgart

Welge MK (1989) Koordinations- und Steuerungsinstrumente (in German). In: Macharzina K, Welge MK (ed) Handwörterbuch Export und Internationale Unternehmung. Stuttgart, pp 1182–1191

Wharton School (2004) Lenovo Chairman Liu Chuanzhi: "We have decided to refocus on PCs". Http://knowledge.whaton.upenn.edu, release order 08/09/2004

Wharton School (2005a) How Lenovo Is Leveraging the Brand from East to West. Http://knowledge.wharton.upenn.edu/index.cfm?fa=viewfeature&id=1282, release order 21/09/2005

Wharton School (2005b) The IBM/ Lenovo Deal: Victory for China? Http://knowledge.wharton.upenn.edu/index.cfm?fa=printArticle&ID=1106, release order 14/01/2005

Wharton School (2005c) Retailers are checking out Chinese consumers' new eagerness to spend. Http://knowledge.wharton.upenn.edu/index.cfm?fa=view Article&id=1201, release order 01/06/2005

Wikipedia (2006) Media-Saturn Holding (in German). Http://de.wikipedia.org/wiki/Saturn_(Elektronikfachmarkt), release order: 01/10/2006

Wilson RW (1970) Learning to be Chinese: The political socialization of children in Taiwan. MIT Press, Cambridge

WIPO (2006) Intellectual Property Digital Library: Madrid Express Structured Search. Http://www.wipo.int/ipdl/en/search/madrid/search-struct.jsp, release order 10/05/2006

Wirtschaftswoche (2003) Spitzenunternehmen. Sonderausgabe China 02/10/2003: 88–95

Wirtschaftswoche (2004) TCL: Neuer TV-Riese. 07/06/2004: N.PAG

Witkowski TH, Ma Y, Zheng D (2003) Cross-cultural influences on brand identity impressions: KFC in China and the United States. Asia Pacific Journal of Marketing and Logistics 15 (1-2): 74–86

Wöhe G (1996) Einführung in die allgemeine Betriebswirtschaftslehre (in German), 19th edn. Vahlen, München

Worm V (1997) Vikings and Mandarins. Munksgaard International Publishers, Copenhagen

Wu YH (2005) Chinese brands needed. China Daily 29/10/2005: 4

Wurm M (2005) Erfolglose Haier will zur IFA neu durchstarten (in German). Computer Reseller News 25/08/2005: N.PAG

Xin yingxiao [New Marketing] (2005) Haixin fali pingban dianshi [Hisense's innovation power resides in flat TV] (in Chinese). 11: 26–27

Xing F (1995) The Chinese cultural system: Implications of cross-cultural management. SAM Advanced Management Journal 60: 14–20

Xinhua (2005) Party calls for GDP to double before 2010. China Economic Information Service 12/10/2005

Xu JG (2000) Entscheidungsstrukturen und Entscheidungsfindung für ein Innovationsmanagement in großen und mittelgroßen chinesischen Staatsunternehmen (in German). Doctoral thesis, Technische Hochschule Aachen

Yan Y (2000) International joint ventures in China: Ownership, control and performance. Macmillan, Basingstoke et al

Yang K (1961): Religion in Chinese society: A study of contemporary social functions of religion and some of their historical factors. University of California Press, Berkeley

Yang MMH (1994) Gifts, favors, and banquets: The art of social relationships in China. Cornell University Press, Ithaca NY

Yang QS (2005) Zuiqiang pinpai [The strongest brands] (in Chinese). China Machine Press, Beijing

Yau OHM (1988) Chinese cultural values: Their dimensions and marketing implications. European Journal of Marketing 22 (5): 44–57

Yi JJS, Ye SWX (2003) The Haier way: The making of a Chinese business leader and a global brand, 1st edn. Homa & Sekey Books, Dumont NJ

Yin RK (1994) Case study research: Design and methods. 2nd edn. Sage Publications, Thousand Oaks Calif London

Yu CS, Taylor GS, Wei T (2003) A cross-cultural comparison of work goals: The United States, Taiwan and the People's Republic of China. In: Alon I (ed) Chinese culture, organizational behaviour, and international business management. Praeger, Westport, pp 169–185

Yu MY (2006) 2006 Zhongguo pinpai baogao [China Brand Report 2006] (in Chinese). Shanghai Jiao Tong University Press, Shanghai

Yuan P, Dawar N (2001) Midea: Globalization challenge for a leading Chinese home appliance manufacturer. Case No. 900A31 Richard Ivy School of Management, University of Western Ontario

Zeng M, Williamson PJ (2004) Die verborgenen Drachen (in German). Harvard Business Manager 3: 37–46

Zhang HY, Bulcke D van den (1996) International management strategies of Chinese multinational firms. In: Child J, Lu Y (eds) Management Issues in China. Routledge, London, pp 141–164

Zhang J (2005) China's urbanization puzzle. China International Business 215 (October): 18–25

Zhang Y (2006) Interview. Group Account Director, OgilvyOne Worldwide, Beijing (unpublished)

Zhang YJ (2003) China's emerging global businesses: Political economy and institutional investigations. Palgrave Macmillan, Houndmills

Zhishi Jingji [Knowledge Economy] (2002) [Interview with Zhou Houjian at Hisense] (in Chinese). 05/05/2002: N.PAG

Zhou DS (2005) Interview. Professor of Marketing, CEIBS, Shanghai (unpublished)

Zhu CJH (2005) Human resource management in China: Past, current and future HR practices in the industrial sector. Routledge, London et al

Zhu SS (2006) China offers new rules to fight product pirates. Shanghai Daily: 28/03/2006: A2

Zhu, Yang (2005): Zhongguo xuan lianxiang wulian [Legend of Lenovo], Harbin Press, Harbin.

Zhu YX (2003) Examining the marketing strategies employed by Chinese sales letters. In: Alon I (ed) Chinese economic transition and international marketing strategy. Praeger, Westport Connecticut London, pp 96–109

Zimmermann R, Klein-Bölting U, Sander B, Murad-Aga T (2002) Brand Equity Excellence. Band 2: BBDO Brand Equity Evaluator. Http://www.bbdo.de/de/home/studien.download.Par.0002.Link1Download.File1Title.pdf, release order 24/08/2006

Printed in the United States
116318LV00001B/121-168/P